CW00566968

Serbia and the Balkan Front, 1914

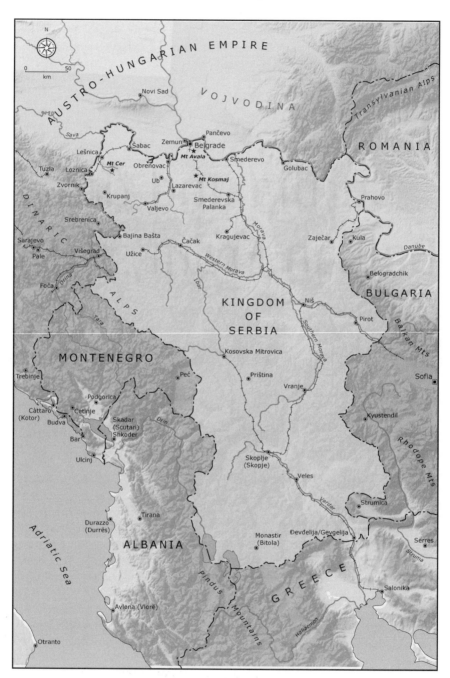

MAP 1 *Serbia and its neighbors, 1914*

Serbia and the Balkan Front, 1914

The Outbreak of the Great War

JAMES LYON

Bloomsbury Academic
An imprint of Bloomsbury Publishing Plc

B L O O M S B U R Y
LONDON • NEW DELHI • NEW YORK • SYDNEY

Bloomsbury Academic

An imprint of Bloomsbury Publishing Plc

50 Bedford Square
London
WC1B 3DP
UK

1385 Broadway
New York
NY 10018
USA

www.bloomsbury.com

BLOOMSBURY and the Diana logo are trademarks of Bloomsbury Publishing Plc

First published 2015

© James Lyon, 2015

James Lyon has asserted his right under the Copyright, Designs and Patents Act, 1988, to be identified as Author of this work.

All rights reserved. No part of this publication may be reproduced or transmitted in any form or by any means, electronic or mechanical, including photocopying, recording, or any information storage or retrieval system, without prior permission in writing from the publishers.

No responsibility for loss caused to any individual or organization acting on or refraining from action as a result of the material in this publication can be accepted by Bloomsbury or the author.

British Library Cataloguing-in-Publication Data
A catalogue record for this book is available from the British Library.

ISBN: HB: 978-1-4725-8003-0
PB: 978-1-4725-8004-7
ePDF: 978-1-4725-8006-1
ePub: 978-1-4725-8005-4

Library of Congress Cataloging-in-Publication Data
Lyon, James B.
Serbia and the Balkan Front, 1914 : the outbreak of the Great War / James Lyon.
pages cm
Includes bibliographical references and index.
ISBN 978-1-4725-8003-0 (hb) — ISBN 978-1-4725-8004-7 (pb) —
ISBN 978-1-4725-8006-1 (ePDF) — ISBN 978-1-4725-8005-4 (ePub)
1. World War, 1914–1918—Serbia.
2. World War, 1914–1918—Campaigns—Balkan Peninsula. I. Title.
D561.L96 2015
940.4'14—dc23
2014042325

Typeset by RefineCatch Limited, Bungay, Suffolk
Printed and bound in India

To my father, James Karl Lyon:
A gentleman and a scholar

CONTENTS

ILLUSTRATIONS

Unless otherwise stated, all illustrations are reproduced with kind permission of the Military Museum, Belgrade.

MAPS

ACKNOWLEDGMENTS

Many people have helped bring together this book. I owe a particular debt of gratitude to the late Dr. Andrej Mitrović (1937–2013) of the University of Belgrade's Philosophy Faculty, whose archival research into Great Power diplomacy prior to and during the Great War is unparalleled among modern scholars. He offered invaluable advice, opened doors to many archives, and provided mentorship that eventually developed into a lasting friendship. His wife, Dr. Ljubinka Trgovčević of the University of Belgrade's Faculty of Political Sciences, has also provided guidance and permitted me access to Andrej's private library when I was unable to find sources elsewhere.

My doctoral committee co-chairs—Dr. Bariša Krekić (UCLA) and the late Dr. Dimitrije Đorđević (UCSB)—opened their homes, libraries, and hearts to me. Both were true old-school gentlemen and scholars (*Bečka škola*), fluent in multiple languages, who willingly shared advice regarding sources and interpretation.

In Belgrade, the employees in the Archive of Yugoslavia's Military History Institute went out of their way to help guide my search for relevant documents. Sadly, this archive was forced to relocate after the building that housed it (the Defense Ministry) took direct hits during the NATO bombing of Milosević's Yugoslavia in 1999. Although the Military History Institute has now been disbanded, many of its holdings have been transferred to Serbia's Military Archive, whose personnel have proven equally kind. In Belgrade, the Archive of Serbia, the Archive of Yugoslavia, and the Archive of the Serbian Academy of Sciences and Arts opened their doors to me, as did the Serbian National Library, the Library of the Serbian Academy's Historical Institute, and the Belgrade University Philosophy Faculty's History Library.

In Sarajevo, the Director of the National and University Library, Ismet Ovčina, and his staff were particularly gracious in permitting access to rare materials from 1914, especially the periodical, map, and photographic collections. Father Vanja Jovanović of the Serbian Orthodox Church permitted me access to heretofore unused archives of the medieval Church of the Holy Archangels Mihailo and Gavrilo in Sarajevo's *Baščaršija*. In addition, countless people in Bosnia and Herzegovina went out of their way to fill in details regarding life in 1914.

Over the years, a number of historians have offered helpful advice, insights, and constructive comments regarding competing interpretations of events. Among these are Dr. Ivo Banac of Yale University, Dr. Dušan Bataković of the Serbian Academy of Sciences and Arts' Institute for Balkan Studies, Dr. Mile Bjelajac of the Institute for Recent History of Serbia, and Dr. Vesna Aleksić of the Institute of Economic Sciences in Belgrade. Dr. Bruce Gudmundsson of the US Marine Corps University offered invaluable advice regarding artillery, and Dr. Joseph Lynn Lyon of the University of Utah willingly shared his expertise about small arms.

I would also like to thank Dr. Kenneth Morrison of De Montfort University, Dr. Adam Moore of the University of California of Los Angeles, Dr. Anna Di Lellio of the New School, Dr. James K. Lyon of Brigham Young University (emeritus), Neil MacDonald, Christopher Bennett, Barın Kayaoğlu, Morgan Tanner, Stephen Schwartz, Alvaro Ballesteros, Neil Howie, and Duško Zavišić for their assistance reading the manuscript.

The photographs and maps in this book came from collections in the archive of the National Library in Sarajevo, the Military History Museum in Belgrade, and the Historical Museum of Bosnia and Herzegovina. The New Zealand Ministry of Culture and Heritage, and Geographx were gracious enough to provide the geographic template for the map "Serbia and its neighbors, 1914."

I am grateful to the people of Bosnia and Herzegovina and Serbia. I have lived in each country for ten years during various periods, both under Tito's socialist Yugoslavia and as independent states. This has helped me contextualize some of the ideas and emotions that were rampant 100 years ago, as they boiled to the surface again in the 1990s.

Finally, none of this could have been carried out without my mother-in-law's homemade *gibanica* and my better half, Maja, who supported me throughout with finding resources, checking footnotes, and warm tea.

Sarajevo and Belgrade

Introduction

Atop Mount Avala on the outskirts of Belgrade sits a magnificent yet somber black granite mausoleum built between 1934 and 1938 by the then-unified Kingdom of Yugoslavia to honor Serbia's dead from the Great War. The shrapnel-pocked Ivan Meštrović-designed Tomb of the Unknown Hero bears an inscription that reads: "Aleksandar I, King of Yugoslavia, to the Unknown Hero." The dates chiseled in stone read "1912–1918." Similar dates appear on war memorials throughout Serbia, where the conflict is often called "the Great War of Liberation and Unification," and viewed as an extension of the First and Second Balkan Wars.[1] The dates and name of the war express the long-term goals of one of the victors—Serbia—that were subsequently adopted at Versailles.

The summer of 1914 is often portrayed as peaceful and uneventful, a time when few suspected war was on the horizon,[2] much less a full-blown world war that would draw in people from across the globe. Yet it was neither peaceful nor uneventful: by that summer, Europe had been engaged in conflict for two years and in low-intensity guerrilla warfare for ten, and had just recently intervened in the northern Albanian city of Scutari (Shköder/Skadar) to dislodge Montenegrin and Serb forces. This war that had already begun in the Balkans would soon draw in all of Europe, include countries as far away as Japan, and eventually come full circle in 1918 to end as a result of military developments in the Balkans.[3]

Just as today, the world order was changing: old empires and alliances tottered, while new forces elbowed their way onto the stage. Along Europe's periphery, change was occurring at a disturbingly fast pace, driven by unresolved national questions, socio-economic frustration, popular unrest, and nationalist leaders. Threats of irredentism, independence, and state dissolution rattled Balkan and Great Power nerves alike. Some of those in power seemed oblivious to the winds of change and clung to their privileges and patronage networks, while others pushed for—or ignored—badly needed reforms to shore up crumbling systems and ideologies. Still others looked for ways to exploit change to their benefit.

During the nineteenth century, one overriding issue preoccupied the Great Powers: the Eastern Question—the collapse of the ever-weakening Ottoman Empire. In practical terms, this meant that each Great Power looked to assure its interests in the territories of the Ottoman Empire.

Yet the contested areas of the Ottoman Empire were in a state of flux. As the Sublime Porte's power weakened in the late eighteenth and early nineteenth centuries, subjugated areas of the Empire began to rebel. In the Balkans alone, during the 99 years between the Congress of Vienna in 1815 and 1914, Albania, Bulgaria, Greece, Montenegro, Romania, and Serbia emerged as nation-states from the ruins of the disintegrating Ottoman Empire. In contrast, the Great Powers subjugated the former Ottoman lands of North Africa, albeit not without the Great Powers' raising tensions among themselves.

The Great Powers were now forced to deal with aggressive programs of national liberation and expansion throughout the Balkans. In 1914, influential elements in both Austria-Hungary and Serbia pressed diametrically opposed geopolitical and national aims that contemplated future programs of territorial expansion at each other's expense. Conflict seemed inevitable. Given this atmosphere, one could well ask why war did not break out earlier, not merely why a small regional quarrel spread into a conflagration that enveloped the entire world.

Since June 28, 1914, tens of thousands of articles and books have been published in numerous languages in an effort to explain the causes of the Great War. Typically, historians cover the events leading up to Sarajevo, point to the assassination as the trigger, jump to the Great Power capitals, follow the flurry of exchanges between foreign ministries, government chanceries, and defense ministries, discuss one or more of the underlying causes (secret alliances, arms races, imperial expansionism, nationalism, the Eastern Question, German aggression, Serb "terrorism," premature Russian general mobilization, the *Schlieffen* Plan, misunderstandings, the Kaiser's blank check, etc.), and then jump to the outbreak of fighting on the Western (or Eastern) Front. With the exception of local language materials published in the Balkans, events on the Balkan Front are largely ignored or mentioned only in passing. This book consciously takes a different approach that begins in the Balkans, and maintains its focus on the Balkans, looking at Great Power interactions only when they directly affected the events of 1914 in the Balkans, or where events in the Balkans affected Great Power decisions.

The exception to the standard approach comes in the numerous post-war German-language apologetics penned by former Habsburg officers and officials hoping to absolve themselves of blame for the war's disastrous outcome: the collapse of empire. During 1914, the Austro-Hungarian Empire's *Balkanstreitkräfte* suffered catastrophic and politically embarrassing defeats at the hands of the Serbian Army. In December 1914, the Serbian Army destroyed the Dual Monarchy's Fifth and Sixth Armies, leaving the Empire's southern border almost completely undefended, causing *Balkanstreitkräfte* commander *Feldzeugmeister* (Lieutenant General) Oskar Potiorek to resign in disgrace. So significant were the defeats that the Empire did not undertake another offensive on the Balkan Front until October 1915, and only then with German and Bulgarian assistance. In the wake of Serbia's initial stunning victories, historians and laymen alike sought to understand how a relatively industrialized Great Power could be so thoroughly and completely humiliated by a small, agrarian Balkan nation with a population one-tenth its size.

After the war, many former Habsburg officers and politicians attempted to exonerate themselves of blame for these catastrophes.[4] Apologists invariably pointed to an allegedly poor state of military readiness and the Empire's low pre-war military expenditures as the cause of these defeats, while portraying their foes as better equipped and supplied. Heavily influenced by these early apologists and lacking readily accessible Western-language translations of Serbian primary sources, most Western historians accepted this basic premise. One frequently quoted measure of the Empire's unpreparedness is that "by 1913 the subjects of the Dual Monarchy were spending three times as much on beer, wine, and tobacco as on defense."[5] According to these interpretations, the Austro-Hungarian Army was ill prepared and trained, equipped with substandard artillery, and hampered by a shortage of artillery ammunition and aircraft, while the Dual Monarchy's multinational makeup weakened morale and caused high rates of desertion and surrender.[6] This view maintains that "the basic cause for the defeat in Serbia was the general unpreparedness of the Habsburg army for war."[7]

The focus on the Dual Monarchy's shortcomings caused most historians to overlook the state of its Balkan adversary, Serbia. The typical portrayal of Serbia maintains that it was looking for a fight, its "army was well-trained, war experienced, and equipped with modern artillery. Its officers were excellent, the rank and file tough and highly motivated."[8] The image of a strong Serbia is further enhanced by claims that Serbian forces possessed weapons that were "in some cases superior to the Austro-Hungarian."[9] This assessment suffers from an excessive reliance on Austro-Hungarian archival sources and post-war Habsburg apologists, while dismissing key Habsburg documentary evidence that downplays the Serbian Army's fighting abilities and readiness.[10] So too, this approach fails to utilize Serbia's rich archival holdings.

In contrast, Serbian sources paint a different picture of Europe on the eve of the Great War. This portrayal, largely unknown outside of Serbian historiography, concentrates on Serbia's unpreparedness for any war, much less one against an industrialized Great Power with a population ten times its size. It depicts a small country with an army exhausted from two previous wars, serious ammunition and weapons shortages, a state budget teetering on the brink of bankruptcy, serious food shortages, constant guerrilla incursions, and a dangerous internal power struggle between a group of rogue military officers and Serbia's democratically elected government. In the first half of 1914, Belgrade actively pursued diplomatic initiatives with its Balkan neighbors—friend and foe alike—to prevent the outbreak of a new war. In spite of longer-term national aims, Serbia's official policy in 1914 was avoidance of war at all costs, and its diplomacy and military preparedness on the eve of the Great War show that although 1914 found the Austro-Hungarian Empire relatively less well prepared than some of its Great Power adversaries, it was definitely prepared for battle against Serbia.[11] More importantly, certain parties in Vienna were actively seeking any excuse to attack Serbia.

The new post-war Kingdom of Yugoslavia produced a substantial number of works on the topic, but few of these were translated into other languages, and in some instances events were ignored when they contradicted the official Serbian narrative. While most post-war Western historians read French and German, few knew Serbo-Croatian, rendering local-language source materials relatively inaccessible. This resulted in the rather unusual phenomenon of the vanquished writing history, as scholars relied on easily accessible German-language sources for information, leading to one-sided and sometimes inaccurate portrayals of events in the Balkans.

Yet during the five months between late July and the end of December 1914, the Balkan Front was of tremendous strategic importance to the Allied war effort. Tiny Serbia tied down large numbers of Habsburg forces that would otherwise have been sent to the Eastern or Western Fronts. Moreover, Serbia's ability to block shipping along the Danube enabled the Allies to effectively cut the shortest and safest supply route between Germany and the Habsburg Monarchy on the one hand, and their Bulgarian and Turkish allies—who relied on German-manufactured weaponry—on the other.

During 1914, the Balkan Front was relatively fluid, with both sides making complex maneuvers, while seeing substantial gains and losses of territory. The Balkan Front also saw a great many "firsts" take place. These included the first battle of the First World War in July 1914, the first attempted amphibious landing, the first aerial combat, the first naval/riverine combat, the first widespread use of artillery according to modern doctrine, the widespread and nearly universal use of camouflage, and irregular guerrilla warfare behind enemy lines. Significantly, the year ended with Serbia's resounding defeat of the Dual Monarchy. These events on the battlefield played a significant role in forming and consolidating national identity in Serbia, and later, Yugoslavia.

This book describes the diplomatic and military battles of 1914, as well as their social context, from a Balkan perspective. It covers the background to the Sarajevo assassination; Serbia's perception of itself in the Great Power diplomatic interactions that followed; the outbreak of war; the first Allied victory of the war (the Battle of Mount Cer); Serbia's abortive invasions of

Austria-Hungary; Serbia's relations with its allies; the bloody ridges and ravines of Mačkov Kamen; mass desertion; Serbia's near-capitulation; and Serbia's destruction of Austria-Hungary's *Balkanstreitkräfte* in December 1914 at the Battle of the Kolubara.

It reveals behind-the-scenes diplomatic maneuvers prior to the Sarajevo assassination: Serbia's secret negotiations with Turkey to realign Balkan borders; struggles with allies over carving up the Habsburg Empire; and discussions with Croats about forming a unified post-war South Slav state. It discusses the role rogue elements played within Serbia's military intelligence and Russia's secret police in planning and financing the Sarajevo assassination. It also provides insights into how Serbia formulated war aims by mid-August 1914, openly calling for the destruction of Austria-Hungary, a Great Power that had constituted a leading force in European politics since the sixteenth century.

During 1914, the still-unresolved conflicts that occurred in 1912 and 1913 took on a larger dimension. By year's end, events both on and off the battlefield created new political realities that enabled Serbia to announce the creation of a South Slav state from the ruins of the Habsburg Empire as its official wartime goal. The same events also gave rise to a historical narrative that permitted the establishment of this new state, both on the field of battle and within the councils of international diplomacy.

Today, new political narratives are being created without trying to verify the accuracy of either the old or the new narratives. When viewed through the prism of Balkans sources, the events of 1914 help us better understand modern-day Balkan political pathologies, where debates over the origins of the Great War still generate controversy. The nature of participation by each country has left lasting and indelible marks on cultural and political identity, particularly in those states that emerged from the ruins of the Austro-Hungarian, German, Ottoman, and Russian empires.

Nothing places an old war in perspective like a new war. Although 100 years have passed since the Sarajevo Assassination, the scars of the Second World War and the more recent Wars of Yugoslav Dissolution remain fresh in the collective memories of the Balkan peoples. These scars have reinforced heavily politicized and polarized views of events surrounding the assassination and the outbreak of the Great War within the region. Debates about the origins of the First World War frequently enter everyday political life.

To better comprehend the neuralgic relationship between the First World War and modern Balkan politics, one must understand that for many Serbs the failure of the West to prevent the breakup of Yugoslavia was viewed as reneging on the deal made at Versailles. For them, it reopened a Pandora's Box of national self-determination. Although such views seemingly fly in the face of the obvious fact that Slobodan Milošević's use of Greater Serb nationalism directly led to Yugoslavia's breakup, they do reflect an all-too-common perception that continues to motivate political choices, as demonstrated by public pronouncements of Serb officials throughout the 1990s. For Albanians,

Bosniaks, Croats, Macedonians, and Slovenes, as well as the numerous other national minority groups that live or lived in the successor states of the former Yugoslavia, the relationship is equally controversial, as their experience of the Great War was different from that of Serbs.

Bosnian Serb assassin Gavrilo Princip offers a prime example of how divisive such questions can be. For many, his is a cut-and-dried case that seemingly offers only two possible explanations: (1) Princip as national hero; or (2) Princip as a terrorist operating on instructions from Serbia. A third, more nuanced explanation would contradict political interpretations on which nation-building myths are based. To see how these competing interpretations have played out, one need only follow their evolution in Sarajevo.

In response to the June 28, 1914 assassination of Archduke Franz Ferdinand and his wife Sophie in Sarajevo, crowds of Catholics, Muslims, Protestants, and Jews went on a two-day rampage through the city and other parts of the Habsburg Monarchy, attacking Serb businesses, homes, schools, and church buildings.[12] Three years later in 1917 on the third anniversary of the assassination, Habsburg officials erected a monument to Franz Ferdinand and Sophie on the corner of the Latin Bridge (*Lateiner brücke*/*Latinska ćuprija*) and Appel Quai, across from Schiller's Delicatessen where Princip stood when the Archduke's car stopped unexpectedly in front of him and he pulled the trigger. The ten-meter high monument rested on two stone pillars topped by crowns, with a bronze medallion of the couple. A rectangular ornamented metal plate the size of a car was set in Franz Josef's Gasse at the spot where the shooting had occurred, with a marble plaque placed high up on the wall of the delicatessen to commemorate where the couple "died a martyr's death by treasonous hands."[13]

After the First World War, the victorious Serbs dismantled the monuments. Yugoslavia's King Aleksandar I Karađorđević, who would himself become a victim of regicide by a nationally motivated terrorist in 1934, refused to officially countenance a monument to the assassins, fearing reactions from foreign capitals and the signal this might send to would-be assassins within his own country.

Nonetheless, in 1920 the bodies of Princip and his co-conspirators were returned from their graves in Czechoslovakia and Bosnia via a special train to a triumphant unofficial posthumous welcome in Sarajevo, where they were reburied together in the Serbian Orthodox cemetery with their martyred hero, Bogdan Žerajić.[14] Due to official concerns over foreign reactions, it was only in 1930 that a black marble plaque with gold Cyrillic lettering was unveiled on the wall high above the spot where Princip stood. It read: "Princip proclaimed freedom on St. Vitus' Day June 28, 1914." Although the Royal Yugoslav government did not officially approve, this plaque clearly represented the near-unanimous thinking of Serbs and Montenegrins: government officials turned a blind eye. The plaque did not survive the 1941 German invasion, and it was removed and presented to Adolf Hitler for his fifty-second birthday that year.

In 1945, following the recent liberation of Yugoslavia from the Wehrmacht, the new Partizan-led leadership held a mass meeting in Sarajevo on May 7, 1945 and erected a marble plaque with the red five-pointed *petokraka* Partizan star. The Cyrillic lettering read: "The youth of Bosnia and Herzegovina dedicate this plaque as a symbol of eternal gratitude to Gavrilo Princip and his comrades, fighters against the Germanic invaders."[15]

Tito's Yugoslavia lionized Princip and the other members of the *Mlada Bosna* (Young Bosnia) youth as national heroes and martyrs, whose sacrifice enabled the liberation of South Slavs from Habsburg occupation and their unification in one South Slav state. On June 27, 1953, the location of Schiller's Delicatessen at the corner of Franz Joseph Street and Appel Quai was turned into the *Mlada Bosna* Museum, with external signage in Cyrillic, Socialist-Realist reliefs in the windows, and shoeprints embedded in concrete at the spot from which Princip fired the fatal shots. A new Cyrillic plaque above the shoeprints read: "From this spot on June 28, 1914, Gavrilo Princip expressed with his shot the national protest against tyranny and the eternal striving of our peoples for freedom." The Latin Bridge was now commonly referred to as Princip's Bridge on tourist brochures and maps, although it does not appear to have been officially renamed.[16]

As socialist Yugoslavia began to violently break apart in the early 1990s, Princip became a highly polarizing litmus test, especially in the polemics leading up to Bosnia and Herzegovina's 1992 independence. During the 1992–1995 Serb siege of Sarajevo, the plaque and shoeprints were removed, and the bridge was redubbed the Latin Bridge.

In the years following the 1995 Dayton Peace Agreement, the museum was recast with a rather neutral focus on what is called the period of "Habsburg Occupation," covering the period from 1878 to 1918, although the exhibit essentially ends with the 1914 assassination. The signs on the outside of the museum are in the Latin alphabet and read simply *Muzej* and *Museum*. In 2004, a simple bi-lingual plaque was installed in Serbo-Croatian (Latin alphabet) and English that reads: "From this place on June 28, 1914 Gavrilo Princip assassinated the heir to the Austro-Hungarian throne Franz Ferdinand and his wife Sophie."[17]

Ten years later, the question of how to treat the legacy of Gavrilo Princip continued to polarize as Sarajevo and Europe began planning 100th anniversary commemorative events. Although there was universal condemnation among all European countries—including Serbia and Russia—of the assassination when it occurred, for Serbs, Princip is a national hero and part of the founding mythology of both Serbia and Yugoslavia. To describe him as anything else is usually condemned as "anti-Serb" by Serbia's cultural and political elites. At the same time, Serbia goes to great lengths to downplay or disavow any official connection between Belgrade and the Sarajevo Assassination, fearing this would tarnish Serbia's image in the twenty-first century and make it appear to have sponsored a terrorist act against a neighbor, justifying the Dual Monarchy's ultimatum and eventual attack. Because the victorious powers were allied with Serbia and acquiesced in the formation of Yugoslavia at Versailles, they had, by default, adopted the official Serb/ Yugoslav narrative that Serbia created Yugoslavia by defeating the Habsburg Empire, then liberating and unifying the South Slavs in Yugoslavia. During the 1990s, Princip became an iconic figure for Bosnian Serbs representing the Serbian struggle against oppression. This narrative remains unchanged.

In contrast to the Serbs, many of Serbia's then-wartime allies continue to condemn Princip's act as one of terrorism, although one that was not sufficiently serious as to warrant Austria-Hungary's ultimatum or subsequent declaration of war. For those countries allied with Austria-Hungary, a common view emerged that Princip was a terrorist doing the bidding of Serbia's government, and that Serbia's response to the ultimatum was disingenuous.

Although one would hope that time and new research would render passé these polarized views, the preparatory events for the commemoration of the 100th anniversary of the assassination in Sarajevo and the successor states to the former Yugoslavia demonstrated that even today, this question touches a raw nerve, not only among the Balkan Slavs, but also inside the European Union and Russia.[18] The "incorrect" interpretation could call into question long-established popular narratives that define today's Europe. In Serbia and Bosnia's Serb-majority entity, Republika Srpska, Serbs cried foul at efforts to portray Princip as a terrorist and launched their own commemorations of *Mlada Bosna* as heroes. On April 23, 2014, the celebrated Serb nationalist film director Emir Kusturica—himself of Bosnian Muslim parentage—unveiled a statute of Princip in the northern Serbian town of Tovariševo, while throughout 2014, numerous pro-Princip conferences were held in Serbia and Bosnia's Republika Srpska. Russia closed ranks with Serbia's interpretation.

For the formerly Habsburg, Catholic-majority countries that split off from the former Yugoslavia (Croatia and Slovenia), the Princip-as-terrorist narrative tends to be more pronounced and is often used to support claims that Serbs are terrorists and hence guilty for the wars and atrocities of the 1990s. This tendency is also seen in the Muslim-majority areas of Bosnia and Herzegovina, where Muslims (Bosniaks) frequently express the opinion that were it not for Gavrilo Princip, today they would have Austrian passports and be inside the European Union.

The abiding importance of this question to twenty-first-century Europe is seen in the reactions of the former Great Powers towards the commemoration of the 100th anniversary of the assassination in Sarajevo itself. Although advance planning for a scholarly conference to commemorate the assassination by the University of Sarajevo's Historical Institute began in 2011, disagreements broke out between France and Austria in 2013 as each struggled to wrest control of the commemoration (i.e., its interpretation) from each other.[19] Reverting to old historical patterns, the Sarajevo Historical Institute sought assistance from Austria, while Serbia and Bosnian Serbs sought support from France to oppose the conference. Although France gained control of European Union funding for the commemoration, the University of Sarajevo teamed up with scholarly institutions in Austria, Bulgaria, Croatia, Germany, Hungary, Macedonia, Slovenia, and the United States of America to hold a three-day academic conference in Sarajevo one week before the commemoration.[20] The conference included over 100 scholars from North America, Europe, Russia, Turkey, Ukraine, and all the Balkan states. Official Serbian and French institutions, as well as French scholars, were notably absent, although four Serb scholars defied official Belgrade and participated.[21]

To seal its historiographic victory, Austria sent the Vienna Philharmonic to play a concert on June 28, 2014 in the recently renovated Sarajevo City Hall. The date and venue were rich with symbolism; this was the last building that Franz Ferdinand and Sophie visited prior to their deaths, and, as the location of the National Library and Archive of Bosnia and Herzegovina during Communist Yugoslavia, it had been one of the first targets of Serb artillery during the 1992–1995 siege. Choosing the precise date of the assassination for the concert was also heavy with symbolism. Croats and Bosniaks interpreted Austria's moves as a message that it shared a common interpretation of events and that Vienna offers support against perceived future Serb aggression. France made do with a Tour-de-France-supported bicycle tour around Sarajevo.

The day before the commemoration, Sarajevo placed a makeshift replica of the Gräf & Stift touring car used by Franz Ferdinand and Sophie at the assassination site, with two costumed re-enactors dressed as Franz Ferdinand and Sophie. Large crowds of tourists gathered, as a Gavrilo Princip re-enactor dressed in a white John Travolta disco suit wielded a fluorescent orange water pistol. The night of June 28, following the Vienna Philharmonic concert, an official commemoration began on the Latin Bridge. It included a sound and light show, a children's choir, popular actors, singers from Turkey, and a Russian choir from Siberia.

Bosnia's Serbs commemorated the assassination quite differently, unveiling a statue to Gavrilo Princip in the Serb-held suburb of Eastern Sarajevo on June 27. The following day, St. Vitus' Day (Vidovdan), the President of Bosnia's Republika Srpska, Milorad Dodik, along with Serbia's Premier Aleksandar Vučić and Serbian Orthodox Patriarch Irinej, gathered to open a tourist attraction in the Bosnian town of Višegrad. Dodik spoke of the Serb struggle for freedom in the past, stated that the Serbs in Bosnia are not yet free, and said that Republika Srpska would soon have "autonomy and then independence."[22]

Hopefully, this book will assist historians and the broader public to understand the events in the Balkans that led to the Sarajevo Assassination, the outbreak of war between Austria-Hungary and Serbia, and the crucial events that led to decisions that eventually resulted in the birth of Yugoslavia.

Perhaps most importantly, it provides insights into the thinking of Belgrade's politicians and generals at a time when nationalist passions were running high following the successes of the Balkan Wars, and when paranoia was ever-present as Great Powers and Balkan neighbors alike fought to acquire territory at each other's expense.

CHAPTER ONE

A Sunday in Sarajevo

The Danube River once formed the heart of a magnificent empire that at various times encompassed all of Austria, Hungary, the Czech Republic, Slovakia, Slovenia, Croatia, and Bosnia and Herzegovina, along with parts of Italy, Montenegro, Serbia, Romania, Poland, Ukraine, Belarus, and Germany. In 1914, one man, the 83-year-old Kaiser Franz Josef I of the House of Habsburg, governed this diverse conglomeration of nationalities and religions known as the Dual Monarchy of Austria-Hungary.[1] At the beginning of the twentieth century, the House of Habsburg was the oldest dynasty to continuously rule a European Great Power. From Vienna, where the Kaiser frequently held court in the *Hofburg* or *Schloß Schönbrunn*, the Danube flows through Bratislava and Budapest to Belgrade, where the tributary Sava River flows in from the west. Should one follow the Sava upstream, one comes to the mouth of the River Bosna, whose spring lies far to the south in the heart of Bosnia.

At the foot of Mount Igman, the River Bosna bubbles up in a series of clear pools surrounded by lush greenery near the town of Ilidža, where thermal springs made it a popular spa since Roman times (*Aquae Sulphurae*) and throughout the Ottoman period. Following the 1878 Treaty of Berlin and the arrival of Habsburg rule in Bosnia and Herzegovina, Ilidža prospered after the *Landesregierung für Bosnien und die Hercegovina* (Habsburg provincial government) constructed a new spa resort on the site of the Roman ruins. The *Landesregierung* erected three hotels—Austria, Hungaria, and Bosna—in neo-Alpine architecture around a central green, each boasting the latest in electric lighting at a cost of 15 *Heller* per hour.[2] By 1914, the spa covered an enormous park complex that offered sulfur baths, Turkish baths, authentic Roman ruins and mosaics, a carousel, three lawn-tennis courts, a shooting gallery, bingo, billiards, a game room, rental horses with guides, fireworks, and carriage rides down a magnificent 2.5 kilometer tree-lined grand *Allee* to the pools of *Vrelo Bosne*. Other modern amenities included not only a post office and telegraph, but also a telephone.[3]

The heir to the Habsburg throne, the Archduke of Austria-Este Franz Ferdinand, and his wife, the Duchess Sophie von Hohenberg, arrived separately in Ilidža on Thursday June 25, 1914 at the small neo-Alpine railroad station. Sophie's train pulled into the station at 9:20 am, having come directly from Vienna via Slavonski Brod; the Archduke's train arrived via Mostar from the Neretva River delta town of Metković at 3:00 that afternoon.[4] At the station, Franz Ferdinand was met by an honor guard, a military band, and *Feldzeugmeister* (Lieutenant-General) Oskar Potiorek, Chief of the *Landesregierung*, who also held the post of *Armeeinspektor* for Bosnia and Herzegovina. The mustached, 60-year-old, three-star general was an ethnic Slovene from the southern Austrian province of Carinthia (*Kärnten*), whose hollow cheeks, taut jaw, slender figure, and close-cropped hair gave him an austere demeanor. Potiorek was known to favor the "war

PHOTO 1 *Feldzeugmeister Oskar Potiorek (reproduced with kind permission of the Historical Museum of Bosnia and Herzegovina).*

camp" in the Dual Monarchy's military, headed by Count Franz Conrad von Hötzendorf, Chief of the General Staff of the Monarchy's Imperial and Royal Army (*Kaiserlich und königliche Armee*, or *K.u.k.*). The war camp sought to annex Serbia and to drastically reduce Magyar (Hungarian) influence and territory within the Empire.

The visit was a major event. Despite the rain, the Ilidža train station was bedecked with bunting, flowers, and flags; the road from the station to the spa was lined with banners and decorations; and a special arch was constructed at the entrance to the resort. In nearby Sarajevo, the city's daily newspapers printed special afternoon editions or ran with full front-page stories and photographs of Franz Ferdinand and what the *Bosnische Post*— Sarajevo's semi-official German language daily—deemed a "High Visit." Page three of the paper carried a large and flattering photograph of Sophie, and the remaining pages largely covered the royal couple and the upcoming military exercises. Other newspapers followed suit,[5] with the Croat Jesuit paper *Hrvatski narod* running a front-page story referring to the Archduke as "our hope."[6] In preparation, one of Sarajevo's main thoroughfares— Ćemaluša Street—was repaved, building façades repaired, while residents bedecked balconies and windows with Habsburg flags and bright oriental rugs to give the city a festive mood.

The lone newspaper to play down the visit was the Serb *Narod*, which ran a back-page story under local news that the Archduke was coming, and that due to his arrival, all Serb and Croat flags had been ordered removed from Ilidža. Another critical article claimed that the adaptation of a hotel room into a chapel for the royal couple—both known for their piety—cost 40,000 gold Kronen.[7] Otherwise, the only hints of unrest in the Balkans were newspaper stories about the peasant uprising in Albania against its ruler, German Prince Wilhelm of Wied, and the defeat of the prince's forces commanded by Prenk Bib Doda near Durazzo (Durrës).

Upon the Archduke's arrival, the Second Battalion of the 92nd Infantry Regiment took up guard duties around the hotel complex and raised a flag with the Imperial Habsburg double eagle. The royal couple was ensconced in a suite of rooms especially furnished with luxurious Ottoman-style lamps, carpets, drapes, needlework, handicrafts, and furniture supplied by the prominent Sarajevo merchant Elias B. Kabiljo, a Sephardic Jew. Kabiljo's wife had personally supervised the refurbishment, and this expenditure of time and merchandise did not go unrewarded. Sophie sent a telegram to Kabiljo expressing a desire to see his showroom, and after settling in, the couple decided to make an impromptu late afternoon shopping excursion. Shortly after 5:00 pm, the Archduke's and Duchess' three-car motorcade set out for Kabiljo's store, some 12 kilometers from Ilidža in the center of Sarajevo at the east end of the valley. The entourage included Sophie's lady-in-waiting, Countess Lanjus, and Count Franz von Harrach, a member of the Volunteer Automobile Corps.

Kabiljo's shop sat at number 56 Franz Josef's Gasse[8] on the corner of Rudolf's Gasse,[9] across from the neo-Oriental Hotel Central, near the neo-Gothic Catholic and neo-Baroque Orthodox Cathedrals. At the time of their arrival, there were few people in Franz Josef's Gasse. However, after an hour inside the shop selecting goods, word spread and a crowd of several hundred gathered outside. Upon seeing the Archduke near the first floor balcony, the crowd began to shout praises of "Živio" (live long). With the shopping finished, they returned to their vehicles and drove down Appel Quai back to Ilidža, where they arrived at the Hotel Bosna by 7:00 pm. Many historians repeat the claim that the soon-to-be-assassin Gavrilo Princip came face to face with the Archduke and Sophie at this time as they walked through the crowd into the Turkish market. However, the Kabiljo shop was not near the Turkish market, and the source of this information is at best dubious and surfaced as hearsay only in 1929.[10]

As the royal couple left Sarajevo, the selection of films that weekend at the city's two main theaters foreshadowed events to come: the Apollo Kino-Theater was showing *Der Schuss um Mitternacht* (A Shot at Midnight), and the Imperial Kino-Theater *Die Welt ohne Männer* (A World Without Men), a comedy starring Madge Lessing.

Franz Ferdinand spent the next two days—June 26 and 27—on maneuvers in the rain with the XV and XVI Corps in the hills and mountains near Tarčin, west of Sarajevo, well distant from the border with Serbia. The maneuvers created a sense of paranoia among many Serbs, who feared they were intended at the very least as a thinly veiled threat against Serbia, as reflected by Belgrade's ambassador to Vienna, Jovan Jovanović, who wrote to Prime Minister Nikola Pašić claiming: "In diplomatic circles these maneuvers are viewed as a demonstration against Serbia."[11]

Rather than basking in the amenities of the spa, Sophie spent time in Sarajevo making formal visits to the Cathedral, the Cloister of St. Augustine, the Catholic Seminary Church and Boarding School, the Cloister of St. Vincent, the Archbishop's Orphanage, the Cloister of St. Josef, the Muslim Girl's School (*Ruždija*), the Muslim Orphanage, the Franciscan Monastery,

PHOTO 2 *Sarajevo Film Repertoire, June 1914 (reproduced with kind permission of the National Library of Bosnia and Herzegovina).*

and the carpet factory. At each stop Sophie was greeted with choirs, musical performances, bouquets of flowers, and speeches of adulation.[12]

On the evening of Saturday June 27, the royal couple attended a sumptuous formal farewell feast (*Höchste hoftafel*) at the Hotel Bosna, to which all Sarajevo's most prominent citizens and officials were invited. The band from the Sarajevo garrison sat on the lawn outside, playing a typical mix of popular music from the era, including the "Blue Danube."[13] Sarajevo's newspapers printed the itinerary for the royal couple's formal visit the next day, giving precise times and places, including the route of the motorcade to the City Hall, and the route after the City Hall visit.

Sunday June 28, 1914 dawned sunny and clear. For Franz Ferdinand and Sophie, their fourteenth wedding anniversary lay only three days away as they attended a 9:00 am holy mass at the special chapel in the hotel.[14] Serbs, however, celebrated the day differently: it was *Vidovdan* (St. Vitus' Day), the anniversary of the legendary 1389 Battle of Kosovo Polje, immortalized in myth and epic poetry, in which the Serbian principality led a valiant fight against the Turks in a Pyrrhic victory that marked the beginning of the end for the already weakened medieval Serbian state.

The royal couple departed Ilidža for Sarajevo at 9:25 am on a special train that covered the distance to the Filipović barracks[15] in roughly twenty-five minutes, five minutes quicker than the usual train. Potiorek and General Appel briefly escorted Franz Ferdinand around the compound and the Archduke reviewed the troops at the barracks. Then he and Sophie sat in the second motorcar of a six-vehicle motorcade.

The drive from the barracks through town was meant to be slow—the official schedule allocated ten minutes to cover 2.7 kilometers—to show off not only the royal couple to the populace, but also to display the achievements of Habsburg rule to the royal couple and the broader world. For during the preceding 36 years, the Habsburg Empire had performed a miracle of transformation in Bosnia-Herzegovina, with Sarajevo as the crown jewel, a city that could fit flawlessly into any *Bezirk* of *fin-de-siècle* Vienna.

When the Austro-Hungarian Army arrived in 1878, it found a backward Turkish province, harrowed by years of turmoil following peasant revolts and wars that had led to international intervention and the 1878 Treaty of Berlin. Ottoman Bosnia was underdeveloped by medieval standards, much less those of the late nineteenth century: approximately 95 percent of the population lived from agriculture, and the country was awash with almost 200,000 refugees who had fled Turkish retaliation during the uprisings.[16] In the 36 years since then, Vienna had built highways, railroads, tunnels, bridges, civic buildings, telegraph and telephone lines, schools, factories, banks, paved streets with asphalt, installed electric lighting and streetcars, constructed grand public structures, and brought western culture in the form of literature, music, architecture, and the other arts.

The capital city of Sarajevo had more than doubled its population from 21,377 residents to over 52,000 and now boasted three theaters and three movie theaters, a *Landesmuseum* (National Museum), and a streetcar, one of the first in Europe and recently electrified.[17] The first factories were built, and the city went from having no banks to eight locally registered banks, along with numerous others from throughout the Empire and other parts of the province. Sarajevo's international importance was reflected in the presence of six Great Power consulates from France, Germany, Great Britain, Italy, Russia, and Turkey, each closely following each other's actions. Numerous schools, both religious and public, were founded. By 1914, Sarajevo had thirty-eight educational institutions, including elementary, *Gymnasium*, and *Hochschule* (college), as well as specialized training in music, crafts, carpet weaving, theology, secretarial work, and teaching.[18] These had raised the level of literacy and culture, which had in turn led to an increased demand for books, the opening of a library, and the publication of twenty-eight different newspapers and periodicals. Cultural life flourished, and by 1914 ninety-seven separate societies had been registered, covering fields of interest as diverse as singing, folklore, homemaking, chess, bicycling, Esperanto, along with Croat and Serb *Sokols*—Slav sports and gymnastic organizations. Notably, a large number of mono-ethnic singing, cultural, and sports societies had opened, which served as hotbeds for various forms of South Slav nationalism. In retrospect, these would prove deadly for the Archduke and his wife.

Lined by verdant mountains to the north and south, the motorcade followed the tracks of Sarajevo's streetcar eastward along *Bahnhofstrasse* towards the town center. Accompanied by the thunder of artillery salutes from the fort on the hill overlooking Kovačići to the south and from the White Bastion perched high on a rock above Bendbaša to the east, they left the barracks and passed the white neo-classical pavilions of the *Landesmuseum* on the outskirts of town, completed only the year before. Across the street on their left was the *Cirkusplatz* (circus ground), the city's main recreation venue. At that point the main thoroughfare forked to the right to become Hisela Dolnja Street, with industrialist August Braun's imposing *Marienhof* ahead on the left, and the tobacco factory on the right. After the *Marienhof*, a row of new residential buildings lined the left side of the street in styles ranging from neo-classical to Secession, with the city's electric plant and gypsy quarter on the right. As they crossed the bridge over Koševo Stream they entered Appel Quai, a boulevard that hugged the bank of the Miljacka River to their right. To their right a George Eiffel-designed cast-iron bridge spanned the Miljacka. To their left rose the large white municipal building. Across the river sat elegant private homes with gardens facing the river, interrupted only by the imposing *Evangelische* (Protestant) church building.

Crowds lined the sidewalks on both sides of Appel Quai, and a series of monumental public and private structures fronted the left side of the boulevard, now lined with trees at its eastern end. These buildings included the recently completed southern façade of the large and grandiose neo-classical Palace of Justice, the newly completed Military Post Office, the Social Hall, the Palace of the Austro-Hungarian Bank, the Hungarian *Handels-Aktien Gesellschaft*, the Great *Realgymnasium*, and the headquarters of the Regional Tobacco Directorate, along with numerous private multi-story residential buildings, all constructed in the Empire's latest architectural fashions.

Yet behind these monumental new façades lurked the unresolved threat that prompted the Great Powers to give Bosnia and Herzegovina to Vienna: the agrarian question. Sparked by Sultan Abdul-Azziz's 1875 order to increase rents from serfs by 25 percent, a Serb peasant revolt erupted in Herzegovina that same year and then spread throughout Bosnia and the wider Ottoman-controlled Balkans. The Ottomans suppressed the rebellion brutally, but Serbia, Montenegro, and later Russia joined in the fight against the Turks. The outcome was Russia's defeat of Turkey in the Russo-Turkish war of 1877–1878, the short-lived Treaty of San Stefano (1878), and then the Treaty of Berlin (1878), where the Great Powers decided to give Bosnia-Herzegovina and the Sandžak of Novi Pazar to the Dual Monarchy to act as protector of the Christians.[19]

The Habsburgs chose to maintain the existing agrarian system in which over 95 percent of serfs were Christian, fearing a potential rebellion by Muslims, who constituted over 90 percent of the landholders. Although Vienna had established a program to help serfs buy their lands and freedom, few had the financial resources to do so, and by 1910 Serbs still constituted almost 73.92 percent of all serf households, Croats 21.49 percent, and Muslims 4.58 percent, while landholders were 91.15 percent Muslim.[20] This contrasted sharply with the overall population structure, in which Serbs represented 43.49 percent, Muslims 32.25 percent, and Croats 22.8 percent.[21] This disparity created a great deal of dissatisfaction among Catholics and Orthodox in rural areas, as well as among the rapidly emerging urban Christian middle class.

A large number of carpetbaggers accompanied the Habsburg administration: Ashkenazi Jews, Croats, Czechs, Germans, Hungarians, Slovaks, Poles, Serbs, and Slovenes descended on Bosnia from throughout the Empire. Some sought new business opportunities. Others sought to advance their careers in the Dual Monarchy's officer corps or administration by accepting posts in the new provinces. Seeking people loyal to the throne, Vienna sent large numbers of officers, policemen, and civilian administrators from the Slav parts of the Empire, especially from Serbo-Croatian speaking regions such as Vojvodina, Slavonia, Croatia, and Dalmatia, all areas with large Serb populations. Thus, from the very beginning Serbs were over-represented in the civilian administration and the military, important stepping-stones for upward social mobility.[22] These officials formed a new and growing middle class; their children attended the newly founded schools and joined the newly founded cultural and social clubs, where they were exposed to modern concepts of Pan-Slav unity, the Yugoslav idea, Bakunin-inspired anarchism, as well as Greater Serb and Greater Croat nationalist philosophies.

The building façades also concealed an even greater threat—the Habsburg Empire was struggling with serious internal unresolved national and political questions that threatened to tear apart its very fabric and lead to its dissolution. The Austrian historian Theodor von Sosnosky described it as:

> A dangerous political drift which allowed internal conditions in the Monarchy to grow steadily more confused while the irredentist movements grew bolder and more hydra-headed, and the process of national disintegration gathered momentum and brought the danger of collapse ever nearer.[23]

Nowhere was this more apparent than in the Empire's South Slav lands, where Greater Serbian nationalist irredentism combined with Croat anger at Hungary's increasing chauvinism to bring Serbs and Croats closer together. Baron Alexander von Musulin, a Croat official in the Dual Monarchy's Foreign Ministry, visited Croatia in 1913 and noted that:

> The differences between Serbs and Croats have largely disappeared among the educated classes and consequently there was a marked weakening of Croatian nationalist feeling . . . impressed by the immense development of the Serb race on the other bank of the Drava. In many places I met with the conviction that national salvation will come only from there . . . The political activity of Serbia makes itself felt everywhere.[24]

As Franz Ferdinand and Sophie's motorcade drove slowly along the crowd-lined Appel Quai, they had no way of knowing that danger lurked ahead.[25] They stopped briefly to admire the façade of the enormous new Military Post Office building, whose director *Präsident* Gaberle handed a telegram to Sophie from her children. As they passed the Austro-Hungarian Bank and approached the Ćumurija Bridge, a young man in the crowd on the right side of the street struck the percussion cap of a bomb against an electric pole supporting the streetcar wires and hurled it at the Archduke's vehicle. The bomb bounced off the rolled-up top of the Archduke's convertible and bounced into the street, where it exploded under the fourth car in the motorcade, injuring a passenger and several bystanders. The bomber jumped over the low retaining wall into the ankle-deep Miljacka and swallowed a cyanide capsule. He was quickly arrested. Franz Ferdinand ordered the driver to stop, got out, examined the damage and returned to his vehicle, after which the car raced to City Hall.[26]

Upon being greeted by Mayor Fehim Efendi Ćurčić on the front steps, Franz Ferdinand's temper momentarily got the best of him, and he upbraided Ćurčić for the bomb attack. Sophie calmed her husband and the two continued their program of official meetings inside the City Hall. Due to the bomb attack, events were behind schedule, and the royal couple left the City Hall five minutes late at 10:45 am with a modified plan. Rather than drive to the *Landesmuseum* as called for by the official itinerary, Franz Ferdinand decided to visit those wounded in the bomb attack, who were now at the military hospital near *Marienhof*. This meant a rapid return down Appel Quai, the most direct route. But no one had informed the drivers of either the first or second vehicles, who followed the original plan and turned right from Appel Quai into Franz Josef's Gasse. Immediately after making the turn, Potiorek ordered a halt; the driver stopped the car and began to back up.

As the vehicle moved slowly in reverse, a young man stepped from the crowd in front of Moritz Schiller's delicatessen on the corner of Appel Quai and Franz Josef's Gasse, pulled out a pistol and shot Franz Ferdinand and Sophie from close range. Chaos ensued. The crowd and police grappled with the assassin. Potiorek ordered the driver to hastily reverse across the Latin Bridge and then race to Potiorek's nearby official residence, the *Konak*, less than a hundred meters distant from Schiller's. En route it became apparent both Sophie and Franz Ferdinand were hit: Sophie was dead on arrival at the *Konak*, and Franz Ferdinand died approximately fifteen minutes later, shortly after 11:00 am.

Telegraph and telephones quickly spread the news of the assassination throughout the Empire, along with an additional piece of important information: the two assassins were Serbs.

The shooter, Gavrilo Princip, was an unemployed student from Bosnia. He had spent the previous two years in Belgrade finishing his education after having been expelled from school in Sarajevo due to participation in nationally motivated student demonstrations and poor grades. The bomber, Sarajevo-born Nedeljko Čabrinović, favored anarchist literature and had bounced around the South Slav areas of the Dual Monarchy organizing strikes and demonstrations, which usually ended in his expulsion from different cities. He had finally settled in Belgrade, where he worked in a print shop. Both were in police custody with serious stomach pains from swallowing old cyanide. Both quickly revealed they had not acted alone.

Realizing the serious implications for them, Sarajevo's leading Serb citizens held an emergency session of the Serbian Orthodox Church School Board under the leadership of its president, prominent Serb businessman and industrialist Gligorije Jeftanović at 6:20 pm. The minutes of the meeting show that the Board composed an official telegram of condolence to His Majesty the Emperor, who was holding summer court in Bad Ischl, in which they expressed "our deepest sympathies with expressions of unwavering faithfulness and loyalty to the most glorious throne and the entire ruling house." The meeting adjourned after thirty minutes and no further entries were made in the record until after 1918.[27] The head of the Serb National Party in Bosnia-Herzegovina, Dr. Milan Hadži Ristić, also sent his official condolences to the Emperor. But by then it was too late.

The anti-Serb backlash

In Sarajevo, several hundred Catholic and Muslim students began to gather in the early evening in Franz Josef's Gasse near the Hotel Central, diagonally across from the Serbian Orthodox Metropolitan Archbishop's Palace. They sang patriotic hymns, chanted "Down with Serbs," "Out with them," and "We don't want them," then moved up the street towards Jeftanović's Hotel Europe, Sarajevo's largest, and began hurling stones through the windows of the ground floor café. They were driven off by police, but shortly after midnight a mob broke into the hotel's café and began ransacking it. The arrival of police again put an end to this, but the mob sought new targets and turned on the Hotel Imperial. Around 3:00 am on the morning of June 29, army and cavalry arrived and stopped the demonstrations.

Anti-Serb demonstrations and riots also broke out that night in Zagreb with greater ferocity.[28] Many Croats viewed Franz Ferdinand as an ally in their struggle against Budapest and the Empire's dualist arrangement. Anti-Serb riots continued in Zagreb for three days.[29]

Overnight, flyers were posted throughout Sarajevo expressing outrage at the assassination and noting Belgrade's hand in it.[30] On June 29, Sarajevo's daily newspapers carried large headlines mourning the victims and lamenting the assassination. The loyalist *Bosnische Post* said that Čabrinović and Princip had carried out their actions under the influence of Serbian nationalists in Belgrade, and had admitted that the bombs came from Serbia. These articles represented the equivalent of a public call for anti-Serb riots.

From early that morning groups of Catholic, Jewish, and Muslim demonstrators wandered the city, encouraged by such luminaries as Croat City Councilman Josip Vancaš, an architect and principle designer of Sarajevo's most prominent public and private buildings. The mobs swept through the city in waves and attacked Serb businesses, schools, homes, and churches, including the Serbian Orthodox Council building, the cultural society *Prosvjeta*, the Serb newspaper *Srpska Riječ*, the Serb Club in Ćemaluša Street, and the Metropolitan Archbishop's Palace. Serbs who attempted to defend their homes were arrested: Serb jeweler Dimitrije Mitričević fired a shot in the air from his pistol to frighten off the crowd and draw the attention of the police as a mob attacked his home, an act which led to his arrest. Jeftanović's home was targeted, as were Jovo Buđanić's grocery store, Đorđo Niković's bakery, and the spice shop of the brothers Spasoje, Tatimir, and Kosta Jovičić, bookshops, and butcher shops, to mention but a few. When one wave finished their destruction, a new wave would follow after an hour or so.[31] In some instances, army officers, military units, and police encouraged this behavior or stood idly by.[32]

A large mob threw rocks, stones, and asphalt through the windows of the Serbian Orthodox Girls' School and Girls' High School. It then broke through both school doors and demolished everything in the office of the Parish and Church Council, rampaged through the corridors and classrooms,

PHOTO 3 *Archduke Franz Ferdinand's death notice on the* Bosnische Post *front page (reproduced with kind permission of the Historical Museum of Bosnia and Herzegovina).*

demolished furniture and tossed it from the window, demolished the plumbing and flooded the school, and ripped all the icons of the Serbian Orthodox Church's patron saint, St. Sava. Among the items damaged was a portrait of Kaiser Franz Josef I. This lasted an hour and a half, at which point a bugle blew outside and the mob moved on.[33] The looting included numerous wine shops and taverns, and by mid-morning many in the mob were intoxicated and beginning to endanger the property of non-Serbs. At this point, the army and police stepped in to calm the situation. Throughout the day, the mobs engaged in running battles with police and army troops, and bugles often signaled the arrival of the army. Order was briefly restored around noon, when troops from the 47th Infantry Regiment arrived to reinforce Sarajevo's overwhelmed 200-man police force.[34]

Around 2:30 that afternoon, another crowd of several hundred gathered in Franz Josef's Gasse and again attacked the Hotel Europe's café, this time destroying it entirely. Army intervention ended this, and the entire Hotel Europe was placed under military guard. Later, a group comprised mostly of Muslims from the lower classes moved through the *Baščaršija* (Turkish market) destroying Serb shops, including that of prominent Serb merchant Simo Prnjatović in *Čurčiluk*. By day's end, Ćemaluša Street had seen four separate waves of rioters and was filled with broken glass, furniture, street signs, and goods from Logavina Street up to the *Baščaršija*, and from the Catholic Cathedral all the way down to the *Landesbank*. Jeftanović's livery stables came under attack, and a large number of carriages were destroyed and thrown into the street.[35]

At 5:00 pm that afternoon, martial law was formally declared in Sarajevo. Ulan cavalry and a trumpeter were placed on every street corner. A 7:00 pm curfew was imposed on all under the age of fifteen, and all cafés and guesthouses were required to shut by 8:00 pm, with the exception of "first-class" establishments. Gatherings of more than three people were forbidden, as was loitering. Violation was punishable by two months jail and a 1,000 Krone fine.[36] Finally, peace descended upon the city. Given the large military forces at his disposal, it is clear that Potiorek intended the anemic response to the rioting as a lesson to the Serbs. Throughout Croatia, Herzegovina, Slavonia, Vojvodina, and other parts of Bosnia, anti-Serb riots and demonstrations continued for several more days in cities such as Zagreb, Mostar, Doboj, Maglaj, Zenica, Šamac, Čapljina, Brčko, and Trebinje.

The two days of violence had taken their toll. Many Serbs were beaten, and the Sarajevo hospitals reported that fifty people had sought medical attention.[37] There were initially two deaths: a Croat who was shot by one of the Jovičić brothers (Tatimir) trying to defend his spice shop, and a Muslim peasant from Kiseljak who committed suicide over rumors a Serb inn-keeper had found a bomb in his possession.[38] Two Serbs, Pero Prijavić and Nikola Nožičić, died several days later from injuries sustained as a consequence of beatings during the riots.[39] Serb stores and homes were robbed of cash, and entire inventories of goods were destroyed or looted. The impact was immediate: although Serbs were a minority in Sarajevo, they held prominent positions in business and industry disproportionate to their numbers.

Events in Sarajevo imperiled the ruling Croat–Serb coalition in the Croatian *Sabor* (parliament). In power since 1903, it had worked to find common cause among South Slavs against Hungarian, Austrian, and Italian interests. On June 30 as *Sabor* Speaker Dr. Bogdan Medaković—a Serb—took his seat, the Croatian Party of Rights deputies (*Pravaši*) began yelling: "Down with the coalition. Down with Serbs. Down with the murderers. That's Belgrade's hand." After fifteen minutes of shouting, Medaković tried to read a statement of condolence for Franz Ferdinand and Sophie, but was shouted down by deputies from the Croatian nationalist right-wing Pure Party of Rights (*Frankovci*), who yelled: "We won't let him speak." Medaković left the hall and the deputies began shouting that Serbs had to leave the coalition, to the applause of spectators in the gallery.[40]

On June 29, the late afternoon *Bosnische Post* reported that Princip and Čabrinović did not deny that the bombs came from Belgrade and that they had failed to show any remorse. It also described Princip as an "extraordinarily intelligent man, who gives precise answers to each question."[41] On June 30, an editorial appeared on the front page of the paper's special edition, stating that no one could believe that Princip and Čabrinović acted of their own accord, and expressed incredulity that they had managed to obtain the bombs along with training in how to use them. The article stated that these were the same type of bombs that had been used in 1906 in Montenegro,[42] that they had also been found the previous year in Brčko, and that all were manufactured in the Serbian arsenal in Kragujevac. The remainder of the editorial laid out a case for direct Serbian involvement in the assassination, and concluded on an ominous note:

> But among the Serb population in Bosnia and Hercegovina there are elements that have the death of the crown prince and his wife on their consciences. Among these Serbs there are those who for years have been pursuing a policy and carrying out activities that must bear fruit precisely like the assassination Sunday. One of the first and most important obligations of those called to positions of influence must be to protect the State against such elements. But it is also the duty of loyal and decent elements of the Serbs in these lands that society be cleansed of these vermin. Only in this way will it be possible that the country, and specifically the Serb population, be freed from the shame that they bear.[43]

On Wednesday July 1, Potiorek issued an order to form military courts in and around Tuzla and Maglaj, with the death penalty for high treason, acts against the military, disturbing the peace, uprising, revolt, public violence, murder, killing, serious physical injury, arson, theft, and aiding in any of the aforementioned crimes.[44]

Habsburg authorities discovered that a total of seven assassins had lined the motorcade route. They subsequently arrested four of them: organizer Danilo Ilić, Vaso Čubrilović, Cvjetko Popović, and Trifko Grabež, all Serbs. The lone non-Serb, Muhamed Mehmedbašić, a Muslim who had once attempted to assassinate Potiorek at the urging of renegade Serbian Army officers in Belgrade, escaped to Montenegro.[45] Authorities also arrested a number of others who helped Ilić, Princip, and Grabež illegally cross the border from Serbia, hide the weapons, and transport them to Sarajevo. All told, twenty-five persons eventually stood trial for the conspiracy. With the exception of four Croats, all were Serb.[46]

Although anti-Serb demonstrations in Zagreb finally ended on July 2, they continued in Slavonski Brod, Djakovo, Osijek, and Metković. In Sarajevo, the Serbian Orthodox Church held a *Parastos* (memorial service) for the royal couple on July 4, presided over by Metropolitan Archbishop Evgenije. That same day the Catholic Church held a mass in its cathedral—draped in black—with Archbishop Stadler leading the service, and Potiorek, Mayor Čurčić (a Muslim), and Vancaš present. In the northeast Bosnian city of Tuzla, Mufti Ibrahim Efendi Maglajlić held a memorial service and called upon Muslim soldiers in the Austro-Hungarian Army to "Be faithful and loyal to the exalted Habsburg House and towards its exalted ruling dynasty."[47]

Anarchists, assassins, and students

Until 1911 student groups in Bosnia were almost exclusively mono-ethnic, each devoted to its respective form of nationalism. The only exceptions were socialists. Catholics, Orthodox, Muslims, and Jews maintained a number of student and cultural organizations, some representing political parties or various philosophies. For example, the Serbian cultural society *Prosvjeta* cooperated with the Serb nationalist cultural society *Narodna odbrana* (National Defense) in Belgrade; the Serbian Radical Organization was under the influence of Serbian Prime Minister Nikola Pašić's Radical Party and met in the Circle of Serbian Sisters; and the Young Croat Organization operated according to the anti-Serb platform of Ante Starčević's Party of Pure Rights (*Frankovci*) who met at the Trebević Singing Society.[48]

Some of the few exceptions to this rule were the Croat Progressive Youth and the Serb Progressive Youth.[49] Under the influence of these two Progressive movements, some students began increasingly to turn to the idea of South Slav unity as a way to protect both Croat and Serb interests from growing Hungarian, Austrian, and Italian interests and chauvinism. Some identified the idea of Yugoslavism with an increasingly assertive Serbia, which they viewed as a possible future South Slav Piedmont.[50] In 1911, Croat and Serb students formed the Serbo-Croat Progressive Organization of High School

Students. This marked a departure from the ethnocentric cultural groups: both the Croat Progressive Organization and the Serbian Progressives aligned themselves with this movement.[51] The first members included Ivo Andrić as president (later to win a Nobel Prize for literature), Gavrilo Princip, Trifko Grabež, Lazar Đukić, and Dragoslav Ljubibratić. Another pro-Yugoslav youth group in Sarajevo was the *Srpsko-hrvatska nacionalistička omladina* (Serbo-Croatian Nationalist Youth), to which some of the conspirators belonged.[52] All seemed to have been deeply influenced by the actions of Bogdan Žerajić, a student who committed suicide following his failed assassination attempt of Marijan Varešanin, the Governor of Bosnia-Herzegovina in 1910.

Many students came under the influence of Vladimir Gaćinović, a Greater Serbian nationalist writer and activist from Herzegovina who maintained close ties with military intelligence circles in Belgrade, and another Herzegovinian Serb, Dimitrije Mitrinović, both writers for the Serb cultural magazine *Bosanska Vila*. Others, especially the Croats, favored cooperation with Serbs for protection against German and Hungarian hegemony, but within a reformed Habsburg Empire or an independent Croatia, and many rejected the notion of unification with Serbia.[53] Anarchist philosophy, the Greater Serbian national idea, the Greater Croatian national idea, the Yugoslav idea, outrage at serfdom and socio-economic inequalities, and anger at outside rule all combined to influence each student, albeit in different ways. Nonetheless, most students remained within the framework of the more traditional nationalist organizations, even though all Orthodox and Catholics seemed united by the injustices of the agrarian question, as well as the possibility of somehow overthrowing or reforming Habsburg authority.

In late 1911 and early 1912, Austria-Hungary passed laws that governed land expropriation along the Adriatic coast. Croats interpreted these laws as favoring Hungarian and Italian interests and significant unrest followed. In February 1912, anti-Hungarian demonstrations erupted throughout Croatia. Croatian high school student leaders—Luka Jukić among them— came to Sarajevo from Zagreb and called a meeting of all socialist and student groups at the premises of the Trebević Singing Society, during which those present sang the Pan-Slav anthem *Ej Sloveni* (Hey Slavs). On February 19 and 20, just after *Fasching* (Carnival), anti-Hungarian demonstrations and riots by mostly Croat students from the *Realschule, Gymnasium*, and Teaching School brought over a thousand demonstrators onto the streets of Sarajevo. Potiorek eventually called in sixty Ulan cavalry and a battalion of infantry with fixed bayonets to restore order.[54] Approximately seventeen people were arrested and twenty students expelled from school, mostly Muslims and Croats. Many others lost their scholarships or stipends. Among these was Princip, who made his way to Belgrade to continue his studies. Serbs in Sarajevo openly expressed their solidarity with the Croats against Hungarian hegemony.[55] Croat dissatisfaction with Hungarian rule would soon express itself in a more violent fashion.

Political assassinations were rather commonplace in Europe during the second half of the nineteenth and first decades of the twentieth centuries. Idealistic students, revolutionaries, and disaffected workers lashed out against Europe's rigid socio-political order and had already claimed the lives of Russian Tsar Alexander II, French President Marie François Sadi Carnot, and Spanish Prime Minister Antonio Cánovas del Castillo, to name but a few.[56] Within Austria-Hungary, such attacks had touched the House of Habsburg directly: Emperor Franz Josef's wife the Empress Elisabeth had fallen victim to an anarchist in 1898, and the Emperor himself had survived two attempts on his own life. Elsewhere in the Dual Monarchy, in 1908 Polish Galician governor Andrzej Potocki died at the hands of an assassin, while the Hungarian-nominated *Ban* (Governor) of Croatia-Slavonia, Slavko Cuvaj, survived two assassination attempts in 1912, including one by Luka Jukić. Between 1900 and 1914, more than forty prominent political assassinations had occurred worldwide.[57]

At the time, these assassins were considered "terrorists," a label they proudly wore. Today we would probably call these acts political assassinations. Certainly they had little in common with the terrorist attacks of the last quarter of the twentieth century and first decades of the twenty-first, which had a goal of spreading fear among broad civilian populations via indiscriminate or targeted mass violence. Similarities, nevertheless, exist. The students, workers, and activists who became terrorists were inspired largely by anger at social injustice, and by ideology. They aimed to convey dissatisfaction and rebellion via the "propaganda of the deed"—setting an example to others by their actions. This usually manifested itself as an attempt to kill members or supporters of Europe's pre-1914 ruling elites.[58] Other motivating factors included passions generated by the nationalism and romanticism that swept through Europe, the successful unifications of Germany and Italy, anarchist philosophers such as Peter Kropotkin and Mikhail Bakunin, and the emergence of new nation-states from the ruins of the Ottoman Empire (Albania, Bulgaria, Greece, and Serbia). In this context, the assassination in Sarajevo could have been seen as yet another in a series of such attacks. Under normal circumstances it would not have led to war.

Sarajevo, however, proved different. During interrogations, Habsburg investigators quickly discovered that the three conspirators who organized the assassination—Danilo Ilić, Trifko Grabež, and Gavrilo Princip—had not acted on their own. They had acquired their weapons and received training in their use from a Serbian army officer in Belgrade; they had also received assistance from Serbian army and government officials and agents to illegally cross the border into the Habsburg Empire. Investigators learned that the three had instructions to find additional people to assist them with the assassination. Although many historians portrayed the conspirators as students, five of the seven had already finished their education (Ilić, Grabež, Čubrilović, Mehmedbašić, and Čabrinović), while Princip kept dropping in and out of school.[59]

Subsequently, most historians and politicians have referred to the conspirators as members of a secret multi-national student organization or movement called *Mlada Bosna* (Young Bosnia) comprised of Croats, Muslims, and Serbs. However, no evidence exists that the conspirators or students in general considered themselves part of a broader organized movement. Certainly the term was not mentioned during the trial or in the newspapers and periodicals at the time. Dragoslav Ljubibratić, a classmate of Princip's who knew all the other conspirators and accompanied Princip to Serbia to volunteer for training with a Serbian guerrilla unit during the Balkan Wars wrote:

> The youth movement in Bosnia and Herzegovina that is today known by the name of *Mlada Bosna*, was part of the general Yugoslav youth movement of that time, and then it didn't carry a particular name. [Vladimir] Gaćinović's article "Young Bosnia" in the calendar of [Bosnian Serb magazine] *Prosvjeta* for 1911 came out at a time when that movement had just begun and was still distant from the meaning it would later receive. Jevtić's article under the same title in *Bosanska Vila* of December 30 1913 related to contemporary Bosnian writers. The name *Mlada Bosna* in its current meaning was used by Božidar Purić in an article under that title that was published in the fourth issue of *Zbavnik* on Corfu in 1917.[60]

Although there was an active South Slav literary movement that attempted to write in Serbo-Croatian and covered a wide variety of topics, the term *Mlada Bosna* was not used contemporaneously to describe it, nor was it organized in any fashion. However, it "gave an impetus to laying the literary and intellectual groundwork for the modernization of not only the local literary scene in Bosnia-Herzegovina but also of the shared cultural space in interwar Yugoslavia."[61] This thesis is also backed by Vladimir Dedijer and the brilliant investigative historian Luigi Albertini, who called it a "collective term."[62] If this is indeed the case, then the term should refer more correctly to the broader generation of students prior to the outbreak of the Great War, who were influenced by Žerajić's suicide.[63] Certainly Žerajić served as a common denominator among most of the conspirators, with Princip stating at his trial that he had visited Žerajić's grave before the assassination.

The first use of the term *Mlada Bosna* to describe the Sarajevo conspirators coincided with the negotiations between the Serbian government-in-exile on Corfu and the Croat-majority Yugoslav Committee, headed by Ante Trumbić and Frano Supilo. As such, it should be viewed as an essential cornerstone of the founding myth of the post-war Kingdom of Serbs, Croats, and Slovenes, later to be known as Yugoslavia. No doubt this myth helped partially win over members of the Serbian parliament-in-exile on Corfu from Garašanin's Greater Serbian program, to the pan-Yugoslav idea enshrined in the Corfu Declaration that was signed on July 20, 1917 by the Serbian parliament and the Yugoslav Committee.

Myth-building aside, at the time the Sarajevo assassination did not appear to be a case of idealistic students acting on their own, because a neighboring sovereign state—Serbia—seemed implicated in state-sponsored terrorism. Since 1903, Serbia and the Dual Monarchy had waged an undeclared cold war. It was now about to become hot.

Immediately after the Sarajevo assassination, official Belgrade sent telegrams of condolence and sympathy to Vienna. Serbia's Prime Minister and Foreign Minister, Nikola Pašić, wrote to all of Serbia's embassies to say:

> The Serbian Government and public opinion in Serbia, upon hearing news of the assassination, expressed not only sympathy for the victims, but also sharp condemnation and disgust towards such a crime.[64]

Popular Serbian reaction, however, was quite the opposite of Pašić's description, as much of the population expressed satisfaction and even joy at the assassination. Beginning on June 29, Serbia's minister in Vienna, Jovan Jovanović, sent numerous telegrams to Pašić pleading with him to curtail the anti-Austrian tone and glee about the assassination in Belgrade's tabloid press, noting that the Habsburg press was exploiting this to whip up anti-Serbian frenzy.[65]

Whereas wiser heads, such as Pašić, understood the seriousness of the situation, popular opinion in Serbia saw this as revenge for Austria-Hungary annexing Bosnia-Herzegovina, and as yet another triumph coming fresh on the heels of the Balkan Wars, one that could lead to the weakening of the Dual Monarchy and perhaps even eventual territorial gain for Belgrade. In early July, the Austro-Hungarian consul in Niš, Herr Hoflehner, wrote to Austria-Hungary's Foreign Minister Count Leopold Berchtold about the level of anti-Habsburg popular opinion in Serbia:

> There was practically no sign of consternation or indignation; the predominant mood was one of satisfaction and even joy, and this was often quite open and without any reserve, and even found expression in a brutal way. This is especially the case with the so-called leading circles—the intellectuals, such as professional politicians, those occupied in education, officials, officers and the students . . . It was painful in the fullest degree to see and hear what a feeling of real delight seized the numerous visitors who were present, with what obvious satisfaction the deed was discussed.[66]

The tabloid feeding-frenzy between Vienna and Belgrade reached such a fever pitch that on July 16 Pašić sent a telegram and a letter to all Serbian embassies informing them that Belgrade's press was writing inflammatory articles about the Dual Monarchy, and that the Austro-Hungarian press was taking the most outrageous of these pieces and using them to whip up further hatred against Serbia. He asked the ministers to inform their host countries of these activities and defend Serbia's position.[67]

In spite of public excitement and approval of the assassination, Serbia's government was more sober in its response, realizing the difficulty of its situation. Yet an election campaign was underway, which meant that any statement appearing less than patriotic could be used against those seeking office. Pašić noted to Serbia's embassies that the Belgrade media was trying to draw Austria-Hungary into a heated polemic. He wrote: "the Serbian Government . . . has tried to give advice to the Belgrade press to remain calm and to simply dispel the tendentiously released false rumors, but efforts were unsuccessful with a significant number of papers." He concluded: "the Serbian Government couldn't prevent this, because complete freedom of the media is guaranteed by constitutional clauses and laws."[68] The increasingly heated war of words strengthened pro-war factions across the continent, especially in Vienna.

CHAPTER TWO

A third Balkan war?

A side order of war

Although not on the menu, the First World War arrived over lunch. On Tuesday July 28, 1914, Serbia's most prominent politician Nikola Pašić, who held the dual posts of President of the Government (Prime Minister) and Minister of Foreign Affairs, sat eating lunch in the *Evropa* café in the central Serbian city of Niš. Famous for his beard of biblically prophetic proportions, horrible penmanship, and non-committal sphinx-like utterances in grammatically questionable Serbian, Pašić was a survivor; his political career had included imprisonment and a death sentence. Shortly after 1:00 pm a Serbian gendarme burst into the restaurant, approached Pašić and handed him an open telegram from the Austro-Hungarian Foreign Ministry in Vienna, which had been routed via Bucharest. The telegram, which had been sent without any urgent markings, read:

> Since the Royal Serbian Government has not given a satisfactory answer to the note which was given by the Austro-Hungarian Minister in Belgrade July 23, 1914, the Imperial-Royal government has found it necessary to resort to arms in order to satisfy its rights and interests. Therefore, Austria-Hungary views itself as being in a state of war with Serbia as of this moment.[1]

Austria-Hungary's Minister of Foreign Affairs Count Leopold von Berchtold had just declared war by open telegram, the first such instance of its kind. After reading the telegram, Pašić arose and announced to the other diners: "Austria has declared war on us. Our cause is just. God will help us."[2] So began the First World War.

In spite of Pašić's statement, there was at first disbelief that the telegram was authentic. Serbia's High Command had received the same telegram from Zemun (Semlin), directly across the Sava River from Belgrade, and the

PHOTO 4 *Serbia's Prime Minister Nikola Pašić.*

ever-cautious Pašić waited to verify the contents, even going so far as to send a telegram to the Serbian embassy in London, telling them that he doubted the authenticity of the declaration, due its method of delivery.[3]

Nonetheless, the declaration of war came as no surprise to Pašić. Five days earlier at precisely 6:00 pm on Thursday July 23, Austria-Hungary's ambassador to Serbia Baron Vladimir von Giesl had delivered an ultimatum—officially a "note"—to the acting President of Serbia's government, the swarthy chain-smoking physician and Minister of Finance Dr. Lazar Paču.[4] The ultimatum, which historian Joachim Remak labeled "a brutal document whose directness had few precedents in diplomatic history," began by accusing Belgrade of complicity in the Sarajevo assassinations.[5] Its ten points demanded that Serbia:

1   Suppress all publications that incited hatred against Austria-Hungary;

2   Dissolve the *Narodna Odbrana* organization;

3   Eliminate all anti-Habsburg teachings from the educational system;

4   Remove all military officers with anti-Habsburg views;

5   Allow the Habsburg security apparatus to operate freely in Serbia to investigate anti-Habsburg movements;

6   Allow the Habsburg Empire to participate in investigations and judicial proceedings against any conspirators involved in the Sarajevo assassination;

7   Arrest Major Vojislav Tankosić and Milan Ciganović;

8   Dismiss all border guards who allowed the assassins to cross into Bosnia-Herzegovina;

9   Apologize for anti-Habsburg statements made by Serbian officials;

10 Immediately inform the Habsburg government of how Serbia would comply with the foregoing demands.[6]

The document also required Serbia to publish a three-paragraph statement on July 26 in the official military newspaper *Vojni List* decrying all anti-Habsburg propaganda and actions, and demanded a response by 6:00 pm on Saturday July 25, a mere 48 hours away. Given the short time-frame and harshness of the demands, it appeared to the Serbs that Vienna had little desire to see Belgrade comply with this ultimatum; rather, it was deliberately written to be rejected so as to provide Vienna the long-awaited *casus belli* against Serbia.[7]

The meeting between Pašu and von Giesl was awkward: Pašu did not speak French, the diplomatic *lingua franca* of the epoch, and he needed the services of General Secretary Grujić, who accompanied him as a translator. Ironically, Pašu spoke fluent German, having studied medicine in Zurich. Von Giesl verbally informed Pašu of the deadline and—without having read the note or opening the folder it was contained in—Pašu told von Giesl that he lacked the legal authority to respond.

The note could not have arrived at a worse moment. All the cabinet members and parliamentary deputies had returned to their home districts to campaign for the upcoming August 14 elections, which meant the entire government was absent from Belgrade. Pašu objected that it was physically impossible for him to convene the Council of Ministers within the time demanded. Von Giesl replied that in the age of trains, telegraph, and telephone, reassembling the government was only a matter of hours. He then left.[8]

In addition to the government and parliament, Serbia's most prominent military figures were also scattered, both abroad and throughout the country, some on leave, others on assignment: the Chief of the General Staff, *Vojvoda* Radomir Putnik, and one of his adjutants, Colonel Živko Pavlović, were in Austria-Hungary at spas; General Stepa Stepanović was in Čačak in western Serbia; Generals Bojović and Božanović were traveling in different areas of Macedonia, far to the south.

Following efforts to locate the elusive Pašić on the campaign trail, he was finally found in Niš, preparing to board the train to Thessaloniki for an incognito rest. Pašić embarked, and didn't seem to wish to deal with the matter, even after the ultimatum was read to him over the telephone at a stop in Leskovac. Finally, the regent, Prince Aleksandar ordered his return to Belgrade.[9] The energetic Pašu met with Military Minister Colonel Dušan Stefanović and ordered him to arrest Tankosić in compliance with the ultimatum's seventh demand. Stefanović relayed the arrest order to Colonel Anđelković, commander of the Danube I Division, who carried it out. Even though it was late in the day, Stefanović took further action. "Without the knowledge of the president of the government, I informed all commanders of the divisions to review preparations for mobilization and to recall all officers on leave or sick leave to their commands."[10] He ordered the recall of *Vojvoda* Putnik and General Stepanović, as well as all other staff officers, then called Director of Railroads Vlada Marković and told him to make preparations for transporting the army. Thus began the flurry of activity intended to precede mobilization.

Answering the ultimatum

Three days earlier, on the morning of Saturday July 25, Stefanović had asked Pašić if the army should mobilize. Pašić answered: "for now touch nothing. This evening it will be known." While waiting for nightfall and the answer, Stefanović returned to the Military Ministry, where he placed the railroads under military control and began preparations to dynamite Serbia's only physical link with Europe, the railroad bridge across the Sava River between Belgrade and Zemun.

On the morning of July 25, Baron von Giesl contacted Đorđe Ćutković, Belgrade representative of the Danube Steamboat Society. The Baron placed his automobile and personal belongings on a barge at the Sava landing and told Ćutković to await his personal instructions. Later that afternoon, prior to the deadline for delivery of Serbia's response to the ultimatum, von Giesl called Ćutković by telephone and told him to send the barge across the river to the Austro-Hungarian border town of Zemun.[11] For Austria-Hungary, the matter had clearly already been decided and Von Giesl obviously did not plan to remain in Belgrade.

Von Giesl's actions aside, there were other indications—unknown to the Serbian government—that Austria-Hungary was intent on war at all costs. On July 23, the day von Giesl delivered the ultimatum to Paču, Count Berchtold sent a secret telegram to the Austro-Hungarian diplomatic and consular missions in Scutari, Durazzo, and Valona. He ordered Habsburg officials to encourage the Albanian population in Serbia (i.e., Kosovo, Macedonia, Sandžak) to begin a revolt. Three days later, on July 26, Berchtold sent a telegram to Consul General August Ritter von Kral in Durazzo, telling him war was imminent and would be declared shortly. He instructed von Kral to spread rumors among the Albanians that war had already been declared, the Serbian government and court had fled Belgrade, and Austro-Hungarian troops had crossed the border with Serbia.[12]

On the evening of July 24 and the morning of July 25, at meetings presided over by Serbia's regent and crown prince Aleksandar Karađorđević, the hastily assembled cabinet pondered over the response, which was drafted by the gravely ill Minister of the Interior Stojan Protić. Knowing in advance that it would not please Austria-Hungary, Serbia began its mobilization at 3:00 pm on July 25, three hours prior to the expiration of the ultimatum.[13]

Nikola Pašić went alone to personally deliver the response to the Austro-Hungarian legation at 5:45, fifteen minutes prior to the 6:00 pm deadline.[14] The Serbian response was humiliating and conciliatory: Belgrade accepted nine of the ten conditions, while equivocating only on one that would require it to violate its own constitution and laws, and offering to submit that matter to the Great Powers or to the World Court at The Hague. After seeing it, Germany's Kaiser Wilhelm II wrote: "with it every reason for war drops away."[15]

Although one historian claimed that the Serbian response was a masterpiece of "diplomatic equivocation," that "the claim often made in general narratives that this reply represented an almost complete capitulation to the Austrian demands is profoundly misleading," and that it was "a highly perfumed rejection on most points,"[16] such analysis demonstrates a profound misunderstanding of the events behind the Sarajevo assassination, Vienna's aggressive expansionist policy and goals in the Balkans after 1903, as well as the legal and constitutional limitations the Serbian government faced in 1914.

The entire Serbian cabinet—with the exception of the gravely ill Protić—gathered at Jovan Ristić's house to await Pašić's return. The wait seemed long: when Pašić "finally" arrived at the Ristić house he wore a formal full length coat, even though the weather was hot and humid, and it appeared that he "was thoughtful and serious."[17] In his diary, Military Minister Dušan Stefanović wrote that Pašić told the assembled ministers:

> It is finished. Giesl is leaving Serbia. He is completely ready for the trip: he was waiting for me in traveling clothes and in the hallway were packed suitcases. Tonight at 22:00 we will leave by train for Niš from the station at Topčider. Don't wait for me. The National Assembly will open immediately in Niš—call all the delegates there. Now, go and finish your most important business.[18]

Pašić told them Austria had decided to declare war on Serbia, and then ordered the Minister of Public Works, Joca Jovanović, to prepare a train at the Topčider station to transport the ministers to the city of Niš.[19] Thus began the evacuation of the Serbian government.

Fifteen minutes after Pašić delivered the Serbian response, Baron von Giesl sent a note stating Serbia's reply was unsatisfactory, and that he and his staff were leaving Serbia immediately, and Pašić should regard the note as formally ending diplomatic relations between the two countries. At the train station, Baron von Giesl and the legation personnel boarded the 6:30 pm train, which took them the 300 meters across the Sava River into Austria-Hungary.[20]

Vojvoda Putnik, who masterminded Serbia's victories in both Balkan Wars, designed Serbia's defensive strategy, and held the key to the safe in which the mobilization plans were stored, was taking a cure for his chronic bronchitis—which had turned into emphysema—at the Austrian spa of Bad Gleichenberg in the company of his daughter. Hearing of the Austro-Hungarian ultimatum on July 24, he left Bad Gleichenberg for Serbia the next day.

While en route to Serbia, Habsburg authorities arrested Putnik in Budapest. With this act it appeared the Dual Monarchy had won a major victory without a shot having been fired. Yet this was an era in which rules of chivalry applied. The following day, July 26, after the personal intervention of the pro-war Hungarian Count von Hoyos of the Foreign Ministry with Field Marshall Franz Conrad von Hötzendorf, chief of the Austro-Hungarian General Staff, the Habsburg authorities released Putnik and allowed him to continue his journey back to Serbia via Romania, under escort by a Lieutenant Colonel of the *K.u.k. Armee* General Staff.[21] According to Austro-Hungarian General Alfred Krauss, the rationale behind releasing Putnik was that it would be better that the Serbs be commanded by the old, uneducated Putnik than by one of the younger officers educated in France.[22]

While traveling through Romania, Putnik contracted the pneumonia that would kill him three years later. Due to the round-about journey and a delay in Turnu Severin caused by pneumonia, Putnik did not arrive at the High Command in Kragujevac until August 5, by which time mobilization was well under way and fighting had already begun.[23]

The absence of *Vojvoda* Putnik became immediately noticeable: the mobilization plans were kept in a safe at the Military Ministry, and only Putnik had the key. The safe had to be dynamited to extract the plans for mobilization.[24] Stefanović named General Stepa Stepanović—who had recently arrived in Belgrade—as acting Chief of the General Staff, pending Putnik's arrival. Around 9:00 pm, Colonel Živko Pavlović, chief of the Operational Section of the General Staff who had been out of the country at an Austro-Hungarian spa, arrived. Shortly after Živković's arrival, Crown Prince Aleksandar entered the Ministry and signed the orders authorizing mobilization. He then left for Niš by automobile.[25] General Stepanović and Colonel Pavlović immediately left for Kragujevac, where they began to form the High Command, which, under Serbia's mobilization plan, replaced the General Staff during wartime. Stefanović stayed at the Ministry, working until 10:00 pm.

The army—at the request of the Governor of the National Bank—began to evacuate the National Bank's treasury. Armed cadets from the Infantry Under-officers School escorted cases of gold bars to the station and loaded them on a special train for Stalać, where they remained until 1915. The military garrison evacuated the Kalemegdan fortress at the confluence of the Sava and Danube Rivers and emptied all ammunition depots. Hospital units left the city, heading south. The various diplomatic missions to Serbia packed their belongings in anticipation of the capital moving to Niš. Belgrade was a flurry of activity as the government evacuated its offices and personnel, and as messengers raced to and from the Military Ministry.

To the south, the normally sleepy city of Niš quickly transformed. On July 26, Dušan Stefanović noted that: "Niš has come to life. All the ministers with their families, foreign emissaries, national deputies, newspapermen, and a large number of refugees have flooded Niš."[26] The Niš Officers Club was converted into a meeting hall for the hastily recalled National Assembly. Crown Prince Aleksandar and his father King Petar established court. The German Minister Griesinger arrived in Niš on July 26 and gave Pašić some good news: "England had taken into its hands the mediation between Russia and Austria-Hungary, and that it appeared that peace will be secured."[27]

Balkan roots of a world war

War between Austria-Hungary and Serbia had been a long time coming and confrontation seemed inevitable. So poor were relations between the two that hostilities had nearly erupted on four separate occasions in the preceding eight years.[28]

The so-called "Eastern Question," a euphemism for the struggle over the decaying carcass of the Ottoman Empire—the "Sick Man of Europe"—dominated nineteenth-century Great Power politics. Just as nature abhors a vacuum, so too does international politics. As the "Sick Man" withered, it created a power vacuum on Europe's periphery, leading to collisions between the Great Powers as they rushed to fill the void. Austria-Hungary, Italy, and Russia all proved anxious to exercise influence over or claim former Ottoman lands in the Balkans. These actions merely represented a continuation of their long-term interests: Austria-Hungary's southward push toward Thessaloniki; Italy's expansion across the Adriatic; and Russia's thirst for unimpeded control over the straits. To a great extent, the origins of the First World War are rooted in Great Power entanglements with the interests of the Balkan nation-states, as they collided in an attempt to fill the vacuum left by decaying Ottoman Turkey and a weakening Austria-Hungary.

For Rome and Vienna, the Balkans provided the only territory directly contiguous with their own into which they could expand without taking land from another Great Power. For St. Petersburg, control of the Dardanelles and Bosphorus was paramount. Both Paris and London wished to parry increased Russian and Austro-Hungarian influence in the Balkans, fearing the prospect of a stronger Dual Monarchy with naval capabilities outside the Adriatic, the growing German naval presence—which would no doubt take advantage of friendly Habsburg and Ottoman ports—and a Russian naval presence in the Mediterranean. Germany sought to follow whatever policies would weaken Britain, France, and Russia and prop up the Habsburgs. To strengthen their positions, the Great Powers created alliances among themselves and with the emerging Balkan nation-states.

In turn, the Balkan states actively sought Great Power patrons, as national groups in the Balkans pursued their own territorial goals. Inspired by the unification of Italy and Germany, the Albanians, Bulgarians, Croats, Greeks, Romanians, and Serbs all formulated greater national programs that laid claim to current and former Ottoman territories, Habsburg lands, or in some cases—the territories of their newly emergent neighbors. All hoped to acquire lands they regarded as rightfully theirs, based on historic, legal, and national claims. In many instances, territorial ambitions overlapped, making a Great Power patron all the more essential to champion one's claim.

Although other Balkan states staked claims to Ottoman territories or those of their neighbors, Serbia's greater national program encompassed substantial portions of the Dual Monarchy's southern lands, thus directly challenging Austro-Hungarian hegemony in the region.

The "Balkan Piedmont"

For the Kingdom of Serbia, it was an era of great excitement and national awakening as the country's star ascended. Following the first and second uprisings against Turkish rule in 1804 and 1815, Serbia had become largely autonomous from Istanbul, and in 1867—guided by Prince Mihailo Obrenović's skillful diplomacy—had achieved *de facto* independence. From 1844 onward, Belgrade followed a national program outlined by then-Foreign Minister Ilija Garašanin in a treatise entitled *Načertanije* (Draft), which called for Serbia to liberate all Serbs and other South Slavs and to annex South Serbia, Kosovo, the Sandžak of Novi Pazar, Bosnia, Herzegovina, Montenegro, and northern Albania, all then within the Ottoman Empire. It also called for Serbia to annex the Hungarian crown lands of Bačka and Srem, as well as the Banat of Temišvar (Timișoara), which covered the areas south of the Maros River, east of the Tisza River, and north of the Danube and Sava rivers, roughly the majority of today's Vojvodina. It spoke of Serbia's fourteenth-century Tsar Stefan Dušan, whose empire extended from the Peloponnesus in the south to the Danube and Sava rivers in the north, from Sofia in the east to beyond the Drina River and into Herzegovina in the west. The document, which was influenced by Polish Prince Adam Czartoryski and Polish ambassador to Serbia Franjo Zach, was intended to ideologically underpin the Serbian national question and as a way to prevent the Habsburgs from dividing the Empire's Slav lands.[29]

The *Načertanije* also implored Serbia to devote its resources to propaganda and education to help prepare the groundwork for future expansion, liberation, and unification, which it actively pursued.[30] Notably, it called for outreach to the Croats, saying "we should act in such a manner that the two peoples, the Eastern Orthodox and Roman Catholic, could reach mutual understanding and an agreement about their national policy, for only then can this policy be successfully brought into effect."[31] This was particularly important as large Serb populations resided inside Croatia's military border, where Serbs made up a substantial proportion of the Empire's most elite fighting units.[32] So, too, were Croats present in Bosnia, Herzegovina, Montenegro, and Vojvodina.

In the Balkans, ideas of Pan-Slav unification had already begun to appear in the seventeenth century.[33] During the first half of the nineteenth century, the Illyrian Movement emerged within the Habsburg Empire, primarily among Croats but with substantial interest from Serbs, such as Vuk Stefanović Karadžić.[34] Although the Hungarians eventually repressed the movement in 1849, the leading Illyrians met in Vienna in March 1850 with prominent Serb scholars Vuk Stefanović Karadžić and Đuro Daničić to sign an agreement on a common language, which they called Serbo-Croatian. This language formed a linguistic and literary basis for future cooperation between Serbs and Croats, who used numerous dialects of the same language, based on region and not nationality. The creation of a short-lived Habsburg duchy between 1848 and 1867 titled the Voivodeship of Serbia and Banat of Temeschwar (*Woiwodschaft Serbien und Temescher Banat*) also served to raise national consciousness among the Empire's South Slavs.

In March 1878, following peasant uprisings in Bosnia-Herzegovina and Russia's victory in the Russo-Turkish War, St. Petersburg attempted to strengthen its influence in the Balkans by creating an independent Greater Bulgaria under the Treaty of San Stefano. This alarmed the other Great Powers, who forced substantial concession from St. Petersburg at the Congress of Berlin (June to July 1878). Vienna sought to weaken Russian influence by championing Serbia's independence as a principality and awarding it the cities of Niš and Leskovac. Bulgaria was forced to relinquish Macedonia and parts of southeast Serbia, while Montenegro received recognition as an independent principality. Significantly, the Treaty of Berlin returned large portions of south Serbia and Macedonia to Ottoman rule. At Berlin, Vienna received the right to occupy and administer Bosnia-Herzegovina and Sandžak, which angered many in Serbia, who viewed both as future areas for Serbian expansion. Although Belgrade had received independence and small chunks of territory, many in Serbia felt dissatisfied; Austria-Hungary's presence in Bosnia-Herzegovina would thwart Serbia's expansion in that direction, and Habsburg occupation of the Sandžak created a barrier between Serbia and Montenegro. This move also suggested Vienna's intent to drive a rail line to Thessaloniki via Bosnia-Herzegovina, Sandžak, Kosovo, and Macedonia, all areas that Belgrade coveted.[35] Writing as a war correspondent in 1912, Leon Trotsky eloquently described the importance of Sandžak:

A railway through the sanjak, a concession for which was granted to Austria during the last days of the old regime in Turkey, would have linked up the Austro-Bosnian line with the Turko-Macedonian one . . . it would open a convenient strategic route for an Austrian drive into the eastern Balkans, and the scheme was completely based on the prospect of an impending dismemberment of Turkey.[36]

Serbia continued its program of education among Slavs in the Ottoman regions, spearheaded by Serbian Orthodox clergy, students, teachers, and government officials.[37] Spurred by the unification of Italy and Germany, many Slavs throughout the Balkans looked to Serbia as an inspiration for what could be achieved. In the coming decades, tensions rose between Bulgaria and Serbia as both countries worked to convert the population of Macedonia to their national cause. Likewise, Serbia also began to increase its propaganda and educational activities in Bosnia-Herzegovina.

Belgrade signed a secret convention with Austria-Hungary in 1881 that essentially formalized Serbia's dependence on the Dual Monarchy as its Great Power patron. In return, Serbia achieved the status of a kingdom in 1882 with full Habsburg support. Consequently, Serbia's ruling Obrenović dynasty usually followed pro-Austrian policies and focused its immediate efforts for expansion on the weakening Ottoman Empire. At the behest of Vienna, Serbia even initiated a short-lived war with Bulgaria in November 1885, after Sofia annexed Eastern Rumelia, creating fears of a Greater Bulgaria that would rival Serbia's pretensions in Macedonia. Following a rapid defeat by Bulgaria at the Battle of Slivnica, Vienna had to step in to prevent Serbia from losing territory. This prompted Serbia to intensify its propaganda and educational activities in Macedonia and the south of Serbia.[38]

Praetorian politics

During the latter part of the 1890s, Serbia's officer corps had become a focal point for the best and brightest men in the country, all inspired by Garašanin's *Načertanije* and all devoted to the idea of creating a Greater Serbia from the Ottoman and Habsburg empires. Between 1898 and 1901, the Military Academy produced approximately 500 officers, all of whom favored expansionist policies, as did the political elites and public at large.[39] One of these was Dragutin Dimitrijević, a large, slightly pudgy and balding bull of a man with a dimple in his chin and a mustache that curled up at the corners. Due to his personality and size, he received the nickname "Apis" after the holy bull in ancient Egyptian mythology.

In October 1902, a group of rogue army officers, led by Apis, signed a secret document that called for murdering the increasingly autocratic King Aleksandar Obrenović and replacing him with the more pliable Petar Karađorđević.[40] On the night of June 10 and 11, 1903, the conspirators broke into the grounds of the royal palace and brutally murdered King Aleksandar Obrenović and his wife Queen Draga Mašin in the residence (*Konak*), tossing their mutilated bodies from the windows. The conspirators—who were led by then-Captain Dimitrijević—also murdered Prime Minister Dimitrije Cincar-Marković, Military Minister Milovan Pavlović, two of the king's aides, and Queen Draga's two brothers.[41]

The regicide shocked Europe's conservative monarchies and led to international censure, as most of them withdrew their ministers and diplomatic recognition from Serbia. On June 15, the conspirators proclaimed 59-year-old Petar Karađorđević of the competing Karađorđević dynasty as king. By year's end, only Greek and Turkish representatives remained in Belgrade. The Great Powers—including Russia and especially Great Britain—brought pressure to bear on King Petar to remove the conspirators from their posts as a condition for renewed diplomatic recognition.

Russia's role in the assassination remains unclear to this day. Almost thirty-six years earlier, immediately after the 1867 assassination of Prince Mihailo Obrenović, St. Petersburg had asked the Porte if it would accept Petar Karađorđević as ruler of Serbia.[42] In the months prior to Aleksandar's assassination, St. Petersburg appears to have subtly withdrawn its support from him, especially its security forces.[43]

Not all Serbs agreed with the regicide: in 1904, the army mutinied in Niš to signal its support for the Obrenovićes; General Živojin Mišić, known for his close ties to Aleksandar—and who would later command the breakout on the Salonika Front in 1918—was forced into early retirement.[44] The regicide established a thirteen-year pattern of power relationships wherein Serbia's security structures directly interfered in political life, manipulating the weak king and threatening the constitutional authorities.

After the coup, King Petar—who left Serbia for exile at age fourteen and lacked a domestic power base—was at the mercy of the conspirators, who acted as a parallel power structure within Serbia, frequently operating without civilian or military oversight. Petar eventually removed some of the conspirators from their posts as aides-de-camp in order to gain diplomatic recognition from most of the Great Powers. Great Britain, however, continued to withhold recognition until 1905 and pressed Belgrade to deal with the conspirators,[45] some of whom Petar simply promoted to higher posts, increasing their influence.

The resulting pathologies proved unhealthy for Serbia's unstable pre-1914 democracy, as the army in general and the conspirators in particular played an influential role in Serbian political life, leading to numerous government crises.[46] Albertini noted: "the army officers implicated in the killings of 1903 had continued to remain in touch with one another and exercised surveillance over the new dynasty and its Governments."[47] Petar relied on the conspirators to remain in power, while he and his sons struggled to create their own power base in the rough-and-tumble world of Serbia's parliamentary democracy. The newly formed civilian government was also at the mercy of the conspirators, fearing that a wrong step could lead to the same fate as King Aleksandar. The conspirators, on the other hand, lived with a Damocles Sword over their heads, as they never received pardons for their act of regicide and feared that one day they could be brought to trial and condemned to death. A number of these officers would later form the nationalist society *Narodna odbrana* in 1908 and the secret society *Ujedinjenje ili smrt* (Unification or Death) in 1911. These pathologies led to the Sarajevo assassination.

Regime change in Serbia also marked a shift in foreign policy. Prior to 1903, the Obrenović dynasty enjoyed relatively good relations with Vienna. But Petar and the conspirators favored St. Petersburg. Petar had fought in Bosnia-Herzegovina during the peasant uprisings of 1875–1878 and was married to a Montenegrin princess, the Montenegrins being well-known for their pro-Russian sympathies, which stemmed in large part from generous Russian financial assistance.[48] The officers turned to Russia in the hope it would abandon Bulgaria's cause and become Serbia's new Great Power patron, while King Petar and the government gradually jettisoned the unpopular Obrenović policy of reliance on the Dual Monarchy. This meant that Austria-Hungary could no longer rely on Serbia to exercise restraint toward the South Slav populations within the Empire. So too, Vienna could now push towards the sea at Thessaloniki and Albania without risk of losing Serbia as a client.

Yet extending Habsburg territories further south came with risks. Since 1878, Vienna had added large chunks of territory inhabited exclusively by Slavs. However, these lands were not fully integrated into the Dual Monarchy's body politic, due largely to Hungarian objections. Budapest feared that more Slavs would enable the Germans to dilute Hungarian power and transform the Dual Monarchy into a triune polity with a third, South Slavic entity that would take away substantial portions of the Hungarian crown lands of St. Stephen.

Some influential figures among Austria-Hungary's Germans—such as Franz Ferdinand—were not averse to a punitive war against Serbia, but wished to avoid dismembering it or seizing its territory.[49] Simultaneously, Franz Ferdinand wished to use the Empire's Slavs to renegotiate an eventual triune solution at the expense of the Hungarians, whom he disliked; in 1906, the Archduke had even gone so far as to threaten Austrian military intervention against Hungary.[50]

Others, such as Conrad, favored aggressive anti-Magyar and anti-Serb policies, up to and including invasion and dismemberment of Serbia between other Balkan states, Romania and Bulgaria in particular.[51] Between 1906 and 1914, Conrad had advocated preventive war against Serbia more than two dozen times, fearing that either the Greater Serb or Yugoslav ideas would weaken the Empire.[52] Yet paradoxically, Conrad also favored a triune solution to weaken Hungary. In spite of Conrad's persistent efforts to draw the Empire into war against Serbia, many in Europe shared the view expressed by the British minister in Istanbul, who told Serbia's minister that the Archduke posed "a real danger to Europe."[53]

Most Magyar politicians feared the addition of new South Slav lands would tip the scales in favor of the triune camp, and thus opposed any military action that would include new South Slav territories. Among these was Hungarian Prime Minister István Tisza.[54]

The Magyarophobic Habsburg diplomat Ottokar von Czernin felt that the Empire should strengthen ties with Romania, and that the preferred option was to attack Serbia and reduce it to a rump state, while awarding substantial portions of its territory to Albania, Bulgaria, Greece, and Romania.[55] Belgrade, however, seemed more concerned with its own narrative of national expansion, and gave little heed to the nuances of Habsburg politics, tending rather to take an "us-against-them" view of both the increasingly chauvinistic Magyars and expansionist Germans as two equally guilty parties of an Empire that occupied Serb lands.

Orthodox Slavs constituted the largest demographic group within Bosnia-Herzegovina and the portion of the Empire's former *Militärgrenze* (military border) that ran from the Dalmatian hinterland through Croatia, Slavonia, and Vojvodina. Serb restlessness within Bosnia-Herzegovina had led to significant unrest and numerous political trials since the Habsburg arrival, while increasing Hungarian chauvinism was alienating all the Empire's Slavs.[56] In 1912, the Hungarians had suspended the Serbian Orthodox Church's autonomy and Church Council within Hungarian crown lands, and following the death of Patriarch Lukijan Bogdanović no new Patriarch was appointed.[57]

After 1904, Serbia entered a ten-year period of robust, albeit chaotic representative parliamentary democracy combined with territorial expansion. This sparked increased interest from the Empire's South Slavs, as well as from some of its other Slavs (Czechs, Slovaks, and Poles), who began to question their political marginalization at the expense of Germans and Hungarians. Although some influential Croat parties espoused a Greater Croatian national program and did not wish to join Serbia in a common Yugoslav state, Serbia nevertheless presented an attractive model to emulate. As Hungarian chauvinism grew increasingly heavy-handed in Croatia and Vojvodina, Croats began to chafe and engage Serb intellectual circles in Belgrade. Serbia encouraged such contacts and increased its cooperation with Croats, as well as its agitation among Serbs in the Empire.[58] In 1914, Serbian intellectual and political circles intensified contacts with Croats, Serbs, and Slovenes inside the Habsburg Empire in the context of the "Slavic South." This espoused a Yugoslav idea under which Serbia would play a role similar to Italy's Piedmont.[59] The officer corps, however, favored the idea of a Greater Serbian state.[60] For Austria-Hungary, a hereditary monarchy with a host of unresolved national questions, Belgrade's actions threatened not only the status quo, but also the Empire's very existence.

In 1902, in response to activities of pro-Bulgarian guerrilla groups in Macedonia known as *Komite*, Serbia formed its own guerrilla organization to operate in Macedonia, the *Četnik* Committee for Military Action

PHOTO 5 *5 Major Vojislav Tankosić.*

(*Četnički komitet za vojna dejstva*), whose members were known either as *Komitej* or *Komitadžija* (from "committee") or *Četniks*. Their first meetings were held in the *Crni konj* (Black Horse) *kafana* (café-restaurant) on the corner of Javorske and Varoš-kapije streets in Belgrade. One of the *Četnik* leaders was army officer Vojislav Tankosić, an unpredictable and sometimes violent hothead with a broad pointy mustache that gave him the appearance of a silent film villain; he too had participated in the 1903 regicide.

In 1904, open guerilla warfare erupted in Macedonia between Bulgarian, Greek, and Serbian *Komitej* as they fought a four-year dirty war that saw numerous civilian casualties and horrific atrocities. Soon Albanian guerillas entered the fray. The state of semi-anarchy in Macedonia lasted until 1908,[61] when the Great Powers pressured Belgrade, Sofia, and Athens to stop supporting these groups. In the meantime, Serb educators, intellectuals, skilled professionals, consuls, and government agents traveled throughout Bosnia-Herzegovina, Croatia, Kosovo, Macedonia, Sandžak, southern Serbia, and Vojvodina establishing schools, cultural societies, sharing ideas, and strengthening Serbdom among South Slavs. The 1903 conspirators played a significant role in organizing these activities.

Relations with Vienna further chilled in 1906, when the Dual Monarchy closed its borders to Serbian agricultural exports, depriving it of 75 percent of its export market. Yet the issues that led to the so-called "Pig War"—named after Serbia's main export to Austria-Hungary—were not agricultural.

Stronger Serbian economic and political ties with Bulgaria, France, and Russia appear to have prompted Vienna's action. Habsburg annoyance over a proposed Serbo-Bulgarian trade union, Serbia's preference for purchasing French *Schneider* cannon over Austro-Hungarian *Škoda* cannon, and closer Serbian ties to Russia only worsened relations between Vienna and Belgrade. The trade war was merely an attempt to re-establish hegemony over Serbia and Bulgaria and wean Belgrade from increasingly closer relations with Russia, France, and Bulgaria.[62] This came at a time when many inside the Empire feared that the unresolved national questions and Magyar chauvinism were pushing it inexorably toward dissolution.[63] Throughout this time the conspirators of 1903 played a noticeable and activist role in Serbia's politics.

Just when relations between Vienna and Belgrade couldn't appear to get any worse, the Dual Monarchy annexed Bosnia-Herzegovina on 6 October 1908. Both countries mobilized their armies and Serbian public opinion turned virulently anti-Habsburg, as Vienna had just annexed a South Slav area with a Serb plurality toward which Belgrade harbored territorial pretensions. Belgrade complained vociferously that the annexation violated the 1878 Treaty of Berlin, and St. Petersburg threw its support behind Belgrade, albeit briefly.

For Vienna, the price of Great Power acquiescence to the annexation meant giving up Sandžak and its plans for a railway via that route to Thessaloniki. But this was no great sacrifice: the railways through Bosnia-Herzegovina were narrow gauge, and the planned route from Sarajevo via Sandžak to Kosovska Mitrovica was torturous. The logical choice was the existing rail line from Belgrade to Thessaloniki via Serbia's Morava River valley and Macedonia's Vardar River valley. In Vienna, focus now shifted to acquiring this route by annexing Serbia and Macedonia into the Empire, a policy favored by the Chief of the General Staff Conrad von Hötzendorf.[64]

On October 21, 1908, in response to popular outrage over the annexation and the Serbian government's helplessness, a group of army officers led by Apis (many of them the 1903 conspirators) together with prominent politicians—some of them cabinet-level ministers—formed a barely secret society called *Narodna odbrana* (National Defense), with the express purpose of using Serbs from within Serbia and the Habsburg Empire (Bosnia-Herzegovina, Croatia, Dalmatia, Slavonia, Vojvodina) to foment armed rebellion inside Bosnia-Herzegovina. One of the society's six points was "to form volunteer units and prepare them for armed action . . . to organize, equip, and exercise Komite *čete* (companies) for special and independent warfare."[65]

The *Narodna odbrana* movement proved enormously popular both inside Serbia and in Habsburg lands, and any hope of secrecy soon vanished. Within one month, *Narodna odbrana* organized 223 committees in various towns and villages throughout Serbia and the Dual Monarchy. Volunteers arrived from Italy, Austria-Hungary, and Russia. Serbian Army officers—using their experience from the guerrilla wars in Macedonia—trained volunteer units, even though forbidden to do so, holding workshops on how to manufacture bombs and explosives. They also trained units for guerrilla warfare within

Bosnia-Herzegovina and sent *Četniks* into Bosnia-Herzegovina to provoke a popular uprising against the Monarchy.[66]

In response, Bosnia's *Landesregierung* and *K.u.k. Armee* reorganized the *Streifkorps* (volunteer border militia) and strengthened the existing *Schutzkorps* (volunteer internal militia) to counter Serb guerillas.[67] These units quickly gained notoriety for their heavy-handed actions against Serbs.

The Annexation Crisis was settled only through Great Power intervention. Under pressure from Germany, fearing further disruption of the status quo in the Balkans, and facing possible embarrassing revelations of inept Russian diplomacy, St. Petersburg dropped its support for Serbia. Isolated and facing the possibility of an Austro-Hungarian declaration of war, on March 31, 1909 Belgrade reluctantly signed a humiliating declaration that read:

> Serbia recognizes that she has not been injured in her right by the *fait accompli* created in Bosnia-Herzegovina and that consequently she will conform to such decision as the Powers shall take in regard to Article 25 of the Treaty of Berlin. Submitting to the advice of the Great Powers, Serbia undertakes already now to abandon the attitude of protest and opposition which she has maintained in regard to the annexation since last autumn and undertakes further to change the course of her present policy towards Austria-Hungary to live henceforward with the latter on a footing of good-neighborliness. Conformable to these declarations and confident of the pacific intentions of Austria-Hungary, Serbia will reduce her army to the position of spring 1908 as regards its organization, its distribution and its effectives. She will disarm and disband her volunteers and bands and will prevent the formation of new units of irregulars on its territories.[68]

The Great Powers forced Belgrade to cease all guerilla and subversive activities inside Bosnia-Herzegovina and transform *Narodna odbrana* into a cultural society that operated only within Serbia. Although Serbia ceased all overt activities, influential individuals within the Army, Police, Customs, and other official institutions were deeply dissatisfied and continued their plans for stirring up unrest in the Habsburg Empire, with the ultimate goal to bring about its collapse and the unification of South Slav lands with Serbia.

More importantly, the die was now cast: Belgrade wanted the Habsburg Empire's South Slav lands, and Vienna wanted to annex Serbia, Macedonia, and Thessaloniki.

The collision course

A war in 1914 came as no surprise to either the Balkan states or the Habsburg Empire. In the days prior to the Sarajevo assassination, all—with the exception of Serbia and Romania—seemed to be actively preparing for a Third Balkan War. In 1912 during the First Balkan War, Serbian national aspirations once again came into direct conflict with Habsburg interests, as Serbia's army conquered Kosovo, Macedonia, and northern Albania, and divided the Sandžak of Novi Pazar with Montenegro. Victory in the Second Balkan War (1913) only increased Belgrade's prestige in the Balkans, while raising tensions with Vienna. Four key matters were at stake.

First, Serbia wanted a seaport, which the Dual Monarchy opposed, as this would have weakened the Empire's strategic position in the Adriatic and permitted Serbia greater economic independence from the Empire. Second, Serbia's successful wartime expansion represented an existential threat to the Dual Monarchy, having fired the imaginations of South Slav nationalists and separatists throughout the Empire. In Vienna and Budapest, it was felt that a strong Serbia would attract the allegiance of the Empire's South Slavs and lead to the dissolution of the Dual Monarchy.[69] The creation of political groups and committees dedicated to Serb-Croat union threatened at best to change the Empire's governing structures from dualism to trialism. At worst, it threatened Vienna with the possible loss of large swaths of territory that could become part of a Serbian-dominated state. Third, Serbia's conquest of Macedonia posed a formidable obstacle to Vienna's drive toward Thessaloniki. Austria would now need to annex not only Serbia, but also a Serbian-ruled Macedonia.[70] Finally, the threat of political or economic union between Serbia and Montenegro raised new obstacles to Austro-Hungarian regional hegemony and its desire to construct a rail line from Bosnia via Sandžak to the Albanian coast.[71]

Belgrade had hoped to acquire a seaport during the First Balkan War. When in October and November of 1912 its forces occupied the northern Albanian ports of San Giovanni de Medua (Shëngjin) and Drač (Durrës, Durazzo), and assisted Montenegro with the siege of Scutari, it collided directly with Habsburg and Italian interests. The Habsburg Army assumed a state of high alert and mobilized along the border with Serbia, as the Scutari Crisis boiled throughout April and May. In the face of increased Serb nationalist agitation inside Bosnia, Potiorek declared a state of emergency in May 1913 and dissolved the Bosnia-Herzegovina parliament, while closing Serb cultural institutions and suspending civil courts.

In the meantime, the Emperor and his ministers again discussed going to war with Serbia and began mobilizing the army to invade Montenegro. Hostilities were prevented when Austria-Hungary stymied Serbian and Montenegrin attempts to occupy northern Albania, but only with Great Power support in the form of Austro-Hungarian, British, French, German, and Italian warships, backed by faint Russian rhetoric and an international conference.[72] Nonetheless, Serbian successes in 1913 during the Second Balkan War only heightened tensions with the Dual Monarchy. At the same time, the alliances that emerged at the conference on Scutari served as a preview of those that would solidify in the summer of 1914.[73]

To block Serbia's expansion, Austria-Hungary pressed for the creation of an Albanian state, and threatened war over it.[74] Rome reluctantly supported

Albania's creation, fearing that to do otherwise would shut Italy out of the Balkans entirely and create an Austro-Hungarian satellite. Although the independent Albania created by the Great Powers in 1913 did not include Kosovo, Macedonia, or Sandžak—as Vienna proposed—it nonetheless thwarted Serbian and Greek plans to partition Albania. Vienna began financing and arming Albanian guerrillas for incursions into Belgrade's newly conquered territories in the hope of destabilizing Serbia. The Great Powers and Serbia viewed the new Albanian state as a Habsburg puppet that was untenable without Austro-Hungarian or German support.[75]

Unsatisfied with its gains in the First Balkan War, Bulgaria had attacked Greece and Serbia on June 29, 1913, hoping to seize contested regions of Macedonia and Thrace. Turkey and Romania took advantage of Bulgaria's attack on Serbia and Greece, to seize lands that they claimed from Bulgaria. The war ended in a significant defeat for Bulgaria, which lost territory to Greece, Romania, and Turkey, and incurred heavy military losses. More importantly, this Second Balkan War destroyed the alliance of Balkan Christian states that had so successfully prosecuted the First Balkan War against Turkey.

Almost from its signing, Bulgaria contested the August 10, 1913 Treaty of Bucharest that concluded the Second Balkan War, and insisted that the boundaries reflect the territorial agreements drawn up prior to the First Balkan War between members of the Balkan alliance. Bulgaria spent the remainder of 1913 and most of 1914 seeking Great Power support to revise the Treaty of Bucharest. Simultaneously, Bulgaria began strengthening its army and making preparations for war. From Romania, Bulgaria wanted the Dobrudja; from Serbia, at the very least, trans-Vardar Macedonia, but preferably all of Macedonia; from Greece, the regions around Kavalla, Serrai, Drama, and Thessaloniki; from Turkey, the region of Thrace around Edirne, and perhaps, Istanbul.[76]

As Bulgaria sought allies among the Balkan states and Great Powers, it supported guerilla raids into contested areas of Greece, Romania, Serbia, and Turkey. In diplomatic circles it became all too evident that "Bulgaria would not make peace as long as it had not received from Turkey and Serbia that which was just."[77] So too, it was obvious that Sofia was not tied to one particular bloc. Bulgaria's Premier Vasil Radoslavov told his cabinet ministers, "Bulgaria will join anyone who will guarantee her rights."[78]

Yet Serbia, Austria-Hungary, and Bulgaria were not the only ones on the verge of war over the Balkan Peninsula. One month before the Sarajevo assassination, tensions between Austria-Hungary and Italy rose to a critical level over Albania. Habsburg moves southward conflicted with Italy's desire to increase its influence in Albania and Montenegro.[79] Tensions grew to the point that Italy's envoy to Montenegro hinted to the Serbs and Montenegrins that Italy would offer Montenegro military aid to defend Lovćen from a Habsburg attack.[80] Only five days prior to the Sarajevo assassination, Serbia's Minister to Vienna Jovan Jovanović referred directly to the poor relations between Italy and Austria-Hungary when he stated: "The danger of a European War is now greater than ever."[81]

In late June 1914, political instability and rebellions within Albania had become so serious that its ruler, German Prince Wilhelm von Wied, sought Great Power support.[82] By early July, many of the Great Powers had reached the conclusion that the creation of an independent Albania was one of their biggest mistakes, and entertained partition between Greece and Serbia as a possible solution.[83] Even Italy considered partition as a solution, and floated the idea of a Greco-Serbian division of Albania, in exchange for which Serbia would satisfy Bulgaria by giving it portions of Macedonia.[84]

Romania alone among Serbia's neighbors seemed relatively content with its Balkan War gains. Its only possible sphere for future expansion was within the Austro-Hungarian or Russian empires, Transylvania and Bessarabia. The only way Romania could acquire these regions would be if the unthinkable happened and one or both empires collapsed. Given the seeming improbability of such a scenario, Romania's leaders made little mention of these desires. In the meantime, Bulgarian agitation and guerrilla raids in the Dobrudja region continued throughout 1914. As border disputes between Sofia and Bucharest worsened, a Bulgarian attack appeared imminent: Romania sought Serbia's support to thwart a Bulgarian attack.

The tense situation between Romania and Bulgaria continued until July 23, the day Baron von Giesl delivered Austria-Hungary's ultimatum to Belgrade. That same day, at Romania's request and with French backing, Serbia's envoy in Sofia delivered a demarche to the Bulgarian government informing it that Serbia would side with Greece and Romania in adhering to the boundaries outlined in the Treaty of Bucharest, and that Serbia would not remain neutral in the event of a Bulgarian attack on Romania.[85] Belgrade's demarche elicited an official response from Sofia that it had no intention of starting a war with Romania, and wished to resolve the situation peacefully.[86]

Greece's plans for future expansion included the Aegean islands, Istanbul, the western shore of Asia Minor, and the Epirus region of southern Albania. Yet Greece was distracted by tensions with Bulgaria, which included constant cross-border raids by Bulgarian *komite*, numerous border skirmishes, and a struggle for control of disputed Eastern Orthodox churches and icons.[87]

In addition to its quarrel with Bulgaria, Greece was also involved in an acrimonious dispute with Turkey over the future of Chios and Mitillini, strategic Ottoman-held Aegean islands with large Greek populations. Relations between Turkey and Greece reached such a low ebb, that in mid-June 1914, immediately prior to the Sarajevo assassination, Greece had sought Serbian military assistance to launch a new war against Turkey. Serbia's Prime Minister and Foreign Minister Nikola Pašić turned down Athens' request for a military alliance, stating that Serbia feared possible

Bulgarian attacks, and that Serbia's army was unprepared for another war. Although Pašić's decision may also have been prompted by the relatively good state of relations between Serbia and Turkey and new Ottoman diplomatic overtures towards Serbia, the overwhelming factor was surely Belgrade's unprecedented internal political crisis and the poor state of Serbia's army. Lacking Serbian support, Athens decided to postpone any war until its army was ready and a suitable ally could be found.[88]

Facing continued Bulgarian guerrilla raids and a possible Greek attack, Turkey actively sought any solution, including a complete redrawing of all the boundaries of the Treaty of Bucharest. In May 1914, Ottoman officials began to sound out Serbian envoys in Vienna and Athens on the subject of a possible Ottoman-Serbian alliance against Greece.[89] Knowing that Austria-Hungary and Italy would never permit a Serbian port on the Adriatic, Turkey offered to compensate Serbia with the Greek port of Thessaloniki.[90] Following Pašić's refusal to betray Greece, Turkey proposed an alliance of Bulgaria, Serbia, and Turkey, operating under Russian protection.[91] In early June, the Porte proposed a wider Balkan alliance consisting of Turkey, Greece, Bulgaria, Serbia, and Romania acting united against the Great Powers. To realize such an alliance, the Grand Vizier proposed realigning all the Balkan borders, including Turkey's.

Under this proposal, Serbia would give Bulgaria portions of Macedonia all the way to Štip, Greece would give Bulgaria Kavala and Kočane, while Serbia and Greece would partition Albania. Regarding Chios and Mitillini, the Porte was "prepared to ensure the widest autonomy for the Greek majority on those islands, and in return give Greece the Dodecanese, and ensure the best conditions for the Ottoman Greeks."[92] To its credit, the Ottoman plan had something for everyone—except the Albanians. It is uncertain how Serbia would have responded, although as late as July 13, Pašić planned to travel to Istanbul to discuss the matter with the Grand Vizier.[93] However, it seems the Serbian envoy to the Porte, Milan Đorđević, exceeded his written instructions from Pašić and either engaged the Turks in excessively detailed discussions, or more probably became involved in Serbia's domestic civilian–military political struggle. Pašić recalled him.[94]

As was the case with all the other Balkan states, Serbia feared another Bulgarian attack and had stationed over half its active army in the "New Regions" of Macedonia to defend against Bulgarian invasion.[95] Serbia was also preoccupied with defending the newly acquired regions of Kosovo, Macedonia, and Sandžak from Habsburg-financed Bulgarian and Albanian guerillas and integrating the new regions into the Serbian economy and state administration. As evidenced by Belgrade's diplomatic stance towards Greece, Turkey, and Bulgaria, war was the last thing Serbia wanted.

Yet Serbia was in no position to ensure peace. Tensions with Bulgaria and anarchy in Albania were overshadowed by poor relations with Austria-

Hungary, the Great Power on Serbia's north and west, which since the First Balkan War had actively prepared for war against its southern neighbor.

Throughout the first half of 1914, Serbia had received reports from its spies and diplomats about Habsburg plans for future expansion at Serbia's expense. Muslim businessmen from Novi Pazar who traveled to Sarajevo spoke of widespread rumors among the Muslims in Bosnia that Austria-Hungary would shortly invade the Sandžak of Novi Pazar.[96] The Sandžak region—occupied by the Dual Monarchy from 1878 until 1908—presented a strategic stepping-stone for Habsburg control over the central Balkans and separated Montenegro from Serbia. Whoever controlled Sandžak controlled access to Kosovo, northern Albania, Macedonia, Montenegro, central Serbia, and Bosnia-Herzegovina. The Sandžak's predominantly Muslim Slav population maintained extensive business and cultural ties with Bosnia-Herzegovina's Muslim community, and its loyalty toward the new Serbian conquerors was suspect.

These rumors were reinforced by ongoing negotiations about railway construction between Serbia and the Dual Monarchy. By mid-June, the Serbs received clear indications from Vienna's negotiators that the Empire wanted right of transit for its troops over Serbian railways "through Sandžak, allegedly to Albania." To Serbia, it seemed that Austria-Hungary was intentionally prolonging the railroad talks until it could assemble an army to dictate a settlement. The Serbian consul in Budapest reported that: "If Serbia agrees to that, it will lose Sandžak, and if it doesn't agree Austria will provoke war."[97]

Throughout the first half of 1914, the Serbian government received reports of accelerated Austro-Hungarian military construction and reinforcement in Bosnia-Herzegovina and along its northern border in Vojvodina. The Serbian government also received various reports of a planned Austro-Hungarian/Bulgarian attack on Serbia, to be launched in conjunction with guerrilla attacks from Albania.[98] In mid-June, Serbian public opinion became inflamed, as Serbia's newspapers printed reports of a secret—and as it turned out, entirely non-existent—Austro-Hungarian mobilization in Bosnia-Herzegovina along the Serbian border to be held in conjunction with the impending military maneuvers.[99] The June maneuvers in Bosnia-Herzegovina, which brought the Archduke to Sarajevo, were interpreted ahead of time by Belgrade as either a cover for an invasion of Serbia, or the beginning of a Habsburg offensive into Albania and Sandžak. Clearly, Serbian paranoia was high and Belgrade was on edge.

In spite of Vienna's entirely factual statements that the maneuvers were merely previously scheduled military exercises, and despite the fact that they were held well distant from Serbia's border in central Bosnia near Tarčin, and despite the fact that they were being overseen by Franz Ferdinand, who was well known for his opposition to war with Serbia,[100] these reports caused a sense of panic in Belgrade.[101] One of the few clear heads at the time was the Serbian military attaché in Vienna, who voiced amazement at how the maneuvers were being interpreted in Serbia, noting that they were intended merely as a political demonstration and that there would not be an Austro-Hungarian attack. Nor did he feel that the Dual Monarchy would attempt to forcefully occupy Albania, and added that the maneuvers were planned long before the Albanian crisis arose.[102] These assurances fell on deaf ears.

CHAPTER THREE

Parallel structures and hostile neighbors

Crna Ruka, éminence grise

Since 1903, the rogue officers who carried out the regicide continued to interfere in Serbia's domestic politics on a regular basis, leading to numerous constraints on the political options available to the King and the civilian government. In addition to the senior officers active in the regicide, there were approximately eighty younger officers who took part in the plot.[1] King Petar proved weak in the face of the plotters, who discussed removing him in 1905, attempted to strengthen their control over the army in 1906,[2] and then attempted to take over the gendarmerie in 1909.[3] During this time the plotters also initiated several government crises and played a leading role organizing *Narodna odbrana*. Clearly, they were a force to be reckoned with.

Dissatisfied with the government's efforts to press the national question in both the Habsburg and Ottoman lands, and angered by the outcome of the Bosnian annexation crisis, the plotters formed a secret organization to conduct operations outside Serbia. On March 3, 1911, ten men met in the apartment of Velimir Vemić in Bosanska Street (today's Gavrilo Princip Street) in Belgrade and drafted the constitution for *Ujedinjenje ili smrt* (Unification or Death), which they founded six days later.[4] Soon it became known by the nickname Black Hand (*Crna Ruka*). The ten consisted of eight army officers—including Tankosić and Apis—and two civilians.[5]

The Black Hand's constitution included among its goals the "achievement of the national ideals—of the unification of Serbdom," "to implement a revolutionary organization in all territories where Serbs live," and "to fight outside the borders [of Serbia] with all resources against all enemies of this idea."[6] It would do so by "placing pressure on all official factors in Serbia as Piedmont, and on all social layers and the complete social life in it [Serbia]."[7]

PHOTO 6 *King Petar Karađorđević.*

Secrets are difficult to keep in Serbia, and word of the society quickly spread. Soon prominent politicians and government officials lent their support or in some cases joined, although the vast majority of members appear to have been army officers, many of them the original conspirators from 1903. At the time of its founding, "no difference of opinion existed between it [Black Hand] and the Government."[8] Apis later said:

> I frequently went to the late [Prime Minister Milovan] Milovanović in his home and his office in Belgrade and immediately began to speak with him about the meaning of our thing . . . I openly told the late Dr. Milovanović that there is a society-organization Unification or Death, which is patriotic and in which the members are mostly officers. He then said to me: "Young friend, place your Black Hand at my disposal and you will see what Milovanović will soon do together with the Black Hand; I would only ask that you be careful and don't let anything happen to me that would not be in keeping with [our] general interests."[9]

Apis appears to have worked closely with Milovanović in 1911 and 1912, as the Prime Minister steered the Black Hand towards guerilla warfare in Macedonia and "Old Serbia" (Kosovo, Sandžak) ahead of the Balkan Wars.[10] At the same time, Apis continued in his role as an *éminence grise* in Serbian politics.

In early September, the newspaper *Pijemont* (Piedmont) appeared in Belgrade; it was immediately viewed as the paper of the Black Hand. Although the Black Hand's Constitution clearly created a Greater Serb organization, *Pijemont* openly espoused a program for public consumption different from that of its constitution, possibly to attract Croat support. The first issue of September 3, 1911 proclaimed:

> A policy of brotherhood and alliance of all Balkan Peoples must be officially adopted, [with] the South Slavs in first place. This is what the Piedmontism of Serbia should consist of. Officially it should be viewed not only that Serbs and Croats are one people, but that Bulgarians and Slovenes are their closest brother and that work towards the unification or alliance of these single-blooded tribes is the only national policy of Serbia and the other two Slav states in the Balkans.[11]

By autumn of 1911, the existence of the Black Hand was known to just about everyone in Belgrade's diplomatic, political, and military elites, as well as among large segments of the general public: even Belgrade's tabloids— *Tribuna, Novo vreme, Jutro*, and *Dnevni list*—all criticized it openly.[12] By early 1912, foreign diplomats were reporting its existence to their capitals, including the Austro-Hungarian embassy, which mistakenly assessed it as a group designed to exert military influence on internal political affairs.[13] Austria-Hungary's Foreign Ministry kept a file of newspaper articles on the Black Hand, and during the first part of 1914 the Monarchy's Minister to Belgrade, Baron von Giesl, was reporting on the conflict between the Black Hand and Pašić's government.[14]

New members were initiated in a mystic ritual loosely inspired by the Freemasons, of which Tankosić was a member. Chief of the General Staff *Vojvoda* Radomir Putnik sympathized with their aims, as did King Petar and many within the cabinet of Prime Minister Nikola Pašić. Because most of the members were military, the overlap between the 1903 conspirators, *Narodna odbrana*, and the Black Hand made it difficult to distinguish these groups from one another. Many in the Black Hand were active in the governing structures of *Narodna odbrana*. Major Milan Vasić was simultaneously Secretary General of both *Narodna odbrana* and *Crna Ruka* until his death in 1913 in the Second Balkan War.[15] Border officers, customs officials, and members of the gendarmerie also joined. This enabled the Black Hand to co-opt the public work of *Narodna odbrana* along with its already established networks and use them as cover for secret activities. These activities required the creation of informal networks of authority outside formal chains of command. It also enabled the Black Hand to leverage the popularity and legitimacy of *Narodna odbrana* among Serbs both inside and outside of Serbia.

The Ottoman territories presented a relatively easy target for Black Hand activities. On the one hand, Kosovo, Macedonia, Sandžak, and southern

Serbia seemed ripe for the picking, and the Great Powers seemed less invested in preserving Turkey's Balkan provinces, as they themselves were busily squabbling over North Africa.

Habsburg territories, however, presented an entirely different matter. Although Serb nationalists coveted Vienna's South Slav lands, Austria-Hungary's Great Power status and its sheer size made it untouchable. Nonetheless, Vienna's visible progress transforming and modernizing Bosnia-Herzegovina represented a threat to Serbia's national program. The greater the Habsburg success in the province, the more likely it became that Vienna—driven by Franz Ferdinand's strong dislike for the Hungarians and desire for federalization of the Empire—might eventually succeed in reconfiguring the Diune German-Magyar structure into, at very least, a triune arrangement, by adding a third, South Slav entity alongside Austria and Hungary.[16] Should Franz Ferdinand ascend to the throne, the probability of such a reconfiguration would increase significantly. If Franz Ferdinand pushed for a South Slav entity, it would most certainly incorporate Bosnia-Herzegovina, and possibly Croatia, Slavonia, Slovenia, and parts of Vojvodina, presenting an enormous and possibly insurmountable obstacle for the Greater Serbian national project. For Belgrade, the Archduke was truly a dangerous man.

The successes in the Balkan Wars, however, changed Serbian attitudes towards the Dual Monarchy: Austria-Hungary was no longer off limits. In late 1912, the French Minister to Serbia, Leon Descos, wrote:

> In the camps and in the towns young and old know that the Balkan question is in the process of drawing to its close for good, while that of the Slavs in Austria is about to be opened and that the present military experiment is only the preparation for a more considerable and more decisive experiment, from which the whole Serbo-Croat people will come out liberated or introduced as a destructive element into the Austro-Hungarian organism. The Serbian officers . . . proclaim this to everybody they meet, the people shout it in the streets of Belgrade.[17]

Shades of grey in the White City

Early twenty-first-century Belgrade resembles that of the early twentieth century in many ways. In spite of growing from 89,000 residents in 1910 to two million during the ensuing 100 years, customs and culture have changed little. All political and economic elites know one another (the two groups are often difficult to distinguish); state secrets are difficult, if not impossible, to keep; domestic security services spend inordinate amounts of time spying on politicians, political parties, and each other; everybody has a favorite *kafana* where he holds court; politically affiliated tabloids spread scurrilous gossip and whip up nationalist passions; all meetings of substance (political and business) take place in a *kafana*; people divide themselves into pro-Western and pro-Russian camps; and conspiracy theories run rampant. Then, as now, influential individuals active in state security structures exerted a strong influence on politics.

In early twentieth-century Belgrade, the *kafana* played an important role in social, economic, cultural, and political life. Each *esnaf* (guild) had its own *kafana*, as did political parties, intellectual, cultural and social societies, clubs, newspapers, and day laborers. Their smoke-filled interiors offered traditional Serbian food at an affordable price, beer, *šljivovica* (plum brandy), live music, billiards, and sometimes less respectable forms of entertainment. A number of *kafanas* surrounded the *Zeleni venac* (Green Wreath) open-air market, an area frequented by Bosnians. These tended to cater to a lower class of clientele than the better *kafanas* further up the hill on Knez Mihaila Street, near the Hotels Moskva and Balkan, and around the *Kosančićev venac* and *Topličin venac* neighborhoods These included *Žirovni venac* (Acorn Wreath), *Zeleni venac*, and the *Zlatna moruna* (Golden Sturgeon), a gathering place for print-shop workers where many Bosnians, such as Gavrilo Princip and Nedeljko Čabrinović, played billiards. Another favorite *kafana* was the seedy *Amerika*, notorious for its short-stay upstairs rooms and underage prostitutes.[18]

Serb youth from throughout the Habsburg Empire visited or studied in Belgrade, attracted by the Greater Serbian idea and the vitality of the young state, as well as the freedom to express pro-Yugoslav ideas. Here they mingled with their counterparts from throughout the South Slav lands. It was in these *kafanas* that the Bosnian conspirators made contact with Black Hand operatives Milan Ciganović, a former member of Tankosić's *Četnik* group in Macedonia, and with Tankosić himself. It was also in these *kafanas* that they conceived the plot to assassinate Franz Ferdinand.

Apis had given one Black Hand member, army officer Čedomir Popović, the assignment of organizing revolutionary groups in Bosnia-Herzegovina that would create an anti-Habsburg uprising in the event war broke out with the Dual Monarchy, all the while keeping this work largely secret from Serbian government and army officials.[19] Because *Narodna odbrana* enjoyed great prestige among Serbs in the Habsburg Monarchy, Popović told the people he recruited that he was working for that group. In September 1911, Vladimir Gaćinović visited Belgrade, joined the Black Hand, and became a member of the Central Committee representing Bosnia-Herzegovina.[20] A Serb nationalist and anarchist writer from Herzegovina whose works heavily influenced Serb and Croat students in the Habsburg Empire, Gaćinović, subsequently formed two secret Black Hand groups in Vienna, one in Zagreb, one in Pakrac (Croatia), and five in Sarajevo. Each group typically had five members and a founder, and they answered to Black Hand members. In early 1914, Gaćinović met with Mehmedbašić in Toulouse, France, the first known contact between the Black Hand and one of the Sarajevo conspirators. In the course of forming Black Hand cells in Sarajevo, he also recruited the main organizer of the Sarajevo conspirators, Danilo Ilić. The only other Sarajevo conspirator who appears to have been a fully inducted Black Hand member was Gavrilo Princip.[21]

Unlike Black Hand members in Serbia, the groups in the Habsburg Monarchy were primarily civilians and were not subjected to an induction ritual; nor did most of them know they were working for the Black Hand. Commenting on the Black Hand groups within the Empire, Popović noted:

> This doesn't mean that those who participated in the movement with their friends were inducted into the organization *Ujedinjenje ili smrt*. Therefore, it is understandable that many participants didn't know where the movement began and where it originated: they cooperated with their friends who ran it.[22]

Put simply, many had no idea they were working for an organized subversive nationalist network that reported to one man, Apis. There were also substantial ideological differences between the Black Hand and many of the Bosnian conspirators.

> Apis heralded Serb supremacy over the other South Slavs (for him Croatia was just a Serb province), while Princip and his friends favored federalism with equality for all South Slavs, or so they said during their trials. Apis' program had elements of an Eastern Orthodox clericalism, while Princip was atheist. Colonel Apis was a general staff officer who favored the use of the Army, while individual terror was the very basis of Princip's credo.[23]

Princip's statements at the trial were entirely pan-Slavic and contained no hint of Serb nationalism. Comments Princip made to the psychiatrist Dr. Martin Pappenheim during his imprisonment in Theresienstadt indicate that he favored a federalized Yugoslav idea.[24] Nonetheless, in the face of a common goal, the Black Hand and the revolutionaries from Bosnia found common ground.

The Central Committee of the Black Hand and the organization mostly ceased to function during the Balkan Wars, as everyone was on active military duty and some of its members were killed.[25] After the Balkan Wars, its Central Committee continued to meet, albeit less frequently, with Čedomir Popović serving as secretary in 1914.[26] Although not officially disbanded, it appears that Apis was now running what was increasingly an informal remnant group of like-minded officers who had first coalesced around the 1903 regicide, the *Narodna odbrana*, and subsequently the Black Hand.

In 1913, Apis—now a lieutenant colonel—became Chief of Serbia's Army Intelligence, and the Black Hand operated at his direction as a parallel organization that answered to no governmental authority. Through Milan Vasić he monitored and manipulated *Narodna odbrana*; through Tankosić he monitored the *Komitej*; through Ljubomir Jovanović he kept his pulse on youth movements; and via Milovan Milovanović he maintained contact with Prime Minister Pašić. Apis enjoyed the favor of Chief of the General Staff Radomir Putnik, and for a brief while he even received support from Crown Prince Aleksandar Karađorđević, who donated a substantial sum to *Pijemont*.[27]

Apis now ran two intelligence operations: one the formal Serbian Army intelligence structures from within the General Staff Headquarters on the Kalemegdan fortress at the confluence of the Danube and Sava rivers;[28] the other the informal parallel structures of the Black Hand from the smoky confines of the large *Kolarac kafana*, where *Narodna odbrana* had been conceived.

Given the level of secrecy and the overlap between the Black Hand and the Bosnian conspirators, it is probable that only a few of the Sarajevo conspirators knew that Tankosić and Ciganović were Black Hand members, or that they were doing the bidding of the officers from that organization. Given Tankosić's reputation as a *Komitej* in Macedonia and in the Balkan Wars and Ciganović's participation in Tankosić's unit, the Bosnians most certainly realized that influential individuals within Serbia's military supported and countenanced the assassination of Franz Ferdinand. From all appearances, the Bosnian youth sought assistance and resources to carry out their plot to assassinate Franz Ferdinand, and the Black Hand—seeing a way to push its agenda—proved willing to help, even though many of the

PHOTO 7 *Lieutenant-Colonel Dragutin Dimitrijević "Apis."*

Bosnians had different aims than the Black Hand. In the words of Vladimir Dedijer:

> The latest historical evidence suggests that the Sarajevo assassination was a result of collusion between the secret revolutionary societies of Bosnia and Herzegovina and Colonel Apis' *Ujedinjenje ili smrt* based in Belgrade—although their motives were by no means identical.[29]

Whether the Bosnians ever met Apis is unknown, and is highly unlikely. From the point of view of operational security and deniability, the idea that the head of Serbian Army Intelligence would permit direct contact with the Bosnians is dubious.

Many historians maintain that Serbia's government somehow knew of or consented to the assassination plot, and the lack of clear information in this regard has tended to cause many to assume the worst. Apis' relations with Prime Minister Nikola Pašić and the Radical Government were strained, and Pašić was "singled out as a personification of all aberrations of parliamentary democracy which were so passionately reviled on the pages of *Pijemont*,"[30] virtually eliminating the possibility of close cooperation or contact between the two. From May 1914 onward, Pašić and Apis were engaged in fierce political combat with each other, virtually eliminating any possibility Serbia's government would have had advanced knowledge or been involved in planning the plot.

Yet secrets are not easily kept in Serbia, and Pašić and the government had indeed learned of Apis' plot ahead of time. It is still unclear what the Serbian government knew and when it knew it. Dedijer noted: "it was the habit of Serbia's statesmen to keep state papers in their drawers at home. In this regard, Nikola Pašić, the President of the Government and Minister of Foreign Affairs in 1914, led the way."[31] What is certain is that one of the Serb peasants who helped Princip cross the border into Bosnia and smuggle the bombs and pistols was also a confidant of *Narodna odbrana*, who informed his superior, who in turn informed the president of *Narodna odbrana* in Belgrade, General Boža Janković, who in turn informed the Minister of the Interior, who passed the report along to Pašić, who then asked *Vojvoda* (Field Marshall) Radomir Putnik, Chief of the General Staff, to investigate.[32]

The chief Serbian agent for Austria-Hungary was now a Croatian Serb, Rade Malobabić, who had developed a network of safe-houses, secret border crossing points, and an entire parallel network of individuals in the army, customs police, and gendarmerie who operated outside their official chains of command in order to assist him, or as many of them thought, *Narodna odbrana*. Although little is known of him or his activities, his close involvement with Apis and the Black Hand was sufficient for Crown Prince Aleksandar Karađorđević to have him sentenced to death and executed alongside Apis in 1917.[33]

In response to Pašić's demand for answers about bombs and pistols being smuggled into Austria-Hungary, Apis wrote a long letter to the Operational Department of the Serbian Army's General Staff on June 21 in which he said the pistols were for Malobabić to use in arming Serbs in Bosnia-Herzegovina, while dropping the names of two other Black Hand members—Majors Milan Vasić and Dimitrije Pavlović—as persons who had vouched for Malobabić. Apis said he had "personally met Malobabić and evaluated him that he is very capable for the service of gathering information about the Austro-Hungarian Army and engaged him for that service in the General Staff."[34] Apis had approved that Malobabić receive four revolvers, and had acquainted him with a "Major Ljub. [sic] Vulović," who commanded the 5th Section of Border Troops responsible for guarding that section of the border, and charged Vulović to tell no one about Malobabić, not even his superiors.

In the letter, Apis noted that there were excessive demands from the police and members of *Narodna odbrana* that were harming his ability to conduct secret operations in Bosnia-Herzegovina and suggested that clear instructions be given both to the police and *Narodna odbrana* so that they stop hampering his work. He denied any knowledge of a suitcase of bombs, attributing it to a probable misunderstanding by the border guards. To further muddy the waters and distance himself from the entire affair, Apis noted that "the commanders of our border companies in Šabac and Loznica have informed me that certain members of *Narodna odbrana* are demanding of our agents—who are also members of *Narodna odbrana*—that they not accept orders from military authorities and that the entire border work of our military authorities be given to *Narodna odbrana*."[35]

Pašić was dissatisfied with this answer: the Military Minister issued an order to the army border units to prevent people from crossing into Bosnia or to transport weapons, and the Chief of the Judiciary Department of the Ministry of War, Colonel Stanko Cvetković, launched an official investigation into Apis' activities.[36] A fuller picture of the plot now began to materialize. Education Minister Ljuba Jovanović claimed that Pašić had learned of the plot in late May or early June and tried to halt it, something Pašić later denied and Jovanović wouldn't refute.[37] Even if Pašić did know something was afoot, which seems highly likely, it is unlikely he knew the full details: Pašić's telegram to Serbia's ambassador Jovan Jovanović in Vienna asking him to transmit a vague warning supports such a thesis.[38]

The parallel structures Apis had put in place were clearly doing their job and causing confusion. The day before the Sarajevo assassination, Commander Prvanović of the 5th Company of Border Troops at Loznica—a town along the Drina River where Malobabić frequently crossed—wrote to Vulović complaining about recent attempts by police and customs officials to try to supervise his troops, and that these officials seemed to be acting on orders coming from a higher level. He complained that the border troops were being spied on by their own people—customs and police—and sought instructions and an official investigation.[39] Prvanović received a response the next day on June 28, in which Vulović told him that he should instruct his troops to take orders only from him, and to try to obtain the original letters of instruction to the police and customs officers.[40] In retrospect, this all seems ironic, as it was Prvanović who helped the Sarajevo conspirators cross the Drina River into Bosnia-Herzegovina.

Realizing how seriously the government was taking the matter, Apis sent word to school teacher Danilo Ilić—the main organizer in Sarajevo—to stop the plot. However, Apis' right-hand man, the notoriously hot-headed and violent Vojislav Tankosić disagreed strongly with Apis and cursed at him, saying: "I don't believe that it has been decided not to shoot! And if it is, I won't go back."[41] According to Ilić's trial testimony in Sarajevo, he argued with Princip in an effort to get him to call off the assassination, but Princip refused.[42] In spite of Pašić's efforts to stop Apis' plot, and Apis' seeming last-minute efforts to do the same, Rade Malobabić was in Sarajevo seven days prior to the assassination, evidently having been won over by Tankosić's arguments. Dragoslav Ljubibratić, a classmate of Princip's, states that one of the conspirators saw Malobabić next to him on the motorcade route on June 28.[43] Malobabić did not attempt to halt the conspirators, and the assassination went ahead as planned.[44]

In late July 1914, Habsburg officials and investigators suspected *Narodna odbrana*, which they considered a semi-official arm of the Serbian government, of organizing and planning the Sarajevo assassination. This occurred in part due to poor examination of the conspirators by Habsburg investigators during interrogation and at the trial in Sarajevo, in part to successful efforts by the conspirators to lie and dissemble about the plot, and in part due to confusion—either by accident or design—as to the role *Narodna odbrana* played.[45] By the time Austria-Hungary issued its ultimatum, its investigators had successfully followed the conspirators' trail back as far as Ciganović and Tankosić, but Apis and the Black Hand eluded them.

Today we know with certainty that Milan Ciganović introduced the Sarajevo conspirators to Tankosić, who approved of their objective. We also know that Ciganović taught them how to shoot and provided them with weapons at Tankosić's orders. Rade Malobabić helped organize the conspirators' journey across the border and to Sarajevo via his "tunnel", what would today be called an underground railway of contacts and safe houses. We also know that they had instructions to find accomplices among their student acquaintances upon their arrival in Sarajevo. In retrospect, it is clear that although the trail led back to Serbia, it led to Apis and his circle of conspirators, and not the government. At his trial in Salonika in 1917, Apis stated unequivocally:

> I engaged Malobabić to organize the assassination on the occasion of the announced arrival of Franz Ferdinand to Sarajevo. I made up my mind

about this only when Artamanov [the Russian Military Attaché in Serbia] assured me that Russia would not leave us without protection if we were attacked by Austria. On this occasion I did not mention my intention for the assassination, and my motive for asking his opinion about Russia's attitude was the possibility that Austria might become aware of our activities, and use this as a pretext to attack us. Malobabić executed my order, organized and performed the assassination. His chief accomplices were in my service and received small payments from me. Some of their receipts are in the hands of the Russians, since I got money for this purpose from Mr. Artamanov, as the General Staff did not have funds available for this increased activity.[46]

Apis repeated: "I engaged Malobabić so that on the occasion of Ferdinand's scheduled arrival in Sarajevo he would organize an assassination on him."[47]

The role Russia played remains murky. After the war, Albertini interviewed several Serbian Black Hand military officers in Belgrade with knowledge of the events, who stated that Viktor Artamanov, an agent of *Okhrana* (the Russian secret police), actually knew of the plot in advance, as did the Russian Minister to Belgrade, Nikolai Hartwig. When Albertini interviewed Artamanov, he denied he had known of the assassination ahead of time, which Albertini found unconvincing.[48] Dedijer notes that Russian archives show Tsar Nicholas personally followed the Black Hand's activities and that he read and annotated a 600- to 700-page dossier on the organization compiled by the Kiev District *Okhrana*.[49] He also claims that up until 1914 St. Petersburg disapproved of the "Praetorian methods" of Apis and the Black Hand. Whatever the level of Artamanov's involvement, Russian money clearly financed Princip, Grabež, and Čabrinović's living and travel expenses, and possibly even the purchase of the pistols.

As befitting a murderer, long-time conspirator, spy-master, and head of military intelligence, Apis was extremely secretive. His sister recalls that on the night of July 25/26, 1914, the last night he spent at his home in Belgrade, he destroyed most of his documents, especially those that dealt with the work of the Black Hand.[50] One thing, however, can be said with certainty: no matter how anxious Tankosić or Apis were to provoke Austria-Hungary or to pick a fight, they were operating on their own, and Serbia's government did not want war in 1914.

What price an ally?

As Austria-Hungary broke off diplomatic relations with Serbia, the immediate questions were those of alliance and neutrality. For Serbia, the most pressing question centered on Russia: would the Tsar honor Russia's commitment to Serbia?[51] A Russian refusal of support to its Balkan ally would mean Serbia must stand alone against Austria-Hungary's 1.4 million strong army. It could also affect Montenegro's alliance with Serbia: the mountain kingdom relied on Russia for weapons, ammunition, uniforms, and financial assistance. It would strengthen the positions of Germanophile factions in Bulgaria, Romania, and Greece, and perhaps influence them to openly side with Austria-Hungary. The best outcome Serbia could hope for from such a conflict would be partial dismemberment and token autonomy within an Austro-Hungarian-dominated Balkan Peninsula.

Serbia lost its strongest advocate with St. Petersburg on the evening of July 10, when Russia's overweight and notoriously anti-Habsburg Pan-Slavic Minister Nikolai Hartwig died of a probable heart attack while smoking cigars with the Austrian Minister in the Austrian legation in Belgrade. This gave rise to conspiracy theories about poisoning and electric chairs, and deprived Belgrade of a strong advocate for Serbia's cause.[52] It also deprived Belgrade of a stabilizing influence: Hartwig had served as a calming factor during the frequent internal political struggles, and had provided invaluable—albeit anti-Habsburg—foreign policy guidance to Serbia during the tense years after 1909.

The Entente, meanwhile, was playing for time and trying to avoid a war. London pushed St. Petersburg to advise Belgrade to "accede to as many Austro-Hungarian demands as possible," while working though Berlin to soften Vienna's position.[53] On July 24, less than twenty-four hours before the expiration of the ultimatum, Russian Foreign Minister Sergei Sazonov:

> Instructed the Russian legation in Belgrade to transmit its advice to the Serbian government that in the case of an attack by the Austro-Hungarian army "no serious attempts at resistance should be made."[54]

Rather, the Serbian Army should withdraw "without combat" into the interior and rely on the mercy of foreign powers. France suggested that Serbia let Austria-Hungary "take Belgrade without resistance,"[55] while Italy suggested acquiescence, as anything would be of a temporary nature. Clearly, the Great Powers felt the matter would need to be settled at yet another major conference.

In spite of Hartwig's death and pressure to acquiesce to all of Vienna's demands, Russia continued to back Serbia, and had sent signals to Vienna throughout July not to interfere in Serbia's internal affairs.[56] On July 26, the day after Austria-Hungary broke off diplomatic relations with Serbia, Miroslav Spalajković, Serbia's Minister to St. Petersburg, relayed Russia's official position to Pašić: "the Russian Army will cross the border the moment Austria-Hungary attacks Serbia." He added that Russia had instructed the Serbian Army to pull back from the Bulgarian border, because "we are guaranteed complete security on that side."[57] The Russian guarantee of Bulgarian neutrality would enable Serbia to free up its troops—most of which were currently on the Bulgarian border—to defend against the Dual Monarchy.

Spalajković's telegram also contained the earliest glimpse of what was to become Serbia's official war aim. Although not ready for a war, and certainly not seeking one, Serbia immediately realized that Russian military backing could allow it to reap long hoped-for benefits. At this early stage, prior even to the outbreak of hostilities, an enthusiastic Spalajković clearly enunciated the possibilities:

> The current moment is unique, since Russia is resolved to go all the way to the end and complete a historic work. In my opinion, a wonderful opportunity has presented itself to us, to use this wise event to create the complete unification of the Serbs. For that [purpose], it is to be desired that Austria-Hungary attack us. In such a case, forward in the name of God.[58]

Although official St. Petersburg does not appear to have supported such wild thinking at this stage, the anti-Habsburg Spalajković had clearly engaged other pan-Slavists in informal discussion. His opinion, although his own, was quite probably widely shared by many in both Belgrade and St. Petersburg, so much so that the unification of the Serbs at the expense of Austria-Hungary was formally published as Serbia's official war aim five months later. From the ruins of the Dual Monarchy, Serbia would finally be able to unite all the Serbs in Bosnia, Herzegovina, Croatia, and Dalmatia with the Serbs in Serbia.[59]

In addition to Russia, Serbia's attention focused on Italy, Romania, Bulgaria, Greece, and Turkey. With the exception of Italy and Romania, which had treaty commitments to the Triple Alliance (Austria-Hungary, Germany, Italy), none of these states had commitments to either the Triple Alliance or the Triple Entente (Great Britain, France, Russia). Both blocs hoped to entice one or all of these countries to their cause. For these states, all of which had territorial aspirations, their position *vis-à-vis* each bloc would be determined by the ability of each bloc to offer territorial compensation in return for an alliance. A complicating factor beyond the already complex issue of territorial compensation was that Bulgaria, Greece, and Romania all had German dynasties on the throne, each of which favored the Triple Alliance. These German dynasties were opposed internally by strong factions that favored the Entente or neutrality. The German dynasties, Turkey's pro-German sympathies, and Austria-Hungary's mutual defense treaties with Italy and Romania seemed to portend the rapid isolation and destruction of Serbia. Given these circumstances, a war on the Balkan Peninsula seemed to favor the Triple Alliance.

Italy's position was important to Serbia, given its proximity across the Adriatic, its border with Austria-Hungary, and its interests in Albania and Montenegro. Although a member of the Triple Alliance, Italy did not find a *casus foederis* in the Sarajevo assassination, Serbia's response to the ultimatum, or Austria-Hungary's attack on Serbia. Italy's diplomats had labored to defuse the crisis arising from the Sarajevo assassination, yet to no avail.[60] In spite of strong German pressure to enter the war on the side of the Triple Alliance, Italy officially declared its neutrality on August 4.[61]

Nonetheless, it was an open secret that Italy might be persuaded to enter the war on the side of the Entente, provided the allies offered sufficient territorial compensation. In return for entering the war, Italy hoped to receive the southern Tyrol, Trieste, Istria, and Dalmatia from the Dual Monarchy, as well as Albania. Dalmatia, Istria, and Trieste had a Slavic population of over 700,000, and figured prominently in nineteenth-century discussions of South Slav unity, including the 1844 *Načertanje*. In the event the Dual Monarchy collapsed, Serbia would not stand idly by and permit Italy to take these predominantly Slavic areas. In the event the Habsburg Empire retained Dalmatia, Kotor, and Bosnia-Herzegovina, Serbia hoped for an outlet to the sea through northern Albania, preferably Skadar or San Giovanni de Medua, both of which Italy coveted as potential ports. No matter the settlement, it was obvious the Entente could not satisfy both Italy and Serbia.

Romania's most powerful statesman, Ion Bratianu, was a Francophile who favored neutrality, while King Carol Hohenzollern favored the Triple Alliance, of which Romania had been a member since 1883. Romania also had an alliance with Serbia, which dated from the First Balkan War. King Carol's pro-German and President Bratianu's pro-neutral stances were offset by a powerful third group of politicians bolstered by strong public opinion that favored the Entente.[62] Although Romania's economy was closely tied to Germany and Austria-Hungary, Romanian relations with Austria-Hungary had soured during the course of 1913, which strengthened Bratianu's position and gave Russia greater influence.

Romania's territorial ambitions lay within countries of both the Triple Alliance and the Entente: Austria-Hungary (Transylvania) and Russia (Bessarabia). The Triple Alliance was not in a position to fulfill Romania's main territorial claim, Transylvania, as this would threaten the territorial integrity of Austria-Hungary. Similarly, the Entente could not promise Bessarabia, as that threatened Russia's territorial integrity. They could, however, promise their opponent's territories.

By 1914, Romania had drawn closer to Russia following the June visit to Bucharest by Tsar Nicholas and his Minister of Foreign Affairs Sergei Sazonov. From that time Romanian participation in the Triple Alliance effectively ceased.[63] Nonetheless, following the Habsburg ultimatum, Germany pressured Romania to join the Triple Alliance. Russia countered by offering Romania all of Transylvania, in exchange for which Romania would join the Entente. Although Bratianu refused to join Russia and the Entente, he informed Serbia that Romania would remain neutral in the conflict, provided Serbia was not attacked by a third party (Bulgaria), or the conditions of the Treaty of Bucharest were not altered.[64] In the event of a Bulgarian attack, Romania would defend Serbia.

Following Germany's declaration of war on Russia, Bratianu secretly informed Germany that guarantees to Belgrade to the contrary, Romania would not defend Serbia against Bulgarian attack. Dissatisfied even with this position, Germany pressed Romania to enter the war on the side of the Triple Alliance, and offered Bessarabia and Serbia's Timok river valley to Romania as incentive.[65] Subsequent Russian diplomatic initiatives towards Romania promised all of Transylvania, a rectification of the boundaries in the Dobrudja, and Russian guarantees of Romanian territorial integrity.[66] The Triple Alliance countered with a territorial offer that included not only Bessarabia, but also autonomy for Transylvania within the Habsburg Empire.

On August 10, the first anniversary of the Treaty of Bucharest, Bratianu proposed to Bulgarian Minister Radev that Romania would remain neutral in the event of a Bulgarian attack against Serbia, provided that Bulgaria renounced all claims to the regions Romania had seized in 1913. Bulgaria's government agreed in principle to such an agreement, provided they received it in writing, to be publicly announced upon mobilization. Bratianu declined to provide such a statement.[67] In spite of strong pressure from King Carol, Bratianu employed what could best be described as a "wait and see" policy that would allow Romania to maintain neutrality. As the fortunes of war became clearer, Romania would be better situated to decide whether to remain neutral or join a bloc. In the meantime, Romania stood to gain either way. If The Triple Alliance won, Romania would gain Bessarabia, the Timok valley, and autonomy for Transylvania: if the Entente won, Romania would gain Transylvania.

In Greece, the powerful Prime Minister Eleftherios Venizelos was a Francophile, in contrast to King Constantine I, the Germanophile brother-in-law of Kaiser Wilhelm II. Greece's French-equipped army and long coastline—which was vulnerable to the British and French navies—caused Entente interests to play a significant role in Greek political calculations. Greece's territorial ambitions lay in Albania, Bulgaria, and Turkey. The question of Greek participation was knotty, due to the Greater Hellenic idea and the complications it posed regarding a final solution for the straits. Russia, which fancied itself the eventual master of Istanbul and the straits, did not want a strong Greek presence in the region. Serbia, on the other hand, needed a strong Greece to protect its flank from Bulgaria and to secure its lines of communication with the Entente. Greek territorial demands also threatened the interests of Bulgaria and Turkey, both of which the Entente wished to remain neutral. Greece, meanwhile, was divided in its domestic politics, with King Constantine's Germanophile faction favoring the Triple Alliance, while Venizelos' faction favored the Entente.

Prior to the war's outbreak, Pašić sounded out Venizelos to find out how Greece would react to an Austro-Hungarian or Bulgarian attack on Serbia. Anxious to oppose a strong Bulgaria, Venizelos assured Pašić that in the event of a Bulgarian attack, Serbia could count on Greece. However, he remained silent about an Austro-Hungarian attack. Upon receiving Austria-Hungary's declaration of war, Pašić telegraphed Serbia's Minister in Athens, Balugđić, instructing him to inform the Greek government that under the terms of Serbia's alliance with Greece, this declaration of war constituted a *casus foederis*.[68] Given Greece's unstable internal political situation, it was uncertain whether Greece would come to Serbia's aid. Greece feared a declaration of war against Austria-Hungary would cause the Dual Monarchy's fleet to take the port of Thessaloniki and destroy Greece's navy. And the situation with Bulgaria was still not settled: as late as August 5, Greece expected an imminent attack by Bulgaria against northern Greece.

King Constantine clarified Greece's position to Balugđić on August 2. Although Constantine expressed interest in helping Serbia, he would do so only inasmuch as it would not lead to the suicide of the Greek state. Greece would maintain strict neutrality and assist Serbia in any way it could, including trans-shipment of munitions, and in the event such a step became necessary defend Serbia against Bulgarian attack.[69]

For Serbia, the Bulgarian position was the most ambiguous and threatening of all the Balkan states. The Germanophile policies of King Ferdinand Battenberg, Prime Minister Vasil Radoslavov, and the Liberal Party contrasted sharply with the Russophile position of the opposition Socialists and Agrarian Union. Bulgarian public opinion looked to Russia as its elder Slavic brother, and the majority of Bulgarians would not countenance war with Russia. Given this situation, Bulgaria's government proved susceptible to Russian diplomatic pressure. Yet Germany and Austria-Hungary had trained and armed Bulgaria's army, and the outstanding territorial grievances against Greece, Romania, Serbia, and Turkey made Bulgaria susceptible to any offer of help to gain the territories it regarded as rightfully hers.

Following a French refusal of help, Sofia had recently taken out a 500-million *Leva* loan from a joint Austro-Hungarian/German banking consortium, headed by Disconto Gesellschaft.[70] Financially, dynastically, and militarily Bulgaria drew ever closer to the Triple Alliance. Nonetheless, Russia's mobilization evoked strong pro-Russian feeling throughout Bulgaria and disconcerted the Bulgarian government. King Ferdinand and the leaders of the Liberal Party realized that an Austro-Hungarian attack on Serbia constituted an attack on Russia: entering the war on the side of the Triple Alliance would align Bulgaria against Russia. This would lead to popular turmoil and might possibly bring an end to the Battenberg dynasty in Bulgaria. Serbia's envoy to Sofia, Čolak-Antić, reported that popular Bulgarian belief in the power and might of Russia, together with the strength of the pan-Slavic idea, had created an atmosphere of depression and indecision in Bulgaria's government.[71]

Immediately after Austria-Hungary broke off diplomatic relations with Serbia, rumors spread that in spite of Russian guarantees to Serbia, Bulgaria was mobilizing its army along Serbia's border. Serbian agents and officials inside Bulgaria and along the border relayed reports confirming this information.[72] Although Čolak-Antić and the Chief of Greece's General Staff quickly labeled these reports false, they caused panic in Serbia.[73] Bulgaria never actually did mobilize; however, it made preliminary preparations for mobilization along the Serbian and Romanian borders.[74]

In spite of St. Petersburg's pressure on Sofia to join the Entente or remain neutral, and Russian assurances of security to Serbia, in late July and early August Bulgaria increased its guerrilla activity along both the Greek and Serbian borders.[75] Greece became so concerned that at the end of July it sought and received an official declaration of Bulgarian neutrality.[76] In the meantime, Russia's envoy to Bucharest passed reports to the Serbs that indicated Bulgaria was massing approximately 8,000 guerrillas to send into Macedonia, and training an additional 7,000.[77] To forestall potential Bulgarian moves, Pašić instructed the Serbian envoy to Bucharest, Ristić, to seek Romanian diplomatic support against Bulgaria.

As a result of this, Romania pressured Bulgaria's government— unsuccessfully—to halt all guerrilla actions.[78] In Sofia, Čolak-Antić sought an official Bulgarian declaration of neutrality, which Radoslavov answered by publicly declaring Bulgaria's neutrality in parliament on July 31.[79] On August 5, Russia informed Bulgaria that an attack on any of Russia's allies would be regarded as an attack on Russia itself.[80] Still, Bulgaria continued to play an ambiguous role, preparing for mobilization but not mobilizing, and escalating guerrilla activity while promising neutrality. These activities, combined with Bulgaria's hostility towards all its neighbors, heightened tensions in the Balkans.

The Ottoman Empire leaned toward the Triple Alliance, both politically and militarily. It's German-trained and equipped army depended on the Triple Alliance for significant quantities of industrial and military supplies. Long-running tensions with France and Britain over the eastern Mediterranean, as well as historic Ottoman antagonism with Russia, meant that Entente overtures for neutrality or alliance were received with suspicion. The Porte's immediate territorial concerns in the Balkans were, first of all, to halt the continued hemorrhage of its Empire, and second, to recover parts of Greece and Bulgaria.

Turkey worried the Entente for several reasons. It had mobilized its army upon hearing of Russia's mobilization. This brought the danger that in the event of an Ottoman declaration of war, Russia would have to divert troops from its western front with Austria-Hungary and Germany toward the south. Two German warships, the *Göben* and *Breslau*, had arrived in Ottoman waters following a chase by a British naval squadron across the Mediterranean.[81] Turkey gave these ships safe haven and announced that it would "buy" the ships from Germany, as compensation for the two dreadnoughts it had ordered from Great Britain, which were confiscated by the British government upon the outbreak of hostilities. The German sailors and officers on the ships simply donned fezzes and continued operating the vessels. A great many German officers were assigned to active duty with the Ottoman Army and Navy, and they exercised a strong influence over Turkey's military and government.

The Russian envoy in Istanbul told the Porte that "buying" the German warships was against international maritime law. France and Britain did not join Russia in this pronouncement, but the Royal Navy blockaded the Dardanelles. In the meantime, the Porte carried out talks with Russia about remaining neutral in return for receiving land in Trachea and islands in the Aegean, all at Greece's expense. The talks were a façade. On August 2, unbeknown to the Entente, the Porte signed a secret agreement with Germany, all the while assuring Entente representatives that it would remain neutral. In November, the Ottoman Empire would openly enter the war on the side of the Triple Alliance.

Pašić hoped the Entente would quickly declare war against the Ottoman Empire, seize Istanbul, and prevent the completion of Turkey's mobilization. This would convince Bulgaria and Romania to lean towards the Entente and radically alter the alignment of forces on the Balkan Peninsula.[82] The Entente, unaware of the secret pact, did not act, fearing Turkey would join the Triple Alliance. On August 17, British Foreign Minister Sir Edward Grey and the Russian and French Ministers in London offered to guarantee Turkey's territorial integrity if it remained neutral.[83]

With the exception of Serbia, each of the Balkan states could play the Triple Alliance and the Triple Entente against each other. Each could accept or reject an alliance based on which bloc offered the most favorable territorial incentives or security arrangements. In most instances, territorial concerns proved the primary motivation behind a country's decision to remain neutral or ally itself with a bloc.[84] Because all of these states had outstanding territorial claims against Serbia, Austria-Hungary, or each other, any attempt to cobble together a cohesive alliance of Balkan states by either the Entente or Triple Alliance would be fraught with difficulty. Given the nature of the competing territorial claims, any comprehensive settlement or alliance would require substantial boundary changes. This eventually led to a situation where the Entente sacrificed the interests of its only Balkan ally, Serbia, in an effort to obtain additional allies on the peninsula, or at least ensure their continued neutrality.

For the Triple Alliance, the task in the Balkans was relatively simple: at the very least, isolate Serbia diplomatically, militarily, and economically; at the most, persuade at least one, if not all, of Serbia's neighbors to enter the war against Serbia. Given the German kings on the thrones of Serbia's neighbors, such an eventuality was possible.

For the Triple Entente, the task was far more difficult. The only effective way to prevent Bulgaria from entering the war on the side of the Triple Alliance was to arrange territorial compensation at the expense of its neighbors, Serbia, Greece, Romania, and Turkey. This would require a complete revision of the 1913 Treaty of Bucharest, as well as involve significant territorial concessions by Serbia, Romania, or Greece, or all three. The Entente faced a situation whereby only a comprehensive Balkan settlement would enable it to attain its diplomatic goals and bring Romania, Bulgaria, and Greece into the war. To achieve such a settlement, Serbia would have to give Bulgaria substantial areas of Macedonia as called for under their agreement preceding the First Balkan War. Serbia stubbornly refused to do this, claiming that Bulgaria had failed to fulfill its portion of that agreement, and that Macedonia was Serbia's compensation for Bulgarian actions in 1912 and 1913, and for Serbia's failure to gain a port on the Adriatic. Given the extent of the Serbo-Bulgarian antagonism, a Balkan-wide settlement appeared distant, if not impossible.

As the war began, Serbia's neighbors all officially declared their neutrality, while privately remaining open to offers from both Great Power blocs. Thus, for Serbia the possibility of an attack by one of its neighbors remained a real threat until October 1915, when Germany succeeded in bringing Bulgaria into the war. Yet more immediately, Serbia faced war with Central Europe's oldest and largest Empire.

Awaiting war

Only a few days before the Austro-Hungarian ultimatum, German military attaché Captain Böhm inquired of Serbia's Military Ministry why it hadn't placed an order with Krupp to repair the cannon captured from Turkey during the First Balkan War, and why it hadn't ordered additional cannon and ammunition.[85] This curious request may have been a German effort to assess the state of Serbia's artillery corps, and it no doubt increased Belgrade's suspicion.

After the assassination, Belgrade received increasingly worrying news from along its borders: reports of increased Habsburg troop movements; construction of fortifications; Habsburg stockpiling of poison gas; Habsburg soldiers repeatedly conducting bridging exercises out to the halfway point in the Danube and Drina rivers; and searchlights repeatedly shined onto the Serbian side of the rivers. Serbian spies in Vojvodina reported that Hungarian troops had moved into forward areas and were lodged in private homes: others concentrated near islands in the Danube and Drina as if preparing to cross. Serbian border guards observed an increase in the number of Austro-Hungarian officers and troops with binoculars examining Serbian positions.[86] Serbian police captured a carrier pigeon with the gothic letter "ẞ" attached to its leg. Tensions inside Serbia increased markedly on July 18, when a company of Austro-Hungarian soldiers crossed the border at Šib in the region of Loznica, and established themselves 300 meters across the Drina river on a piece of high ground, well within Serbian territory.[87] Austro-Hungarian boats sailed down the Danube carrying visible military cargos—such as cannon—to Bulgaria.

In the meantime, another danger loomed: famine. The two years of mobilizations and wars had disrupted the typical cycles of planting, as had the sudden mid-summer crisis in 1914 and bad weather. As a result, the harvest was poor throughout the Balkans that year. Serbia asked Bulgaria for wheat, but Sofia had suffered a poor harvest and had insufficient for its own needs,[88] as did Greece, which banned wheat exports pending the arrival of wheat from the United States.[89]

Despite Russian assurances that it would guarantee Bulgarian neutrality, guerrilla raids against Serbia continued from Bulgaria, and new reports, many false, brought rumors of Bulgarian mobilization, military and guerrilla activity.[90] On the eve of total war, Serbia feared the prospect of hostilities with not only Austria-Hungary, but also Bulgaria.

Back in Sarajevo, the Reis-l-Ulema issued an order on July 24 that Muslims should not participate in anti-Serb demonstrations and pogroms, saying: "we live with other non-Muslim citizens in our homeland, with whom we were born and with whom we will live and with whom we will die. Therefore, we should never forget that each of our wicked acts towards them could bring with it very ugly repercussions." Although other Muslim clerics followed suit, Habsburg authorities forbade such public statements.[91]

After the assassination, within Bosnia-Herzegovina and the other South Slav parts of the Empire, authorities began a crackdown not only on Serbs, but also Croats suspected of having pro-Yugoslav or pro-Serb sympathies, fearing they would comprise a potential fifth column. The *Schutzkorps* were particularly noted for their viciousness in Herzegovina, where they participated in looting and anti-Serb pogroms. Once war was declared, this would turn into both targeted and indiscriminate killings of prominent Serb clergy, intellectuals, and peasants. On the night of July 25, shortly after Baron von Giesl handed the ultimatum to Paču, Habsburg police began arresting *Sokol* functionaries in Banja Luka and Split, as well as throughout the remainder of Bosnia-Herzegovina.[92]

Once Vienna declared war, the *Schutzkorps* began mass executions of Serbs in Herzegovina, including hanging seventy-nine of the most prominent Serbs in the Trebinje region.[93] The Ban of Croatia-Slavonia closed a number of newspapers deemed subversive—that is, pro-Serb, pro-Yugoslav, or anti-Hungarian: these included Serb, Croat, and German papers.[94] Habsburg officials began taking Serb hostages, clergy in particular, and placing them on troop and supply trains, vital railroad bridges, and other installations that could be targets for Serb *Komitej*.[95] If a train was attacked, the hostage was executed.[96] During early August, prominent Croat and Serb civilians were taken as hostages to ensure the good behavior of their respective communities. Arrests took place in Istria, Omiš, Split, Knin, Dubrovnik, Šibenik, and on the island of Hvar, and included Catholic and Orthodox clergy, as well as politicians.[97] In late August, Habsburg officials transported 274 political prisoners to Rijeka from Dalmatia, including the mayor of

PHOTO 8 *Austro-Hungarian troops hanging Serbian civilians in Trebinje.*

Dubrovnik, Melko Čingrija, two representatives from the Emperor's Council, the mayor of Šibenik, numerous attorneys, doctors, four Orthodox priests, the former Orthodox Archbishop of Zadar, one Catholic priest, and many professors and students.[98] Once Habsburg forces invaded Serbia, atrocities against civilians would worsen.

CHAPTER FOUR

"A peasant mob"

Ready or not . . .

War could not have come at a worse time for Serbia. In July 1914, Serbia faced an adversary that could muster overwhelming military force, both quantitatively and qualitatively. In contrast, Serbia was completely exhausted and unprepared—economically, socially, financially, politically, and militarily—and had spent the previous six months seeking to avoid war at all costs. The Balkan Wars of 1912 and 1913 exacted a terrible toll on Serbia's economy, nearly bankrupted the state budget, and killed or maimed large numbers of able-bodied men. The country's internal political structure was in turmoil, and the military had worn out or used most of its equipment during the preceding two years of war. During the Balkan Wars, Serbia spent more than three times its entire state budget for 1912 by maintaining 400,000 men in uniform for approximately ten months. By early 1914, the government faced a severe fiscal crisis that forced it to take out a 250-million Franc loan at a 5 percent interest rate.[1]

In addition to an exhausted treasury, the army's manpower demands deprived the largely agrarian economy of its most productive workers during two crucial harvest seasons (1912, 1913), which caused food shortages, sent food prices soaring, and touched off localized famines.[2] The drop in agricultural production caused a comparable drop in state revenues.

Although the Balkan Wars nearly doubled Serbia's territory from 48,300 to 87,300 square kilometers, and increased its population from 2.9 million to 4.4 million, the country paid a terrible human price. The Serbian Army suffered at least 36,500 deaths, 4,300 from cholera alone, 12,000 from other illnesses, and the remainder from battlefield causes. At least 55,000 men were seriously wounded; many became invalids. All told, the Serbian Army lost approximately 91,000 men, one-quarter of its fully mobilized strength. In addition to Balkan War losses, Serbia lost another 3,000 men killed or wounded while fighting against Austro-Hungarian supported Albanians in the new regions of Serbia and northern Albania.[3]

The newly acquired territories were far from peaceful: Serbian Balkan War atrocities against civilians and prisoners of war in Kosovo, Macedonia, and Sandžak, along with heavy-handed and often violent post-war efforts at enforced Serbification of the population in these regions, meant that the possibility of violence always loomed.[4] And if the financial and manpower difficulties were not enough, a political dispute developed over the newly annexed regions of Macedonia, Kosovo-Metohija, and the Sandžak of Novi Pazar, as to whether military or civilian authorities should take precedence in administration.

In September 1913, while the Chief of Serbia's General Staff—Black Hand sympathizer *Vojvoda* Radomir Putnik—was out of the country on convalescent leave, Apis and the Black Hand officers engineered the dismissal of General Živojin Mišić, Putnik's aide-de-camp. This was the second time Apis had engineered Mišić's forcible retirement, the first in 1904.[5] Although Mišić was publicly charged with everything from improper collection of customs fees at Kriva Palanka to endangering Serbia by improperly guarding the border with Albania, the real reason appears to have been Apis' distrust of Mišić, who had been adjutant to the assassinated King Aleksandar Obrenović. More significantly, Mišić did not want the military to intervene in civil affairs in the new regions, favoring civilian institutions. As a result, Mišić—who was recalled to active duty when war broke out and would later prove to be Serbia's most capable general—was forced to resign.

The political struggle between civilian and military authority continued through the first half of 1914. Concerned about the Black Hand's growing intervention in civilian affairs, Nikola Pašić removed Miloš Božanović—a Black Hand sympathizer—from the post of Military Minister in January 1914. Pašić initially attempted to replace Božanović with the Minister of Internal Affairs Stojan Protić, a civilian, but death threats from the Black Hand forced Protić and several other candidates to decline the post. The drawn-out attempt to find a new Military Minister led King Petar to give Pašić an ultimatum: either find a new Minister, or have the entire government resign. This forced Pašić to name Colonel Dušan Stefanović to the post.

In an effort to reassert civilian control over the army, on March 21, 1914, Interior Minister Stojan Protić issued the "Priority Decree," which gave precedence to civilian officials in the newly conquered regions.[6] This led to a near revolt among the officer corps, especially the Black Hand members. Apis attempted to engineer an uprising against Pašić's government in Macedonia using his Black Hand connections, but the officers refused to support him. In April, strong support in the *Skupština* enabled Pašić to force the resignation of Black Hand member General Damjan Popović, who was commander of the new regions, a conspirator in the assassination of King Aleksandar Obrenović, and a leader of the military opposition to the Priority Decree.[7] The animosity between the Black Hand and Pašić had now reached a dangerous level, and both sides were no doubt looking for external pressure to resolve the matter. But resistance to the Priority Decree continued, and King Petar favored the Black Hand, on whom he relied for support, and was reticent to support Pašić. Refusing to reverse their position, Pašić's ministers resigned on June 2. On June 10, Pašić resigned.

At this point, external pressure did come to bear, as the representative of a Great Power stepped in to resolve the crisis. Russia's Minister to Belgrade, Nikolai Hartwig, strong-armed King Petar, who reversed himself and threw his support behind Pašić: on June 11, Pašić's government was back in power, unchanged. Russian support for Pašić also quieted rebellious spirits in the army. On June 24, four days before the Sarajevo assassination, a weary and ill King Petar disbanded the *Skupština*, and appointed his son Aleksandar as regent with the explanation that poor health prevented him from carrying out his royal duties. Parliamentary elections were scheduled for 14 August.

Some within the Black Hand may also have been waiting for external factors to intervene in their favor to get rid of Pašić. When the Serbian Army arrested Vojislav Tankosić as part of its compliance with the Austro-Hungarian ultimatum, he was asked why he organized the assassination. He replied: "To spite Pašić."[8]

Prince Aleksandar, although energetic, serious, well educated, and experienced in the Balkan Wars, was regarded by some of Serbia's leading politicians as not equal to the task at hand.[9] During the crisis, Aleksandar had had to navigate between the military and civilian camps, while maintaining working relationships with both the government and opposition. Although Aleksandar maintained cordial relationships with the Black Hand officers, he had also benefited from a group of officers known as the "White Hand," who opposed the Black Hand and around whom Aleksandar hoped to create support within the army loyal to the crown. Aleksandar disliked Pašić, but also realized that as newly appointed regent he needed to tread carefully and could not risk offending Russia.

In addition to the civilian–military controversy, Pašić was in the midst of preparing for secret negotiations with the Ottoman Empire, which would completely redraw the Balkan boundaries, and give half of Albania to Serbia, while giving portions of Macedonia to Bulgaria.[10] The government was in no shape to deal with a major international crisis, such as the Sarajevo assassination or the Austro-Hungarian ultimatum, much less a war. "It can be said unequivocally that Pašić did not desire war with anyone in 1914, and this was true of all Serbian leaders."[11]

Yet Serbia's unpreparedness for war extended far beyond economic chaos, human casualties, the absence of key politicians and generals, and political chaos. In 1914, the army had yet to repair the damage and losses suffered during two years of war. The Balkan Wars had dramatically reduced the material readiness of the army's one cavalry and eleven infantry divisions, while two years of fighting had seriously depleted stocks of artillery and rifle ammunition, cannon, rifles, pistols, uniforms, boots, winter clothing, and field equipment (tents, field kitchens, etc.), horses, oxen, carts, medical supplies, and so on. Many cannon and rifles were broken or in a state of disrepair; wagons were broken or missing; there was an insufficient number of horses and animals, etc. The wars had severely damaged artillery carriages and ammunition caissons, requiring extensive repairs that did not even begin until after the outbreak of hostilities.[12] To make matters worse, Serbia's army had not received any new supplies—including artillery or rifle ammunition—since 1912.

Manpower and formations

After January 1883, Serbia organized its military around three levies. The first levy consisted of men from twenty-one to thirty-one years of age; the second levy, which was also considered a front-line levy, was composed of men between the ages of thirty-one and thirty-eight; the men of the third levy, affectionately nicknamed *Ćića* (uncle), were between the ages of thirty-eight and forty-five. An additional group, the *Poslednja odbrana* (final defense), consisted of men aged eighteen to twenty and over fifty,[13] "wearing peasant clothes, with lambskin caps and opanci."[14] Although the army supplied weapons and ammunition to soldiers of all levies, only soldiers of the first levy received military equipment and uniforms.

All other levies were expected to provide their own clothing, footwear, and shelter, although second levy soldiers would also receive a cap and a coat.[15] Rarely used as part of the operational army, troops of the third levy formed special local defense units, and carried out guard duties along railroads, highways, and bridges.[16] In peacetime, second and third levy units were inactive.

In 1903, Serbia reorganized its army into five divisional regions (Danube, Drina, Morava, Šumadija, and Timok), each based in the corresponding geographic region.[17] Each divisional region recruited and equipped one first levy infantry division and one second levy infantry division. For example, the Danube divisional region equipped the Danube I Division (first levy) and the Danube II Division (second levy), the numbers corresponding to the levy. Each divisional region also provided men, horses, and other matériel in equal ratios to the Cavalry Division and a Combined Infantry Division (first levy). Under this organizational scheme, Serbia's operational army totaled eleven infantry divisions and one cavalry division: Danube I, Danube II, Drina I, Drina II, Morava I, Morava II, Šumadija I, Šumadija II, Timok I, Timok II, the Combined Division, and the Cavalry Division.

A first levy Serbian infantry division on war footing consisted of two infantry brigades of two regiments each: each regiment was comprised of four battalions of 1,000 men each.[18] Each battalion was to have one machine gun detachment. On paper, a first levy infantry division could field 16,000 rifles (enlisted men). Each infantry division maintained three cavalry squadrons, and forty-eight cannon divided into twelve batteries of four cannon each. Each division had four field hospitals, field kitchens, transportation and supply trains, an artillery repair shop, an engineer battalion, a telegraph section, regimental bands, chaplains, a bridging unit, a veterinary hospital, a quartermaster section, butcher company, and a craftsman company (blacksmiths, shoemakers, etc.).

A Serbian second levy infantry division on war footing consisted of one infantry brigade composed of three regiments, totaling twelve battalions of 1,000 men each. Without adding the various staff formations, each division could field approximately 12,000 rifles. There were also cavalry, engineers, artillery, and the other ancillary units associated with a first levy formation. The second levy divisions were much more poorly equipped than first levy divisions, and usually had antiquated weapons. Their daily food ration was smaller, the second levy soldier receiving a daily 860 grams as opposed to the 1,060 grams provided the first levy soldier.[19] Second levy divisions also received less field equipment and fewer uniforms than their first levy counterparts.

PHOTO 9 *First levy troops.*

Third levy troops were usually formed into company, battalion, and occasionally regiment size units, assigned to such regionally based units as the *Defense of Belgrade, Užice Army*, and *Obrenovac Detachment*. They participated in *Četnik* (guerrilla) operations behind enemy lines and in occupied territories, guarded communication lines, and patrolled rear areas for deserters. They received no military clothing, and usually carried the oldest weapons. Their unit sizes varied widely.[20]

In spite of manpower losses during the Balkan Wars, as well as the relatively large size of these divisional formations,[21] at the war's start Serbia managed to fully man most of its first and second levy units. However, following the initial manpower losses in August at the Battle of Mount Cer, and the loss of approximately 60,000 soldiers to desertion during the first five months of the war,[22] its units would not again reach full strength until mid to late 1915. In fact, during the first five months of the war (August to December 1914), such first levy units as the Combined Division, Morava I, and Drina I were often at one-third of their effective strength.[23]

Weaponry

In contrast to the other armies of 1914, whose infantry carried standardized quick-firing, magazine-fed, bolt-action rifles, Serbia's front-line infantry units used several different types of rifles of varying calibers. The most prevalent was the so-called "Serbian" rifle, a Model 98 *Mauser* firing a 7-mm rimless cartridge from a five-round magazine. Četnik units used a *Mannlicher* M1895 firing an 8-mm rimmed cartridge from a five-round magazine, quantities of which were captured from Bulgaria in the Second Balkan War. Small numbers of *Mauser* 7.65-mm Model 1893 and 1903 rifles captured from Turkey during the First Balkan War also saw limited use.[24] In early August, the High Command received its first shipments of the "Russian" rifle, an M1891 *Mosin-Nagant* firing a 7.62-mm cartridge from a five-round magazine. This rifle saw its first service in September.[25]

At the war's outbreak, the Austro-Hungarian *Armeeoberkommando* estimated that Serbia's army lacked at least 150,000 rapid-fire rifles.[26] Colonel Živko Pavlović, Chief of the Operational Section of the High Command, claimed that Serbia possessed sufficient modern rifles to equip only 180,000 men. This may have been optimistic, as other figures show that the army had only 137,609 modern rifles and carbines. The army had lost approximately 65,000 rifles during the Balkan Wars, due to damage or because they were distributed to Serbs behind the Turkish lines preparatory to the First Balkan War.[27] Because Serbia's meager industry lacked the ability to manufacture rifles, the weapon shortage forced Serbia to rely on large numbers of antiquated rifles for its second and third levy troops.[28] The Serbian Army issued some of its front-line troops with 11-mm M.80 (Model

1871) *Mauser-Koch* single-shot, black powder rifles, which had been refitted with magazines and smokeless powder ammunition, as well as some that had not been refitted. In addition, a quantity of Russian-made single-shot, black powder .42 caliber *Berdan* II rifles—which pre-dated the M.80—were in service with the third levy. The use of antiquated rifles placed the Serbian soldiers at a severe disadvantage on the battlefield. The black powder meant that the moment a soldier fired, he revealed his position, and the single-shot action meant that his adversary could get off several shots for every one the Serbian soldier could fire.[29]

The lack of standardization created not only logistical difficulties, but also posed problems for transferring battalions and regiments between larger units. Because the supply trains were organized on the regimental and divisional levels, standardization of equipment among the units of a division was preferred. Therefore, when a regiment or battalion was sent from one division to another, it would often have to wait in a rear area to be re-equipped with the necessary rifles, causing unwanted delays, due to insufficient quantities of the new rifles and the amount of time required to exchange weapons.[30]

The machine gun, a weapon synonymous with the bloody trench warfare of the Firsct World War, was in short supply. At the war's start, the Serbian Army possessed 210 machine guns,[31] approximately half the European average of one machine gun per 1,000 troops.[32] Only in the front-line divisions did the army come close to the 1/1,000 ratio: at the war's start, the average Serbian first levy division had one machine gun per battalion. All told, a first levy division had sixteen and a second levy division twelve *Maxim* water-cooled heavy machine guns.[33]

In 1914, Serbia's standard field artillery piece was the *Schneider* field gun, a lighter export version of the famous *modele 1897* "French 75," which the Serbs designated the M907 (M907A for second levy divisions) and referred to by the Serbian Army as *Schneider-Creusot*, due to the factory that manufactured them.[34] Due to insufficient numbers of the M907, Serb forces relied on the antiquated French 80-mm Model 1885, colloquially called the *de Bange*, a screw-breech, black-powder cannon with no recoil mechanism or crew shields. Although the Serbian Army had substituted smokeless powder for the M1885 *de Bange* (and other larger-caliber, black-powder weapons), its short range, lack of shields, and slow rate of fire endangered its crews. The lack of a recoil mechanism created difficulties aiming concentrating fire. In July 1914, of Serbia's 488 operational field guns, 272 were quick-firing and 216 were *de Bange*.[35]

The standard mountain gun was a 70-mm version of the *Schneider*, also designated the M907, alongside two batteries of 75-mm *Danglis* guns—an innovative modification of the French 75.[36] These were supplemented by 80-mm *de Bange* mountain guns. In July 1914, the Serbian Army had fifty-five operational mountain guns, of which eight were *Danglis*, twenty-nine M907s, and eighteen *de Bange*.[37]

In addition to field guns, Serbia had fifty-four *Schneider* 120-mm howitzers, thirty-two of which were the quick-firing M910, the remainder being the slower M97, which lacked a recoil mechanism, but now used smokeless powder. Six M97 120-mm mortars and eight M910 150-mm howitzers were also used.[38] There were also two dozen 120-mm *de Bange* heavy artillery pieces. Although the heavier weapons were theoretically controlled at the army level, many were distributed to the infantry divisions.

Serbia had captured substantial quantities of artillery from Turkey and Bulgaria during the Balkan Wars. From the Turks, they had taken 126 *Krupp* 75-mm quick-firing field guns, six *Krupp* 75-mm quick-firing mountain guns, thirty *Krupp* 120-mm howitzers, a battery of obsolete *Broadwell* mountain guns, and almost 25,000 shells.[39] Not all the captured guns were battle-worthy, and in July 1914, Serbia initially incorporated three *Krupp* quick-firing batteries into front-line service.[40] Throughout 1914, this number varied and grew to include Habsburg Škoda 80-mm and 104-mm guns, depending on the availability of ammunition for the captured pieces.[41] In addition, Serbia's many fortresses were defended by obsolete artillery, including some muzzle-loaders.[42]

Although Serbia's organizational chart called for each division to be equipped with forty-eight quick-firing field artillery pieces, each first levy division typically fielded between twenty and twenty-four pieces, along with up to a dozen howitzers, the sole exception being the Combined Division, which had only twelve field artillery pieces. A second levy division had from eleven to thirteen cannon plus a few howitzers.

Altogether, of Serbia's 617 artillery pieces, only 381 were the rapid-fire weapons needed for modern war, and not all these cannon were available to face Austria-Hungary. Due to the unsettled situation along the Bulgarian and Albanian borders, Serbia was forced to assign some of its scarce artillery to Macedonia, as well as to the eastern border cities of Zaječar, Pirot, and Niš. To worsen the situation, at the war's outbreak Serbia sent almost 100 cannon to Montenegro, which had no modern breach-loading artillery of its own.

By August 1914, very little of the artillery ammunition used during the Balkan Wars had been replenished, and Serbia's army lacked adequate ammunition reserves. Although Serbia's small military arsenal at Kragujevac could turn out only 250–260 75-mm field artillery shells per day (the French 75 could fire twenty shells per minute), it could manufacture only 200 fuses per day. Nonetheless, Serbia's arsenal was unable to produce sufficient gunpowder for more than 80–100 shells per day.[43] Therefore, most artillery shells were purchased from France or Russia. The first replacement shipments of artillery shells for Balkan War losses did not begin to arrive until early July 1914.[44]

In July 1914, Serbia's air force was so unknown that Serbia's Ambassador to Rome had to ask the Foreign Ministry if Serbia even had an air force.[45] The fledgling Serbian Air Force consisted of two observation balloons, three aircraft, and 192 homing pigeons.[46] The aircraft, two of which were Bleriot monoplanes, were considered obsolete, even by the embryonic standards of 1914 military aviation,[47] and only one was barely flight-worthy at the outbreak of the war, which led to a pilots' revolt.[48] Due to mechanical and other difficulties, these aircraft were often out of service until mid-August, and then again through much of the fall and winter.[49]

The Serbs' lack of familiarity with aircraft may be seen in their attempts to differentiate between Serbian and Austro-Hungarian aircraft. Until the end of August, Serbian aircraft towed a 2-meter long colored flag from their tail, changing the color on a daily basis to prevent the enemy from mimicking Serbian aircraft.[50] So unfamiliar were the Serbian ground forces with aircraft, that after the war had been under way for several months, an aircraft flown by Captain Stanković and Second Lieutenant Novičić ran out of fuel and landed near a bridge behind Serbian lines. The pilots were "captured" by the local third levy *Čiča*, who refused to believe that Serbia had an Air Force.[51] The presence of homing pigeons on the High Command's rosters only underlined the shortage of modern communication equipment—telephone and telegraph—in the Serbian Army.

Mobilization

The state of the weaponry aside, there was the question of an effective mobilization, particularly since the army had no funds with which to carry it out. On July 20, eight days prior to Austria-Hungary's declaration of war and five days prior to Serbia's mobilization, Military Minister Stefanović received a letter from the General Staff that accompanied a twenty-six-page report more than one year in the making, compiled by a special railway commission. This report discussed the state of the country's railways and their suitability for mobilization. Prior to the First Balkan War, the mobilization was accomplished relatively easily and without heavy strain on the railroad. The report acknowledged that, although not without its problems, "before the war of 1912, the mobilization of our army was very simple," due to Serbia's relatively small size, the fact that all the divisions were located in their divisional recruiting regions, and that the only front was in the south.[52] At that time, the army had needed twelve trains per day devoted entirely to troops, military supplies and equipment. In addition, there had been two to three commercial trains per day.

Now, only five days prior to mobilization the report's author stated ominously: "I cannot provide more than seven trains for military use."[53] This situation was due to Serbia's newly enlarged borders, the dislocation of troops from their area of recruitment, and the new political situation in the Balkans: post-Balkan War hostility with Bulgaria and the continuing anarchy in Albania had forced Serbia to station large numbers of troops in Macedonia, the southernmost area of the country. Contrasting the situation with that in 1912, the report continued:

> Today it is completely different: 17 infantry regiments, 5 field, 3 mountain, and 1 howitzer artillery division, 1 heavy artillery and 1 engineering battalion; 5 hospital companies, 5 transport sections, and 2 cavalry squadrons are located outside their area of mobilization in newly seized regions.[54]

In other words, much of the regular army was in Macedonia and would need to be transported the length of the country to the Northern and Western Fronts. The report continued:

> When the transport of troops in 1912 was unable to take place without difficulty, when the territory was smaller, the mobilization simpler, and the railroad more capable than it is today, how then will it be carried out when there are so many potentials—in the negative sense—for the needs of our troops?[55]

The report added that in 1912 half of the troops marched to the front. But, "if war were declared tomorrow, 70% of our army would have to be transported by train."[56]

The commission's report stated that a major area of concern was the physical state of Serbia's railways. Although most of the lines within the old borders were, by and large, in adequate condition, in 1912 the north–south Belgrade–Niš–Vranje line, the most important for mobilization, had been "unprepared for carrying out concentration for the Serbo-Turkish war." When the section of the line that extended south from Vranje to Skopje and down to the Greek border had been seized from the Ottoman Empire in 1912, its condition was extremely poor. These lines, which had been built by the *Oriental Railway Society*, were poorly constructed and maintained: in Macedonia alone the Serbian state railway had to change over 30,000 railroad ties since 1912. The report went on to say that the rail lines in the south were dangerous for travel, and were judged inadequate for military use. The rail facilities in Macedonia were so poor that they were unable to adequately handle the regular commercial and passenger traffic. All this on the Skopje–Vranje–Niš–Belgrade main line, which would need to transport the majority of troops from Macedonia to the Northern Front.

Many locomotives and wagons had broken down during the Balkan Wars, leaving Serbia with fewer locomotives and wagons than in 1912, and double the length of track. These losses had not yet been replaced. Many of Serbia's locomotives were over thirty years old and had outlived their usefulness, while approximately 20 percent of the locomotives needed for military trains were in the repair shop. Serbia needed 2,023 type *H* freight wagons to transport its army, yet had only 1,877. Of this number, 280 were being repaired, leaving a total of only 1,597 wagons.

And then there was the question of coal. Even during peacetime, Serbia had difficulty obtaining sufficient quantities of coal for its engines: many passenger and freight trains, both domestic and international, were delayed by a lack of coal, to the point that international passengers often missed their connections. This situation had led to protests from foreign railways and travelers. The only available domestic coal—from the Ravnorečki and Senjski mines—was of poor quality and quickly deteriorated in bad weather. The coal's poor quality also caused the locomotives to break down. Yet even this was not available in sufficient quantities to form a strategic reserve sufficient to fight a two-month war.[57]

Matériel readiness

An example of the Serbian Army's poor condition may be seen in a pre-war readiness report on the Morava I and II Divisions sent to the General Staff on June 2, 1914 by General Gojković. The report gives only generalities, yet these provide a frightening picture of an army less than two months away from total war. In terms of manpower, the number of conscripts was "in general satisfactory," most regiments and battalions being close to adequate peacetime strength. However, the divisions lacked sufficient technical personnel, officers, and non-commissioned officers (NCOs). Gojković blamed most of these deficiencies on wartime losses. The loss of NCOs—who form the backbone of every army—was especially troubling, because inexperienced reserve NCOs and officers were having to replace them, and their quality was poor.

The divisional livestock and transport equipment—consisting mainly of oxen and ox-drawn wagons (komora)—was labeled "unsatisfactory." Dead and missing oxen were not yet replaced, while wagons were worn out and not yet repaired; the actual number of oxen was deemed insufficient for divisional needs. The number of pack and riding horses was also well below strength. So bad was their condition, that Gojković predicted the transport train would be far less effective in a future war than in 1912.

The divisions' weapons were also in terrible shape. The divisional artillery was largely worn out. Numerous rifles and pistols were missing parts and were described as completely inoperable: revolvers were few, and those that existed were in poor shape. Although stocks of rifle ammunition had been mostly replenished, artillery ammunition had not.

All units lacked basic field equipment, such as tents. What little they had was worn out, and could be used only in case of extreme need. Engineering and other technical equipment was in the process of being repaired. The divisions' few motor vehicles were worn out and needed repair. Medical supplies had been exhausted during the wars and were not yet replenished. Gojković concluded that, although the divisions' manpower was adequate for mobilization and war, "in general the state of military readiness could be described as barely satisfactory only in the most extreme necessity."[58] This situation was mirrored throughout the Serbian Army.

For some of the Serbian troops stationed in Macedonia, the state of peacetime housing was so poor that many had fallen ill and died. There was no money left to update, repair, or improve housing conditions: the army's need to keep 20,000 reservists on duty had bankrupted the treasury.[59] Although the troops were fed, they were not paid. Budget difficulties prevented Serbia from sending a military attaché to Paris, the source of Serbia's artillery ammunition and cannon.[60]

The post-mobilization situation proved equally serious. On average, the typical infantry division lacked rifles for one-quarter to one-third of its men.[61] The Morava I Division lacked approximately 1,900 rifles and two machine guns per regiment. The divisional artillery had sufficient draft animals to pull only twenty cannon and forty-four caissons. The division's cavalry regiment was missing 240 horses. The ammunition supply column lacked sixty horses, while the quartermaster column lacked 170. The Morava II Division had only 8,709 rifles for 11,210 men, leaving three entire battalions without rifles. These battalions were to wait near the front: when enough men had been killed or wounded, they were to take their rifles and move into the front lines.[62] The divisional artillery had only sufficient draught animals to pull four cannon, while the supply train was missing 200 ox-carts. And, of course, there was no field equipment.

The Danube I Division was missing 3,700 rifles and four machine guns. Its cavalry regiment lacked 100 horses, and two of its machine guns lacked pack-horses. The artillery lacked 418 horses, ninety carts, and nineteen caissons. The field hospitals lacked tents and other equipment.

The Danube II Division's entire VII Regiment was equipped with M.80 Mauser-Koch rifles, which required reloading after every shot. Most of the VIII and IX Regiments were equipped with M.80 single-shot rifles that had been refitted with magazines, to provide a faster rate of fire, although some soldiers still carried the single-round model. Each soldier's uniform consisted of a tunic and a *šajkača* cap. There were only sufficient greatcoats for every second soldier. Approximately 10 per cent of the division's recruits showed up in worn-out footwear; after a few weeks they were essentially barefoot. In a war that was to become famous for trenches, there were only forty entrenching tools per company.

The Drina I Division lacked rifles for the entire III Supernumerary Infantry Regiment and all the replacement battalions. The III Regiment's reservists were forced to wear their peasant clothing, due to a lack of uniforms. They also lacked 500 shovels and 500 pickaxes, and had no tents or shelter halves. Ammunition bandoliers and rucksacks were non-existent: because the typical peasant trousers did not have pockets, the soldiers carried their rifle ammunition in their hands. The artillery ammunition and troop supplies were exhausted and there were no food reserves.

The Drina II Division's regiments, although having numbers of modern magazine-fed bolt action rifles, were partially equipped with the M.80 single-shot rifles, especially V Regiment. Most of the troops wore their peasant clothes; only the officers had uniforms, making it impossible to distinguish between non-commissioned officers and enlisted soldiers. Due to a lack of manpower, this division used a number of third levy units in its formation: these troops were equipped with the black powder Berdan II single-shot rifle. Much of the divisional artillery consisted of the antiquated *de Bange* system, and there was a complete lack of field equipment.

The Šumadija I Division lacked rifles: on average, one battalion per regiment was entirely without arms. The artillery lacked sufficient draught horses and was forced to use oxen instead. The howitzer battery had 250 shells per barrel. And, as usual, field equipment was in short supply.

The Šumadija II Division lacked 2,500 rifles. Because its replacement battalions all lacked weapons, they were sent to Kruševac under the aegis of the *Reserve Army*. A lack of horses forced oxen to be used for pulling the artillery. There were only sufficient uniforms for approximately one-third of the soldiers: the remainder wore peasant clothes. Most units received no field equipment. The little equipment that was distributed was worn out and next to useless. There were no food reserves, and the number of draught animals was 10–12 percent below the required number.

The Timok I Division lacked uniforms and field equipment. The XX Regiment alone lacked 550 rifles, 650 bayonets, twenty sabers, twenty revolvers, two machine guns, ten riding and sixty pack horses, 300 shovels, 1,900 tent halves, 250 great coats, 450 šajkača caps, and more. The situation was similar throughout the division's other regiments. The artillery train had only eight caissons per battery, and the supply train lacked wagons, oxen, and horses.

The Timok II Division lacked 6,757 rifles, which meant fully 50 percent of its soldiers were unarmed. Those soldiers fortunate enough to be issued rifles had no bandoliers, and were forced to carry ammunition in their pockets or hands. The Division was missing large numbers of its officers, many of whom had gone abroad to find work. The Divisional artillery consisted of three batteries totaling twelve cannon, one caisson per battery, and a complete lack of horses or oxen to pull the artillery. Because of this the division was capable only of limited action.

The Cavalry Division lacked 280 sabers, 390 carbines, eighty revolvers, 400 sets of uniforms, and 760 horses.[63] No precise figures are available for the Combined Division in the immediate post-mobilization period, but, judging from later figures, it can be supposed that its matériel state was similar to that of a second levy division.

After mobilization, the stark reality of the army's unpreparedness sunk in. Many soldiers showed up for mobilization—in Military Minister Stefanović's words—"completely barefoot."[64] The army had neither boots nor shoes for its soldiers. Instead, they were issued *opanci*, a leather, curled-toed moccasin worn by the Serbian peasants.

Under battlefield conditions, *opanci* could last anywhere from one to three months, depending on the quality of the materials, workmanship, and the climate. Unfortunately, many were made from inferior materials, including a consignment of cardboard *opanci* from Romania that disintegrated almost immediately under battlefield conditions, leaving portions of the Danube I Division barefoot.[65] The footwear shortage became so serious that the government arranged to have *opanci*-makers excused from military service so that they might make footwear.[66]

In essence, the Serbian Army of August 1914—half uniformed, poorly equipped, barefoot, and in many cases dressed entirely in peasant clothes—resembled what one prominent Serbian historian termed a "peasant mob."[67] Nikola Pašić bemoaned the state of Serbia's army and the lack of support from its allies: "Our army was left, so to say, completely without clothes, shoes, and camping equipment."[68] So thoroughly exhausted were Serbia's troops and stocks of military supplies and equipment that in mid-June 1914, immediately prior to the Sarajevo assassination, Nikola Pašić turned down a Greek request for a military alliance against the Ottoman Empire, explaining that Serbia's army was completely unprepared for another war.[69]

The soldiers

Yet, in spite of the poor state of matériel readiness, contemporary foreign observers described the Serbian soldiers as some of the best in the world. The British military attaché in Belgrade, Colonel Thompson, said:

> It is very difficult to overpraise the Serbian infantry. They are brave, enduring, obedient, good-tempered, and can live on next to nothing under conditions which would appall the average Britisher. Attacks are sometimes made without officers ... the private soldier has a fund of common sense which enables him to do the right thing when acting independently.[70]

The US Ambassador to Serbia, Charles Vopicka, commenting on the hardiness of the Serbs, said: "give the Serbian soldier bread and an onion, and he is satisfied." This was not mere hyperbole: an onion and bread was often more than the average Serbian soldier received to eat. On July 28, Military Minister Stefanović wrote to Pašić asking him to expedite food deliveries from abroad, stating that "in the nation and in our warehouses there is no food."[71] The shortages were so great that the Serbian government even explored the possibility of purchasing flour from its enemy, Bulgaria.[72] The Habsburg general Alfred Krauss, who commanded the Austro-Hungarian

Combined Corps against Serbia in 1914, described the Serbian soldiers as "satisfied by small amounts, skilled at orienting themselves, cunning, exceptionally mobile, well-armed, . . . skilled on the terrain, very well-led."[73]

The Serbian generals readily admitted the hardiness and durability of their troops, saying their soldiers had a "love for the Fatherland, founded on great and strong traditions from their glorious past, connected with the successes in the Balkan Wars, [which] raised the spirit and morale of the Serbian soldiers to an exceptional height."[74] The experience of the Balkan Wars proved critical, as Serbia was the only European country in 1914 to enter the First World War with soldiers who had fresh combat experience. The US Ambassador to Serbia, Charles Vopicka, wrote that the Serbian conscripts dressed in their peasant clothes "looked like bands of tramps coming to the front, but they made excellent soldiers."[75]

In spite of the Entente's glowing opinion of the Serbian private soldier, the Serbian generals were considered below average by their foreign peers. The British Army attaché in Belgrade, Colonel Thompson, said "good officers are lacking." He considered *Vojvoda* Radomir Putnik and Second Army commander General Stepa Stepanović too old, and said that First Army commander Petar Bojović was slow to take initiative and "does not exert himself as he might."[76] The Austro-Hungarian *Armeeoberkommando* shared this low opinion of Serbian officers: for this very reason they had released the elderly Putnik after Serbia began mobilizing its army, certain that his age, poor health, and lack of formal military training would hinder Serbia's war effort. Wartime experience would show these assessments of Serbia's officer corps to be highly flawed.

On the eve of battle, Serbia could field a woefully equipped first and second levy operational army totaling 250,000 men, armed with only 180,000 modern magazine-fed bolt-action rifles, 200 machine guns, three obsolescent aircraft, 192 homing pigeons, and 617 artillery pieces, of which 381 were modern rapid-fire weapons.[77] When third levy troops and other non-operational forces were added, Serbia's army totaled 320,000 men, many of whom had to be deployed along the borders with Albania and Bulgaria in irregular formations.[78] Serbia's 250,000 man operational army would face the 320,000 first levy soldiers of Austria-Hungary's *Balkanstreitkräfte*, armed entirely with modern rapid-fire rifles, 486 machine guns, forty-eight aircraft, 744 modern cannon, and an abundance of the latest equipment.[79]

In stark contrast to the Serbian Army, the Austro-Hungarian Army entered battle well-equipped, rested, and possessing ample supplies: there are no recorded instances of Habsburg soldiers entering battle barefoot, dressed in peasant clothes, armed with black powder single-shot rifles and carrying ammunition in their hands. The Empire's rail system—designed specifically for a military mobilization—functioned with Germanic precision. Underdeveloped Serbia, with a war-ravaged agrarian economy, rag-tag military, and population of four million people, would face the industrialized

PHOTO 10 Vojvoda *Radomir Putnik*.

Austro-Hungarian Empire, with its well-equipped army and fifty million subjects to draw upon. On paper, the outcome seemed predetermined.

Rumors of wars . . .

Serbia's capital Belgrade sits on a hill at the confluence of the Danube and Sava rivers. On the promontory stands the Kalemegdan, an enormous fortress dating to Roman times, when, as the fortified border outpost of *Singidunum* it guarded the empire against barbarians from the Pannonian plain and the Carpathians. In the early Byzantine period, Belgrade served as that empire's northernmost outpost. In the late medieval period, the Hungarian ruler Janos Hunyadi used it as a base against the Ottoman Turks. At some point in the middle ages, the fortress-city's white limestone walls and towers earned it the name "Beograd," or "white castle." From 1739 until 1878, it was the northernmost outpost of the Ottoman Empire. Although Belgrade was officially part of the Ottoman Empire until 1878, it became the capital of an autonomous Serbian principality following the 1804 and 1815 Serbian uprisings. Until the second reign of Serbian prince Mihailo Obrenović in 1860, Belgrade was a provincial Turkish border town. Serbian princes such as Mihailo's father, Miloš Obrenović, built palaces after the Turkish style: numerous Turkish fountains throughout the city lent their names to the various neighborhoods and districts. Radiating out from the Kalemegdan fortress, narrow winding streets—faced by dilapidated, tilting Ottoman buildings—wound their way down the hills towards the Danube and Sava rivers. Mihailo Obrenović, the father of modern Serbia, tore and burned down entire districts of the city and replaced many of the Turkish structures with buildings in the latest European architecture.

By 1914, Belgrade boasted many of the accouterments of a modern European capital: a university, a national museum, a royal academy, a hospital, libraries, a royal palace, numerous hotels and *kafanas*, a Bohemian district, a tobacco factory, mills, a telephone exchange, an extravagant officers' club and casino, government ministries, several breweries, electric lighting, banks, embassies, upper-class mansions, a train station, churches, the homes of the emerging middle class, and street cars. Parks and broad boulevards radiated outward from the city's old center around the Kalemegdan fortress, and French and Austrian cultural influences were strong.

Although Belgrade's new civic architecture was European, even its newest buildings had a distinct flavor that mixed European style with subtle hints of its Turkish and Byzantine past. In spite of these accouterments, when compared with other European capitals—Budapest, Vienna, Berlin, London, Paris, Rome, St. Petersburg—Belgrade was tiny. Unlike Sarajevo, which boasted main streets paved with asphalt, Belgrade's main street had just begun to be paved in 1912, and with wooden blocks no less.[80] Assuming one was not run over by the ox-carts that plied the main thoroughfares, a pedestrian could walk from the city's eastern-most Dorćol district on the banks of the Danube, to the western outskirts of Senjak along the Sava, in an hour. In an equal amount of time, he could walk from the Kalemegdan's northern river wall to Kumodraž, the birthplace of General Stepa Stepanović on the city's southern outskirts.

Immediately across the Sava River from Belgrade lay the Habsburg provincial border town of Zemun (*Semlin*), a thriving commercial city that gained much of its income from river traffic and trade with Serbia. Spread out along its main street *Herrengasse*, numerous shops and businesses—owned by Slavs, Germans, Hungarians, and Jews—catered to river and border traffic, as well as the needs of the town's garrison. Zemun's Orthodox, Catholic, and Protestant churches, customs offices, and military barracks formed a microcosm of the Austro-Hungarian Empire. On a hill overlooking the Danube stood an enormous tower, erected in 1896 to commemorate 1,000 years of Hungarian history. As was the case with many of the Austro-Hungarian regions bordering Serbia, Zemun's garrison and military installations had grown since 1912, as though preparing for war.[81] Given Belgrade's small geographic area, the entire city was well within range of Austro-Hungarian artillery batteries around Zemun and across the Danube at Pančevo.

After severing diplomatic relations on July 25, the Dual Monarchy cut all telephone, telegraph, and rail traffic with Serbia, and most residents of Belgrade expected an artillery bombardment to commence as soon as von Giesl crossed the river.[82] As Serbia's government and army evacuated Belgrade, foreign diplomats followed. Most of the shops and factories closed, expecting war to break out momentarily. Tensions ran high throughout Belgrade and large numbers of people began to leave the city.[83] But nothing happened.

On July 26, Austro-Hungarian armored river monitors captured the Serbian steamer *Vardar* far to the east on the Danube and forced it to dock at Orșova on the Austro-Hungarian side of the river.[84]

After two days of calm, shops and workplaces reopened on the morning of July 27, prompting one observer to note that Belgrade was beginning to calm down.[85] Early that same morning the last steamboat departed Belgrade's Sava landing for Zemun, leaving behind an enormous crowd of people who had been unable to obtain passage back to Austria-Hungary. Most were Habsburg citizens—mainly Serbs—vacationing at Serbian spas. Across the river at the Zemun landing large crowds of Serbs waited in vain in the hot, humid late-July weather for passage back to Serbia. Because telephone and telegraph connections were cut, there was no way to make arrangements for the passage of the stranded civilians.

Around 11:00 am on July 28, the German Consul Count Spee and his counselor Baron Scharfenberg, now in charge of Habsburg interests in Belgrade, rented a private Serbian motor launch with the help of Đorđe

Ćutković, an agent of the Danube Steamboat Society. After paying thirty dinars for the boat they set off for Zemun flying the German flag, in an attempt to negotiate passage for the stranded Austro-Hungarian travelers. En route to Zemun a sudden and fierce thunderstorm forced them onto a sandbar: a passing Austro-Hungarian patrol boat pulled them off. Refusing to believe German diplomats were on board, the captain of the patrol boat towed the Serbian craft to Zemun, where the Austro-Hungarian authorities verified the German diplomats' identity.

Upon disembarking, Consul Spee met with the military commander of Zemun to discuss passage for the stranded travelers. Although it was midday, the streets of Zemun were nearly deserted and the shops closed. The only people on the streets were Austro-Hungarian officers in full battle dress. Among the large crowd of people waiting at the Zemun landing Ćutković found the Russian military attaché to Serbia, accompanied by his wife and family. They had been at a spa in Austria-Hungary when the ultimatum and declaration of war caught them by surprise. Ćutković spent the next hour in the Hotel Grand waiting for Spee to finish his discussion. When Spee returned he appeared optimistic and informed Ćutković he had made arrangements to transport the stranded travelers early the next day. He told Ćutković that "judging by everything, it appears that it won't come to war."[86] The party, which now included the Russian military attaché and his family, left for Belgrade. When they arrived at the Sava landing around 3:00 pm, they were met by Belgrade's chief of police, who informed them that Austria-Hungary had declared war, and that further movement on the rivers was prohibited.

Belgrade received Berchtold's declaration of war before Nikola Pašić did. Even though the telegram was destined for Niš, and was only being relayed by the Belgrade station, the fact that it was an open telegram meant that within moments of its arrival everyone in the Belgrade telegraph office knew of its contents. Shortly, the entire city seemed to know. The open telegram also meant that everyone in the telegraph stations at Kragujevac and Niš would know of the declaration before Pašić.[87] In Belgrade, the news of war prompted the shops to close once again. People rushed to those few shops still open and began buying food and supplies. A rumor that the city's water supply would be turned off prompted crowds to form around the many public fountains, as people filled every available dish and vessel with water. To further confuse the situation, the Ministry of Internal Affairs in Niš, when told of the declaration by telephone, categorically denied the existence of a declaration of war.[88]

Ćutković walked from the Sava landing up the hill to the *kafana* at the Hotel Moskva. En route children sold newspapers for five *para* a piece: large headlines proclaimed the declaration of war. On one street corner gendarmes seized newspapers from the children and cut them up, proclaiming loudly that war had not been declared and that they were rumors—a Polish-Jewish attempt to make money off of war fears.[89] At the *kafana* in the Hotel

Moskva, the conversation centered on war rumors. All present seemed to think that war had not really been declared. From the *kafana*, Ćutković called his wife and assured her that the reports were merely false rumors.

The confusion increased throughout the late afternoon and early evening as the German Consul Count Spee claimed to have no knowledge of a declaration of war, and maintained that the military commander in Zemun, to the best of Spee's knowledge, knew nothing of an impending declaration. In order to quell the rumors the newspaper *Politika* published a special late edition with an enormous banner headline that took up half the front page—it read, "WAR IS NOT DECLARED." The paper then reported on Count Spee's trip to Zemun, as well as the assurances of the Zemun military commander that war had not been declared.[90]

Around 6:00 pm, a semi-official telegram arrived in Belgrade from the government Pressburo in Niš, further confusing the situation. It stated that the Royal government was attempting to confirm the authenticity of the telegram from Berchtold, and that the German Ambassador in Niš—who was handling Austro-Hungarian interests—knew absolutely nothing of a declaration of war. In the early evening crowds milled around the Grand Hotel, the Hotel Moskva, and the Greek Queen Hotel, discussing the rumors and whether or not war had been declared. By late evening the situation was still unclear, and Belgrade fell into what an editor of *Politika* termed a "deadly silence."[91]

CHAPTER FIVE

The guns of July

Hej trubaču s bojne Drine,
ded' zatrubi zbor!
Nek' odjekne Šar-planina,
Lovćen, Durmitor.
I nek' Drina jekne Savi
Sava-Dunavu,
Dunav bujni Tisi, Dravi:
u boj! . . . U slavu! . . .

A city that is set on a hill . . .

From a military standpoint, Belgrade would be difficult to defend, located just a few hundred meters across the river from Austro-Hungarian territory. When the Serbian government evacuated Belgrade on July 25, Military Minister Stefanović ordered that all soldiers, artillery, and stocks of ammunition be withdrawn from the Kalemegdan fortress.[1] Given the length of time necessary for Austria-Hungary to concentrate its troops, Stefanović believed that the Dual Monarchy would not commence hostilities until August 4 at the earliest.[2] Therefore, any decision to defend the capital could wait for a few days.

The Danube I Division—commanded by Colonel Milivoje Anđelković— was responsible for defending Belgrade and its environs, and had concentrated most of its troops and artillery to the west of the city on Banovo Hill or up at Banjica to the south of the city. As of late in the evening on July 28, neither the High Command nor Colonel Anđelković had yet decided to defend Belgrade.[3] In the meantime, there were no artillery pieces or machine guns in place, and the city was defended only by an unorganized group of gendarmes, customs police, a few Četniks from Vojislav Tankosić's

Detachment, a company from the 18th Infantry Regiment, and members of the gymnastic society "Dušan The Mighty," who kept weapons at their club house near the Saborna Church.[4] The city seemed ripe for the taking.

At approximately 11:30 pm on the night of July 28, rifle fire broke out along the Serbian side of the Sava River. It began near the river wall of the Kalemegdan's lower fortress (*Donji grad*), and then moved upstream towards the Sava landing. The small arms fire was followed by loud cannon fire and explosions along the Serbian side of the river. The financial police and gendarmes, armed with rifles, ran along the river bank, shooting at dark shapes on the water. Three Austro-Hungarian tugs pulling barges with infantry had tried to land near the *Donji Grad* (lower fortress) section of the Kalemegdan, but veered away after coming under intense rifle fire. The barges were escorted by a heavily armored river monitor, which began shelling the Kalemegdan and city with its 120-mm cannon.

The move was brilliant. If the amphibious landing succeeded, Vienna would capture Serbia's capital city and present the other Great Powers with a *fait accompli* before their mobilizations were complete. Not only would Vienna be able to claim that it had achieved partial satisfaction for the Sarajevo assassination, but it would increase Habsburg leverage at the subsequent peace conference. So too, it might forestall a general European war. Should Russia continue to mobilize, Austria-Hungary could transfer substantial forces from the Balkans and send them to the Russian Front. It could also give the wavering neutral countries—Bulgaria, Greece, and Romania in particular—reason to ally with Austria-Hungary against Serbia and Russia in exchange for territorial concessions. A *fait accompli* might also dissuade France from keeping its commitments to Russia and demonstrate St. Petersburg was incapable of protecting Serbia. Crucially, it would send a message to the South Slavs in the Habsburg Empire that Serbia was not their hoped-for Piedmont. Millions of lives and the fate of empires and countries rested on this midnight amphibious descent.

Colonel Krsta Smiljanić, chief of the General Military Section of the Military Ministry in Niš, maintained constant telephone contact with Belgrade and was on the line when the shooting erupted. As the monitor began shelling the city and fortress, the staff at the headquarters of the Danube I Division fled, as did the staff at the telephone exchange. As a result, the telephone line to Niš went dead at ten minutes past midnight.[5]

As the first tug and its barges veered away from the river wall, they headed up the Sava towards the railway bridge, with the financial police and gendarmes in hot pursuit on foot. The monitor stayed near *Donji Grad* and continued shelling the city and fortress. As the tug approached the railway bridge, by now early on the morning of July 29, the Serbs encountered small arms fire from the Austro-Hungarian side of the bridge. Fearing that Habsburg forces were preparing to cross the bridge, the Tankosić Detachment quickly dynamited the span nearest the Serbian shore shortly after 1:00 am, cutting off Serbia's last contact with Europe.[6] At 1:10 am, an off-duty telephone operator ran to the deserted telephone exchange, called Niš and informed the government that the shelling and shooting had stopped, and that all was now quiet.[7]

In this brief skirmish, the first of the war, the first Serb to die was Dušan Đonović, a student at the Commercial Academy and a member of Jovan Babunski's Četnik group.[8] Rifle fire from the Serbian defenders killed the captain of the first tug, Karl Eberling, and his helmsman, Mikhail Gemsberger, the first Austro-Hungarian casualties of the war. Under fierce small arms fire, the tug ran aground on the Austro-Hungarian side of the river and the panicked soldiers dove overboard from the barges; those that could, swam to the north shore of the Sava. Others drowned. At first light on the morning of July 29, one steam tug and eight empty barges were visible, aground under the Habsburg side of the ruined railroad bridge. A second tug with a string of barges had run aground across from the Sava landing, at Ušće, nearby modern Belgrade's Old Fairground. The third tug returned safely to Zemun with its barges.

The Austro-Hungarian soldiers in the crowded barges were sitting ducks. The chief of the hospital in Zemun, Dr. Sava Nedeljković, a Serb, reported heavy Habsburg casualties that filled the hospital's 100 beds and forced the wounded to be lodged in private homes or lie in the streets. The Zemun police force went door to door on the morning of July 29, collecting bedding for the wounded.[9]

Around 5:00 am that morning, the Military Ministry in Niš received a telephone call reporting that Austro-Hungarian artillery batteries at Zemun and Bežanija had opened fire on Belgrade and were shelling various parts of the city and the Kalemegdan. By 6:00 am, shells had hit the Second Gymnasium, the Grand Hotel, the Novi Majdan Hotel, the Franco-Serbian Bank, the Andrejević Bank, and had completely destroyed the house at 9 Bitoljska Street. Perhaps the single greatest blow was the destruction of the government's Tobacco Monopoly factory, which had been hit and set ablaze, effectively depriving Belgrade of cigarettes, a catastrophe for any civilian population under siege.[10]

Throughout the day shells fell on the city and Kalemegdan at the rate of approximately eleven per hour, hitting numerous buildings. The shelling prompted the Italian and British ambassadors to approach Colonel Anđelković and ask him whether the army intended to defend the city. Yet neither Anđelković nor the High Command had yet decided what to do. Reacting to the Italian and British ambassadors, Anđelković telegraphed the High Command for instructions, noting that the city was poorly defended and that evacuation would probably save the city from shelling.[11] At 4:00 pm, the foreign diplomatic representatives still in Belgrade raised a white flag on the roof of the General Staff building, hoping to negotiate neutral zones for foreign citizens. As soon as the flag was raised, the Austro-Hungarian artillery ceased firing. Because the telephone and telegraph links had been cut, all efforts to make contact with the Austro-Hungarian forces failed: after an hour of futile attempts to make contact, the diplomats took the flag down and the shelling resumed, with most of the shells landing around the General Staff building.[12]

By 5:30 pm, still lacking instructions from the High Command, Anđelković decided to defend Belgrade. He informed the High Command of his decision and asked Putnik to send ammunition for the 150-mm howitzers. Shortly before dark, Austro-Hungarian artillery began to shell Topčider Hill and Banovo Hill, two pieces of high ground to the southwest of the city center that overlooked *Ada Ciganlija* (Gypsy Island) in the Sava River. The shelling lasted until 9:00 pm. At the same time, Habsburg troops began to build a bridge from the north bank of the Sava out to Little *Ada Ciganlija*, a small, occasionally flooded island 200 meters from the Serbian bank. Around one in the morning, artillery began shelling the rail line running east of the city between Smederevo and Grocka.[13] All along Serbia's border with the Dual Monarchy similar events occurred. To the east of Belgrade on the Danube, the town of Veliko Gradište came under heavy artillery fire which lasted for several days, as did Grocka, Smederevo, and Ram.[14] On the Drina River, the town of Loznica came under fierce artillery fire. On the Sava, the city centers of Šabac and Obrenovac were hit with incendiary shells.[15]

The world learned that war had started when Nikola Pašić sent a telegram on July 30 to all Serbian embassies, telling them to announce that "yesterday at 2:00 am an Austrian monitor began a lively bombardment of Belgrade."[16] The shelling of Belgrade continued without respite for eight days and nights.[17]

Throughout this period, the Austro-Hungarian Army made constant and visible preparations to cross the Danube and Sava. On July 30, they landed men and matériel to the southeast of Belgrade on an island in the Danube across from the town of Vinča. On the night of August 1, spotlights from the Habsburg shore lit up the Kalemegdan, Banovo Hill, and *Ada Ciganlija*. Shelling from artillery batteries and river monitors continued without interruption. On August 3, the first aerial attack of the war occurred, when an Austro-Hungarian reconnaissance plane, flying over the town of Ralja, dropped a hand-held bomb on Serbian troops. The bomb failed to explode.[18] By August 5, when the Austro-Hungarian forces employed their enormous 305-mm siege mortars,[19] citizens had begun to seek shelter in the cave under Tašmajdan.[20] In the meantime, Belgrade's city authorities cut off all electricity at night.[21]

By the time the shelling stopped on August 6, much of Belgrade had been hit: the Greek Queen Hotel, the Hotel Bristol, the Serbian Crown Hotel, the Grand Hotel, the Novi Majdan Hotel, the Hotel Kragujevac, the Commercial Bank, the Andrejević Bank, the Jugoslavija Bank, the Franco-Serbian Bank, the British Embassy, three private homes on the *Terazije*, a girls' home, three homes in the *Sava Mali* district, the tobacco factory, twenty-eight private homes in the *Dorćol* district, the Second Gymnasium, the Academy of Science in Brankova Street, the state printing press, the city's main church—the *Saborna Crkva*—the Zaharija mill, the train station, the general staff building, the main post office, and the officers' club and casino. All the coal on the Danube landing had been set ablaze, and the National Museum was completely destroyed. Remarkably, during the course of the entire bombardment only one civilian had been killed. By the end of the year, the Royal Palace, Royal Stables, Military Academy, General State Hospital, and even the Austro-Hungarian Embassy would be hit by artillery shells.[22] The shelling was in clear violation of Article 27 of the Hague Convention—of which Austria-Hungary was a signatory—that prohibited bombardment of churches, schools, museums, cultural objects, hospitals, and other civilian targets.[23] By late August, Vienna would declare Belgrade a fortified military target "in its entirety," laying the groundwork for indiscriminate artillery fire.[24]

In wartime, truth is usually the first casualty. Throughout the first days of the war, in spite of the bombardment, the Belgrade press carried sensational reports of allied support for Serbia and patriotic editorials. On August 3 the newspaper *Depeša*, flush with patriotism, threatened to publish the names of all who left Belgrade during the bombardment, and asked residents to report the names of their neighbors who fled the city. The exodus of refugees from the besieged city was so great that *Depeša* eventually turned to publishing only the names of those who stayed. Large headlines inflated minor skirmishes into major Serbian victories, as the Serbian Army repulsed small Habsburg reconnaissance crossings of the Danube and Sava. On August 4, one report confidently (and erroneously) spoke of a major battle in which the French Army had repelled a German attack.[25] On August 5, another report confidently placed the victorious Russian Army at the outskirts of Budapest, and stated that it would take the city by 9:00 am the next morning; another said the Serbian Army was crossing the Drina into Bosnia-Herzegovina at Zvornik against light Austro-Hungarian opposition; yet another indicated the German Army had not yet mobilized.[26] In the midst of this patriotic fervor, one news item stood out. In a published interview, an anonymous foreign diplomat spoke against the popular belief that the war would be short and swift. Prophetically, he foretold that "the war will be bloody and terrible and will be waged until one side is completely incapacitated for war."[27]

After a brief respite between August 6 and 8, the shelling of Belgrade resumed anew with the heaviest bombardment to date on August 9. Shelling now continued unabated through the end of August.[28] Shells hit the water pumping plant and the power plant, cutting off water and electricity to the city.[29] Yet in spite of the bombardment, life in Belgrade continued. The Swiss Consul, Mr. Fegeli, opened his house to the citizens of Belgrade, whom he served white coffee, chocolate, and weak glasses of cognac. He allowed several whose homes had been destroyed by the shelling to sleep on his sofas.[30] Fears of shortages caused prices to rise. Millers raised the price of flour so high that bakers threatened to stop baking bread.[31] For the residents who remained behind in Belgrade, however, life was made bearable, as the *Weifert* and *Bajlon* Breweries kept operating.

Mountains everywhere

In the Balkans, geography is destiny. In contrast to events on the relatively flat Eastern and Western Fronts, geography decisively shaped the battlefield and war.[32] The modern nature of the Great War notwithstanding, the same geographic features that confronted the Greeks and Romans two millennia earlier and molded the peninsula's historic trade and communication routes, limited the Austro-Hungarian and Serbian Armies. In 1914, the peninsula's geography directly affected the strategic and tactical objectives of the combatants, limited their available options, and in some cases circumscribed the possible outcomes of any given campaign or battle.

Mountains characterize the Balkan Peninsula, some as high as 8,000 feet, many of which carry snow until August. The Dinaric mountain range covers most of Dalmatia, Bosnia-Herzegovina, Montenegro, much of Serbia, Albania and Macedonia, and together with the Balkan and Rhodope mountains in Bulgaria, forms a barrier across the peninsula. Characterized by range and basin topography (similar to the Great Basin region of the United States), the Balkan Peninsula boasts "remarkably straight and abrupt" mountains, separated by deep trenches which run northwest to southeast. Only two north–south trenches traverse the peninsula's entire length. Whoever controlled these routes controlled the Balkans.[33]

The northwest to southeast direction of the mountains meant that travel on this axis was far easier than from west to east. Travel between the Balkan hinterland and Constantinople was easier than travel to the Dalmatian seacoast, even though the distance to the seacoast was much shorter. Only the northern port of Rijeka (Fiume) provided relatively easy contact between the Adriatic and the interior. None of the rivers running from the Balkan hinterland to the Adriatic were suitable for navigation, and their valleys could carry little more than the most rudimentary wagon traffic. In 1914, with the exception of the northern port of Rijeka, only the rail line from Sarajevo to Metković near the mouth of the Neretva River connected Bosnia to the Adriatic. Nor did any rail lines connect Serbia to Bosnia-Herzegovina. The narrow-gauge Bosnian line running southeast from Sarajevo ended beyond Višegrad, just short of the Serbian border, while the Serbian line stopped at Užice, over 40 kilometers—as the crow flies—across the mountains from Višegrad. The only transportation link of any significance on the entire peninsula was the railroad along the main north–south corridor.

Geographically, the Balkans gained importance from its position at the juncture of Asia Minor and Europe. Throughout history it was *the* conduit for most cultural, ethnic, and political contact between Europe and the Near East. For certain regions in central and eastern Europe—the lands of present-day Austria, Belarus, the Czech Republic, Germany, Hungary, Poland, Romania, and Slovakia—from which a sea voyage proved too long or impractical or which did not have a seacoast, the Balkan peninsula was the most direct—or the only—route to the Near East.[34]

In 1914, the Ottoman Empire depended on Germany for cannon, artillery shells, rifles, bullets, and machine guns. Because the Entente controlled the sea lanes, the only land route between the Ottoman Empire and Germany ran overland across the Balkan peninsula. Serbia sat astride one-third of this land route, which gave it the opportunity to block all contact between the Triple Alliance and the Ottoman Empire. For Russia, which depended on its allies Britain and France for significant amounts of military and industrial material, the Balkans was also important. During the winter months, cold weather forced Russia's northern White Sea ports to close, while Germany's North Sea fleet rendered the Baltic inaccessible. After the Ottoman Empire entered the war on the side of the Triple Alliance, Russia could no longer receive supplies via the Dardanelles. This left the partially completed rail line from Thessaloniki (Salonika) to Serbia's eastern Danubian port of Prahovo as the only route for trans-shipment of cargo to Russia via Serbia and Romania.[35] Thus, control of the Balkans assumed an importance to the Entente and the Triple Alliance that went far beyond the initial Austro-Hungarian objective of avenging Sarajevo.[36]

Immediately after the Austro-Hungarian occupation of Bosnia-Herzegovina in 1878, the Serbian general staff began to plan for an Austro-Hungarian attack, and in the 1880s they surveyed possible invasion routes from Austria-Hungary and Bulgaria into Serbia's interior.[37] On the northern (Sava and Danube rivers) border they identified several routes, most of which centered on the north–south Morava River valley. From the western border (Drina River), all routes followed the Jadar and Kolubara valleys toward Belgrade, or toward the Western Morava watershed at Užice. Along the Bulgarian border, possible routes centered around Zaječar and Pirot, as well as points further south in Macedonia, where small rivers penetrated the mountainous frontier. Although this planning began prior to construction of the Orient Express line and before Serbia's gains in the Balkan Wars, the geographic imperatives remained the same: defend the north–south trans-Balkan corridors.

The north–south routes

The first of the north–south trans-Balkan routes, the Morava–Marica corridor, was the only land route from Central Europe to Istanbul (Constantinople). In the ancient world, the Romans and Byzantine Greeks used it as a major trade route; in 1189 during the Third Crusade, the German Emperor Frederick Barbarossa marched his army to Jerusalem via this route; during the late medieval period, the Ottoman Turks used it to invade the heart of Europe, overrunning Hungary and advancing to the gates of Vienna. After the construction of the railway in 1888, it was the primary land link between Eastern, Central, and Western Europe on the one hand, and Istanbul on the other. The Orient Express and Berlin–Baghdad railway followed this route, and it quickly became the main supply route between Germany and the Ottoman Empire. Serbian acrimony with Bulgaria meant that the Bulgarian government prohibited trans-shipment of Russian military supplies for Serbia over this route via its Black Sea and Danube ports, purportedly due to Bulgaria's desire to maintain its neutrality.

The Morava–Marica corridor followed the courses of the Morava and Marica rivers. The Morava River entered the Danube almost 50 kilometers east of Belgrade. Along its lower course, the river flowed through a broad valley flanked by low rolling hills that offered few natural defenses against an enemy attempting to enter the corridor from east or west. Therefore, any attack had to be stopped prior to reaching the valley. Upstream, approximately 45 kilometers south of the Danube, the river valley narrowed and mountains rose on either side, preventing entry to the corridor from east or west. Still, the valley remained relatively broad as far south as Niš. A road accompanied the river most of the way to the city of Niš, making only two detours away from the valley, at points where it narrowed to a gorge.

From Niš the corridor branched off to the southeast and followed the Nišava River's narrow valley, and in two places the road left the valley entirely. The rail line followed the valley to the broad basin at the town of Pirot. A border town of strategic significance, Pirot had fortresses to guard against Bulgarian invasion. From Pirot the road continued upward to the border with Bulgaria near the Dragoman Pass (2,500 feet), and then descended to the broad floor of the Sofia basin. After Sofia the road crossed the Vakarel Pass and descended to the headwaters of the Marica River, traveling southeast toward Edirne and then Istanbul.

The other main trans-Balkan route, the Morava–Vardar corridor, connected the Pannonian Plain with the Aegean Sea via Thessaloniki, both by rail and road. This corridor provided the most direct route from Eastern and Central Europe to the Mediterranean, other than the road through Rijeka, whose proximity to Italy rendered it strategically vulnerable. In classical times, the Greeks, Romans, and Byzantine Greeks used this corridor as a major trade route; in the sixth century, the Slavs used it to invade Greece and besiege Thessaloniki and Byzantium; during the medieval period, the Ottoman Turks used it as an invasion route into the central Balkans; and in 1690, the Habsburg general Louis of Baden followed it with his armies in a campaign against the Ottoman Empire, in which he penetrated as far south as Macedonia. After it began to administer Bosnia-Herzegovina and the Sandžak of Novi Pazar in 1878, and spurred on by the completion of the railway to Istanbul in 1888, the Austro-Hungarian Empire began to consider this route as an avenue of expansion to the Mediterranean. After Serbia's conquests in the Balkan Wars, three-quarters of this corridor ran through Serbian territory.

The Morava–Vardar corridor followed the Morava River all the way to Niš, and then continued south along the southern Morava River, crossing the divide between the Morava and Vardar watersheds (1,500 feet) just north of Kumanovo, where it entered Macedonia. At Kumanovo, the road and rail entered a broad triangular basin of strategic importance. At the northern corner of the basin lies Kumanovo, at the western corner Skopje, and at the southeastern corner Veles. From Skopje the line ran to Veles, south of which it entered the Vardar river gorge. In 1914, the gorge had both a railway and a poor road. At Demir Kapija, the valley narrowed to an almost impassable gorge. The route then crossed into Greece at Ðevđelija, and continued to the port of Thessaloniki. The section of the rail line from Kumanovo to Ðevđelija was in extremely poor repair and was not considered suitable to support an Entente field army.[38]

The Morava–Vardar corridor was protected on the east by the Balkan and Rhodope mountains, which rose steeply from the valley floor. Serbia's frontier with Bulgaria ran along the crests of these rugged and heavily forested mountains. Nonetheless, several routes existed for an invading army to enter the corridor. These were: the Nišava river valley, guarded by the fortress town of Pirot; the Timok river valley, guarded by the fortress town of Zaječar; the Vlasina river valley, which entered the corridor at the Leskovac basin; the Kriva river valley, which entered the corridor at Kumanovo; and the Bregalnica river valley near Veles. The Strumica river valley also provided access to the corridor through several passes in the southernmost areas of Macedonia. In many places, the border with Bulgaria reached the mountain crests directly overlooking the corridor: between Leskovac and Vranje, the border was less than 19 kilometers from the rail line.

In 1914, the Morava–Vardar corridor was Serbia's vital lifeline to the west and the only way it could receive ammunition and other supplies from Great Britain and France. The close proximity of the Bulgarian border as well as the dilapidated state of the railway in Macedonia and northern Greece—which only two years earlier had been Turkish—meant this route was at best tenuous. Cutting it at any point would destroy Serbia's only source of war matériel. Fortunately for Serbia, Greece's loose interpretation of neutrality allowed this route to remain open to such shipments. This corridor's vulnerability caused concern at the highest levels of the Serbian Army and government, and protecting it from Bulgarian Komite attacks was a high priority. Weak points notwithstanding, the terrain favored the defenders. If adequately manned and defended, the eastern frontier could prove a formidable obstacle to any invader. Unfortunately, the Serbian Army's manpower shortages made this impossible: in October 1915, this shortage would prove disastrous.

The northern border

The Danube and Sava rivers formed Serbia's northern border with Austria-Hungary. The broad Pannonian Plain lies to the north of these rivers and provides a stark contrast with Serbia's wooded hills on the south banks. These rivers formed the boundary of the Byzantine Empire with Hungary until the twelfth century, as well as the boundary between the Ottoman Empire and the Habsburg lands for almost 200 years. An excellent defensive line, in 1914 the Danube and Sava reprised their historic role as a great natural moat.

A tributary of the Danube, the broad Sava meanders across a marshy flood plain, forming Serbia's northern border from the Drina River in the west to its confluence with the Danube at Belgrade in the east. The Sava was too deep to ford and was crossed by a bridge only at Belgrade. The many swamps on either side of the river and extensive flooding in spring and autumn often made the river impassable, save at a few points. A frequently shifting channel and sandbars made navigation difficult. In many stretches the low hills and bluffs on the southern Serbian side provided a stark contrast to the flat marshland on the northern Austro-Hungarian side. Several large islands along its course offered cover for crossings, the most worrisome being *Ada Ciganlija* near Belgrade, *Podgorička Ada* east of Šabac, as well as islands near the villages of Skela and Drenovac.

The Danube was from one to several kilometers wide at various points and comprised Serbia's northern border from Belgrade in the west, to the Romanian border at Orşova in the east. It was unfordable and unbridged: large islands near Pančevo, Starčevo, Vinča, and Grocka offered cover for an armed crossing. At Smederevo (*Semendria*), the width between the islands and the Serbian side was only 200 meters. Similar to the Sava, large stretches along the southern Serbian side had bluffs and low hills, in marked contrast to stretches of wooded marsh on the northern Austro-Hungarian side. At Golubac, the river entered the Iron Gate's narrow gorge, with steep cliffs and deep swift waters.

The Danube also played an important role for transportation between Central Europe and the Black Sea. Its shipping connected the Pannonian Plain and the Black Sea—provided Romania, Bulgaria, and Serbia cooperated.[39]

The western border

The Drina River formed most of Serbia's western border with Bosnia-Herzegovina. Characterized by heavily forested mountains rising sharply on either side of the river, steep shores, and a water level that fluctuated dramatically depending on the season, this unnavigable river was relatively shallow and fordable at numerous points. The Austro-Hungarian and Serbian General Staffs had surveyed the major fords, and their depths and positions were well known.[40] In Serbia's northwest corner, where the confluence of the Drina and Sava rivers formed the Mačva Peninsula, the Serbian bank was flat and marshy. In 1914, no bridge crossed the Drina's frontier region.[41]

Along the Drina, a wide belt of mountains formed a natural barrier to Serbia's Morava–Vardar corridor. Near Višegrad, the border deviated east of the Drina and formed an Austro-Hungarian enclave on the east bank, which removed the river's role as a barrier. Yet the mountains in this region were more imposing than those further north, thereby compensating for this deviation. Although these mountains were rugged and difficult to traverse, once crossed, three east–west valley systems offered access to the Morava–Vardar corridor and the interior of Serbia. In medieval times, Serbian and Bosnian rulers—such as Serbian Despot Stefan Lazarević and Bosnian King Tvrtko I—traveled these valleys, as they fought to control Bosnia's silver mines along the Drina. The Romanian *Vojvoda* Vlad III "Ţepeş" (Dracula) campaigned in this region as a Hungarian vassal in the second half of the fifteenth century. During the First Serbian Uprising of 1804–1813, the Ottoman Empire used some of these valleys as invasion routes in their attempts to defeat Karađorđe Petrović's Serbs.

The northernmost and easiest to invade of these valleys was the Jadar–Kolubara corridor. From its mouth on the Drina between the towns of Loznica and Lešnica, the Jadar River ran east to within 12 kilometers of the town of Valjevo. On the Jadar's north side lay the Vlašić ridge, with Mount Cer (2,254 feet) at its western end. Cer commanded the entire Jadar valley to the south, as well as the flat Mačva region and the Sava river plain to its north. If an enemy penetrated the Jadar valley, it could not be considered secured until the Vlašić ridge had been taken. The Maljen ridge ran along the southern side of the Jadar valley, with Mount Rudnik (3,714 feet) on its eastern end. Rudnik commanded the Jadar valley to the north, as well as the Kolubara valley and Valjevo basin.

From Valjevo, the Kolubara river valley ran east and then north through Mačva into the Sava. By following the Jadar, crossing the Jadar–Kolubara watershed and following the Kolubara toward the Sava, an enemy could gain quick access to Belgrade. From Belgrade, the Morava lay open to the east across low rolling hills. A narrow-gauge railway line in the Kolubara river valley connected Valjevo to Obrenovac. In spite of this route's appeal, caused by the relatively easy terrain, an invading army was vulnerable as long as the defenders held the Vlašić ridge or Maljen ridge. Although this was the most direct route from Bosnia-Herzegovina into Serbia, the roads were rough and muddy, and it was at best a long and roundabout path to central Serbia.

Another corridor through the western mountains lay south of the Jadar River across the Maljen ridge. Near Višegrad, the border shifted several kilometers to the east of the Drina, passing close to the towns of Uvac and Vardište. The Dual Monarchy had built two narrow-gauge rail spurs from the Sarajevo–Višegrad line: one to Vardište and the other to Uvac. On the Serbian side, only 34 kilometers from the border as the crow flies, lay the headwaters of the Western Morava River and Užice. From Užice, the Western

Morava flowed east through a narrow valley and gorge, then widened as it passed through Čačak, Kraljevo, and close by Kruševac, after which it turned north and flowed into the Morava. A narrow-gauge rail line connected Užice with the Orient Express line, and the road was in relatively good repair. This route provided an enemy the chance to bisect Serbia's heartland. Yet the terrain in the 34 kilometers between the Drina and Užice was so rough that a relatively small force could hold the border almost indefinitely against a much larger and better-equipped force. It was a defender's dream and an attacker's nightmare.

Lastly, a route existed through the former Sandžak of Novi Pazar, which until two years earlier was part of the Ottoman Empire. Not far from Višegrad—site of Turkish Grand Vizier Mehmed Sokolović's famous bridge built in 1577—the Rzav River flowed into the Drina. Following the Rzav southeast from its mouth, this rough route crossed a ridge to the Uvac River, passed through the town of Uvac at the confluence of the Lim and Uvac rivers, and followed the Lim as far as Prijepolje. From Prijepolje the road followed a tributary of the Lim, and crossed over into the Uvac watershed at Sjenica. From there it crossed the 4,278-foot high Pometenik ridge into the Ljudska river watershed and followed that river into the market town of Novi Pazar. An administrative center under the Ottoman Empire, Novi Pazar sat in a small basin surrounded by the medieval Serbian monasteries of Sopoćani and Đurđevi Stupovi, and St. Peter and Paul, Serbia's oldest church. Yet more than an historical curiosity, Novi Pazar provided access to an important north–south corridor in the heart of old Serbia.

In addition to the two main trans-Balkan corridors, there lay another north–south corridor within Serbia's borders, with Novi Pazar near its center. Although only an internal route, it centered on the Ibar River and offered access to the Morava–Vardar corridor at two points, allowing an enemy to cut the corridor at its center and in the south. Starting at Kraljevo on the Western Morava, this corridor passed south through the heart of old Serbia—the mineral-rich areas around the Ibar valley and Kosovo—and ended at Skopje. Historically, the southern and central portions of this route provided the most direct access to Bosnia-Herzegovina via Sandžak.

From the corridor's northern end in Kraljevo, a poor road followed the course of the Ibar River south, passing some of Serbia's oldest medieval monasteries—Žiča, Studenica, Gradac—through an extremely narrow and precipitous gorge. Local legend has it that in 1216, the man who one year later was to become Serbia's first king, Stefan the First-Crowned, planted this gorge with flowers to impress his new wife Anna Dandolo, granddaughter of the famous Venetian Doge Enrico Dandolo. As the gorge widened to a narrow valley near Raška, the road followed the Ibar River, entered the broad Kosovo basin near Kosovska Mitrovica, and continued on to Priština near the site of the famous Battle of Kosovo Polje. From Priština, the route headed south through Uroševac, over the pass at Kačanik into Macedonia and the Vardar watershed. The route then followed the Lepenac River—a tributary of the Vardar—to Skopje. An Ottoman-built rail line connected Skopje with Priština and Kosovska Mitrovica.

Although this route offered interesting strategic possibilities, it suffered from the same problems associated with the route through Užice and the Western Morava valley: high mountains, narrow gorges and valleys, and poor roads. The terrain between Bosnia and Novi Pazar was more rugged, the mountains higher, and the roads worse than the routes to the north. Although adequate for caravan traffic between Sarajevo and Novi Pazar, the poor roads through the Sandžak would challenge a modern army's supply train, while the region's rough terrain offered enormous advantages to the defender.

Geographically and strategically, anyone invading Serbia was compelled to gain entrance to the Morava–Vardar corridor. This could be accomplished from the east through the Zaječar and Pirot gaps in the Balkan Mountains, as well as through several smaller gaps. An invasion from the east would sever Serbia's lifeline to the world. From the west, an invasion across the Drina would sweep through the Jadar–Kolubara valley corridor, take Belgrade, and then cross into the northern Morava valley. Or it could cross the Drina near Užice and sweep down the Western Morava valley, cutting the country in two. For the truly foolhardy, the route through the Sandžak beckoned. Any invasion of the Western Morava valley that reached Kraljevo or Novi Pazar could proceed south along the Ibar River to mineral-rich Kosovo, and from there on to Skopje, cutting the southern portion of the Morava–Vardar route. From the north, a river crossing could occur at any of several points, all offering access to the Morava's mouth. No matter the invasion route, geography dictated that all roads led to the Morava and Vardar. Therefore, the Serbian High Command based its entire defensive strategy on protecting Serbia's heart and the Morava–Vardar valleys from the enemy.[42] Topography simplified everything: capture the Morava valley or cut the Vardar rail line and win the war. The rest of Serbia could be left to wither on the vine.

Defending the fatherland: Serbia's defensive strategy

Even the most well thought-out mobilization plan is bound to encounter setbacks and difficulties. Amazingly enough, in spite of numerous difficulties, Serbia's army managed to mobilize in a manner that the Serbian High Command characterized as relatively trouble-free.[43] Because of the recent Balkan War experience, the mobilization proceeded relatively quickly: most combat units were ready within four to six days, with their support units in place within twelve days. All troop concentrations were completed

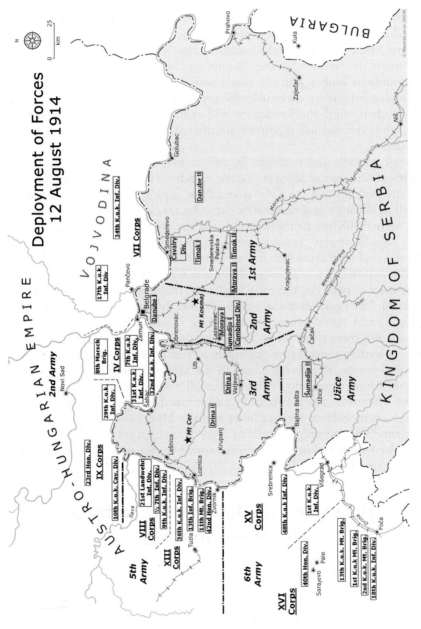

MAP 2 *Deployment of Austro-Hungarian and Serbian forces, August 1914.*

by August 10, two days prior to the first Austro-Hungarian offensive.[44] Nonetheless, in some units as many as one-quarter of the men marched to the front carrying shovels, due to a lack of rifles.[45]

Serbia's General Staff understood the strategic importance of the Morava–Vardar corridor, as well as the defensive advantages afforded by the country's mountains and rivers, and incorporated these natural obstacles into their defensive plans. In 1914, Serbia had four general plans for war, including one against Austria-Hungary. These plans were drawn up by *Vojvoda* Putnik, with help from his deputy General Živojin Mišić.[46] Serbia's strategy depended entirely on when and if an Austro-Hungarian attack came, and what if any Balkan countries entered the war. Should any of the other Balkan states enter the war, either on the side of the Triple Alliance or the Entente, Serbia's strategic situation could change dramatically, for better or worse.

In the High Command's first operational directive to the commanders of all armies on August 6, the Commander in Chief of the Army, Crown Prince Aleksandar stated clearly that "until the political situation clarifies, we will maintain the defensive; later, we will act according to opportunities."[47] This reflected the diplomatic uncertainties and Serbia's military weakness of July 1914; Serbian was content to wait.

The primary defensive challenge facing Serbia in 1914—other than its complete lack of preparedness—was the length of its borders. In addition to the 600-kilometer northern and western border with Austria-Hungary, there was the 690-kilometer eastern border with Bulgaria and the southwestern border with Albania. In spite of Russian pressure on Bulgaria to remain neutral, Sofia's half-hearted public assurances of neutrality meant the eastern border was still vulnerable. Nonetheless, acting on St. Petersburg's assurances of Bulgarian neutrality, Serbia's High Command pulled most of its troops away from the Bulgarian border and concentrated them against the expected Habsburg assault, leaving primarily third levy units to man the eastern border. The only borders which did not require large numbers of troops were the relatively short Romanian, Montenegrin, and Greek borders.

The length of the borders and the overwhelming Habsburg superiority meant that Serbia could not anticipate exactly where and when the invasion would occur. An invasion straight across the Danube at Smederevo and up the Morava river valley was strategically the most logical choice. An attack across the Sava at Šabac or Obrenovac, then on down the Kolubara valley to Valjevo was the next most likely option. After these two options, an attack across the Drina at Loznica and along the Jadar and Kolubara valleys towards Belgrade was the third most likely possibility. A major attack in the direction of Užice or Novi Pazar seemed so unlikely as to be discounted. Serbia's High Command fully expected the Austro-Hungarian attack to come from the north, across the Sava and Danube rivers, with only minor diversions along the Drina.

The first three potential invasion routes in northern Serbia formed a geographically unitary battlefield across relatively flat terrain with few natural defenses, other than rivers. In contrast, the potential invasion routes around Užice and Novi Pazar were geographically separate from the northern areas and possessed plentiful natural defenses. Serbia, therefore, placed ten of its eleven infantry divisions and its only cavalry division facing the Northern Front in expectation of a Habsburg assault across the Danube or Sava: only one infantry division faced west toward the Drina, at Užice.[48]

To defend against the expected attack from the north, Serbia's main forces were concentrated between 40 and 60 kilometers south of the Danube and Sava rivers, on a line running from Mount Belasica in the east, through the towns of Svilajnac, Palanka, Aranđelovac, Lazarevac and Valjevo, and anchored on the western end by Mount Medvednik. This line was roughly at the point where the foothills of the Sava and Danube plains reached the mountains, and prevented access to Serbia's interior and the Morava–Vardar corridor from both the north and northwest, and offered excellent possibilities for maneuver and defense in depth. To guard the borders, Serbia's High Command detailed second and third levy troops operating under the auspices of regionally based detachments. Many of these were irregular Četnik formations with substantial guerrilla experience operating behind enemy lines in Macedonia, during the Balkan Wars, and in Bosnia-Herzegovina. The largest of these—the Užice Army—guarded the approaches to the headwaters of the Western Morava watershed near Užice. Other units protected the regions from which they derived their names: the Lim Detachment, Ljubovija Detachment, Loznica Detachment, Šabac Detachment, Obrenovac Detachment, the Defense of Belgrade, and the Braničevo Detachment. These detachments usually consisted of one to three battalions, and were equipped with obsolete *de Bange* artillery. In essence, the High Command had withdrawn the operational army's main strength well into the interior and left second and third levy units and irregular guerrilla units to defend the borders and conduct reconnaissance.

According to the High Command's strategy—based on Putnik's 1911 manual *War Service*[49]—the regional detachments along the borders would carry out defensive (guerrilla) actions against the Austro-Hungarian forces and delay them, while the Serbian High Command assessed the situation. When the direction of the main enemy advance became clear, the body of the Serbian operational army would maneuver and attack the enemy's force with its entire strength. But until the direction of the main thrust was determined, Serbia would hold its operational army well back and wait for the situation to develop.

Serbia's operational army consisted of three armies, each approximately the size of an Austro-Hungarian corps and divided into a forward and a main group. The First Army, headquartered at Rača and commanded by General Petar Bojović, was deployed on the right flank. Its forward group was concentrated along the Danube, from Veliko Gradište in the east to the mouth of the Morava River in the west and comprised the Braničevo Detachment and elements of the Danube II Division. Further back, the main group comprised the First Army's main operational force and included the Timok I and II Divisions, and the Morava II Division, deployed between Svilajnac, Palanka, and Topola.

Headquartered at Aranđelovac, General Stepan "Stepa" Stepanović's Second Army held the center of the Serbian line. Its forward group included the Defense of Belgrade unit and the Danube I Division, concentrated along the Sava and Danube from Grocka in the east to the mouth of the Kolubara in the west. The main group—the Combined Division, Morava I Division, and Šumadija I Division—was deployed between Topola, Aranđelovac, and Lazarevac. Once the direction of the main enemy advance became known, the Second Army would act as the operational army's main maneuver force.

On the left wing, General Pavle Jurišić-Šturm's Third Army was headquartered in Valjevo. By far the weakest of the three armies, its forward group comprised the Obrenovac, Šabac, Loznica, and Ljubovija Detachments, and the Detachment on Debelo Brdo, which were stretched thin from Obrenovac on the Sava to Rogačica on the middle Drina. This army's main body was comprised of the Drina I and II Divisions, concentrated near Valjevo. In addition to defending the lower Drina and Mačva regions from invasion, the Third Army was expected to protect the flanks of the First and Second Armies when the expected invasion came from the north.

General Jurišić-Šturm was an anomaly in Serbia's army: an ethnic German, born in Germany to German parents. Bespectacled, with a broad, bushy mustache that covered half his face and ended in upswept points, his expression was that of a kindly old grandfather. He had attended the Prussian Military Academy in Breslau and the French War Academy in Nancy, and come to Serbia as a German officer in 1876 to volunteer in the Serbo-Turkish War. He remained, changing his name from Paul Sturm to Pavle Jurišić-Šturm, the first part of his newly hyphenated last name being the Serbian equivalent of the German "*sturm*." He worked his way up through the ranks to command a first-levy division during both Balkan Wars.[50] Highly capable, he held what would turn out to be the most crucial assignment of any Serbian general in 1914.

The Užice Army, the largest regionally based defensive unit, was headquartered in the city of Užice, under the command of former Defense Minister and Black Hand sympathizer General Miloš Božanović. It comprised an infantry brigade at Bajina Bašta, a few units around Vardište, and the Šumadija II Division in Užice. It was responsible for defending the Drina border between Rogačica and Priboj in Sandžak, and for defending the headwaters of the Western Morava watershed. The six-battalion Lim Detachment—responsible for defending the route into the Sandžak of Novi Pazar, was also under the command of the Užice Army. In addition to its purely defensive role, the Užice Army was to operate in conjunction with Montenegrin forces in a diversionary invasion of Bosnia-Herzegovina.

The Cavalry Division was responsible for scouting and defending the relatively flat plain near the mouth of the Morava between Smederevo and

PHOTO 11 *General Pavle Jurišić-Šturm.*

Grocka. Near the Romanian border, the detachment at Donji Milanovac—comprised of two third-levy battalions—guarded the eastern-most reaches of the Danube.

Each army and regional detachment had Četnik (guerilla) units attached to it. They would often don Austro-Hungarian uniforms and infiltrate the Dual Monarchy's rear areas, where they gathered intelligence, conducted raids, sabotaged supply lines, and exhorted the local Slav population to rise up against the Habsburg Empire. They often preceded invading Serbian and Montenegrin army units into occupied or enemy territory.[51]

The strength of the fully mobilized Serbian Army is difficult to assess with accuracy. Serbian High Command documents show an initial mobilization of approximately 320,000 men, which included all officers, men, and auxiliary personnel throughout the entire country.[52] Colonel Živko Pavlović, chief of the Operational Section of the High Command, wrote that Serbia's operational army (actual combat units) had 250,000 men in 213 battalions. Of these, 153 were first levy, thirty-three second levy, and twenty-seven third levy battalions.[53] The Austro-Hungarian High Command estimated only 200,000 men in 202 infantry battalions, which more closely agrees with the Serbian High Command's internal figure of 202,000 enlisted men.[54] Whatever the actual number, the Serbian Army's operational effectiveness was hampered by the availability of only 180,000 modern bolt-action rifles and 200 machine guns. Thus, the actual operational combat strength of the army numbered approximately 180,000 men, while the remainder of the troops awaited rifles in replacement units. After sending cannon to Montenegro, the army was left with 528 artillery pieces of all calibers, of which only 381 were modern quick-firing weapons.

Vienna's strategic plans

In the initial stages of mobilization, the Austro-Hungarian *Armeeoberkommando* (AOK) fully expected the Romanian and Italian armies to mobilize in accordance with their pre-war treaty obligations and assist Austria-Hungary. This meant the Dual Monarchy had planned for the possibility of war on two fronts, against Russia and Serbia. The AOK prepared two mobilization plans: *Kriegsfall "B"* for a localized Balkan war, and *Kriegsfall "R"* for a two-front war against Russia and Serbia.[55] These plans divided the *Kaiserlich und Königlich Armee (K.u.k.)* into three groups: *A Staffel*, *B Staffel*, and *Minimalgruppe Balkan*. *A Staffel* comprised those units permanently assigned to the Russian Front, while *Minimalgruppe Balkan* comprised those units permanently assigned to the Balkan Front. *B Staffel* was a swing force of eleven infantry divisions and five brigades that could be deployed to either the Russian or Balkan Front as needed.[56] In the event of *Fall "B,"* the troops of *B Staffel* would join *Minimalgruppe Balkan* on the Balkan Front and prepare for offensive action against Serbia. In the event of a two-front war involving

Russia, *B Staffel* would deploy to the Russian Front, where it would give the *K.u.k.* the needed strength to cope with the much larger Russian Army: *Minimalgruppe Balkan* would adopt a defensive posture against Serbia.

Austria-Hungary's Chief of Staff Field Marshall Franz Conrad von Hötzendorf acted on the faulty assumption that Russia would not enter the war, and that hostilities would be limited to the Balkans. On July 25, the day the Habsburg ultimatum expired, Conrad ordered a partial mobilization against Serbia. In accordance with *Fall "B,"* the AOK began preparations to send *B Staffel* to Serbia's northern border. According to the plan, *B Staffel* would join with *Minimalgruppe Balkan* to form *Balkanstreitkräfte* (Balkan Armed Forces) under the command of Bosnia-Herzegovina's military governor *Feldzeugmeister* Oskar Potiorek.

The units of *B Staffel* sent to the Balkans to join *Minimalgruppe Balkan* comprised General Eduard von Böhm-Ermolli's Second Army, headquartered at the enormous fortress of Petrovaradin (*Peterwardein*) across the Danube from the city of Novi Sad (*Neusatz/Újvidék*). The Second Army deployed its forces along the length of the Sava and Danube rivers and consisted of the IV Corps from Budapest (31st and 32nd *K.u.k.* Divisions); the VII Corps from the ethnic Romanian regions of Timişoara and Grosswardein (Nagyvárad/Oradea—the 17th and 34th *K.u.k.* Divisions, the 107th *Landsturm* Brigade, and the 7th *Marsch* Brigade); the IX Corps from the Czech regions around Theresienstadt (*Terezin*—29th *K.u.k.* Division); the 27th *Honved* Division from Szeged, the 7th *K.u.k.* Division from Osijek (*Esseg*) in Slavonia, and the 10th *K.u.k.* Cavalry Division from Budapest. Altogether, the Second Army could muster approximately 135,000 rifles in 135 battalions, along with 43½ cavalry squadrons, backed by 300 cannon.

Minimalgruppe Balkan consisted of the Fifth and Sixth Armies. The Fifth Army, commanded by General Liborius Ritter von Frank and headquartered in the northeastern Bosnian town of Brčko, was concentrated along the lower Drina between Zvornik and the Sava. Its VIII Corps was from Prague and had two infantry divisions (9th *K.u.k.* and 21st *Landwehr*). The remainder of this army came from the South Slav regions of the Empire. The Thirteenth Corps—considered one of the Austro-Hungarian Empire's best units—had two infantry divisions (36th *K.u.k.* and 42nd *Honved* Divisions), both based in Zagreb (*Agram*) in Croatia. Although the commander of the 36th Division's 71st infantry Brigade, Major-General Johann Salis-Seewis, was Swiss by ancestry, he has been proclaimed a Croat by Croatian historians. He was later to command the 42nd *Honved* Division.[57] At the war's start, the 42nd Division was under the command of General Stevan Sarkotić, a Croat. It had the honorary title of *Slavonski Domobrani* (Slavonian Home Guard), but its official title was *Vražija Divizija* (the Devil's Division), and it used Serbo-Croatian as the official language of command. The Thirteenth Corps included a number of nationally mixed Serb and Croat units which traced their heritage directly to the Empire's famed military border regiments. These included the 16th Varaždin, 53rd Zagreb, 78th Osijek, 79th Otočac, and

96th Karlovac *K.u.k.* Regiments. There were also the 25th Zagreb, 26th Karlovac, 27th Sisak, and 28th Osijek *Honved* Regiments.[58] Among Potiorek's Fifth and Sixth Armies, almost 40 percent were South Slavs (i.e., Serbs, Croats, or Muslim Slavs).[59]

In addition to the *K.u.k.*, *Honved*, and *Landwehr* formations, Potiorek had at his disposal the famed *Bosniaken*, four *Bosnisch-Herzegowinische* (BH) mountain regiments modeled on the elite Tirolean *Kaiserjäger* regiments. The ethnically mixed Serb, Croat, and Muslim troops of these BH formations wore a special uniform featuring a grey fez with a grey tassel and pants cut wide above the knee in Turkish style; on parade they wore powder blue uniforms with red epaulets, collars, cuffs, and a bright red fez.[60] Although these units were of mixed South Slav national composition, most of their officers were Croats, Czechs, Germans, and Poles, as they were considered more loyal to the Empire than Bosnia's Serbs. Because Bosnia-Herzegovina formed an administrative district outside the 1867 *Ausgleich* between Austria and Hungary, these units belonged neither to the *K.u.k.* nor the *Landwehr* or *Honved* formations. Nonetheless, they operated as regular *K.u.k.* formations.[61]

At the war's start, the BH regiments were scattered around the Empire on garrison duty—Graz, Trieste, and Bruck an der Leitha. Their ethnically mixed character notwithstanding, the Serb, Croat, and Muslim troops of these units served the Emperor valiantly throughout the war.[62] However, prior to being transported to serve with the *Balkanstreitkräfte*, Potiorek insisted and the AOK concurred, that all ethnic Serbs be removed from these formations. Although this action was left to the discretion of each regimental commander, the 2nd and 3rd BH Regiments placed all Serbs in labor companies.[63]

In addition, the Fifth Army had other independent units from Bosnia-Herzegovina and Croatia: one infantry brigade, one mountain brigade, one *Landsturm* infantry brigade, and a *Marsch* brigade, the equivalent of two divisions. In total, the Fifth Army could field approximately 93,000 rifles in 79½ battalions, along with 14½ cavalry squadrons and 212 cannon.

The Sixth Army, headquartered in Sarajevo and concentrated along the upper Drina around Višegrad and Goražde, was personally commanded by Potiorek. With the exception of the 40th *Honved* Division and 109th *Landsturm* Brigade from Budapest, which operated under the direct command of Sixth Army headquarters, all the units of the Sixth Army were recruited entirely from the Dual Monarchy's South Slav regions: Bosnia-Herzegovina and the Adriatic coast (Mostar, Sarajevo, Nevesinje, Herceg Novi, and Dubrovnik). The XV Corps from Sarajevo had two infantry divisions (1st and 48th *K.u.k.* Divisions), each divided into two mountain brigades. The large XVI Corps from Dubrovnik maintained two infantry divisions (18th and 47th *K.u.k.*), of which the 18th Division—an unusually heavy unit—had four mountain brigades, making it the size of two divisions. In addition, the XVI Corps had four independent mountain brigades (1st, 2nd, 3rd, and 13th *K.u.k.*). In total, the Sixth Army could field approximately 118,000 rifles in 94½ battalions, along with 5½ cavalry squadrons and 162 cannon.[64]

These three armies were supported by thirty-six battalions of garrison and security troops (approximately 36,000 men) with six machine guns and twelve field artillery pieces, as well as eighty-four fortress artillery companies, each with its own cannon. There was also the Danube Flotilla operating on the Danube and Sava rivers, comprised of six heavily armored river monitors mounting 120-mm cannon (*Temes, Bodrog, Szamos, Körös, Maros, Leitha*) that could be used for close artillery support on the rivers. These were supported by five patrol boats and a number of auxiliary vessels, such as mine layers, mine sweepers, tugs, transport vessels, and so on.[65] The operational forces of *Balkanstreitkräfte* totaled 319½ infantry battalions (approximately 320,000 rifles), sixty cavalry squadrons, 744 cannon, and 486 machine guns.[66] The mismatch with Serbia's woefully equipped 250,000-strong operational army, armed with only 180,000 modern rifles, was striking.

Yet in spite of overwhelming Austro-Hungarian superiority, several factors would work in Serbia's favor.[67]

Vienna's battle plan: crushing the Balkan rabble

The Austro-Hungarian battle plan was driven by political—not military—considerations. Vienna wanted to limit the war to the Balkans, quickly avenge the Archduke, and restore the Empire's prestige by subduing Serbia before Russia stepped in: a quick victory was imperative. Vienna also feared an uprising among Serbs in Bosnia-Herzegovina and thought a quick victory would defuse this and encourage Bulgaria, Greece, Romania, and perhaps Italy to side with the Triple Alliance. For Potiorek, who had been in charge of security arrangements during Franz Ferdinand's assassination, a strong sense of humiliation and personal disgrace still lingered. He hoped to personally avenge Franz Ferdinand, present the Emperor Franz Josef with a major victory for his birthday on August 18, and thereby erase the shame of Sarajevo once and for all.[68] Potiorek received support for swift action from the AOK chief of staff Field Marshall Conrad and the Imperial Court's General Bolfras.[69]

Yet the Empire's pre-war planning and troop deployment augured against speed. The AOK's mobilization plans created troop concentrations at points that would not permit a rapid invasion of Serbia. In the regions of Srem and Banat, eight standard-gauge rail lines led directly to Serbia's northern border, all of which could be used for troop concentration and supply. Yet the majority of the Dual Monarchy's troops were deployed in Bosnia-Herzegovina, where only three narrow-gauge rail lines led to the Drina River, one of which—near Zvornik—stopped 20 kilometers short of the border.

The Sixth Army, the largest in Bosnia-Herzegovina, was deployed around Sarajevo, Višegrad, and Goražde, where mountainous terrain hampered movement, rendering the army's size less relevant. From a defensive standpoint, this concentration of force made little sense, as a much smaller force could have held the region against even a major Serbian incursion. From an offensive standpoint, the only logical route of attack for the Sixth Army was toward Užice or Novi Pazar. The terrain in these areas was so rugged and easily defensible that the Serbian High Command dismissed both as potential invasion routes and had stationed minimal forces in the region. Mountains made it difficult for the Sixth Army to maintain effective contact with or provide operational support to the Fifth Army to its north. Given the topography, the Sixth Army was effectively isolated from the remainder of the Habsburg forces; troops could not be easily shifted around the operational theater from army to army.

The Fifth Army was also out of contact with the northern Second Army across the Sava River in Srem. The Fifth Army was well situated to prevent a Serbian invasion of northern Bosnia. However, from an offensive standpoint it would be forced to cross the Drina River, the marshy Mačva Peninsula, and fight along the circuitous route leading up the Jadar and Kolubara valleys, a region noted for poor roads that turned to muddy quagmires with the slightest rain.

The Dual Monarchy's largest force in the Balkans, the Second Army, was not only out of contact with the Fifth and Sixth Armies, it was in a state of limbo. Following Russia's full mobilization on July 31, the AOK rescinded Conrad's earlier decision to implement *Fall B*, and ordered the Second Army to the Russian Front. Once the initial mobilization began, troops could not be re-routed without causing disruptions to the complex train and troop movement schedules. As a result, the Second Army would have to remain in Srem on Serbia's northern border until after other mobilizations and troop concentrations were completed on the Russian Front. Only on August 18 would it to be able to start embarking for Galicia. In the meantime, the Second Army's operational status as part of *Balkanstreitkräfte* was ambiguous. Although the Second Army was battle-ready, the AOK permitted Potiorek to use it only for diversionary purposes, as they wished it to arrive intact in Galicia. In spite of the Dual Monarchy's larger and better-equipped army, uncertainty as to its use and poor deployment made the numerical advantage less effective. Poor Habsburg planning might offer Serbia a fighting chance.

The commotion before the storm

The first week of war saw only limited engagements, mostly in the Sandžak region along Austria-Hungary's southern border with Serbia and Montenegro. On August 3, three Serbian battalions from the Lim Detachment crossed into Bosnia-Herzegovina and besieged the towns of Rudo and Uvac, near Višegrad. On August 5, following Montenegro's declaration of war on Austria-Hungary the previous day, Montenegrin artillery on Mount Lovćen shelled (rather ineffectually) a few Austro-Hungarian positions at the Bay of Kotor (*Bocche di Cattaro*). On August 6, Serbian and Montenegrin forces skirmished with Habsburg troops near Vardište, Uvac, and Rudo, and on August 7 the Lim Detachment skirmished with Habsburg forces near Višegrad, while the Montenegrins fought around Čajnice and Čelebić. Serbian forces seized the Drina River towns of Višegrad, Stari Brod, Goražde, and Foča, all inside Bosnia-Herzegovina, while Montenegrin and Serbian *komite* (guerrillas) carried out raids throughout southern and eastern Herzegovina. These were accompanied by the flight of some Montenegrin Muslims into Bosnia-Herzegovina.

From a practical standpoint, Herzegovina—especially the region between Foča and Višegrad—was so heavily defended, by garrisons, *Schutzkorps*, gendarmes, and the Sixth Army, that the Serbo-Montenegrin actions posed little more than a nuisance, serving largely as tabloid fodder for Sarajevo and Belgrade newspapers.[70] During this period, however, *Schutzkorps* actions against Serb civilians in Herzegovina intensified to include mass executions and widespread looting and destruction of property.

From the end of July until the second week of August, Austro-Hungarian artillery subjected Serbia's border towns and cities to constant bombardment. Other than Belgrade, the worst shelling occurred to the west of the capital in the Mačva region, where artillery severely damaged the town centers of Šabac, Obrenovac, and Loznica. Between August 9 and 11, small Habsburg units operated under cover of heavy infantry and artillery fire to cross the lower Drina and probe Serbian defenses at various places. On the lower Danube, Habsburg forces captured four Serbian steamboats, one of which was carrying a valuable cargo of fifty wagons of wheat.[71]

Is this the real invasion?

Late on the evening of August 11, the commander of the Loznica Detachment informed the Serbian High Command that he had observed Austro-Hungarian forces massing across the Drina, and he suspected a major crossing would occur that night or early the next day.[72] *Vojvoda* Putnik was acutely aware that the most logical invasion route was from the north, and he hesitated to shift his forces toward Mačva until the situation was clarified. Although the heaviest Austro-Hungarian shelling was in the Mačva region along the lower Drina and the Sava, no Habsburg troops had crossed in force. Was this a diversion? Only after a lengthy consultation with his aide-de-camp General Živojin Mišić and the Chief of the Operational Section Colonel Živko Pavlović, both of whom favored redeploying the army toward Mačva, did Putnik give the order. Upon emerging from the meeting, Pavlović is reported to have victoriously exclaimed: "Aaah. We broke the *Vojvoda*."[73]

Anticipating an attack somewhere along the lower Drina, yet still uncertain as to when and where it would come, Serbia's High Command

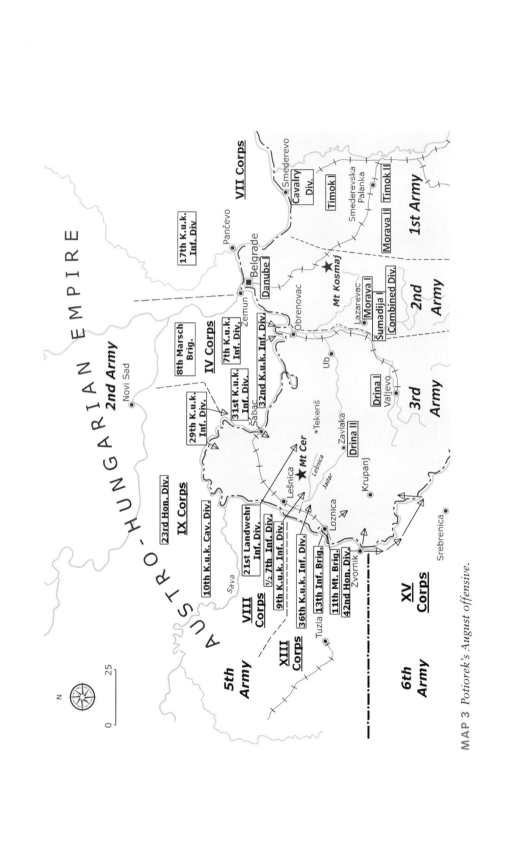

MAP 3 *Potiorek's August offensive.*

began to gradually shift forces westward from defensive positions further east near the mouth of the Morava river valley. The High Command informed its army commanders that: "according to the latest reports, the enemy is attempting a strong disturbance along the Obrenovac–Šabac–Loznica border front, probably with the aim of a crossing."[74]

Early on the morning of August 12, the High Command ordered General Pavle Jurišić-Šturm's small Third Army, which had previously been solely responsible for defending the entire Mačva region, to advance to forward positions between Šabac and Loznica that were at greatest risk of attack. The High Command also ordered the Cavalry Division—far to the east near Smederevo—to ride the approximately 100 kilometers west to Mačva, where it would form the Third Army's right flank. Cavalry was well suited to Mačva's corn fields and flat terrain.

Putnik ordered General Stepa Stepanović's Second Army to move northwest to defend the Sava River to the north of the Third Army between Šabac and Obrenovac. The Second Army was to place two divisions approximately 12 kilometers south of the Sava, and General Petar Bojović's First Army would shift westward and occupy the positions being vacated by the Second Army. This left the mouth of the Morava River only lightly defended.

At 9:00 am on August 12, shortly after the three Armies had received their marching orders but before they had begun to move, the Serbian High Command received a report from Third Army headquarters that Austro-Hungarian troops had crossed the Drina at 4:20 am between Loznica and Lešnica at *Ada Kurjačica* island with approximately 10,000 to 15,000 men. The Loznica Detachment, comprised of several second and third levy battalions, had been pushed back from the Drina and was fighting a delaying action. The telegram also reported that Austro-Hungarian forces had crossed the Sava on pontoons and taken the town of Šabac.[75] At Šabac, the Austro-Hungarian pre-crossing bombardment began around 3:30 am and destroyed all telegraph lines, leaving the telephone lines intact. To the east of Šabac, the Obrenovac Detachment engaged in a heated infantry battle at 3:00 am, followed shortly thereafter by a heavy Habsburg artillery bombardment. Around 4:30 am, positions in and around Obrenovac came under direct fire from field artillery, while heavy artillery began to shell the town center. Heavy fighting was reported at other points along the Sava, particularly in the vicinity of Prahovo and Mrđenovačka islands, where Habsburg forces had landed artillery and bridging material in preparation to cross the river.[76]

Putnik was still uncertain that the crossings at Šabac and Loznica represented the main invasion thrust and suspected they might be diversions to distract Serbian forces away from a larger Austro-Hungarian crossing at some point further east near the Morava or Belgrade. From a topographic and strategic standpoint, the routes from Loznica and Šabac were among the least advantageous for an invasion. An invasion near Obrenovac, Belgrade, or Smederevo seemed far more logical. Therefore, Putnik delayed committing the entire operational army to Mačva, fearing a diversion. Instead, he decided to block the road leading up the Jadar river valley from Loznica to Valjevo, and the roads leading from Šabac to Valjevo, with the aim of delaying Habsburg forces until the situation crystallized.[77]

Putnik instructed the Third Army to send cavalry towards Šabac to determine the extent of the Austro-Hungarian crossing, to send reinforcements to Loznica and Koceljevo, reinforce the second levy infantry units already in place, and block all main roads leading from the Austro-Hungarian bridgeheads. Jurišić-Šturm ordered Drina I Division to take up positions between the roads leading from Loznica and Šabac towards Valjevo, which would give Drina I the opportunity to move toward whichever sector of the front became most critical.[78] Putnik ordered the Second Army's Šumadija I Division to march from Lazarevac to Šabac, via Ub and Koceljevo, a distance of over 90 kilometers, and repulse the Habsburg units across the Sava. The High Command placed the Cavalry Division—still some 100 kilometers to the east at Smederevo—under the command of the Second Army and ordered it to Mačva. The remainder of the Second Army, except for the Danube I Division, was to "gather at Ub, follow the development of events, and act energetically in the direction where the main enemy force appears, in its movement towards Valjevo along the Obrenovac–Šabac front."[79] In the south, Putnik directed the Užice Army to launch an offensive toward Višegrad and Sarajevo in conjunction with Montenegrin forces, in hopes of creating a diversion and tying down Austro-Hungarian forces.[80]

Reports of Austro-Hungarian advances continued to pour in to the High Command throughout the morning and early afternoon of August 12. The third levy forces defending Šabac withdrew without a fight, and there had been no communication with the commander of the Šabac Detachment. There were also reports that Austro-Hungarian forces had crossed the Sava at Sremska Mitrovica and *Samurović Ada*, and pushed back the defenders.

Along the Drina, the troops of the Loznica Detachment withdrew from the river banks under fierce fire and took up positions at a previously prepared defensive line on the heights east of Loznica, and along the elevated railroad embankment that paralleled the Drina west of Loznica. A few kilometers to the north, units of the Lešnica Detachment (approximately 1,500 second and third levy troops, 500 Četniks, and two artillery pieces) withdrew from the Drina to previously prepared defensive positions on the heights east of the river to avoid being outflanked by Austro-Hungarian forces crossing upriver at Loznica.

At 3:40 pm, as Jurišić-Šturm prepared to send the Drina I Division—the Third Army's only first levy unit—to Loznica to reinforce Drina II, Putnik ordered him to send infantry to both Loznica and Šabac. Lacking sufficient forces, Jurišić-Šturm split Drina I and sent one of its regiments to Loznica to reinforce Drina II, another regiment toward Šabac, and the remaining two regiments to an area between Jautina and Valjevo to await further instructions. Drina I's cavalry was to reinforce the front around Šabac and block the roads leading south from Šabac to Koceljevo and Valjevo.[81] The change in orders forced Jurišić-Šturm to cancel his previous plans, and new orders were not ready until 7:30 that evening. In the meantime, the Third Army remained in place.

Throughout August 12, reports trickled in sporadically. During the afternoon Lieutenant Miodrag Tomić, a pilot attached to the Danube I Division, flew an observation mission in his Bleriot monoplane along the Sava and around Šabac. Tomić told the High Command that contrary to initial reports, there were no pontoon bridges at Šabac, and that the Austro-Hungarian forces seemed to have crossed using boats. There were, however, bridges under construction or already in place at other points upriver of Šabac.[82]

Around 4:00 pm, Colonel Dragutin "Apis" Dimitrijević, now commander of Drina II, contacted the commander of the Šabac Detachment, who claimed he had attempted to carry out a flanking attack on the Habsburg forces. However, it appeared he had wandered from place to place during the day, and held back reserves from the front. With one minor exception, the Šabac Detachment appears to have avoided battle.[83] Apis reported that the Habsburg forces at Šabac were weak and could have been easily defeated by the Serbian defenders. At Apis' recommendation, the Šabac Detachment was placed under the command of Drina II's cavalry commander, who redeployed the Šabac Detachment 5 kilometers south of Šabac on the road to Koceljevo.[84]

By nightfall of August 12, the situation was still unclear. Although Austro-Hungarian troops had crossed the Drina and Sava in force at several places, the crossings occurred at points that seemed ill-suited for an offensive. In the face of incomplete and confusing information, along with continued shelling and infantry attacks along both the Sava and Danube, the Serbian High Command waited, fully expecting the main thrust to occur momentarily, either near Obrenovac or further east, closer to Belgrade.

But this was the main offensive, and the forces crossing the Drina and the Sava on August 12, 1914 belonged to the Austro-Hungarian Fifth and Second Armies, commanded by a vengeful *Feldzeugmeister* Oskar Potiorek.

CHAPTER SIX

Lightning on Mount Cer

Haste makes waste

When Conrad changed the war plan from *Fall B* to *Fall R* on August 1, *Minimalgruppe Balkan* should have assumed a defensive posture and awaited transport to the more critical Russian Front. Under *Fall R*, the Austro-Hungarian Armies were ideally deployed to prevent a Serbian or Montenegrin invasion of Bosnia-Herzegovina, but not to invade. In spite of the changed plan, both Potiorek and Conrad wanted to defeat Serbia first.[1] Without the presence of von Böhm-Ermolli's Second Army on the Balkan Front, victory would be less sure. Therefore, both Conrad and Potiorek decided to quickly launch an attack before the Second Army departed for Galicia on August 18. This meant attacking immediately, even if all of *Balkanstreitkräfte*'s units and matériel were not in place, and even if units were poorly positioned.

Following Russia's mobilization, the Austro-Hungarian Second Army's role had been ambiguous. Although positioned along Serbia's northern border, it was not allowed to engage in any offensive action, other than artillery fire, pending its transport to the Russian Front. Following Conrad's decision to declare *Fall R*, the *Armeeoberkommando* (AOK) removed command of the Second Army from Potiorek. Thus, any offensive action by the Second Army had to be approved directly by the AOK. Potiorek, who in the words of Field Marshall Conrad was *persona gratissima* at the Imperial Court and Military Chancellery, wanted to use the Second Army against Serbia. Beginning on August 2, Potiorek used his court connections to lobby for operational control over the Second Army.[2]

By August 7, Potiorek had received almost complete autonomy of action from AOK for the Fifth and Sixth Armies, as well as permission to use the Second Army for diversionary actions across the Sava. On August 9, Second Army commander Ermolli—wishing to play a decisive role in what he thought would be a short war and quick victory—telegraphed Conrad that the success of Potiorek's offensive depended on the Second Army taking a more active role, and asked to use the Second Army in an offensive role against Serbia.[3] Conrad responded by allowing the Second Army to expand its diversionary activities to the west of Šabac, but refused to permit it to launch an offensive.[4]

However, August 18 was not only the Emperor's birthday; it was also the date by which the Sixth Army would be fully deployed and ready for offensive action. This meant the Fifth Army would need to attack on its own, with only limited support from the Second Army. But the Fifth Army was also not ready; two train wrecks had slowed its troop concentration, and by August 12 it still lacked a number of bridging and artillery units, and ammunition supply columns.[5] Although Fifth Army commander General von Frank protested to Potiorek that he could not attack until August 14, Potiorek ordered the attack to begin on the twelfth. When the offensive began on August 12, not all Fifth Army units had reached their jumping-off points; each Corps had only one pontoon bridge, the Sixth Army was not yet in position to attack, and it was unclear whether the Second Army would be permitted to cross the Sava and engage in combat.

In spite of these obstacles, Potiorek began his main offensive across the Drina through a region which the Serbian High Command considered an unlikely invasion route. The drawbacks of the invasion route became evident almost immediately. Along the lower Drina, General Liborius Ritter von Frank's Fifth Army—which consisted of VIII Corps commanded by the former Ambassador to Belgrade, Cavalry General Baron Artur Freiherr Giesl von Gieslingen, and General Adolf Freiherr von Rhemen zu Barensfeld's XIII Corps—was to make a two-pronged attack toward Valjevo. The XIII Corps would cross the Drina near Loznica, seize the mouth of the Jadar valley and advance upriver toward Valjevo. The plan called for VIII Corps to dislodge the Serbian defenders from the heights east of Loznica and Lešnica and free XIII Corps to advance at Lešnica. In the north, VIII Corps would cross the broad Mačva plain, also with Valjevo as the goal. Separating them stood Mount Cer.

The offensive begins

On August 12, VIII Corps (21st *Landwehr* Infantry Division, 9th Infantry Division—26,000 men and ninety-eight cannon) tried to cross the marshy lower reaches of the Drina at Osmi Šib, an island near Amajlija, roughly 9 kilometers east of the Bosnian town of Bijeljina. They encountered stiff resistance from the Lešnica Detachment and failed to bridge the Drina until early evening. Once across the river, high cornfields hampered movements; mid-August corn, well over the heads of the soldiers, interfered with Austro-Hungarian observation and reconnaissance and provided excellent hiding places for Četniks to snipe at the advancing troops. The sniping caused

Habsburg forward elements to advance in large groups without sending out scouts, while marshy terrain hampered the movement of horses and men, forcing the *K.u.k. Armee* to spend time improving paths and roads so that artillery could be brought forward. The heat and lack of potable water also took a toll on morale.[6] By nightfall, the 9th Division had advanced 2 kilometers from the river, the 21st Division was still on the left bank of the Drina, and the heights remained in Serbian hands.[7]

To the south, XIII Corps (33,000 men and 114 cannon) also made slow progress. When the 36th Division waded across the shallow Drina between the towns of Loznica and Lešnica, two third-levy companies of Serbian defenders mounted such fierce resistance that by noon only seven battalions had crossed. The full division crossed only later in the day when engineers erected a pontoon bridge. Other units of XIII Corps that attempted to ford near Koviljača encountered such fierce resistance that they marched north to the bridge near Batar, where they arrived that evening. The southernmost unit of XIII Corps, the 42nd *Honved* (Domobran) Infantry Division, marched south along the Drina through Zvornik to cross at Ljubovija, from where it could assist either the Fifth or Sixth Army as needed.

The XIII Corps' objectives were the town of Loznica, the heights east of town, and the mouth of the Jadar river valley. Yet by nightfall of August 12, more than half the Corps was still on the left bank of the Drina. Serbian defenders stopped the only unit that managed to cross (the 36th Division) 2 kilometers from the river, using the raised rail embankment running

PHOTO 12 *Third levy infantry scout.*

parallel to the Drina as a defensive line.[8] Serbian fortifications on the heights east of Loznica and Lešnica included not only trenches and foxholes, but also numerous concealed artillery positions. Because of the rough terrain, good camouflage, and thick foliage, Habsburg observation aircraft had not spotted these prior to the offensive.[9] These defenses proved too difficult for XIII and VIII Corps to overcome the first day.

The Austro-Hungarian Second Army's IX and IV Corps were to create a diversion to the north along the Sava to distract the Serbian Army from the main thrust across the Drina. When units of the Second Army's IX Corps (29th Infantry Division) crossed the Sava by boat early on the morning of August 12, Serbian defenders at Srpska Mitrovica fled without a fight.[10] The 29th fared much worse at *Samurović Ada*, where a single Serb battalion held them for over ten hours.[11] The 31st Infantry Division sent one regiment, the ethnic Hungarian 44th, which took Šabac following a brief skirmish, but provided no reinforcements. Ironically, the only Habsburg forces that achieved any significant progress that day—the Second Army at Šabac and Srpska Mitrovica—were not permitted to exploit their bridgeheads.

The first day of the offensive proved disappointing. Although the 9th and 36th Divisions had crossed the Drina, the 21st and 42nd Divisions, and the 13th Infantry and 11th Mountain Brigades were still in Bosnia-Herzegovina. To the south, the Sixth Army continued concentrating its forces and was still several days from entering combat. The transport and supply trains of VIII Corps had become hopelessly confused, and it proved nearly impossible to feed or supply troops, worsening the water shortage. Nonetheless, Potiorek sent a congratulatory message to General von Frank noting the "successful crossing of the river," and stated that he looked forward to "brilliant and exceptional acts."[12] Yet Austro-Hungarian first-levy troops had incurred losses at the hands of irregular Četnik formations and poorly armed and equipped second and third levy troops.

Lacking aerial reconnaissance, the river crossing left Putnik uncertain as to which direction the invasion was coming from.

The next day, August 13, Habsburg forces continued shelling and probing Serbian defenses along the Sava and Drina rivers. Near the outskirts of Belgrade, the Austro-Hungarian 7th Infantry Division created a diversion by crossing the Sava on Belgrade's western outskirts at *Ada Ciganlija* island, but were repulsed.

Along the Drina, VIII Corps—which comprised the Fifth Army's left wing—spent much of the day reinforcing their bridgehead and skirmishing with Serbian defenders. The 9th Division again struggled with marshy conditions, poor roads, high corn, oppressive mid-August heat, and the Lešnica Detachment, as the 21st Division finally began to cross the Drina. The Fifth Army's center at the mouth of the Jadar river valley finally crossed two Brigades of XIII Corps to join the 36th Division at Loznica. Both Corps spent the day reinforcing their bridgeheads and fortifying their positions, engaging only in minor skirmishes.

On the Fifth Army's right wing, the 42nd *Honved* Infantry Division crossed at Zvornik against light Serbian opposition from third-levy reservists and a small detachment of Četniks. The 42nd—accompanied by some 500 Muslim civilian looters from Bosnia driving wagons and wearing yellow armbands—began plundering and burning villages.[13] The 42nd was now positioned to penetrate northeast through the mountains to Krupanj on the Third Army's exposed left flank, from whence it could swing north into the Jadar valley and attack Valjevo.

At Šabac, Drina I's cavalry scouts accurately assessed Austro-Hungarian strength at one regiment, reporting that Habsburg forces remained inside the town and were not being reinforced. They were, however, seen to be plundering, setting homes on fire, and taking their booty across the river on boats.[14] Yet Putnik still remained uncertain as to whether Šabac represented the main offensive, and refused to commit the Serbian Army's main Strike Group, Stepa Stepanović's Second Army. In the meantime, he waited for further developments.

Lacking specific instructions from the High Command and noting the failure of Habsburg forces at Šabac to expand their bridgehead, while those along the Drina appeared more active, General Jurišić-Šturm ordered the commander of Drina I, Nikola Stevanović, to march from Valjevo down the Jadar valley to reinforce Drina II at Loznica.[15] The Third Army's forward elements withdrew to defensive positions on the slopes of the Cer/Iverak ridge.

Although Putnik had not yet ordered Stepanović's Second Army into battle, Stepa had begun to move towards Mačva on his own initiative. Following a late start, troops of the Second Army's Šumadija I Division arrived at Ub late in the evening of August 12, following a forced march of approximately 25 kilometers. Ub was some 42 kilometers southwest of Šabac as the crow flies, and almost double that on the windy roads. They set out early on the morning of August 13, and by noon Šumadija I's forward elements had covered more than 20 kilometers, followed closely by the Combined and Morava I Divisions.

Both sides' strategies now became evident. Potiorek envisioned a pincer movement to encircle the Serbian center at Valjevo, with his left wing (VIII Corps) sweeping across Mačva, while his right wing (XIII Corps) moved up the Jadar valley. The center of the line on Mount Cer was crucial, because the ridge separated the two Austro-Hungarian Corps from each other. The first army to arrive at Cer would have a tremendous advantage.

In spite of Austria-Hungary's invasion, on August 13, Russia—which had promised to defend Serbia against Austria-Hungary—sent a troubling signal: Grand Duke Nikolai Nikolaievich asked Belgrade to launch an offensive against Austria-Hungary to relieve pressure on the Russian Army in Galicia. Serbia's government now faced a serious dilemma: the Great Power that was supposed to be its protector was itself in dire need of assistance. Conrad's desire for a swift victory over Serbia had already delayed the deployment of

PHOTO 13   Vojvoda *Stepan Stepanović "Stepa."*

Ermolli's much-needed Second Army to the Russian Front, and now Serbia was under attack. There was little Belgrade could do.

Pašić responded that Serbia was already on the offensive against Austria-Hungary on Serbian territory, and that an order had been given to attack Bosnia-Herzegovina. He added that Serbia would cross the Sava and attack Austria-Hungary in Srem and Slavonia as soon as it received 1,000 meters of bridging material it had requested from its allies. He also mentioned that Serbia still awaited new rifles from Russia, and that 120,000 Serbian soldiers carried obsolete weapons.[16] He tactfully avoided mentioning that Russia was the ally that had failed to deliver the bridging equipment and was slow in delivering the rifles.

After its main body crossed the Drina, on August 14 the Fifth Army resumed its advance, attacking the Loznica and Lešnica Detachments. At Loznica, XIII Corps spent much of the day waiting in vain for VIII Corps to launch a flank attack against Serbian positions on the heights east of the town. Around noon, Fifth Army commander von Frank—frustrated by the delays—ordered the 36th Division to attack the heights. Initially, it made some progress and took Tršić hill east of Loznica. Still, it failed to dislodge the Loznica Detachment, despite three charges that resulted in heavy losses to both sides. However, by evening the 36th took the village of Gornji Dobrić on the slopes of Cer in hand-to-hand fighting. The Loznica Detachment—which lost approximately 900 men during eight hours—withdrew eastward up the Jadar valley to avoid encirclement,[17] where it joined the newly arrived Drina I. General von Rhemen's XIII Corps fared poorly. During the day's fighting, the 36th lost approximately 600 men, including all the officers of the 16th Regiment.[18]

At Lešnica, the 2,000-man Lešnica Detachment offered fierce resistance to the 25,000-strong VIII Corps as it advanced along the western slopes of Mount Cer in an effort to flank the Loznica Detachment's positions. Due to rough terrain and heavy resistance, the VIII Corps' 21st Division advanced only 8–10 kilometers from its starting point, suffering heavy losses.

Around noon on August 14, Šumadija I's lead elements began arriving at the Šabac Detachment's positions near Mišar and Jevremovac, some 5 kilometers east of Šabac. The Šabac Detachment spent much of the afternoon trying to retake the town, but without success. The Serbian High Command then gave the task to the Second Army. In the meantime, General Ermolli ordered the remainder of the 29th Division to abandon Šabac and withdraw across the Sava. The ever-cautious Putnik sent the First Army to deploy between Ub and Valjevo as a strategic reserve.

Although the Habsburg forces ended the day some 15–25 kilometers from their objectives, Potiorek received an encouraging telegram from Conrad, in which he stated that the AOK would accept "full responsibility" for launching the offensive against Serbia. On a less encouraging note, Conrad added that Bulgaria refused to enter the war, but expressed hope that a swift victory against Serbia would change Sofia's mind.[19] Pressure on Potiorek was mounting.

As VIII Corps slowly advanced across Mačva and onto the northern slopes of Cer, and XIII Corps drove back the Serbian defenders between Lešnica and Loznica, the battlefield took shape. It was now evident to most Serbian commanders that Habsburg forces were driving towards Valjevo, a major city and rail center in northwest Serbia, approximately 60 kilometers east of the Drina as the crow flies.

Nonetheless, on the afternoon of August 14 a hesitant Putnik still agonized over whether the Austro-Hungarian thrust up the Jadar valley represented the main offensive. Sometime during the evening, he finally decided this was indeed the case, and that Šabac was a diversion. Around 3:15 on the morning of August 15, Putnik ordered Jurišić-Šturm's Third Army to hold the Austro-Hungarian forces near Lešnica and Loznica as long as possible. He then ordered Stepanović's Second Army to perform a maneuver that would require a complicated forced march westward along circuitous roads to the junction at Tekeriš, a small village on the northern slopes of Cer. At Tekeriš, roads led west into the Jadar valley, north to Šabac, and west over Cer to the Austro-Hungarian bridges on the Drina. From Tekeriš, the Second Army would continue across Cer and hit the left flank of XIII Corps' columns advancing up the Jadar valley.[20]

The maneuver presented numerous difficulties for the Serbian Second Army, not the least of which was the forced nighttime march over rough terrain. An army with modern communications would be hard pressed to complete such a maneuver. The poorly equipped Serbian forces were severely challenged. One of Putnik's biographers, reflecting on the difficulties inherent in the unfolding Serbian plan of attack, noted fawningly that:

> Putnik, prior to making this very daring decision, had in mind the extraordinary quality of the non-commissioned officer cadre of the Serbian army, and the unusual enthusiasm and sacrifice with which the regular Serbian soldiers—Serbian peasants—set out to defend the attacked fatherland from the aggressor.[21]

To Putnik, the maneuver seemed within the army's capabilities. If successful, he would drive a wedge between the VIII and XIII Corps. If the Serbs held Cer, the Fifth Army would be unable to force the Jadar valley, and XIII Corps would be cut off from VIII Corps, leaving both open to flank attacks and Serbian penetration into the Fifth Army's rear, threatening the pontoon bridges on the Drina and supply routes with Bosnia.

Potiorek, however, anticipated a decisive battle between the Fifth Army and the main Serbian forces on either August 16 or 17. Given the initial Serbian army positions far to the east and the time necessary to redeploy, Potiorek expected this battle to occur on the heights west of Valjevo. The resulting victory would allow him to present a triumphant birthday gift to the Emperor on the 18th. To meet this timeline, the Fifth Army's ambitious objective for August 15 was a line approximately 25 kilometers east of the

Drina, stretching from Krupanj in the south to Zavlaka in the Jadar valley, and Tekeriš on the north.

The collision between Serbia's Second Army and the Austro-Hungarian Fifth and Second Armies was about to become a battle of maneuver and envelopment that would require long marches over forested and mountainous terrain. And, as in all battles, plans were discarded as they were overtaken by events.

The eve of battle

The fifteenth of August dawned hot and humid, as Von Frank deployed the entire Fifth Army without any troops in reserve. On the left, the 21st Division advanced along the northern slopes of Mount Cer; directly to the south, the 9th Division advanced up the Lešnica river valley. In the center, the 36th Division advanced up the Jadar valley, while the 11th Mountain and 13th Infantry Brigades advanced southeast from Loznica toward Krupanj, where they hoped to link up with the 42nd Division. On the Fifth Army's far right flank, the 42nd Division advanced eastward toward Krupanj.

The Fifth Army advanced against relatively light opposition, mostly from Četnik and irregular formations. Yet, by 8:00 am, none of its units were even close to their objectives. On the far left, Field Marshall Artur Przyborski's 21st *Landwehr* Division advanced furthest, its left column's lead elements reaching Culjković, almost 20 kilometers from the Drina. However, the artillery remained more than 5 kilometers behind with the main body of the division. The 21st Division's right column had advanced only 5 kilometers after running into fierce Četnik resistance and rough terrain. Przyborski ordered the right column to stop when it reached Tekeriš.

During the evening, a severe thunderstorm descended on Mount Cer. Heavy lightning and a torrential downpour turned the night pitch black. Yet the 21st Division's right column continued its advance until it reached Tekeriš around midnight. Strung out along the northern slope of Mount Cer and blinded by darkness and the downpour, the Division's regiments lost contact with each other.

On the right flank, the 9th Division advanced slowly up the Lešnica river valley, slowed by destroyed bridges, extreme heat, a lack of water, and fierce resistance from remnants of the Lešnica and Loznica Detachments. By evening, the Division reached the village of Milina, 18 kilometers from the Drina, and forward elements had advanced further to the peaks of Popov Parlog and Rašuljača.

To the south, XIII Corps—which was supposed to be pushing up the Jadar valley—had difficulty regrouping following the fighting around Loznica and did not begin advancing until noon. The 36th Division reached Brezjak, some 14 kilometers east of the Drina, where it halted after making contact with Serb forces. The 11th and 13th Brigades spent the night on the road from Loznica to Krupanj, while the 42nd Division defeated the Ljubovija Detachment (two third-levy battalions) and advanced to Jagodnja. The 42nd's forward elements reached Krupanj, where they encountered Vojislav Tankosić's Rudnik Četnik Detachment. After a brief skirmish, the 42nd withdrew to Jagodnja for the night.

Although the Fifth Army encountered no serious resistance during the course of the day, both Potiorek and von Frank requested that the AOK delay the Second Army's transport to Galicia and permit it to participate in the upcoming battle. Second Army commander Ermolli also desired to participate in the anticipated victory. A sympathetic Conrad ordered the 10th Cavalry Division and 23rd *Honved* Infantry Division to entrain for Galicia according to schedule, but now permitted the remainder of the Second Army—General Karl Tersztyanszky von Nadas' IV Corps (31st and 32nd Divisions) and the 29th Division—to actively assist the Fifth Army south of the Sava.[22]

Further south along the upper Drina, the Sixth Army finally entered action on August 15. Four of the Sixth Army's five infantry divisions were comprised entirely of mountain brigades recruited in Bosnia-Herzegovina, giving the Sixth excellent mountain warfare capabilities. The 18th Infantry Division, a heavy formation from the Mostar region of Herzegovina, consisted of four mountain brigades—the equivalent of two divisions.

Potiorek ordered the 12th Mountain Brigade to Ljubovija to protect the Fifth Army's right flank, while Feldzeugmeister Wenzel Wurm's XVI Corps (18th Infantry Division, 1st, 2nd, and 13th Mountain Brigades) was sent to retake Čajniče and Čelebić from Montenegrin and Serb forces.

Even now, Putnik still feared an invasion from the north, as Austro-Hungarian artillery shelled Obrenovac and Belgrade with increased intensity. As a precaution, Putnik halted the redeployment of Petar Bojović's First Army and held it at Lazarevac, a three-day march from Cer.

That day, while in mid-march toward Šabac, Stepanović's Second Army received orders to swing left and strike the Austro-Hungarian forces in the Jadar valley on their left flank, which required crossing Mount Cer. The Combined and Morava I Divisions, which formed the Second Army's Strike Group, marched towards Tekeriš. The Cavalry Division was now well on its way to Mačva to reconnoiter and protect the Second Army's right flank against Ermolli's Second Army.

On the afternoon of August 15, Stepanović ordered the acting commander of the Combined Division, Svetislav Mišković, to take the highest peak on Cer, Kosanin Grad.[23] The Combined Division sent its 2nd Supernumerary Regiment and a battery of field artillery to Trojan, the easternmost peak of Cer. From Trojan, several smaller hills descended toward Tekeriš, encircling it on three sides. On the evening of August 15, the 2nd Supernumerary Regiment advanced through the storm and darkness to Parlog, a hill one kilometer north of Tekeriš. Unbeknown to Stepanović, VIII Corps had the same objectives: Tekeriš and Kosanin Grad.

Things that go bump in the night

Around midnight of August 15/16, the Combined Division's 2nd Supernumerary Regiment literally stumbled across the Austro-Hungarian 21st Division's right column, which had stopped for the night at Parlog to await the body of the division. The heavy rain, lightning, thunder, and blackness had rendered reconnaissance ineffective, and neither side expected an encounter. Coming off the march, the Serbs caught some of the Austro-Hungarian troops asleep and bayoneted them in their bedding, but the battle quickly intensified.[24] Each side sent new units piecemeal into battle as they arrived. The 21st sent its 6th, 8th, and 28th Regiments, while the Combined Division—exhausted by three days of forced marches—sent the 1st, 2nd, 4th, and 6th Supernumerary Regiments as soon as each reached the battlefield. Even though the Combined Division had marched over 40 kilometers that day, the Serbs are reported to have "flown" into the enemy lines at a dead run as they came off the march, which sowed confusion and panic among the Habsburg troops.[25]

In the darkness and driving rain, units from both sides became mixed with each other, sometimes firing on their own troops. The panic among the Habsburg ranks demanded heroic efforts from the Austro-Hungarian officers and non-commissioned officers to hold their troops. The 21st Division commander, General Przyborski, took up a rifle and fought in the trenches alongside his men; the 28th Regiment commander, Colonel Friedel, was killed while defending a hill with his unit.[26] Darkness, rain, unfamiliar terrain, and the chaos of battle made reinforcing units difficult, and it was often impossible to tell who was attacking whom, and from which direction. Here the Serbs' previous combat experience from the Balkan Wars came into play, as they took advantage of the heavily wooded terrain on Cer to attack the 21st Division from the front, flanks, and rear. Amidst the chaos and darkness, the 21st broke and fled, some as far as the Drina, spreading panic in rear areas.

The commander of the 21st Division's right column, General Othmar Panesch, managed to regroup a few scattered units on a hill east of Trojan. However, he had lost contact with all other Habsburg forces. On the morning of August 16, Panesch informed von Giesl that his troops needed food and water, and that it was no longer possible to stay on Cer. Many troops had eaten only once in three days, lacked water, and were openly complaining to the officers about the situation.[27] In spite of this, von Giesl ordered Panesch to hold. Panesch ignored him and withdrew the remnants of the 21st Division's right column from Cer.

The battle at Tekeriš left a large gap in the Habsburg line. Yet the troops of the Combined Division were too exhausted to exploit the victory, having been on a forced march for three days, and Morava I was still marching toward Tekeriš.

On the morning of August 16, the crippled 21st Division tried to advance towards Trojan, but encountered the Cavalry Division and Šumadija I.

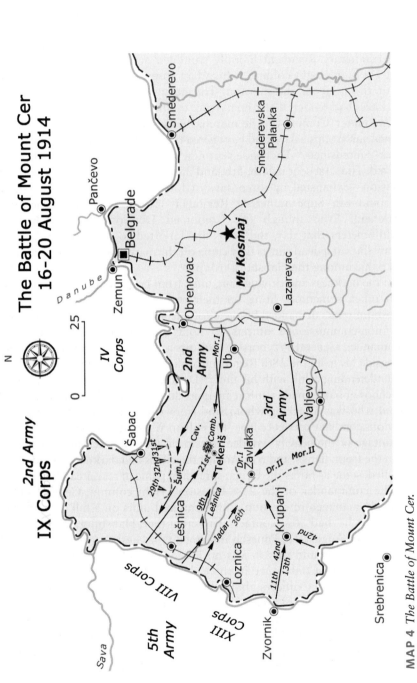

MAP 4 *The Battle of Mount Cer.*

The Serbs attacked the 21st Division's left column from the front and both flanks. The deadly crossfire caused the Habsburg troops to break and run: even artillerymen abandoned their cannon and rode off on draught horses. The commander of the right column, Colonel Karl Hinke, held his position with one battalion and five batteries until noon, at which time he ordered a withdrawal. A regiment from the Cavalry Division pursued the retreating Habsburg forces as far as Bobija, where it captured two complete artillery batteries (eleven cannon, five officers, and 215 men), as well as large amounts of war matériel.[28] The 21st Division would now be *hors de combat* for almost an entire week.

That same day, the Austro-Hungarian 9th Division advanced up the Lešnica valley and hit the Combined Division, forcing it to withdraw, the 6th Regiment having lost all its battalion commanders. The 9th Division also suffered heavily: the ground around its 73rd Regimental headquarters on Rajin Grob was covered with "innumerable wounded on stretchers" and numerous shell-shocked men.[29] The Combined lost forty-seven officers and 2,995 men during the night, and withdrew eastward to a series of hills, where the 5th Supernumerary Regiment finally caught up with the main body of the Division.[30]

Around 10:00 am, Morava I arrived at the front. When General Stepanović arrived, he unified the Combined and Morava I Divisions under his personal command, then immediately ordered Morava I to advance toward Popov Parlog to the west of Tekeriš. Morava I made rapid progress, with a reconnaissance in force to Trojan.

To the north of Cer, the Cavalry Division's right column, reinforced by troops from Šumadija I, encountered the Habsburg 29th Infantry Division's 57th Brigade between the villages of Dobrić and Maovi, 10 kilometers southwest of Šabac. The Habsburg troops had halted their advance for the day and stacked their rifles as they prepared to pitch camp, but Šumadija I surprised them. Although the 57th had artillery support, it lost over 1,000 men and fled toward Šabac, with many troops abandoning their rifles. While fleeing, the 57th encountered the 58th Brigade, also from the 29th Division, mistaking it for a Serbian unit. The two attacked each other, causing further losses: the two brigades left over 500 rifles and six caissons on the battlefield. Serbian losses were relatively light: ten killed and twenty-five wounded.

South of Cer, XIII Corps attacked Jurišić-Šturm's Third Army, now reduced to eighteen battalions, three cavalry squadrons, and thirty-nine cannon. Unable to hold with this small force, Jurišić-Šturm withdrew to a new defensive line, regrouping his troops in the Jadar valley to block the road from Loznica to Valjevo. In response to Jurišić-Šturm's pleas for reinforcements, Putnik ordered Morava II to reinforce the Third Army.

Along the upper Drina, XVI Corps advanced against the Užice Army Group and the Montenegrin Army's Pljevlje Division, quickly dislodging the poorly equipped Montenegrins from Metaljka and pushing them back toward Pljevlje inside Sandžak.

By the evening of August 16, Serbia's High Command faced a serious situation. It had used all available forces to defeat the 21st Division on the Fifth Army's left wing, while to the south, the 42nd Division threatened to penetrate the rear of the Third Army and encircle it. This would destroy not only the Third Army, which Belgrade could not afford to lose, but would also ruin Putnik's plan to have Stepanović's Second Army attack the Austro-Hungarian left flank in the Jadar valley. To bolster the Third Army's critically weakened left wing, Putnik ordered the 12th Cadre Regiment to reinforce Jurišić-Šturm, and had the First Army send Morava II to hold the road to Valjevo and prevent the 42nd Division from enveloping the Third Army. The High Command also began to shift its strategic reserve to Ub, from whence it would be better positioned to help Stepanović's Strike Group and contain the Habsburg forces at Šabac. That same day, Putnik finally decided the invasion was not coming from the north and that the main threat was from Bosnia-Herzegovina.

Unknown to the Serbian High Command, the Austro-Hungarian Fifth Army's situation was critical. Spread out along a mountainous, relatively waterless 55-kilometer front with no reserves, it had lost contact with Ermolli's Second Army to the north following the 21st Division's destruction. Because *Balkanstreitkräfte* lacked a strategic reserve, Potiorek could only reassign troops from other areas of the front. Upon learning of Przyborski's catastrophic defeat, Potiorek asked the AOK for permission to use the Second Army to reinforce the Fifth Army's broken left wing.

In the meantime, Second Army commander Ermolli, acting on a personal plea for help from Fifth Army commander von Frank, sent Tersztyanszky's IV Corps (31st and 32nd Infantry Divisions) across the Sava to Šabac. The AOK instructed Ermolli to create only diversions and mask IV Corps' imminent departure for Galicia. Ermolli ordered IV Corps commander Tersztyanszky to gather his units near Šabac, but not to engage in offensive actions. Whether from poor communication or a lack of understanding, "it is evident that the Austro-Hungarian High Command, in spite of the pleading of Generals von Frank and Potiorek, did not comprehend all the difficulties of the situation in which the 5th Army found itself on the first day of the Battle of Cer."[31]

The second day of battle

On August 17, the Serbian Second Army's Strike Group (Combined and Morava I Divisions) continued west along the Cer/Iverak ridge. The 9th Division halted both Morava I and the Combined Division, inflicting heavy casualties, forcing Morava I to withdraw, and opening a potentially dangerous hole between Serbia's Second and Third Armies. A reconnaissance in force toward Trojan by the Combined Division forced a Habsburg withdrawal and closed the hole.

Combined Division commander General Mihailo Rašić then divided his division into two columns, which advanced west toward Trojan and met little resistance. Having secured the peak, the Combined Division now advanced westward along the spine of Cer towards the Drina. This forced the 9th Division to protect its left flank, which would soon become its Achilles Heel. Although the 9th Division was now isolated on Cer with both flanks exposed, its constant counterattacks meant that the Second Army's Strike Group was unable to exploit the situation.

To the north of Cer in Mačva, the Cavalry Division advanced as far north as the Šabac–Loznica rail line. It cut the line and attacked a Habsburg infantry battalion traveling by train from Šabac to Loznica, forcing the train to return to Šabac. To the west, the Cavalry Division's 3rd Regiment followed a column of the retreating 21st Division as it fled toward Prnjavor. Penetrating deep into the Austro-Hungarian rear, the cavalry took Prnjavor and pursued the 21st toward the pontoon bridges on the Drina, capturing an entire battalion. As the cavalry chased the 21st, the Austro-Hungarian troops guarding the pontoon bridges mistook their own retreating troops for Serbian forces and opened fire on them. Toward late afternoon, Habsburg forces surrounded the 3rd Cavalry Regiment between the villages of Prnjavor and Petkovica. The 3rd held its positions until the middle of the night, when it slipped through Austro-Hungarian lines under cover of darkness and rejoined the Cavalry Division. The Cavalry's actions on August 17 effectively cut all remaining contact between the Habsburg Fifth and Second Armies and prevented the 21st Division from regrouping and re-entering the battle.

Even though outnumbered more than two to one by Tersztyanszky's IV Corps, Šumadija I went on the offensive near Šabac: its artillery destroyed the pontoon bridges across the Sava, causing panic in the Austro-Hungarian transport train. Šumadija I's left flank pushed the Habsburg forces back to the edge of Šabac, a distance of almost 4 kilometers. On the Division's left wing, its 10th Regiment ran into fierce fire while crossing open ground near Pričinović, some 4 kilometers from the edge of Šabac. Lacking entrenching tools, soldiers dug foxholes with their bare hands. Around 6 pm, Austro-Hungarian forces counterattacked, supported by heavy artillery from land and the river monitors on the Sava. The 10th managed to hold, but only after sending all available reserves into battle. Šumadija I's right column advanced, but was quickly halted by Habsburg artillery fire. Although Šumadija I succeeded in forcing Tersztyanszky's IV Corps to withdraw toward Šabac, it suffered heavy losses, and withdrew during the night.

Although reluctant to commit the entire Second Army, the AOK was now ready to permit Tersztyanszky's IV Corps to undertake offensive actions south of the Sava. When informed of Šumadija I's attack at Šabac, Ermolli ordered IV Corps to forgo its scheduled transport to Galicia. At the AOK, Conrad agreed. Upon receiving reports of the 21st Division's destruction, Potiorek asked the AOK to authorize the entire Second Army to invade Mačva to aid the Fifth Army. Now the remaining forces of the Austro-Hungarian Second

Army entered the fray. Despite previous AOK desires that this be avoided at all costs, Conrad postponed the Second Army's transport to the Russian front in Galicia indefinitely. This would have direct and catastrophic consequences on the Habsburg Eastern Front.[32] Potiorek and Frank hoped the Second Army would turn the tide in the battle for Mačva and Cer. Bad news, however, continued to arrive: the destruction of the 21st Division meant VIII Corps was unable to continue the offensive. Therefore, Frank ordered XIII Corps to continue alone.

Serbian successes in the north notwithstanding, the Third Army faced a serious situation south of Cer. The XIII Corps now comprised the 36th Division and the Krupanj Maneuver Group (42nd Division, 13th Brigade, and 11th Mountain Brigade), and held a three-to-one advantage over the Third Army in troops and artillery. Morava II, which was supposed to reinforce the Third Army, had just arrived in Valjevo, and would not reach the front until August 18 after noon.

Yet the Habsburg forces failed to attack, because 36th Division commander General Claudius Czibulka demanded his troops have a rest. While waiting for Czibulka, the remainder of XIII Corps strengthened local positions and conducted reconnaissance in force. This allowed the beleaguered Third Army time to reinforce and regroup. Yet so weak was the Third Army that even the limited actions conducted by XIII Corps seriously threatened its lines: the Habsburg 13th Brigade nearly broke Drina I's front, and Serbian soldiers had begun to abandon their positions when reinforcements arrived. Only by committing all its reserves did Drina I hold.

After assessing the situation on August 17, Putnik decided the Third Army's left wing would stabilize as soon as Morava II arrived the following day. Along the upper Drina, the Sixth Army did not pose a serious threat to the Užice Army Group and the Montenegrin Pljevlje Division. Thus, defeating the Austro-Hungarian forces on Cer remained the main task, and Putnik sent Timok I to reinforce the Second Army's Strike Group.

The Emperor's birthday gift

The eighteenth of August was Emperor Franz Josef's 84th birthday, and Potiorek had wished to present him with a decisive victory over Serbia. But the situation in the field was tenuous for both Austro-Hungarian and Serbian forces, and the Fifth Army's offensive faced increasing difficulties on this, the third day of battle.

On August 18, Potiorek realized that the desired grand battle near Valjevo would not take place as hoped, and he instead decided that defeating the Serbian forces on Mount Cer was the key to victory. To do this he would use XIII Corps and IV Corps to envelope the Serbian Second Army on Cer: IV Corps would push southward from Šabac toward Valjevo, while

XIII Corps would continue its push eastward up the Jadar valley toward Valjevo, surrounding the Serbian Army. For the plan to succeed, von Giesl's weakened VIII Corps would have to hold the center on Cer; otherwise, the flanks of XIII and IV Corps would be exposed.[33]

In contrast to Potiorek, who wanted to win the battle on the wings, Putnik felt the key was the center. If the Serbian wings could hold IV and XIII Corps, then the Cer Strike Group could dislodge the 9th Division, open a hole in the Habsburg center, and expose the flanks of XIII and IV Corps. The battle thus became a contest to see which would collapse first: the Austro-Hungarian center or the Serbian wings.

On the afternoon of August 18, the Combined Division went on the offensive along Mount Cer. However, stubborn defense by the Austro-Hungarian 9th Division's artillery and infantry at Rasuljača prevented progress. Morava I, which was supposed to take Rasuljača, was held up by a late start, bad weather, and heavy fire from Habsburg artillery.

In spite of enjoying a two-to-one advantage over the Habsburg troops, the Second Army's Strike Group lost an opportunity on August 18 to destroy the 9th Division, whose commander General Viktor von Scheuchenstuel could barely hold his forces, and then only because he had been told that Tersztyanszky's IV Corps was advancing to his aid from the north.

To the north, Tersztyanszky was indeed advancing to von Scheuchenstuel's aid: he sent all available forces into action—the 31st and 32nd *K.u.k.* Divisions, the artillery of the river monitors *Maros* and *Leitha*, and IX Corps' 29th Division. Against this force stood a single Serbian division, Šumadija I, already weakened by the previous day's losses.

Early on the morning of August 18, IV Corps attacked Šumadija I supported by artillery fire from batteries across the Sava. Among the 31st Division's units was the Bosnia-Herzegovinian 3rd Regiment. These Habsburg forces marched out of Šabac in high style, accompanied by a military band playing the popular Hungarian Rakoczy March.[34] One eyewitness said the 3rd Regiment advanced "as on the practice field . . . in overly thick formation and without seeking shelter."[35] Serbian artillery and rifle fire quickly decimated the regiment, wounded its commander Colonel Brenner, and his replacement Lieutenant-Colonel Janošek, leaving Lieutenant-Colonel Čanić in command. One Croat newspaper in Sarajevo described this engagement thus: "The Bosniaks fall among the bravest, who with boldness go into fire and no remonstrance is heard."[36] Following a fierce charge, the 31st Division penetrated Šumadija I's line at the center near Pričinović, forcing it to withdraw eastward to a more tenable position across the Dumača River. The Serbian Cavalry Division withdrew to guard Šumadija I's left flank.

Tersztyanszky misinterpreted this withdrawal as a general Serbian retreat and reported to Ermolli at Second Army Headquarters that IV Corps would pursue the Serbian forces as far as the Dobrava River. As IV Corps moved south from Šabac on the two main roads, the 29th and 31st Divisions ran into unexpected and stiff Serbian resistance, which halted IV Corps for the day. Although IV Corps had advanced 6 kilometers on August 18, by nightfall it was still some 20 kilometers distant from its objective, the beleaguered 9th Division on Cer.

In the Jadar valley on the Habsburg right wing, XIII Corps (thirty-nine battalions, eight squadrons, 126 cannon) attacked the Third Army (twenty-two battalions, four squadrons, sixty-six cannon) at Zavlaka, a crucial junction on the road to Valjevo, 25 kilometers east of Loznica.[37] In a pincer movement, the 36th Division and 11th Mountain Brigade advanced up the Jadar valley from the west, and the 42nd Division and 13th Brigade advanced from Krupanj in the south.

Drina I came under heavy attack, which it repulsed after intense fighting, exposing the 42nd Division's right flank. The 42nd then halted its attack and spent the day shelling Serb positions. In the early evening, the 36th and 11th pushed Drina II off Marjanovića Vis, a prominent hill to the northeast of Zavlaka. During the battle, Serbian officers and NCOs lost control of their men, many of whom panicked and fled. The loss of Marjanovića Vis opened a gap between the Serbian Second and Third Armies, nearly severing all communications between them. Around 6:00 pm, the 11th Mountain Brigade advanced to exploit the situation, but was driven back by Serbian artillery, narrowly averting the collapse of the Serbian left wing.

Along the upper Drina, little took place: despite AOK demands, Potiorek didn't want his Sixth Army to continue the offensive until it was completely battle-ready.

During the day, overly optimistic reports from Tersztyanszky misled Potiorek about the state of affairs in Mačva. After receiving Tersztyanszky's report of a complete withdrawal by the Serbian forces, Potiorek wrote in his diary: "Now I firmly believe that with this blow, the battle of the Fifth Army will be resolved in our interest." He then sent a message to Tersztyanszky congratulating him on the victory that he had achieved on the Emperor's birthday.[38] Relying heavily on Tersztyanszky's reports, Potiorek began planning an extension of the offensive: von Rhemen's XIII Corps would continue toward Valjevo; the Second Army toward Ub; and the Sixth Army would advance deep into the heart of Serbia via Užice and the Western Morava valley, which would surely bring Bulgaria into the war. Unaware of the actual state of VIII Corps, Potiorek ordered the battered 9th Division and the remnants of the 21st Division to attack toward Tekeriš on August 19. Neither could comply.

In contrast to Potiorek, who had placed all his strength on the wings, Putnik concentrated his forces in the center. Following Morava II's arrival on the afternoon of August 18 to bolster the Third Army, Putnik no longer worried about the left wing. Still uncertain about the Austro-Hungarian forces around Šabac, Putnik ordered Stepanović to hold Timok I in reserve. Lacking adequate aerial reconnaissance, Putnik had to hedge his bets, as the small and poorly equipped Serbian Army could ill-afford to lose a single battle.[39]

Late on the night of August 18/19, Second Army's Stepanović realized the Austro-Hungarian forces on Cer were wavering. He committed Timok I to

PHOTO 14 *Field hospital at Tekeriš.*

Cer and informed Putnik accordingly. Putnik was now firmly convinced that the attacks around Šabac were diversions and that Šumadija I could contain the Austro-Hungarian bridgehead. Stepanović urged Putnik to send Timok I and the Cavalry Division around the northern slopes of Cer toward Lešnica and Loznica through the gap between the Austro-Hungarian Fifth and Second Armies and seize the pontoon bridges on the Drina, cutting the supply lines to VIII and XIII Corps. Instead, the ever-cautious Putnik sent Timok I to Cer via Tekeriš to the left flank of Morava I.

Make or break: the fourth day

On Wednesday August 19, rain fell as Tersztyanszky's IV Corps—now reinforced by the 7th Division—advanced south toward the Serbian line in the belief the Serbs had withdrawn from Mačva and the road to Cer lay open. Not expecting resistance, IV Corps advanced in densely packed, close-order marching columns. Šumadija I's artillery and infantry opened fire from concealed positions near Sančevo and Leksić Mehana, decimating the 31st Division's lead regiment, which lost over 240 men during the initial moments. This slaughter sowed confusion in the Habsburg ranks, as Šumadija I continued to pour fire into the advancing troops. The 31st became completely demoralized, and the Division commander withdrew the lead regiment to Pričinović. The 31st Division's 3rd and 44th Regiments—which had not been involved in the earlier fighting—attacked Šumadija I's center, forcing Šumadija I to commit its last reserves. After very fierce fighting, Šumadija I managed to hold the line. Austro-Hungarian officers—perhaps expecting set-piece warfare of the early nineteenth century—subsequently condemned the Serbian use of camouflage and concealed positions as "dishonorable tactics."[40]

The lead regiment of the 32nd Division came under heavy infantry and artillery fire from Šumadija I's concealed positions as it advanced along the Šabac–Valjevo road, and also suffered heavy casualties. The 32nd continued to press its attack, but was forced to halt twice: the first time because of heavy Serbian artillery fire, the second because of "friendly" artillery fire.

Observing the battle from a bell tower in the main church in Šabac, Tersztyanszky ordered the 29th Division—marching southwest toward Tekeriš—to wheel east and attack Šumadija I's left flank. In the confusion of battle, the 29th emerged at the front directly in front of the 31st Division's positions, which delayed the Habsburg assault while the divisions reassembled. Šumadija I took advantage of the delay to shell the 31st and 32nd Divisions, causing further casualties. Šumadija I then used the Austro-Hungarian confusion to withdraw unhindered to the right bank of the Dobrava River, the Cavalry Division protecting Šumadija I's left flank. Although again forced to withdraw, Šumadija I had single-handedly halted the advance of four Austro-Hungarian divisions.

In Šabac, Tersztyanszky assumed that he faced three Serbian divisions and halted all further attacks until the next day. This not only prevented him from relieving the beleaguered VIII Corps on Mount Cer, but also removed any threat to the flanks and rear of the Serbian Second Army.

On Mount Cer, the Combined Division launched its attack well before dawn on August 19 and advanced west along Cer's northern ridge, Iverak. By 4:00 am, the division had overrun Kosanin Grad, Cer's highest peak, threatening the 9th Division with encirclement. As it advanced, the Combined Division's right column ran into heavy resistance from the 9th Division and surviving elements of the 21st Division. Although it was forced to stop around noon, partly due to exhaustion, but also because of ammunition shortages, it resumed its advance and reached Veselinov Vrh, a peak from which it could see the Austro-Hungarian defensive positions facing Morava I across the Lešnica valley. The Combined Division's left column took Rašuljača at the head of the Lešnica valley, where it captured sixteen cannon and large quantities of war matériel.

By now the 9th Division had broken and begun to flee. An Austro-Hungarian diarist wrote: "The army is defeated and finds itself in headless, wild, chaotic flight . . . a general flight, which pulled us in. One beaten army, no, one unbridled mob hurried in mindless fear towards the border."[41] Through pouring rain and Serbian artillery fire, the 9th Division retreated toward the Drina.

The Combined Division's left column now pursued Habsburg forces down Iverak into the Lešnica valley. Advancing closely behind the fleeing

Habsburg forces, they sent artillery to Vidojevica, a town on the heights overlooking Lešnica at Iverak's western tip, from whence shortly after midnight they began shelling Habsburg troops retreating down the Lešnica valley.

On Cer's southern ridge, Morava I advanced toward the two highest peaks, but had to wait for the Combined Division to overrun the Austro-Hungarian artillery at Rašuljača before it could advance. Morava I then took the remaining peaks. By now all Austro-Hungarian forces on Cer were in full retreat toward the Drina. The Habsburg center had collapsed, leaving the flanks of the Second Army and XIII Corps completely exposed.

As Habsburg troops fled in panic on the afternoon of August 19, Frank asked Baron von Giesl if VIII Corps could hold the heights east of Lešnica and Loznica. The Baron replied that VIII Corps would not even be able to spend the night on the right bank of the Drina. Hearing this Frank ordered the Fifth Army: "All back across the Drina."[42]

In the Jadar valley, von Rhemen's XIII Corps lacked fresh forces to follow up the previous day's success at Marjanovića Vis. Early in the morning, the 36th Division and 11th Mountain Brigade prepared to attack Drina II— now reduced to just seven battalions and twenty-eight cannon—at Zavlaka. As the troops advanced to their jumping-off points under cover of artillery fire, von Rhemen received orders from von Frank to turn his Corps north and help VIII Corps at Cer; otherwise it would be forced to withdraw, exposing the XIII Corps left flank to the Serbian Second Army on Cer. General von Rhemen continued shelling Drina II until late afternoon, at which time he withdrew XIII Corps toward the heights east of Loznica.

Throughout the day, the Third Army's Jurišić-Šturm received reports that the 42nd Division and 13th Brigade were withdrawing toward Krupanj. Fearing the Habsburg forces were merely regrouping for a new attack, he held his forces in place. Then, that evening, the Third Army retook Marjanovića Vis from XIII Corps following fierce hand-to-hand fighting. The Third Army was now too exhausted to continue, which allowed XIII Corps to withdraw unhindered toward Loznica during the night. Thus ended the tiny Third Army's heroic holding action at the Battle of Mount Cer.

Undermanned and facing vastly superior Austro-Hungarian forces, Jurišić-Šturm's Third Army carried out its duty in superb fashion. Although facing the equivalent of three well-equipped first-levy Austro-Hungarian divisions, Third Army's single first-levy and single second-levy division, complemented by a smattering of irregular third-levy formations, held Habsburg forces long enough for the Second Army to conduct its maneuver on Mount Cer against VIII Corps.

On the morning of August 19, Putnik ordered Stepanović to send Timok I to reinforce the Third Army, thinking the Third Army was still in serious trouble. Whether General Jurišić-Šturm exaggerated the size of the Austro-Hungarian threat, or whether Putnik was truly concerned by the Austro-Hungarian wedge at Marjanovića Vis, the surviving High Command documents do not say. Whatever the case, Putnik again overrode Stepanović's desire to send Timok I and the Cavalry Division around the north side of Cer, where they could have cut the Austro-Hungarian bridges at Lešnica and Loznica, and encircled the Habsburg Fifth Army. Instead, at 1:50 in the afternoon on August 19, Putnik ordered Timok I to march south toward Zavlaka to assist Jurišić-Šturm. Arriving in the middle of the night of August 19/20 after a forced march, Timok I found no Habsburg troops. There can be no doubt that "sending the Timok I division in the wrong direction saved the Austro-Hungarian Fifth army from a catastrophic defeat."[43]

On August 19, Potiorek received a telegram from Frank informing him of the "critical" state of the Fifth Army. This came as a shock to Potiorek, who was expecting imminent victory. Alarmed, he hurriedly ordered the Sixth Army's 15th Mountain Brigade and the 109th *Landsturm* Brigade to march north and reinforce the Fifth Army at Ljubovija. Potiorek also ordered General Lütgendorff to reinforce Tersztyanszky's IV Corps with the 8th *Marsch* Brigade, and General Ermolli to reinforce the Second Army with the 14th Infantry Brigade.

Hoping to divert Serbian forces from the Jadar valley, Potiorek ordered Wurm's XVI Corps to attack Rudo in the Serbian part of Sandžak as soon as possible, while General Michael von Appel's XV Corps would attack Višegrad and Stari Brod, all of which had been seized by Serbian and Montenegrin forces during the first week of August. Potiorek ordered the Fifth Army to hold its positions at all costs until help arrived from the Second Army in the north and the Sixth Army in the south. Wurm's XVI Corps finally began its long-awaited advance into Sandžak, crossing the Lim River at Priboj and Rudo, taking Pljevlje, and advancing toward Prijepolje, while von Appel's XV Corps spent the entire day preparing to attack the Serbian forces at Višegrad and Stari Brod.

But these moves came too late. As VIII Corps collapsed and retreated from Cer, it threatened the flank and rear of XIII Corps. Hoping to avoid political embarrassment and to hold—at the very least—the heights east of Lešnica and Loznica, Conrad and AOK pressed Frank to maintain his line. However, the rapid collapse of VIII Corps made this impossible. On the evening of August 19, the AOK ordered all Austro-Hungarian forces back across the Drina to prevent a Serbian attack against Habsburg soil. The Fifth Army used the night of August 19/20 to withdraw across the Drina into Bosnia. The Serbs, too exhausted from forced marches and fierce fighting, could not effectively pursue the retreating Habsburg troops.

Fearing a possible Serbian invasion of northern Bosnia or Srem, Potiorek called off the Sixth Army's offensive, ordered it back across the Drina and to swing north to the Zvornik-Rogačica regions. This left only one Austro-Hungarian division to defend the southern regions of Bosnia-Herzegovina. Taking advantage of this sudden redeployment, the Serbian Užice Army and the Montenegrin Sandžak Army immediately reoccupied Pljevlje, Višegrad, Čajniče, Goražde, and Foča.

On the morning of August 20, the Combined Division advanced with caution, unable to believe Habsburg forces had abandoned Cer. Arriving at Vidojevica around noon, they shelled VIII Corps as its columns withdrew across the Drina; entering Lešnica around 2:00 pm, they took scores of prisoners and captured large quantities of war matériel. The 9th Division, however, escaped across the Drina with its organization relatively intact, other than the heavy manpower and matériel losses it had incurred during the fighting on Cer and during the retreat. As Morava I advanced along Cer's southern ridge, it shelled the troops of XIII Corps retreating toward Loznica. Neither Morava I nor the Combined Division tried to cut off the Habsburg forces.

The Timok I Division, weary after days of marching and counter-marching, arrived at the Third Army in the vicinity of Zavlaka, only to be ordered to march east back through Tekeriš to Mrovska, more than 20 kilometers distant and await further orders. During the night of August 19/20, the Third Army lost contact with Habsburg forces. In spite of this, it did not advance until the afternoon of August 20, at which time the Austro-Hungarian retreat was well under way. This permitted XIII Corps to withdraw to the heights overlooking Loznica, where it fought a rearguard action for another twenty-four hours, permitting the 13th Brigade to escape across the Drina. The 36th and 42nd Divisions were also able to withdraw unhindered.

North of Cer, IV Corps continued to attack Šumadija I, but during the day Tersztyanszky received orders to withdraw across the Sava. He halted the attack, leaving the 29th Division behind as a rearguard. Šumadija I commander Stevan Hadžić mistook the dust clouds of withdrawing troops for new Habsburg reinforcements. Anticipating an attack, Hadžić ordered his forces to hold their positions on the Dobrava River until the footsore Timok I arrived from Zavlaka via Tekeriš.

Timok II, which had also been sent to reinforce Šumadija I, was in the process of re-arming with the newly arriving Russian Mosin rifles. As a result, half its troops were *hors de combat* as they awaited new weapons. Timok II did not move toward the front until the night of August 19/20, and then made a forced march toward Šumadija I's position, a distance of almost 60 kilometers. Although the division did not arrive until the night of August 20/21, First Army Commander General Petar Bojović ordered it directly into battle. As the half-strength Timok II attacked the 29th Division on the morning of August 21, it pressed Habsburg forces back to the outskirts of Šabac. During the engagement, Bojović was wounded by shrapnel while inspecting front-line artillery positions, and was replaced by General Vukoman Aračić.

Following the attack by Timok II, Tersztyanszky ordered the 29th Division to abandon Šabac, which it did that day. Serbian forces did not enter or reconnoiter the town during the night of August 21 or the morning of the twenty-second. Therefore, Tersztyanszky ordered the 29th Division

PHOTO 15 *General Petar Bojović.*

back across the Sava to reoccupy the town on August 22. That same day, Timok II and Šumadija I advanced on Šabac. During the night of August 22/23, Tersztyanszky sent the entire IV Corps across the Sava to assist the 29th Division. Early on the morning of August 23, the 31st and 32nd Divisions advanced south along both sides of the Šabac–Valjevo roadway in massed formations. Serbian artillery and infantry opened fire and decimated the close-order Habsburg formations, causing panic among the ranks. As IV Corps began to disintegrate, Tersztyanszky ordered all his troops back across the Sava under covering fire from the river monitors.

The cost of battle

When Serbian forces re-entered Šabac around 9:00 am on August 24, they found a ruined town. Nearly every building had been hit several times by artillery fire. The buildings in the center were almost completely destroyed, and the retreating Austro-Hungarian troops had looted and burned the cathedral. In the city itself, 486 homes were destroyed or damaged.[44] The civilian population had mostly fled: those that remained had been subjected to torture and execution by the occupying Austro-Hungarian troops. Habsburg officers ordered their troops to loot and plunder entire villages in retaliation for shots which were alleged to have come from civilian homes. Discipline disintegrated among the Habsburg troops. Drunken troops ran rampant, aided by the presence of a liquor factory in the town: numerous accounts testify of inebriated Habsburg troops creating problems in the front lines and among civilian rear areas, including murder and rape.[45] The Sarajevo newspapers noted that Habsburg troops found large quantities of wine and chocolate in Šabac,[46] which also had a chocolate factory. The discipline problem became so severe that Austro-Hungarian commanders forbade all drinking, except for official celebrations, such as the Emperor's birthday.[47]

Austro-Hungarian officers distributed written orders to their troops telling them to "act towards everyone with the greatest strictness . . . anyone who showed the least mercy would be severely punished."[48] One dead Croatian soldier was discovered to have on his person a parody of the famous Serbian epic poem "Destruction of the Serbian Empire": its closing verses called for Serbia to be leveled to the ground.[49]

In Sarajevo, newspapers reported the Battle of Mount Cer as an Austro-Hungarian victory that pushed the Serbs all the way back to Valjevo.[50] These same papers also carried accounts of wounded Habsburg officers and soldiers who claimed the Serbs had engaged in guerrilla activities that violated the rules of warfare, and that in entire occupied towns—Šabac in particular—the civilian population initially accepted the occupying forces peacefully, then during the course of the night, rose up *en masse* against Habsburg troops, with women, children, and old men firing and throwing hand grenades from their homes. After subduing these insurrections, the Austro-Hungarian forces executed many civilians.[51] Although many Habsburg troops no doubt had vengeance on their minds when they invaded Serbia and carried out horrific atrocities, so too there can be little doubt that Serbia's irregular units broke numerous articles of The Hague Convention of 1907 as they had during the Balkan Wars.[52] The use of irregular troops certainly blurred the lines of proper conduct for many Austro-Hungarian officers and soldiers, as they encountered a type of warfare for which they were unprepared.

Both the Serbian and Austro-Hungarian sides accused each other of using dum-dum bullets, shelling field hospitals, and committing horrible atrocities against prisoners of war and civilians, including murder. Since many of the Serbian irregular and regular units had seen action in Kosovo, Macedonia, and Sandžak during the Balkan Wars, and had engaged in numerous atrocities against civilians and prisoners of war, there is little reason to believe this behavior changed. Given the available evidence, there can be little doubt the fighting was nasty, and neither side was particularly inclined to show mercy or give quarter. In Sandžak, the atrocities by Hungarian units on the one hand, and Serbian/Montenegrin forces on the other, appear to have been particularly vicious.[53]

The Swiss criminologist and physician Archibald Reiss counted 1,658 burned buildings in the region around Šabac. The Habsburg forces engaged in an orgy of looting, rape, murder, mass extermination, and other atrocities. One diarist recorded: "prior to his departure, the opponent left behind everywhere in the villages traces of his wildness. In the villages they slaughtered women and little children. In Loznica itself they slaughtered nineteen people and lined them up alongside the road: some they disfigured."[54] Throughout Mačva, in towns and villages such as Radjevina, Šabac, Prnjavor, Krupanj, Ljubovija, and Zavlaka, groups of peasant men, women, and children were tied together and shot.

Reiss recorded that people were shot, hanged, massacred, clubbed to death with sticks and rifle butts, burned alive, and pinioned. Some had their arms, legs, ears, noses, breasts, and genitals cut, torn or broken off; eyes were gouged out, skin was cut off people in strips, portions of entire faces were detached, small children were thrown to pigs, pregnant women were disemboweled, and wounded prisoners of war were shot.[55] This left its mark on the civilian population that stayed behind the retreating Serbian forces. In the Šabac region alone, more than 2,500 civilians were killed and over 700 homes burned. Reiss indicates that in the broader Mačva region, a minimum of 4,000 civilian deaths may have occurred.[56] The story was similar in the Jadar valley, at Loznica and Lešnica, and in the contested areas of Bosnia-Herzegovina along the upper Drina.

Reiss also verified the use by Habsburg forces of *Einschusspatronen*, explosive bullets forbidden by Article 23 of The Hague Convention of 1907 at the specific behest of Germany. Such bullets had been used by the combatants during the Balkan Wars, along with improvised dum-dum bullets.[57]

PHOTO 16 *Austro-Hungarian troops hanging Serbian civilians in Mačva.*

The Austro-Hungarian Empire, renowned at the turn of the century for the high culture of Klimt, Strauss, Brahms, Liszt, Kafka, Freud, Schnitzler, and Mahler, had now debased itself by committing the worst sorts of atrocities and massacres against an unarmed civilian population. The worst offenders appear to have been the Hungarian and Austrian soldiers. The Empire's South Slavs in general seem to have behaved somewhat better: in Jarebica, Habsburg Serb and Croat troops collected 600 Krone for the looted village's Orthodox church.[58]

As the first Entente victory of the war, the Battle of Cer represented a magnificent triumph for the Serbian Army. The Belgrade papers trumpeted it with headlines shouting "God Is With Us!" and "Glory To The Heroes."[59] In Niš, the entire populace went wild with jubilation and began a celebration that lasted for days. Military Minister Stefanović recorded that on August 19 the nervous Bulgarian Ambassador Čaprašikov "came several times to the building where the ministers hold their meetings to ask whether there was anything new from the front. He had expected and rejoiced at our defeat."[60] Coming as it did when the French were in retreat before the German Army, and when Russia faced the combined onslaught of Germany and Austria-Hungary, the victory at Cer was the sole note of encouragement for the Entente in an otherwise discouraging first month of war.

Repercussions from the Battle of Mount Cer went far beyond the battlefield. The Serbian victory delayed the transport of Austria-Hungary's Second Army to the Eastern Front, with disastrous results for Habsburg forces: on August 27 to 30 the Russian Army inflicted a serious defeat on the Dual Monarchy at the Battle of Lemberg (*L'vov/L'viv*) in Galicia, captured large quantities of matériel, and forced the Austro-Hungarian forces to surrender that strategic fortress. The delayed arrival of Ermolli's Second Army from the Balkan Front directly contributed to the Russian victory. So too, the Second Army needed time to re-equip its battered units. Perhaps most importantly for Belgrade, Serbia's victory damaged the Dual Monarchy's prestige in the Balkans and persuaded Bulgaria's wavering Coburg dynasty to remain neutral.

In addition to lost prestige, Austria-Hungary paid a heavy price for Potiorek's failure. The *Balkanstreitkräfte* lost 600 officers and 23,000 men, of whom 4,500 were taken prisoner. Among the prisoners of war was a wounded lieutenant, the Emperor Franz Josef's cousin Prince Windischgrätz.[61] Putnik later estimated Austro-Hungarian losses at 15,000 to 16,000 dead and wounded. During the battle, the Serbian Army captured more than fifty cannon and howitzers, eighty-six caissons, three field hospitals, one field telegraph, thousands of rifles, six field kitchens, and numerous other items, while losing 259 officers and 16,045 men, approximately 12 percent of the Serbian forces that saw action.

At Cer, a disturbing trend appeared in the Austro-Hungarian Army. At the beginning of the offensive, almost 40 percent of soldiers in the Fifth and Sixth Armies were South Slavs. There were many "disturbing instances of surrender or outright defection among Yugoslav troops," with the ethnic Serbs being the worst. The Croats and Muslim Slavs suffered twice the casualties as did the Habsburg Serbs. The 2nd Bosnian Regiment suffered particularly high casualties among its Croats and Muslims, while the Regiment's Serbs escaped with only light casualties.[62] One Serbian officer recorded that "the opponent is surrendering in masses . . . all the opponent's soldiers who are surrendering speak very good Serbian."[63]

Two weeks after the victory, the newspaper *Politika* referred to the war for the first time as "The Great War for Liberation and Unification of the Serbian People," a name, which in slightly altered form—the Great War for Liberation of Serbs, Croats, and Slovenes—lasted through most of the twentieth century.[64]

CHAPTER SEVEN

The Battle on the Drina, invasion of Srem, and Mačkov Kamen

The days after

The guns fell silent, as the Serbian and Austro-Hungarian armies regrouped behind their respective borders for the next two weeks, the exceptions being the ongoing Habsburg shelling of Serbia's border towns and cities, joint Serbo-Montenegrin skirmishes along the upper Drina valley, and Četnik actions inside Bosnia-Herzegovina.

The Serbian Army desperately needed to regroup, resupply, and re-equip. Captured Austro-Hungarian equipment only slightly alleviated shortages. Rifle ammunition was in short supply, and stocks of artillery ammunition—low before Cer—were now critical. New replacements arrived slowly to fill Serbia's rapidly thinning ranks. Basic equipment such as uniforms, boots, shovels, picks, and shelter halves were still in short supply or non-existent. The Serbian government searched frantically for whatever food, medicines, shelters, or uniforms it could obtain, appealing to its allies for loans, food, and clothing.

Even though Serbia's allies eventually provided a few small loans, France, Great Britain, and Russia judged their own needs too great to provide sufficient assistance. France refused to export either provisions or war matériel, while Russia had little to spare. Although Britain allowed the export of certain non-strategic materials and foods, it hesitated to export war matériels for fear its own armies might need them.[1]

Newspapers throughout the Balkans ran stories about food shortages. Belgrade even attempted to purchase grain from Bulgaria, whose animosity toward Serbia—as well as the preceding year's disastrous wheat harvest and resulting high prices—prevented any sale.

Desertion

Serbia suffered significant manpower losses at Cer. By late August, the army fell from its initial mobilization strength of 319,000 men to below 300,000, having lost 33,293 men in the first month of war.[2] Heavy fighting aside, some of the losses were to desertion. Sarajevo newspapers reported Serbs deserting to both Habsburg forces and the Bulgarians.[3] The Serbian High Command first realized there was a problem in the closing days of the Battle of Mount Cer on August 23, while Bojović's First Army still battled Tersztyanszky's IV Corps near Šabac. At this point the High Command received reports that large numbers of armed soldiers were loitering in the rear area cities of Niš, Zaječar, and Paraćin. These troops refused to return to the front and claimed ignorance of their regiments' locations. Another report arrived several days later from the military commander of Požarevac, who reported large numbers of active duty troops loitering in the city: once again, all refused to return to the front.[4]

Desertion was directly connected to the poor state of Serbia's military after the Balkan Wars, and became evident prior to the outbreak of hostilities. In May 1914, the Serbian Army lacked regular pay and its troops were inadequately fed, clothed, and housed.[5] The primarily agrarian economy meant that troops often left their units to help with harvests and feed their families.

On September 5, the worsening manpower shortage forced the army to strip rear-area garrisons of all able-bodied men and replace them with soldiers from the *Poslednja odbrana* (Last Defense), those unfit for service in the first three levies. To its consternation, the army found a "significant number" of able-bodied active-duty soldiers and reservists who "remained" in the rear areas among the ranks of the *Poslednja odbrana*. On September 7, General Mišić ordered the commanders of divisional recruiting regions to take all necessary measures to get the "large number" of military-age loiterers into uniform. In particular, the commanders were to prevent them from wandering from town to town to evade induction.[6] Nonetheless, loitering and draft-dodging continued and seemed to worsen.

In mid-September, Minister of Internal Affairs Stojan Protić complained of frequent cases where soldiers were issued rifles but refused to join their units, then wandered through the rear areas and committed crimes. Gendarmes proved unable to stop them, and some deserters had killed gendarmes. Military Minister Stefanović ordered that all soldiers be disarmed prior to leaving the front lines.[7] Still, the problem continued. *Vojvoda* Putnik noted the "great disorder" caused by large numbers of deserters "who are wandering in rear areas and around the roads, stations, and settled areas." Putnik ordered NCOs to exercise greater control over the troops and to assist the local gendarmerie in apprehending deserters.[8] Yet the army continued to lose soldiers to desertion in increasing numbers.

Allied pressure for an offensive

In early September, the two sides launched offensives against each other. Most of the fighting took place along the Drina river valley, causing Serbian historians to label this period the "Battle on the Drina." This was not one single engagement confined to a single battlefield. Rather, it included Serbia's invasions of Bosnia-Herzegovina and Srem (southern Hungary), and several Austro-Hungarian offensives in Mačva.

Following defeat at Cer, Tersztyanszky's IV Corps entrained for Galicia on the Eastern Front. The AOK transferred other units—most notably the massive 305-mm siege mortars used to bombard Belgrade—from the Balkan Front to Belgium to destroy Entente fortresses. These actions weakened the Habsburg defenses, leaving only the 29th *K.u.k* Division and half of the 7th *K.u.k* Division to defend the entire Sava. Consequently, the Entente increased pressure on Serbia to invade Austria-Hungary.

Beginning in early August, Russia and France pressed Belgrade to invade the Dual Monarchy, hoping to divert German and Austro-Hungarian troops from the Eastern and Western Fronts. Seemingly insensitive to Serbia's lack of preparedness for even a defensive war, much less an offensive one against superior forces, St. Petersburg and Paris continued to press Belgrade throughout August. On August 14, two days after Potiorek's invasion of Serbia, the Russian and French military attachés, Colonels Artamanov and Fouriet, visited Military Minister Stefanović in Niš and "represented that it was absolutely necessary that the Serbian Army undertake an offensive as soon as possible, so as to make it easier for its allies." To Stefanović "it was evident that the Frenchman and Russian were under a lot of pressure."[9] The Serbian government resisted, claiming truthfully that it lacked resources to launch an offensive.

Prior to the Battle of Cer, in an effort to forestall Russian pressure, Pašić informed St. Petersburg of Serbia's urgent need for pontoon bridges: he said that Serbia needed at least 1,000 meters of bridging material and lacked the ability to bridge either the Sava or Danube rivers. Pašić stated that Serbia lacked ammunition and pontoons, and that both "were urgently needed in the interest of an offensive and crossing against Austria-Hungary."[10] On August 16, the first day of the Battle of Cer, Serbia's Minister to Paris Milenko Vesnić, met with French Minister of Foreign Affairs Theophile Delcasse, who demanded Serbia immediately launch an offensive against Austria-Hungary. Delcasse had been erroneously informed that Austria-Hungary was already sending troops from the Balkan Front against France and Russia.[11] Although the Dual Monarchy had planned to transfer its Second Army and heavy artillery, such transfers were now delayed.

In late August, Russian Grand Duke Nikolai Nikolaievich became increasingly insistent, and the Grand Duke went so far as to write a personal letter to Crown Prince Aleksandar.[12] The French High Command vocally supported the Grand Duke's proposal. On August 25, the Russian High Command promised aid and said it was assembling a pontoon bridge for

Serbia: the Russians asked the width of the Danube at the crossing point, and whether or not the bridge would be used for cavalry and artillery.[13] On September 4, Serbia's Minister in Petrograd, Miroslav Spalajković, approached the Russian General Staff and asked that it send Serbia a bridging unit with 345 enlisted men, thirty-eight non-commissioned officers, and ten officers, to assist in an upcoming invasion of Austria-Hungary.[14] In spite of repeated Serbian requests for bridging material, as well as Russian pressure for Serbia to invade, assistance failed to materialize. The Russian General Staff eventually turned down Serbia's requests, claiming that the Russian Army required all available bridging materials for its own use.[15]

Putnik urged Pašić to respond to the allies by saying Serbia would attack as soon as its troops were rearmed with Russian rifles, and as soon as sufficient bridging equipment arrived from Russia. Given the rate at which military supplies were arriving, Serbia could easily have used this as justification until at least early 1915. This, however, was not sufficient for the Entente. Serbia's artillery ammunition came from France, and its rifles and ammunition from Russia: both expected something in return. Under continued pressure from Petrograd, Pašić urged Putnik to attack. The political pressure led Putnik and the High Command to mount a limited offensive in early September.

On August 31, Putnik met with the commanders of all Serbian Armies in Valjevo to discuss an offensive. Putnik's plan called for the left and right wings of the Serbian Army (Užice Army Group on the left, the First Army and part of the Second Army on the right) to launch offensives, while the center (Second and Third Armies) would hold its position. The Užice Army Group would attack westward into Bosnia-Herzegovina in conjunction with Montenegrin forces and push toward Sarajevo. The First Army would cross the Sava into Srem (*Sirmium*), a predominantly South Slav region of the Dual Monarchy's Hungarian crown lands and push north toward the wooded Fruška Gora hills and the enormous Austro-Hungarian fortress of Petrovaradin (*Peterwardein*) at Novi Sad. Stepanović's Second Army would create a diversion by sending Timok I across the Sava near Sremska Mitrovica, where it would draw Habsburg forces away from the First Army's main crossing. Putnik viewed this operation as largely without risk: in the event of a serious enemy threat to the invading forces, he could easily withdraw the First Army from Srem, while the topography in Bosnia-Herzegovina where the Užice Army Group would be operating lent itself to an easy withdrawal. On September 4, Putnik ordered the invasion to begin the next night, the same day as the Battle of the Marne.[16]

David invades Goliath

On the Serbian Army's right wing, the First Army (Šumadija I, Danube I, and the Cavalry Division) was to cross the Sava slightly to the west of

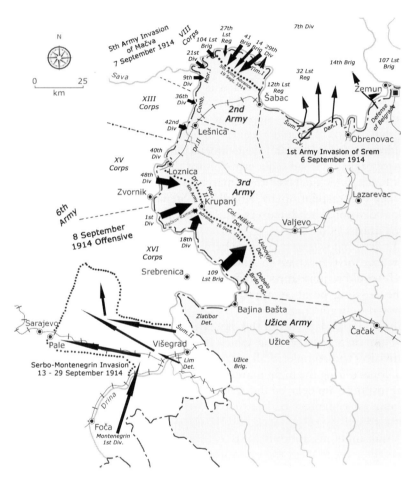

MAP 5 *The September offensives.*

Obrenovac at the villages of Skela and Novo Selo. Further west, the Second Army's Timok I would create a diversion for the First Army.

For Timok I, the crossing quickly became a fiasco. Stepanović—recently promoted to the rank of *Vojvoda* following his success at Cer—received orders at 11:00 am on September 4 to cross the Sava the following night. Although Stepanović had known of the invasion plans since August 31, he failed to inform Timok I commander General Vladimir Kondić, nor had he made any significant preparations to support a crossing. Stepanović called General Kondić half an hour later and told him to prepare the Division to march, without informing Kondić of the proposed crossing, and told him to report to Second Army headquarters at 7:00 am on September 5.

Kondić claimed that Timok I was ready to march at 5:00 am on the morning of September 5, and he arrived at Stepanović's headquarters half an hour early at 6:30 am. Stepanović informed him of the planned invasion and that Timok I would receive support from three additional cavalry squadrons, the Mitrovac Detachment, and some obsolescent fortress artillery. Stepanović subsequently claimed that Kondić ordered his troops to cook lunch, which delayed their march by four hours. Whatever the cause, whether procrastination by Kondić or Stepanović, Kondić didn't arrive back at divisional headquarters until 9:30 am, and Timok I did not begin its march until 11:00 am.

The crossing was to take place between Sremska Mitrovica and Šabac at the village of Čevrntija, 45 kilometers from Timok I's position, and the march would require approximately twelve hours. This would put Timok I at the crossing point at approximately midnight, the exact time it was supposed to begin crossing.[17]

Timok I's lead elements did not arrive at the jumping-off point until 11:50 pm on September 5, at which time Kondić informed Stepanović that the division had completed all preparations for crossing. In reality, little had been done: during the night march, columns became mixed and sick oxen in the transport train delayed the arrival of bridging material until early on the morning of September 6. The first pontoon was not launched in the Sava until 5:15 am.

Četnik units in captured Austro-Hungarian uniforms preceded Timok I across the river to clear the opposite bank.[18] The defenders on the wooded north shore responded so fiercely that it took two hours to establish a bridgehead. Around 8:00 am, Stepanović arrived at the crossing site, where for two-and-a-half hours he observed Timok I cross the river on pontoons and small boats. He was rather surprised to learn the crossing had started late. When he left at 10:20 am, the pontoon bridge was still being assembled onshore.

Around 1:30 pm, Stepanović received a message from Kondić that Timok I had begun to bridge the river at 12:40, and that two regiments (eight battalions) and one artillery battery had crossed the river on ferries. Kondić reported that the two regiments were engaged in combat with

Austro-Hungarian forces near the village of Jarak. The actual situation was quite different. By 1:30 pm, only six battalions and one battery of three cannon had crossed the river. Under the impression there were no enemy forces nearby, Kondić ordered the division to stop ferrying troops, cannon, and supplies across, and to begin building the bridge, leaving only six battalions to hold the bridgehead. Due to material shortages, the bridging unit lacked sufficient pontoon sections to span the entire river, and the bridge ended 55 meters from the north shore.

Unknown to Kondić, General Krauss' 29th Infantry Division, as well as other units totaling thirty infantry battalions, five cavalry squadrons, and twelve artillery batteries, were in the immediate vicinity of Jarak. An entire Habsburg regiment was attending Sunday church services in nearby Šašinci. This regiment offered fierce resistance and held the Serbian forces while reinforcements arrived.[19] Hearing of the Serbian crossing, Krauss immediately ordered the entire 29th Division to attack,[20] and the six Serbian battalions near Jarak came under heavy fire. Stepanović received a message at 3:00 pm, informing him of heavy fighting and that the bridge was only partially completed. After this, a lapse of five hours ensued, during which time Serbian Second Army headquarters heard nothing from Timok I.

At 6:00 pm, the Austro-Hungarian 58th Brigade attacked and encircled the Serbian left wing while the 57th Brigade broke through the Serbian right flank. The fierce Habsburg counter-attacks broke Serbian morale, and Serbian soldiers began to waver and flee. The center and left wing of the 13th Regiment disintegrated and withdrew in disarray, and its second battalion panicked and fled toward the still uncompleted bridge. As a battery of Serbian horse-drawn field artillery galloped toward the uncompleted bridge, it raised clouds of dust, causing the commander of the 13th Regiment's 3rd Battalion to mistake it for enemy cavalry. He ordered his bugler to signal defense against a cavalry charge, which sowed panic among the wounded waiting on the riverbank for evacuation.[21] Many of the lightly wounded, joined by healthy soldiers, rushed the ferries and pontoon boats and swamped them while others swam or floated on logs and wood toward the end of the pontoon bridge, 55 meters away. Some seized on the tripods, stakes, ropes, and cables anchoring the unfinished bridge in place, while others tried to swim across the Sava. Officers and NCOs tried in vain to restore order, but the majority of troops in the water did not know how to swim and drowned.

Around 7:30 pm, the remaining officers and NCOs managed to restore order and formed a battalion approximately 600 meters from the bridge. Around 8:00 pm, Kondić informed Stepanović that the Habsburg forces had attacked and caused a panic among the troops, but that order had been restored. Stepanović discovered the truth of the situation from a reporter, Aura Genčić, who arrived at Stepanović's headquarters in Bogatić around 8:00 pm with a team of foreign war correspondents.[22] Failing to reach Kondić by telephone, an angry Stepanović sent his chief of staff, Colonel Vojislav Živanović, to Čevrntija.

That evening at 9:00, the 57th and 58th Brigades again attacked the Serbian positions. Low on ammunition, the troops of Timok I panicked and fled toward the bridge, which collapsed under the weight of those who managed to reach it. As the Austro-Hungarian soldiers reached the shoreline, they began shooting at the pontoons, holing some and further damaging the bridge. Many Serbian soldiers drowned. The next morning, September 7, the remaining elements of the 15th Regiment—by now out of ammunition—surrendered to Habsburg forces. Colonel Živanović described Kondić as having "lost his head," and very depressed and almost immobile.[23] Živanović took temporary command of the division and ordered the troops to launch the remaining pontoons and pick up soldiers from the Sava. All the bridging engineers had fled, so the task was left to the artillerymen. Upon finally hearing an accurate assessment of the situation, Stepanović sent reinforcements to defend against an Austro-Hungarian crossing.

The fiasco cost Timok I dearly. In the course of twenty-four hours, it lost eighty-four officers and 6,282 NCOs and men—nearly half the division's strength. Three cannon and twelve machine guns, which the Serbs desperately needed, were also lost, as well as more than 6,000 of the new Russian Mosin bolt-action, rapid-fire rifles. An additional seven officers and twenty-nine NCOs, all wounded, eventually managed to make it back across the river. What was intended as a minor diversion effectively annihilated two of Timok I's four regiments, and called into question the division's effectiveness as an organized fighting unit. Timok I represented 20 per cent of the Serbian Army's first levy strength: it was a major catastrophe.

The High Command quickly replaced Kondić with Živanović, and retired Kondić from active service: Kondić was subsequently court-martialed and jailed.[24] Stepanović came under heavy criticism because he had known of the invasion plans since late August, yet had failed to inform his divisional commanders and to allow them time to prepare.[25] Military Minister Stefanović blamed Stepanović directly for much of the disaster, claiming that Stepa chose to ignore the High Command's recommendation for a crossing at a different point, and that he ignored the commander of the bridging train, who reported that he lacked sufficient material to make a crossing. Others placed blame on Serbia's High Command for bowing to allied pressure and ordering its troops on the offensive, even though they lacked the resources.[26] Following the war, a number of prominent politicians and generals—including Military Minister Dušan Stefanović—supported Kondić in an effort to restore his pension and rescind the stigma of court-martial.

To the east, the Serbian First Army's crossing went well. On September 5, First Army commander General Petar Bojović ordered his forces (Šumadija I, Danube I, and the Cavalry Division) to cross the Sava during the night and early morning hours of September 5/6 at an ox-bow bend in the river, not far to the west of Obrenovac where a narrow peninsula of Habsburg territory known as Kupinski Kut jutted south toward Serbia. Given the low water level of the Sava in early September, the river was no more than 250 meters wide at this point, and many of the marshes on the northern side were relatively dry and passable.[27]

Under artillery cover, the First Army crossed the Sava against relatively light resistance from the 32nd *Landsturm* Regiment and advanced rapidly northward through Srem. By the evening of September 6, the First Army had established itself north of the Obedska Bara marsh, some 5 kilometers from the crossing point. Although not adequately equipped or prepared for an invasion, the Serbian advance progressed rapidly across the flat plains of Srem, aided by Habsburg Serbs who provided intelligence and reconnaissance. By September 11, the First Army—which was now engaged with the 29th and 7th *K.u.k.* Divisions—had reached the outskirts of Stara Pazova, 15 kilometers from the crossing point. This offensive sufficiently worried the Imperial Court in Vienna that it placed all Austro-Hungarian forces in Srem and Banat under the command of General Alfred Krauss.[28]

On September 6, when the First Army and Timok I crossed the Sava, Serbian artillery at Belgrade—which had been silent the previous week—began a heavy bombardment of the Habsburg artillery positions at Zemun and Bežanija Ridge.[29] On September 7, small elements of the Defense of Belgrade crossed the Sava and reconnoitered. They quickly made contact with First Army cavalry patrols near the village of Jakovo, and continued to scout the region. During the night of September 8, the Defense of Belgrade launched attacks across the Sava at *Ada Ciganlija*, but all were repulsed.

During the night of August 9/10, following several days of intense artillery duels and infantry skirmishes, units from the Defense of Belgrade crossed the Sava at *Ada Ciganlija*, and entered Zemun early on the morning of August 10. Fearing encirclement, Habsburg troops, mostly from the 7th *K.u.k.* Division, abandoned their positions at *Ada Ciganlija* and Zemun during the night, offering only token rearguard resistance.[30] Most of the German and Hungarian residents of Zemun fled with the retreating Austro-Hungarian troops, leaving behind mostly Slavs.

The outpouring of public emotion and joy in Belgrade and across the river in Zemun was enormous and spontaneous. As Serbian soldiers entered Zemun and walked the length of its main street, *Herrengasse*, they were welcomed as liberators by a cheering populace, which hugged and kissed the soldiers, and showered them with flowers, bread, and wine. Serbian soldiers freed a number of prominent local Serbs, who had been taken hostage by Habsburg authorities at the war's start to ensure the good behavior of the town's Serb population. At 6:00 am on the morning of September 10, thanksgiving services were held in Zemun's main Serbian Orthodox church, as church bells pealed throughout Zemun and Belgrade. By 7:00 am, large crowds had formed along the docks at Belgrade's Savamali district, and residents of Belgrade began crossing the river to visit Zemun.[31] Members of the Zemun *Sokol*, a Serbian gymnastic/cultural organization, crossed the Sava by boat, paraded through Belgrade's streets in their *Sokol* uniforms,[32] and attended thanksgiving services in Belgrade's main cathedral, the *Saborna Crkva*, after which they were toasted by the citizens of Belgrade at the *Ruski Car* (Russian Tsar) restaurant. The confusion that resulted from sightseeing civilians crossing the river forced the military to restrict cross-river traffic.[33]

The Serbian occupation of Zemun brought an end to the constant Habsburg artillery bombardment. This prompted official announcements that the waterworks would be fixed within six days, Belgrade's telephone system would be repaired, telephone and telegraph service to Zemun would be restored, and electricity and streetcar service would be functional within four days. The festive atmosphere increased when two boxcars of tobacco and cigarettes arrived in Belgrade on September 11. Since the destruction of the tobacco factory during the opening days of the war, Belgrade had been without a regular supply of cigarettes.[34]

Fighting fire with fire: Potiorek's second offensive

Humiliated by the disastrous outcome of what should have been a quick and easy campaign against Serbia, from his Sarajevo headquarters Potiorek insisted that the negative diplomatic and political results of Cer could be nullified only by launching a new offensive. The AOK, on the other hand, forbade action and warned Potiorek not to do anything that would risk further failure. Using his connections at the Imperial Court, Potiorek complained that the AOK was limiting his independence, but he was opposed on this by AOK Chief of Staff Conrad, who lobbied hard against an offensive.[35] Supported by the Chief of the Court's Military Chancellory, General Bolfras, as well as Counts Tisza and Berchtold, both of whom harbored grudges against Serbia, Potiorek received Imperial approval.[36] On August 21, Potiorek received a telegram from the Emperor that unified all the Balkan forces—including the remnants of the Second Army in Srem— under his command. This gave Potiorek near *carte blanche* to direct affairs on the Balkan Front with little or no AOK supervision. In Vienna, this created dissent over who would direct the war—the AOK or the Imperial Court.

Potiorek asked Conrad to seek permission from Archduke Friedrich— nominally in command of the Balkan forces—for a new offensive against Serbia to begin on September 3 or 4. In spite of the numerous disadvantages and disastrous defeat at Cer, Potiorek envisioned attacking along the same route used previously. Potiorek wanted the Fifth Army to invade Mačva, supported by the Sixth Army further south on the lower Drina. On the Fifth Army's left wing, the 29th Division would cross the Sava at Šabac, while on the right wing the Sixth Army's XVI Corps would drive toward Krupanj.

The center would mount the main push, while the wings maintained a largely defensive posture and kept the Serbian forces pinned down.

News of Serbia's invasion of Srem and capture of Zemun, coming on the heels of the defeat at Mount Cer, was a great embarrassment to Vienna. Knowing that this meant weaker defenses along the Drina, Potiorek decided the best way to parry the invasion of Srem was to invade Mačva, which would force Putnik to withdraw the Serbian First Army to reinforce Mačva. Potiorek may also have counted that the physical and matériel exhaustion of the Serbian Army would give his better-equipped forces an advantage. Habsburg intelligence reports accurately noted that Serbian troops were exhausted from long forced marches, poorly fed, lacked ammunition, and their equipment was worn out. In short, they were in poor condition to undertake offensive operations.[37]

On September 7, Potiorek ordered his forces to attack the following day. Unlike August, this time all the Habsburg forces were ready. The Sixth Army[38] was deployed along the upper Drina from Zvornik to Ljubovija. The main force of the Fifth Army[39] was deployed along the Drina from its confluence with the Sava as far south as Zvornik. To the north of the Sava, General Lütgendorff's Group[40] was joined to the Fifth Army on August 29. This force, now renamed the Combined Corps, was deployed westward from Zemun to Sremska Mitrovica. Additional Austro-Hungarian units included the 107th *Landsturm* Brigade defending the Banat region (north of the Danube), and the 3rd and 8th Mountain Brigades on the upper Drina.

These units outnumbered the Serbs nearly two to one, had plentiful artillery, were well equipped, and at full strength. The Fifth Army had eighty-nine battalions and 250 cannon, against the Serbian Second Army's fifty-four battalions and 123 cannon, while the Sixth Army had 125 battalions, ninety-two machine guns, and 165 cannon against the Serbian Third Army's sixty-six battalions, forty-three machine guns, and eighty-eight cannon.[41] The Serbian Army had not yet been able to resupply all its units with men or rifle ammunition, and the Serbian artillery now suffered from an acute shortage of ammunition, which prevented it from responding to Habsburg shelling unless repelling attacks.

The invasion of Mačva

Following a day-long artillery bombardment on September 7, the Austro-Hungarian Fifth Army attacked Stepanović's Second Army early on the morning of September 8, when the 104th *Landsturm* Brigade of Feldmarschal Viktor von Scheuchenstuel's VIII Corps[42] crossed the Sava in the northwestern most corner of Serbia near Ravnje, at the marshy confluence of the Sava and Drina rivers as did the 21st Division against the defending Morava I. The 9th Division crossed the lower Drina near its mouth, also against

Morava I. The terrain favored the defenders, and by nightfall the Serbian Second Army had forced all Austro-Hungarian units back across the Drina and Sava. To the south of VIII Corps, the 36th Division of von Rhemen's XIII Corps was also turned back by Morava I. Further south, on Morava I's left flank, the 42nd "Devil's Division" created a diversion on the Combined Division's front in the vicinity of Loznica, but did not attempt a sustained crossing.

For Morava I it had been a good day: it had single-handedly repulsed three enemy divisions. One of Morava I's officers recorded that the Serbian defense was so tenacious that "the front battle lines of this regiment didn't allow even a single step forward."[43] For Potiorek, the offensive had begun inauspiciously.

By dawn of September 9, Stepanović was convinced that the main Austro-Hungarian assault was coming near the mouth of the Drina against Morava I, and that the 42nd Division was only a diversion. Stepa sent urgently needed reinforcements from his army reserve—Timok II—to reinforce Morava I. On Morava I's right wing, the 21st Division again attempted to cross near the marshy Parašnica Peninsula, supported by the 9th Division. Timok II's troops arrived at Parašnica after a forced march of 16 kilometers and attacked directly from the march. This sudden attack threw the 21st Division back, causing it severe losses. Due to the marshy terrain, Timok II could not exploit this victory, as its troops lost their way in the swamps. The 21st escaped across the river, although losing large quantities of matériel. The 9th Division was repulsed by artillery fire, which cost it more than 2,000 men. Morava I again repulsed the 36th Division, which took heavy casualties after Morava I hit it with flanking artillery fire: the 79th Regiment alone lost fourteen officers and 1,500 men, causing Division commander General Salis-Seewis to abandon further crossings.

Although performing valiantly against overwhelming odds, Morava I did not escape unscathed: the Division's 3rd Regiment suffered 102 killed, 575 wounded, and 129 missing.[44] Other regiments suffered similarly. Eyewitnesses to the carnage claimed that one island—*Bujuklića Ada*—was so covered with Austro-Hungarian corpses that the Serbian soldiers and medics who retook the island could not avoid walking on them.[45]

Upon hearing of this setback, Potiorek told Frank that "forcing the Drina must be repeated until it succeeds."[46] Yet heavy losses forced the Fifth Army to halt all offensive operations until September 13. In the meantime, Austro-Hungarian soldiers of the 36th Division—most of whom were Croats and Serbs—cursed and yelled at their Serbian counterparts. In one such exchange, the 36th Division's troops, which included large numbers of Serbs from Lika, shouted: "Do you think that we are Turks or Bulgars, who run away? No, the Emperor's border troops don't run away or surrender!"[47]

In spite of Stepanović's success in halting the Fifth Army, another assault threatened Serbia's interior. Aided by heavy fog along the middle and upper Drina, the Austro-Hungarian Sixth Army crossed the river quickly on the morning of September 8. By September 11, it had pushed the Serbian Third Army back from the Drina to the summits of Gučevo, Boranja, Jagodnja, and Sokol, the main mountain peaks lining the Drina valley. The Serbian High Command, which had initially foreseen another Habsburg attempt to force the Jadar valley, now guessed—accurately as it turned out—that the Sixth Army would attempt to reach Valjevo via the southern route through Krupanj. If successful, this would encircle Serbian forces in Mačva from the south.

Although the Serbian First Army was still advancing steadily against Krauss' 29th Division in Srem, the Sixth Army's offensive threw Putnik off-guard, just as Potiorek had hoped. Over-extended with almost one-third of his operational forces in Srem, and lacking a strategic reserve, Putnik recalled the First Army. Beginning late on the night of September 11, the High Command began the withdrawal: Danube I marched to Valjevo as a reserve for the Third Army; Šumadija I and the Cavalry Division were to follow.[48] By noon of September 14, the entire First Army was back on Serbian soil. Only a few small units—at Zemun and Bežanija ridge—remained behind. Potiorek's strategy to defeat the Serbian invasion of Srem had succeeded: he had fought fire with fire and won.

The defense of Mačva

Following the withdrawal from Srem, the Serbian High Command transferred the Combined Division from the Second to the Third Army, and placed the battered Timok I in the Second Army reserve. Although welcome news to the hard-pressed Third Army, this reduced the Second Army by one division, while lengthening its front to 100 kilometers.

On September 13 after regrouping, the Habsburg Fifth Army resumed its offensive in Mačva. The XIII Corps' 42nd Division ceased its diversions, went on the offensive and crossed eight battalions into a narrow bridgehead at *Ada Kurjačica*. The 42nd suffered heavily that day, with over 1,000 men killed or wounded. Lead elements of the 36th Division crossed at *Samurović Ada*, but Serbian resistance was so fierce that by day's end two entire Austro-Hungarian companies were destroyed entirely—either killed or taken prisoner. On September 14, in spite of the previous day's heavy losses, the 42nd finally constructed a pontoon bridge and crossed six more battalions. Yet it failed to expand its bridgehead, as Serbian forces kept it pinned down on the riverbank.

On September 16, the Second Army faced a new threat as units of the Habsburg Fifth Army's Combined Corps (including the 29th Division) crossed the Sava to the Second Army's rear at the village of Jarak, where Timok I had undergone its fiasco. Even though the region was lightly defended, the Combined Corps made slow progress, due partly to the marshy terrain. Nonetheless, by September 18 Habsburg forces had taken the village of Pričinović, some 10 kilometers from the crossing point. This threatened to encircle the entire Second Army.

The Combined Corps' offensive came as a surprise to the Serbian High Command, and coincided with a renewed frontal attack by VIII Corps. Lacking sufficient reserves to strengthen the line, Stepanović redeployed Šumadija I and the weakened Timok I to face the Combined Corps, leaving only Morava I to hold off the 9th, 21st, and 42nd Divisions. Yet the move paid off. A costly Serbian counterattack on September 19, in which the already decimated Timok I lost another 1,900 men, halted the 29th Division's advance at Pričinović. Although successful, the counterattack severely weakened the Second Army's fighting spirit, prompting one Serbian officer to write in his diary: "you can't count on the morale of our soldiers. They fight because they have to: there are many exhausted soldiers."[49]

Following Timok I's counterattack at Pričinović, the Austro-Hungarian Fifth Army's bridgehead comprised a narrow strip of land approximately 10 kilometers deep and 25 kilometers wide that stretched along the Sava from Pričinović in the east to Zasavica in the west. In addition, the 21st Division took the swampy Parašnica Peninsula at the mouth of the Drina. The remaining Habsburg forces—the 9th and 42nd Divisions—were once again forced to withdraw across the Drina. In Mačva, the troops of the Fifth Army became quickly bogged down, and both sides dug trenches in the marshy soil. An uneasy calm, punctuated by daily Austro-Hungarian shelling, settled upon the narrow front.

The Sixth Army returns

General Jurišić-Šturm's thinly stretched Third Army—consisting of only two second-levy divisions (Morava II, Drina II) and one first-levy division (Drina I)—was assigned an 80-kilometer stretch of the Drina from Lešnica in the north to Ljubovija in the south. To the east of the Drina, mountains ran parallel to the river, separating it from the Jadar and Western Morava watersheds. From north to south, the peaks in this range were: Gučevo, Boranja, Jagodnja, and Sokol. Their western slopes—those facing the Drina—were steep and thickly forested, offering the Serbs excellent defensive positions. This range was penetrated at several points—Krupanj and Pecka being the most important—by a number of streams and narrow valleys that offered access to the Jadar valley. This mountain range was an important barrier and comprised Serbia's chief western defensive bulwark.[50] The manpower shortage forced Jurišić-Šturm to rely on the terrain as his primary asset, and he assigned only one division (Morava II) to defend the Drina along this mountain range. Of greater worry was the relatively open mouth of the Jadar valley, the target of Potiorek's previous offensive, to which he assigned his remaining forces—Drina I and Drina II.

The Austro-Hungarian Sixth Army had seen little action during the August offensive, and its limited battlefield experience was more favorable than that of the Fifth Army. Morale was high and defeat unknown: it had withdrawn from Serbia in mid-August only because of the danger posed to its left wing by the retreating Fifth Army. In early September, it outnumbered Jurišić-Šturm's Third Army by more than two to one and had among its formation twelve mountain brigades, making it a formidable opponent. Potiorek was extremely confident of its capabilities.[51]

Potiorek knew of the Serbian Third Army's concentration at the mouth of the Jadar and ignored this area. Instead, he attacked the Third Army at its weakest point: the steep mountain range defended by the thinly stretched Morava II. Prior to the attack, Potiorek kept the Sixth Army's troop concentration and intended invasion route a secret from Serbian spies by evacuating all civilians from within five miles of the Drina. When the offensive came, it took Serbia's High Command by surprise.[52]

Crossing along a front that ranged from Han Brasina just north of Zvornik to Ljubovija in the south, the XV and XVI Corps quickly pushed the outnumbered Third Army back from the Drina.[53] Jurišić-Šturm committed his entire reserves to battle on September 8 to prevent a breakthrough, but it robbed him of the ability to counter any further Habsburg maneuvers.[54] The XV and XVI Corps advanced steadily toward Krupanj and Pecka, with the intention of pushing the Serbian forces from the mountain range and entering the Jadar valley behind the Second and Third Armies.

Serbia's High Command initially thought the September 8 attack was a diversion to draw attention from the Fifth Army's invasion in Mačva. Yet it continued on September 9, when the Sixth Army fought straight uphill on the slopes of Gučevo, Boranja, and Jagodnja and pushed back the Serbian defenders. Rough terrain, heavy forests, and fierce Serbian resistance notwithstanding, Habsburg artillery and numerical superiority proved overwhelming. On September 10, some units of the XVI Corps had reached to within 300 meters of Serbian positions at a crucial point called Mačkov Kamen.

Jurišić-Šturm faced a critical situation. Lacking reserves, and with his front lines wavering and breaking in many places, on September 11 Jurišić-Šturm ordered the beleaguered Morava II to withdraw from Mačkov Kamen to the east banks of the Brištica and Bogoštica rivers, beyond the mountain crests; on Gučevo, Drina I also withdrew. Fortunately for Jurišić-Šturm, the First Army's Danube II Division (at half strength with only two regiments) arrived from Srem in time to shore up the detachment of Colonel Mišić, which had begun to falter.[55]

By day's end, the Austro-Hungarian troops reached the now empty Serbian positions at Mačkov Kamen and Košutnja Stopa, where they stopped, exhausted from four days of continuous uphill fighting and having outpaced their artillery support. Potiorek ordered XVI Corps to spend

September 12 resting and regrouping. The Sixth Army's achievement was significant: it had pushed Serbian forces from the crests of Jagodnja and Boranja overlooking the Drina.

Serbia's situation was now serious. Putnik realized the Third Army couldn't halt the Habsburg Sixth Army, and that substantial reinforcements were needed. Late on September 11, the High Command ordered the Second Army—which had by now halted the Fifth Army's initial offensive in Mačva—to expand its area of operations to the south, permitting Drina II to shorten its line and transfer troops south to defend against XV Corps. The High Command also ordered the Užice Brigade and a third levy regiment to attack XVI Corps' right flank as it approached Pecka. These paltry reinforcements were all the assistance the High Command could offer at this point. Thus, Putnik called off the Srem invasion and sent the First Army to the Drina, to avoid an Austro-Hungarian breakthrough to Valjevo via Krupanj and Pecka.[56]

A desperate Jurišić-Šturm ordered Drina II to send all but five battalions to reinforce the Third Army's front against XVI Corps, and shifted the entire Drina I Division south to the slopes of Gučevo. This left only five battalions from Drina II to hold a 30-kilometer front near Loznica at the mouth of the Jadar valley.

Serbia's shortage of artillery ammunition was now being keenly felt. Third Army gunners were allowed to fire only on visible troop concentrations and all counter-battery fire was suspended: commanders sent entire batteries to the rear for lack of ammunition.[57]

PHOTO 17 *Fourth Regiment, first levy, September 1914.*

On September 13, the 42nd *Honved* Division crossed the Drina near the mouth of the Jadar at *Ada Kurjačica*, against Drina II's skeleton force. Drina II immediately sought help from the Second Army's neighboring Timok II. Elements from both divisions mounted a tenacious defense that cost the 42nd Division over 2,000 killed and wounded and contained the 42nd to a narrow bridgehead, but the situation along the western front was worsening.

Also on September 13, the Sixth Army continued its efforts to push the Third Army off the mountain range. The next two days saw fierce fighting along the entire Third Army front, as the Sixth Army continued to push back the overwhelmed Serbian forces. By September 15, the Sixth Army had pushed Jurišić-Šturm's Third Army either off the crests of the mountain range or back to their very peaks.

The Third Army was exhausted from the constant combat and demoralized due to the shortage of artillery ammunition. Ammunition was now so scarce that more batteries had to be withdrawn from the front, and cannon could be fired only upon approval of the divisional commander: each shell had to be accounted for.[58] Potiorek's Sixth Army was also worn out, having suffered heavy losses over the rough terrain.

Following several long forced marches, the main body of Petar Bojović's First Army finally began to arrive from Srem. This enabled the Serbs to regroup and plug holes in the front. Serbia's High Command decided the best way to stop Potiorek's latest offensive was to have Bojović's First Army turn northwest and follow the mountain ridges, from Sokol to Jagodnja, Boranja, and finally Gučevo, catching the Sixth Army in the rear and rolling up its exposed flank.

On September 16, Bojović attacked XVI Corps' right wing. The Ljubovija Detachment and Danube I successfully crushed the XVI Corps' right flank, which had been advancing along the Ljubovića stream from Ljubovija toward Pecka. During the night of September 16/17, the 109th Brigade fled 9 kilometers back to the Drina and crossed into Bosnia, ending the threat to Pecka and exposing the XVI Corps' right flank. Danube I and the Ljubovija Detachment turned northward into the XVI Corps' rear, causing elements of the 18th Division (*K.u.k.* 2nd Brigade) to flee northwest toward Mačkov Kamen. To the immediate north, Danube II pushed the *K.u.k.* 18th Division off the crest of Sokol and forced it to withdraw toward Mačkov Kamen. The Third Army, which also participated in the counter-offensive, proved unable to dislodge Habsburg forces from the crests of Gučevo, Boranja, and Jagodnja.

Thinking the entire Sixth Army was in headlong flight, on September 17 Bojović pursued the rapidly disintegrating 18th Division. Descending the heavily wooded slopes of Sokol on the morning of September 18 through thick fog and rain, the First Army ran into unexpected and fierce resistance from Austro-Hungarian troops on the slopes of Jagodnja. Although a few brigades of the *K.u.k.* 18th Division were indeed in disarray and disintegrating, the same was not true of the remainder of the Division or the

Sixth Army as a whole, which had successfully defended Gučevo, Boranja, and Jagodnja against Third Army counterattacks the previous two days. The First Army's Danube I and Danube II Divisions spent the remainder of the day regrouping on the eastern banks of the Ćumurana and Selenački streams, within sight of the two highest hills on Jagodnja—Košutnja Stopa and Mačkov Kamen.

The battle at Mačkov Kamen

Beginning on September 19, Mačkov Kamen saw the bloodiest engagement on the Balkan Front in 1914. Mačkov Kamen is an uneven plateau approximately half a kilometer long, southwest of Krupanj on Jagodnja. It overlooked the road running from Krupanj to the Drina, which provided the shortest and most direct route to the Jadar valley from the middle Drina. Control of Mačkov Kamen meant control of all communication between the middle Drina and the Jadar valley, and the mountain ridge on the east bank of the Drina. Rising sharply from surrounding mountain streambeds, the sides of Mačkov Kamen are steep and heavily forested, with many sharp ravines and gullies, while the top is a relatively barren clearing of approximately 500 square meters.

Mačkov Kamen, together with the higher Košutnja Stopa to the north, formed a narrow ridge about 2 kilometers long. A small, thickly wooded hill rose on the ridge line between Košutnja Stopa and Mačkov Kamen. The combination of steep slopes, thick forests, and numerous ravines and gullies made it difficult to deploy large troop formations.[59] Any attempt by the Serbs to retake Jagodnja would require seizing Mačkov Kamen as a prerequisite. To halt the First Army, Potiorek formed a defensive line anchored by Mačkov Kamen and Košutnja Stopa.[60]

On the morning of September 19, Bojović ordered Danube I and Danube II to take Jagodnja—that is, Mačkov Kamen and Košutnja Stopa—and the surrounding hills. Danube II attempted a direct assault on Mačkov Kamen and immediately ran into heavy resistance from the *K.u.k.* 7th Mountain Brigade backed by artillery, which forced Danube II to withdraw. Serbian artillery couldn't offer effective counter-battery fire, due to an ammunition shortage, and fired only at visible Habsburg troop concentrations. This allowed Habsburg artillery to fire with impunity. In the afternoon, Danube I combined its 9th and 5th Regiments into one formation, abandoned its attacks on the surrounding hills, and together with Danube II renewed the direct assault on Mačkov Kamen. The two regiments were placed under one command due to the difficulty of simultaneously deploying two regiments in such a confined space. Following a fierce three-hour battle, Serbian forces broke the Austro-Hungarian 7th and 6th Brigades and took Mačkov Kamen shortly before nightfall.

On Perunika, a hill directly south of Mačkov Kamen, elements of Danube I broke the 9th Brigade's lines, causing it to flee. Danube I and Danube II pursued the broken 6th and 7th Brigades down the slopes of Mačkov Kamen, whereupon they ran into the *K.u.k.* 1st Brigade, which had been brought up from reserve to hold the line. After a fierce fight, the 1st Brigade pushed the Serbian forces back up the slopes of Mačkov Kamen, where they remained for the night. At nightfall, the Austro-Hungarian lines were approximately 400 meters downhill from Serbian positions on Mačkov Kamen. Darkness, rain, and fog prevented further contact between the two sides for the remainder of the night, although infantry and artillery fire continued unabated,[61] preventing the First Army from regrouping. At day's end, Bojović informed the Serbian High Command that Mačkov Kamen had been taken, and that the following day he would pursue the retreating Habsburg forces, who he thought to be in full retreat.

But Potiorek was not retreating. If he allowed Bojović's Army to maintain its position on Mačkov Kamen, then the Serbian forces would be able to force XVI Corps back across the Drina. For the Sixth Army as a whole, the loss of Mačkov Kamen posed even greater problems. The fierce combat on Gučevo, Boranja, Jagodnja, and Sokol had taken a heavy toll: most of the battalions in XV Corps and XVI Corps had fallen to half strength and the Sixth Army lacked a strategic reserve.[62] If it withdrew across the Drina, it would be unable to mount offensive operations anytime in the near future. The commander of XVI Corps realized the seriousness of the situation and ordered a counterattack the following day to retake Mačkov Kamen. It was to comprise elements of the 1st, 2nd, 6th, 7th, and 9th Brigades.

The fate of Mačkov Kamen would influence not only the success of the Sixth Army's offensive, but that of the Fifth Army also. With the Fifth Army and Combined Corps clinging to tenuous footholds in the muddy trenches of Mačva, the withdrawal of the Sixth Army across the river would free Serbian forces to dislodge the Fifth Army from Mačva.

Such a loss would have serious international repercussions for the Habsburg Monarchy. The embarrassment of a second Habsburg defeat at Serbian hands would influence those Balkan nations leaning toward the Triple Alliance (Bulgaria and Greece in particular) to reconsider their policies. Even more disturbing, reports now arrived at Potiorek's headquarters of a combined Serbian/Montenegrin invasion of Bosnia-Herzegovina that was rapidly advancing toward Sarajevo and threatened to cut the Sixth Army's main rail supply lines.

During the night of September 19/20, rain fell on Jagodnja; on the morning of September 20, thick fog enveloped most of the mountain.[63] Because of this, neither side attacked immediately. The first assault came when the 1st Mountain Brigade attacked Danube I's 9th and 5th Regiments. This assault failed, and Habsburg forces were thrown back with heavy losses. Fortunately for Potiorek, the fog of war literally intervened: thick mists prevented Serbian forces from assessing the extent of Habsburg losses. Had they been able to do so, they most likely would have pursued the broken and disorganized Austro-Hungarian troops. Yet the First Army waited for the fog to burn off, and for the arrival of several field artillery batteries with ammunition, losing the opportunity to pursue the broken 1st Mountain Brigade. This allowed Habsburg forces time to regroup. When the Serbian forces on Mačkov Kamen finally went on the offensive in the late morning, Habsburg troops were ready and repulsed the Serbian attack.

In the afternoon, elements of Danube I's 5th and 9th Regiments and Danube II's 8th and 9th Regiments launched an assault. On the southern and western edge of Mačkov Kamen, the 5th Regiment advanced in the direction of Smajino Brdo, a hill to the west of Mačkov Kamen. On the northern edge of Mačkov Kamen, the two 9th Regiments (first and second levy), aided by Danube II's 8th Regiment, pushed north along the ridge-line toward Košutnja Stopa. They were met by four Austro-Hungarian Brigades (1st, 2nd, 6th, and Combined), which simultaneously were launching attacks against the Serbs.

The far larger Habsburg force halted the Serbian advance with concentrated rifle and artillery fire, causing Danube I's 5th Regiment to waver. Only a hasty withdrawal to Mačkov Kamen prevented a general panic. In spite of its ammunition shortage, Serbian artillery brought several field pieces into the very front firing lines. Although fog limited visibility, the Serbian artillery neutralized the Austro-Hungarian artillery and slowed the advancing infantry.[64] This enabled the 5th Regiment to hold its line.

Meanwhile, on the northern end of Mačkov Kamen, the two 9th Regiments from Danube I and Danube II came under increased pressure, causing the First Army to send the 4th Regiment to Nešino Brdo, a hill immediately east of Mačkov Kamen, to act as a reserve. Although Danube I and Danube II succeeded in repulsing the Habsburg counter-attacks of September 20, the cost was high: Danube I's 9th and 5th Regiments, as well as Danube II's 9th Regiment, lost more than half their officers, and nearly half their men.[65] Immediately to the south of Mačkov Kamen at Perunika and Javornik, Danube I spent much of the day fighting off attacks from the 2nd, 6th, 7th, and 13th Brigades. Paradoxically, Serbs considered their artillery useless during this particular engagement, while Habsburg forces considered it the most effective encounter to date.[66]

Colonel Milivoje Anđelković, the commander of Danube I, informed Bojović that the route along the spine of Jagodnja-Boranja-Gučevo was now effectively blocked: the First Army could no longer continue to advance along Jagodnja. He suggested that Danube I hold Mačkov Kamen, and Danube II swing to the north, where it could attack southward from the direction of Krupanj.[67] Bojović approved the move.

Potiorek, whose Sixth Army had lost 20,000 men since the offensive began,[68] thought the Serbian forces had suffered far heavier losses than his. He therefore ordered the Sixth Army to hold its current positions and await XIII Corps, which would enter the fray on September 22. The commander of the *K.u.k.* 18th Division, Ignaz Trollman, had other ideas. He felt the

Serbs were beaten, and that he could retake Mačkov Kamen: he ordered his Division to prepare to attack on September 21.

On the morning of September 21, the commander of Danube I's 5th Regiment noticed movement to the west near Smajino Brdo. Assuming it was a rearguard formation protecting the withdrawal of Habsburg troops, he sent a battalion from the 9th Regiment on a reconnaissance in force northward along the ridge toward Košutnja Stopa to ascertain whether the Habsburg forces had withdrawn. Unexpected rifle and artillery fire from Trollman's 18th Division on Košutnja Stopa shattered the Serbian battalion and forced it to flee: the 18th Division charged from Košutnja Stopa in headlong pursuit of the 5th Regiment's reconnaissance battalion.

The retreating Serbian troops spread panic through Danube I's entire 9th Regiment, causing it to abandon its forward positions. Only heroic efforts by the officers succeeded in halting the flight. Officers and men from Danube II's 9th Regiment helped restore order, allowing Danube I's 9th Regiment to return to its forward positions. The engagement of Danube II's 9th Regiment delayed its withdrawal from the front, which disrupted the planned Serbian envelopment of the Sixth Army from Krupanj.

By 10:00 am on September 21, heavy artillery fire from Košutnja Stopa and Smajino Brdo, accompanied by heavy infantry fire, caused Danube I's 9th Regiment—now back at its positions on Mačkov Kamen—to waver. Once again the regiment began to withdraw, and once again its officers barely held the troops. Shortly thereafter, the Habsburg troops attacked, wounding the newly appointed regimental commander Major Petar Mađarević. This proved the last straw for the 9th Regiment and it withdrew from Mačkov Kamen, costing the First Army its positions on the hill's northeast side.

The commander of Danube I's 4th Regiment acted on his own initiative, deployed his troops on Mačkov Kamen, and attempted to regroup the 9th Regiment while occupying its positions. During the confusion, Danube I's 5th field artillery battery, which had been positioned in the front, was left stranded in no-man's land. The only other available artillery battery on Mačkov Kamen, the 2nd field battery, was firing so rapidly that it quickly used up all its ammunition as well as that of the 5th battery, whose caissons had been salvaged along with the cannon's breach-blocks. After using all its own ammunition and that of the 5th battery, the 2nd battery then used up all the ammunition from the 8th battery, which could not deploy due to the intense fighting.

Sensing uncertainty among the Serbian ranks, Trollman launched another attack on Mačkov Kamen at 4:30 pm with the entire 18th Division. The battered 9th Regiment once again began to break, permitting the 18th Division to capture the 5th artillery battery from no-man's land. Once again Danube I's 4th Regiment stepped in to hold the line. The 4th and 9th Regiments then launched a counterattack, which enabled them to recapture their positions on the northeast side of Mačkov Kamen, which had been lost earlier that day. They also recovered two of their captured cannon, the

Habsburg forces having taken the other two. At the end of a long day of bloody fighting, Mačkov Kamen remained in Serbian hands. During the course of the day, both Danube I and Danube II suffered very heavy losses, as did the 18th Division.

During one of the 4th Regiment's charges, the regimental commander, Colonel Dušan Purić, is reported to have shouted at the Habsburg troops: "Surrender, don't die so stupidly!" The opposing Austro-Hungarian forces consisted of large numbers of Serbs from the Lika region of Croatia, descendants of the famed Habsburg border regiments. They responded to Purić by shouting back: "Have you ever heard of Serbs surrendering?"[69]

It now became apparent to Bojović that Košutnja Stopa could not be captured from the south. He ordered Danube I to relieve Danube II on Mačkov Kamen, and Danube II to march north toward Krupanj and attack Košutnja Stopa from the north.

On September 22, the now reinforced Austro-Hungarian 18th Division, with elements of seven different brigades totaling twenty battalions, attacked the three Serbian regiments on Mačkov Kamen. For this new assault, the 18th Division borrowed a Serbian tactic and brought its mountain guns into the front lines for direct fire against Serbian positions.[70] Austro-Hungarian forces approached the Serbian lines shortly after midnight and began to attack during the early morning hours. By 5:00 am Danube I had beaten back three charges with heavy losses to both sides. Nonetheless, Habsburg forces closed to within 30 meters of the 4th Supernumerary Regiment's positions and threatened it with encirclement. Fearing entrapment, the 4th Supernumerary Regiment began to waver and abandon its positions. Once again, the Serbian officers and NCOs barely managed to hold their troops. Fortunately for the Serbian forces, early morning darkness prevented the Habsburg forces from seeing the chaos among the Serbian ranks.

Shortly after 5:00 am, the Austro-Hungarians attacked once more, from the north, west, and south. All attacks were repulsed. The 4th Regiment launched a local counterattack, but failed to move the Habsburg troops more than 150 meters. During the morning's fighting, the Serbian 9th field artillery battery ran out of ammunition, further weakening defenses.[71] At the center of the Serbian line the 4th Supernumerary Regiment found itself under heavy machine gun, artillery, and rifle fire. After heavy fighting, it succeeded in pushing the Habsburg forces back only 30–150 meters from Serbian lines. The close proximity of Habsburg forces exposed the 4th Supernumerary Regiment to artillery and infantry fire from the flanks and rear, forcing Colonel Anđelković to send reinforcements from the Divisional reserve.

Around 7:00 am, Habsburg forces unsuccessfully attacked the 8th Regiment on the southern (left) wing of the Serbian position. In the center of the Serbian line, the situation rapidly became desperate, as elements of the 4th Regiment and 4th Supernumerary Regiment once again panicked and fled, abandoning some of their positions to Habsburg forces. The collapse of the 4th Regiment was especially worrisome, as its commander Colonel Dušan Purić had been killed during the morning's fighting. To prevent the center from collapsing, Colonel Anđelković deployed his last available regiment—the 18th. These reinforcements enabled the Serbian troops to counterattack around 8:30 am and dislodge Habsburg troops from the Serbian positions they had taken earlier that day. But the counterattack cost the 18th Regiment dearly: flanking artillery fire killed and wounded half its officers and men and shattered morale. The horror of large numbers of casualties was enhanced by the Austro-Hungarian use of *Einschusspatronen*, explosive bullets, which caused horrific wounds.[72] The narrow terrain on Mačkov Kamen further contributed to losses as it forced large troop formations into confined areas, exposing them to enemy artillery fire.[73]

Throughout the morning as various Austro-Hungarian units mounted attacks, different Serbian units wavered and withdrew from their positions, only to retake them by counterattack. This fluid situation worsened around 10:00 am, when Colonel Dragutin Dulić, commander of the 4th Supernumerary Regiment was wounded. Prior to this time, all the regiment's battalion commanders and their replacements were either wounded or killed, leaving no one to assume command of the battered unit. This forced the chief of Danube I's Divisional staff to assume operational command over the regiment.[74] At 11:30 am, the situation became so desperate that the 18th Regiment sent the last of its reserves into action.

The fighting ebbed back and forth throughout the remainder of the morning and afternoon. The Habsburg forces took Serbian positions in costly assaults, only to lose them to Serbian counterattacks. Lacking artillery and machine guns, the Serbian troops resorted to mass charges, suffering heavy losses in the confined space. By mid-afternoon, Potiorek's advantage in numbers, artillery, and machine guns prevailed. Around 3:00 pm, a new assault broke the center of the Serbian lines, where the 4th Supernumerary Regiment and 18th Regiment were intermingled. Under constant artillery and infantry crossfire, these two regiments had by now lost most of their NCOs and officers; they broke and fled. Only the troops of the 4th Regiment managed to hold their positions on the slopes of Mačkov Kamen, where they fought a rearguard action. This enabled Danube I to withdraw without being pursued by Habsburg forces.

The struggle for Mačkov Kamen was now over.

This battle was by far the bloodiest and costliest on the Balkan Front during the first year of the Great War.[75] The small, narrow ridge and steep slopes forced the Serbian and Austro-Hungarian soldiers to bunch together in exposed spaces, where they rapidly fell victim to artillery and infantry fire. By late afternoon of September 22, the 500 square-meter clearing on top of Mačkov Kamen was covered with over 2,000 corpses.[76] The fierceness of the fighting was attested to by the hill itself: rifle and artillery fire had almost completely denuded the thickly wooded slopes of both Mačkov Kamen and Košutnja Stopa.[77]

All told, Danube I lost 5,772 officers and men during the five-day battle, while Danube II lost 2,246 men. During the eleven-day offensive, Danube I and Danube II lost a total of 11,490 men. The 18th Regiment alone lost thirty-four of its fifty-eight officers. The 4th Supernumerary Regiment lost thirty officers, including the regimental commander and commanders of three battalions. The 4th Regiment lost ten officers, including the regimental commander and three battalion commanders. The 8th Regiment lost ten officers, including the regimental commander and one battalion commander. The 9th Regiment lost thirty-one officers, including the regimental commander and three battalion commanders, and had only 1,000 men and seventeen officers left. The 5th Regiment also lost its commander and commanders of three battalions, and was reduced from 3,500 to 910 men. The battle spared no one: King Petar Karađorđević's oldest son, Prince Đorđe, was wounded.[78]

After seizing Mačkov Kamen on the afternoon of September 22, Habsburg forces immediately dug in against a counterattack, not realizing the extent of Serbian losses. The Habsburg XVI Corps was also unable to capitalize on the Serbian defeat, having itself lost large numbers of men. Its soldiers were exhausted and worn out, physically unfit for further battle without rest and replacements. The XV Corps commander General von Appel notified Potiorek that he had lost 12,000 men since the offensive began. Altogether during the two weeks since crossing the Drina, the Sixth Army had lost over 30,000 men.[79]

Thus, at the end of September the Serbian First and Third Armies had barely managed to stop the Austro-Hungarian Sixth Army, shortly after the Fifth Army bogged down in the mud of Mačva. The exhausted Serbian Third Army, which still clung tenaciously to Gučevo and Boranja, lacked the strength to mount an offensive. So too, the Austro-Hungarian Sixth Army and the Serbian First Army were exhausted and worn out. Potiorek wouldn't be able to send replacements to the Sixth Army until October: all available soldiers were being sent to the Fifth Army. For the First Army, no help was on the horizon. In a state of sheer exhaustion, the opposing sides dug in along both sides of the mountain crests, waiting for replacements and fresh supplies.

CHAPTER EIGHT

Defeat and hemorrhage

Distraction and diversion

Following the carnage at Mačkov Kamen, Potiorek launched diversionary attacks along Serbia's northern border, hoping to divert attention from the battered Fifth and Sixth Armies while they regrouped.

The heaviest fighting took place on the western outskirts of Belgrade at *Ada Ciganlija* early on the morning of September 22, when the *K.u.k.* 32nd Regiment crossed the Sava and pushed Serbian forces back along part of the narrow 4.5-kilometer long island. At 5:00 pm, the Austro-Hungarian military commander of Zemun, General Gustav Goglia, sent a monitor across the Sava flying a white flag. The monitor carried a surrender demand—written in Serbo-Croatian—to Joksim Gajić, commander of the Belgrade city defense, ordering him to surrender by 6:00 that evening. The Serbian forces were to strike the Serbian colors on the Kalemegdan and replace it with a large white flag. General Goglia offered to let the Serbian officers keep their swords. He was also polite enough to warn the Mayor of Belgrade of the potential for fires when the bombardment resumed.[1] Gajić's response was blunt: he ordered the Russian coastal artillery battery on the Kalemegdan to shoot two shells at the monitors moored next to the Zemun landing.[2]

That evening fighting resumed on *Ada Ciganlija* and raged for two days, as the Defense of Belgrade fought desperately to repel the Habsburg forces. On September 24, Serbian forces finally routed the Austro-Hungarian forces on the island. Losses on both sides were heavy, and Lieutenant Colonel August Schmidt, the crew-cut, handlebar-mustached commander of the mostly ethnic Rumanian 32nd *Landwehr* Regiment was killed: in the confusion of retreat his troops left his body on the island.[3]

On September 25, the Dual Monarchy liquidated a Serbian bridgehead at Ostružnica in southern Srem, which remained from the First Army's early-September offensive into Mačva. On the Danube, Austro-Hungarian forces began to build a pontoon bridge several kilometers east of Belgrade near Vinča, under cover of two monitors.[4]

PHOTO 18 *Serbian artillery near Ostružnica.*

To stop the constant shelling of Belgrade, Serbian forces crossed the Sava and re-took Zemun on September 28. This caught the Austro-Hungarian troops by surprise and they fled in panic, leaving Zemun undefended. The Defense of Belgrade quickly began construction of a bridge across the Sava at *Ada Ciganlija*, with the intention of expanding its bridgehead, but high, swift water slowed progress. After completion, three Habsburg river monitors steamed up the Sava and destroyed the bridge, preventing reinforcements and forcing the Serbian forces to withdraw from Srem on the night of September 29 with several captured cannon and machine guns. Belgrade's civilian population now settled back to its normal routine of constant shelling.[5] Civilian morale suffered a terrible blow when Habsburg artillery hit the Weifert Brewery, removing a popular source of liquid courage.[6]

As an uneasy lull descended along the Sava and Danube and the mountains east of the Drina, events further south caused new concerns for both Potiorek and Vienna. A combined Serbian-Montenegrin invasion of Bosnia threatened to cut the Sixth Army's supply lines, capture Sarajevo and large parts of Bosnia-Herzegovina, and provoke an uprising among the Empire's Serbian and South Slav populations.

The road to Sarajevo

On the upper Drina, the joint Serbian-Montenegrin offensive got off to a late start. The combined force—operating under the operational direction of Serbia's High Command—consisted of Montenegro's Sandžak Army (one division of 13,500 men and twenty cannon) under the command of *Serdar* Janko Vukotić, and Serbia's Užice Army (42,000 men and fifty-eight cannon) under the command of Black Hand member and former Military Minister General Miloš Božanović. The Užice Army's troops were mostly second and third levy, supplemented by irregular Četnik formations. Parts of the Sandžak Army consisted of the rag-tag, semi-trained peasant militia that passed for an army in Montenegro. Although armed with modern Russian Mosin rifles, many Montenegrin soldiers wore peasant dress. Experienced from the Balkan Wars, they had little formal military training; in addition to being known for their fierceness, they had a reputation as an undisciplined lot.

The two armies had seized the east bank of Bosnia-Herzegovina's upper Drina valley in August. They now awaited orders to cross the river. The original plan called for both armies to go on the offensive shortly after the First Army invaded Srem, and make a two-pronged advance in the direction of Sarajevo and Vlasenica. When Potiorek launched his September 8 offensive, Putnik ordered both Vukotić and Božanović to delay their offensive in case their troops were needed to reinforce Serbia's Second or Third Armies, a prescient move, as Putnik was forced to send two regiments from the Užice Army to assist Jurišić-Šturm's embattled Third Army. In the meantime, the Užice Army was told to attack only if the opportunity presented itself, which it quickly did.

The Sandžak Army crossed the Drina at Foča on September 11, and at Goražde on September 14. The Užice Army crossed the Drina at Višegrad, Stari Brod, and Međeđa, also on September 14. The crossings went slowly due to a lack of bridging equipment. Rather than immediately expand their bridgeheads, the Serbian and Montenegrin commanders held their troops at the bridgeheads, which allowed the *K.u.k.* 8th Mountain Brigade and the 9th *Landsturm* Brigade—the only Austro-Hungarian units in the area—to withdraw safely to Han Pijesak, up in the mountains. Had the Serbian and Montenegrin commanders acted more quickly, they could probably have destroyed both units, leaving Sarajevo and Vlasenica almost completely undefended. In spite of light Austro-Hungarian resistance, the Serbian and Montenegrin forces proceeded slowly and did not enter Rogatica until September 17. The tardiness of their entry appears to have been caused by mutual disagreement over whose forces should enter the town first.[7] Given the track record of the Montenegrin troops, substantial time was probably devoted to such traditional Balkan tasks as looting. Putnik ordered them to remain in Rogatica until the situation in Mačva became clearer, and until the First Army's counter-offensive bore fruit.

Only on September 22, when Putnik realized the First Army would not be able to defeat the Austro-Hungarian Sixth Army at Mačkov Kamen, did he order Vukotić and Božanović to resume the advance toward Sarajevo and Vlasenica. He ordered Božanović to drive north toward Vlasenica, and Vukotić's Sandžak Army to advance northwest toward Sarajevo. The Užice Army's goal was to destroy the rail line in the Krivaja river valley—the Sixth

Army's main supply line—and wreak havoc in that Army's rear area, forcing Potiorek to withdraw the Sixth Army from western Serbia. This would relieve pressure on the hard-pressed Serb First and Third Armies.

On September 25, the Sandžak Army advanced from Rogatica up the Prača valley toward the high Romanija plateau, east of Sarajevo. By the early morning hours of September 26, lead elements of the Sandžak Army entered Pale, a mountain village some 12 kilometers up the Miljacka river gorge from Sarajevo. Vukotić's troops also reached the village of Podromanija, which sat at the junction of the main road running from Olovo in the west to Višegrad in the southeast, and which was intersected by another main road that ran from Sarajevo to Vlasenica and Tuzla.

The Užice Army advanced along a line running from Rogatica to Žlebovi, and from there toward Han Pijesak. The offensive progressed quickly: by the end of September the Užice Army had taken much of eastern Bosnia, including Srebrenica, Han Pijesak, Sokolac, and Glasinac. Božanović's troops cut the rail line from Olovo to Đile, which ran through Han Pijesak and carried supplies and reinforcements to Wurm's XVI Corps. The Užice Army then advanced toward Kladanj, Olovo, and Vlasenica, the main rail head and supply depot in the Sixth Army's rear area.

The invasion of Bosnia threatened the exhausted Austro-Hungarian Sixth Army not only with the loss of supplies and reinforcements, but also encirclement. Of even greater concern was the response of Bosnia's Serbs, who actively supported the Serbian and Montenegrin forces. The Bosnian Serbs caused serious concern in Vienna, which feared a general uprising of the Empire's South Slavs and havoc in the *Balkanstreitkräfte*'s rear areas. Even worse, the fall of Sarajevo would present an overwhelming political embarrassment for the Austro-Hungarian Empire.[8] The Sarajevo assassination was ostensibly the *casus belli* for the war, and a Serbian seizure of the city would not only irreparably damage the Dual Monarchy's prestige among neutral Balkan nations, but would also quickly raise the specter of the Empire's dissolution and the rise of a South Slav state at the expense of Habsburg territory, with Serbia at its head. It would no doubt cause some of Austria-Hungary's allies to question the further utility of war.

To forestall this impending military, political, and existential disaster, the AOK diverted part of its strategic reserve—which was badly needed on the Eastern Front in Galicia—along with units on the Italian border, to reinforce Potiorek's Sixth Army. Potiorek pulled the 18th Division from XVI Corps on the Drina's east bank. He also sent the *K.u.k.* 50th Division—newly formed from previously independent brigades of XVI Corps—into battle. As a result, most of XVI Corps was withdrawn from western Serbia back across the Drina to combat the threat in the Sixth Army's rear area, easing pressure on Serbia's hard-pressed First and Third Armies.

On October 5, the 18th Division attacked the Užice Army. Upon running into the first real Habsburg resistance since the invasion of Bosnia began in early September, Božanović quickly withdrew: over a five-day period, the Užice Army retreated 20 kilometers from its furthest point of advance at Han Pogled.[9] After running into determined Serbian resistance on October 10, Potiorek halted his counteroffensive until the *K.u.k.* 50th Division arrived at the front. In Valjevo, an angry Putnik forced General Božanović to retire for failing to offer more effective resistance against the 18th Division, and replaced him with General Vukoman Aračić.[10] The situation stabilized along the new line for several weeks while Potiorek awaited the arrival of reinforcements and supplies. On October 18, the *K.u.k.* 50th Division attacked the weaker Sandžak Army at Glasinac and Romanija. The Montenegrins held their positions for three days, at which point they suddenly withdrew 30 kilometers to Jabuka, completely exposing the Užice Army's left flank.[11]

The Montenegrin withdrawal was caused every bit as much by internal discipline problems as by the Austro-Hungarian offensive. The Serbian military liaison officer with the Montenegrins, General Božidar Janković, placed the blame for the failure of the Bosnian offensive squarely on the lack of discipline among the Montenegrin. Lacking an adequate supply train, the Sandžak Army was poorly fed and lived largely off the land. Since entering Bosnia, the undisciplined Montenegrins had engaged in massive looting. The old Montenegrin tendency to view wars as a legitimate means of economic gain certainly played a role in their behavior: traditionally, Montenegrin military operations focused on raids and plundering. Montenegrin soldiers were unaccustomed to taking territory and holding it for a protracted period of time. In the face of determined enemy opposition, many Montenegrin soldiers simply wanted to return home as quickly as possible with their booty. The idea of allegiance to a centralized state was relatively new in Montenegro, and many of the soldiers lacked a firm commitment to King Nikola. Eleven of the thirty-five Montenegrin battalions in Bosnia suffered serious desertion problems. Many battalions simply renounced their loyalty to King Nikola and began plundering their areas of operation.[12]

After losing contact with the Sandžak Army, General Aračić ordered the Užice Army to shorten its lines and withdraw to positions east of Rogatica. The Užice Army remained there until the night of October 23/24, when it came under heavy attack from Wurm's XVI Corps. It then withdrew across the Drina, marking an end to large scale Montenegrin and Serbian forays into Bosnia-Herzegovina.

Although the incursion ended with a Serbian and Montenegrin withdrawal across the Drina, it succeeded as a diversion. It delayed the start of Potiorek's planned offensive toward Valjevo by at least a month, forced Potiorek to withdraw much of the XVI Corps from Serbia to secure the rear area and supply lines, and gave the beleaguered Serbian Third and First Armies time to regroup and reinforce. Finally, the AOK was forced to send its strategic reserve—which was urgently needed in Galicia—to the Balkan Front, relieving pressure on the Russian Army.

A muddy stalemate

In the last week of September, with the two sides too exhausted to mount offensive operations, the Serbian and Austro-Hungarian forces settled into trench warfare, where they remained until the end of October. During this time Putnik transferred Morava II from Jurišić-Šturm's Third Army to Bojović's First Army, which also included Danube I and Danube II. The Combined Division was transferred from the First Army to the Third Army, which now included Drina I and Drina II. The lull was used to replenish units with what little men, ammunition, and equipment remained.[13]

During this period of static trench warfare, the Dual Monarchy enjoyed a tremendous advantage. Serbian troops lacked such basic equipment as entrenching tools, field kitchens, boots, winter coats, and shelter halves. Potiorek used the time to replenish all his units to full strength and resupply them. But all was not entirely well among the Austro-Hungarian ranks. In early October, an outbreak of cholera in the *K.u.k.* Army spread to civilian areas along the Russian Front. In only a very short time, the cholera traveled south to the Balkan Front.[14]

Trench war proved disastrous for Serbia's army. Many units lacked sufficient replacements and were under half strength. Thinly stretched over a long front, soldiers could not be given leave and were forced to remain in the trenches. Because the war started in late July, few soldiers brought winter clothing or coats with them. By mid-September the Serbian Army still lacked sufficient uniforms for its first levy soldiers, much less the soldiers of the second and third levies, who wore their own clothing, prompting Nikola Pašić to tell Serbia's Minister to Petrograd Miroslav Spalajković:

> A large number of the conscripts fight in their peasant clothes, which are worn out: many times in their pants and shirts, without any kind of military insignia, so that the opponent doesn't consider him a soldier from the ranks and shoots him immediately when he falls into their hands. There are regiments, which half-barefoot undertake forced marches of long distances and enter into battle completely barefoot.[15]

The situation became so desperate that the Serbian High Command sent a mission to Russia to requisition used Austro-Hungarian clothing captured during the Russian victory at Lemberg (L'vov).[16]

As cold weather set in, many Serbian soldiers fell ill. The situation was worst among the Serbian First Army along the cold mountain peaks of Boranja: on September 29, Bojović complained to the High Command that "the troops will not be capable of any type of action unless they are quickly supplied with warm clothes and shoes." Poor roads and bad weather made many roads impassable. Food arrived irregularly, and the troops began to forage. Bojović asked that all artillery and transport livestock be kept far from the front lines to prevent their being slaughtered and eaten. He also reported the lack of food and clothing caused many troops to break their weapons, throw away their ammunition, and go home.[17] As winter approached, Serbia's army showed signs of internal dissolution.

During the trench warfare, Serbian and Austro-Hungarian troops often conversed back and forth between the trenches, and even traded food and goods.[18] Hungry Habsburg soldiers even traded their overcoats for bread. The commander of Serbia's 4th Regiment (first levy) used this method to equip most of his soldiers with overcoats.[19]

The trench stalemate did not mean the end of fighting. On the night of October 13/14, Drina II attacked the 42nd Division's bridgehead at *Ada Kurjačica*. Heavy rains and the rising Drina flooded the Habsburg trenches and destroyed the pontoon bridge, making the Austro-Hungarian positions untenable. Drina II took advantage of this to push the 42nd back across the Drina and destroy that bridgehead.[20]

The only large-scale Serbian action occurred at the end of October, when the Combined Division tried to take Gučevo from XV Corps. The 4th Supernumerary Regiment drove a tunnel under Habsburg lines, which it filled with explosives. On October 28, it detonated the explosives, collapsing a large section of the enemy's forward trenches and defensive positions and creating an enormous crater. The explosion frightened the Habsburg troops so badly that many fled back across the Drina. Yet Serbia's lack of artillery ammunition severely affected the outcome of this particular engagement. Unable to answer the Austro-Hungarian artillery effectively or provide a pre-attack bombardment, the Combined Division lost 1,400 men in a series of futile charges and XV Corps held Gučevo.

Both sides proved innovative: hoping to disrupt the enemy's supply lines, the Užice Army floated large logs and rafts down the Drina to wreck Austro-Hungarian pontoon bridges, while Austro-Hungarian troops shot signal rockets directly at Serbian troops, a tactic that created panic among the Serbian lines.[21]

Serbia's tiny industrial base and its inability to manufacture artillery shells now became critical, as the Serbian Army began to suffer heavy casualties from artillery. Habsburg superiority in artillery increased, as *Balkanstreitkräfte* received more cannon of larger caliber. The effectiveness of Habsburg artillery had improved since early August, and was heightened by the use of high explosive shells—ideal for destroying trenches and field fortifications. Serbian field guns lacked high explosive and fired shrapnel, which was of limited effect in trench warfare.[22] The Serb Third Army's Combined Division lost an average of 100 men per day to artillery fire: over a period of fifty days, the Division lost 12,000 men, of whom 2,000 were killed.[23] In Mačva, where the flat, marshy terrain offered little natural cover, the Austro-Hungarian artillery proved especially deadly.

The shortage of artillery ammunition became acute. On September 28, total reserves were only 9,000 field artillery shells and 800 mountain artillery rounds; there were no reserve stocks for howitzers or heavy artillery. On the front lines, each field artillery piece had 200 shells, heavy howitzers 100, light howitzers 200, mortars 300—sufficient ammunition for two days of heavy action.[24] The High Command forbade Serbian artillery officers to fire without explicit permission from their divisional commanders, who in turn demanded a strict account of each shell fired. During one twenty-four-hour period, Habsburg batteries fired over 1,500 shells at Morava I, while Serbian artillery remained silent.[25]

Serbian artillery could only be used to fight off attacks, and even then sparingly. Serbian batteries were not permitted to shell Habsburg troop concentrations or engage in counter-battery fire. Even when fending off Habsburg attacks, the Serbian Army used artillery sparingly. Under constant bombardment, Serbian troops were pinned in their trenches for long periods, while Austro-Hungarian troops could leave their trenches freely.[26] Constant bombardment took a heavy psychological toll on Serbia's army and morale plummeted.[27] The Austro-Hungarian forces, for their part, understood the use of artillery and its ability to reduce their own casualties and destroy the Serbian Army.[28]

Many Serbian soldiers decided to desert until the army received more artillery ammunition, and some blatantly told their officers: "why should we die when we have no artillery ammunition?"[29] Using the ongoing bombardment as an excuse, many soldiers wandered the front lines, claiming they had suffered concussions from the shelling. Threats and cajoling failed to return them to their units. Between September and December 1914, desertion would claim almost 25 percent of the mobilized army's enlisted strength.[30]

Serbian commanders pleaded for more ammunition. At the end of September, the commander of Timok I telegraphed Second Army commander Stepanović, saying: "I beg you . . . to send me ammunition, that for once I can free myself of this terrible state in which I endlessly find myself, fearing that in the most critical moment I will be left without one single shell."[31]

The situation became so desperate that the High Command kept record of the number of shells for individual batteries. When a battery ran low, the Army commander divided its shells among other batteries and sent the battery to the rear.[32] Serbian infantry dug their trenches to within less than 100 meters of the Austro-Hungarian lines, hoping Habsburg artillery would not fire for fear of hitting its own troops. This tactic worked especially well for the troops of the 6th Supernumerary Regiment, who dug trenches to within 10 meters of enemy lines.

Putnik telegraphed Prime Minister Nikola Pašić on October 10 that if the current state of affairs continued the army would be incapable of further resistance. In response, Pašić and Military Minister Stefanović visited Putnik on October 12. Putnik bluntly told them: "the army cannot be allowed to be wasted in battle because they lack [artillery] ammunition for even one battle."[33] After the meeting, Pašić instructed Serbia's envoys in Paris,

Petrograd, and London to renew their efforts to obtain matériel, but the Entente itself was short of matériel, and little help was forthcoming.

Throughout the second half of September and most of October, the Serbian Second Army held three Austro-Hungarian Corps in Mačva. Lieutenant Mirko Ćurović of the Second Army's Morava I observed the artillery's effect on the Serbian soldiers:

> It cannot be said that the morale of our troops is good, because the soldiers excessively are physically and spiritually wavering as a result of the constant fighting, and lying in trenches next to the Drina, which are always wet.[34]

Constant bombardment, bad weather, sniping, and frequent Austro-Hungarian forays against the Serbian positions, took a heavy psychological toll on the Serbian Army and morale plummeted.[35] For the First and Third Armies, the situation was similar to that of the Second Army, except that in the mountains the weather was colder than in Mačva. In one notorious instance, poor-quality Rumanian *opanci* disintegrated after several days' use, leaving several regiments of the Danube I Division completely barefoot.[36]

The only substantial allied aid came in the form of Russian, French, and British naval missions that began to arrive at Belgrade in late September. Using a combination of mines, naval artillery, and land-based torpedo launchers, they effectively halted all river traffic on the Danube: no longer could the Dual Monarchy's monitors ply the waters around Belgrade with impunity. Russian and French naval batteries forced the monitors to move their anchorage from the now vulnerable Zemun landing, and stopped Austro-Hungarian river traffic on the Danube, including vital supply convoys to Turkey.[37]

On the diplomatic front

Throughout the fall, the struggle on the battlefield was accompanied by equally intensive diplomatic efforts that concentrated primarily on Bulgaria, Italy, and Romania. Both Italy and Romania possessed relatively large armies, and their entry into the war could decisively tip the balance of power, while Bulgaria's entry into the war would decisively influence the outcome on the Balkan Peninsula. To gain the backing of these countries, both the Entente and the Triple Alliance struggled to satisfy their various territorial appetites. Italy wanted Trieste, Istria, Dalmatia, the Montenegrin littoral, and northern Albania, all areas coveted by Serbia. To gain Bulgaria as an ally, the Entente would have to convince Serbia to cede at least a portion of Macedonia. This created a dilemma for the Entente: any attempt to satisfy Bulgaria or Italy would inevitably cause friction with Serbia, which unlike Italy, was actually fighting. And in the case of Bulgaria, only Serbian willingness to cede Macedonia would satisfy Bulgarian demands. At this point, Bulgaria's entire foreign policy centered on acquiring Macedonia.[38]

Toward the end of summer, Pašić instructed Serbia's envoy in London, Mateja-Mata Bošković, to inquire discreetly of the British government as to whether or not the Entente had entered into talks with Romania. Bošković reported that England and the Entente had not yet begun efforts to win over Romania.[39] By mid-September, following the Austro-Hungarian defeat at Cer, the Serbian invasion of Srem and the Russian victories at Lemberg on September 3 and Grodek on September 12/13, Romanian public opinion shifted heavily in favor of the Entente. Pašić received reports from Serbian Minister in Bucharest Mihajlo Ristić that Romania planned to declare war on the Dual Monarchy within the next several days. The Romanian government needed only another significant Entente victory as impetus.[40] However, such a victory remained elusive and Romania remained neutral.

Serbia's most immediate concern centered on Italy and the price the Entente would pay to gain that country as an ally. Since the very beginning of the war the Entente engaged Rome in discussions, with Russia leading the way through the Italian Legation in Petrograd, and through Anatoli Nikolajević Krupenski, the Russian Minister to Rome. When asked what Italy desired, the Italian Minister of Foreign Affairs, Antonio Paterno Castello di Sangiuliano, said that Italy would enter the war only if allowed to keep all the territory her army could occupy, including Dalmatia. Knowing this would create problems with Serbia, Krupenski answered that Serbian interests deserved to be protected. Italy then expressed concern that Russia was using the larger part of its army against Germany, and not Austria-Hungary. Italy wanted assurances that if it entered the war, Russia would devote greater resources to Galicia and the Carpathians, thereby diverting Habsburg troop strength away from Italy. This met with an unenthusiastic Russian reaction. Given the Italian response, on August 30 the Russian, French, and British envoys to Rome met and declared the talks unsuccessful.[41] Following the failure of the initial round of talks, the Entente moved the negotiations to London.

The Entente excluded Serbia from negotiations with Italy, both in Rome and London, and the Serbian government received only second-hand information from the Entente Ministers. During late September, unconfirmed reports reached the Serbian government that the Entente had promised Valona and Trieste to Italy. These did little to assuage Serbia's fears, particularly since the question of Dalmatia—perhaps the Habsburg Empire's most pro-Serbian and pro-Yugoslav region—still hung in the balance.[42] Although Serbia expressed no interest in acquiring either Trieste or Valona, the very idea that these Slav territories to the north and south of Dalmatia were being given away gave cause for concern.

In England, public opinion wanted the war prosecuted to the very end and to create radical changes throughout Europe that would ensure long-lasting continental peace. Hopefully, new boundaries could be drawn up that would prevent all future attempts at hegemony and revenge. This included dismantling the Dual Monarchy. In direct contrast to English public opinion, English Foreign Minister Sir Edward Grey opposed the destruction of the Habsburg Empire and favored its survival, if for no other reason than for Central European stability and the maintenance of the Great Power system. Because of this, Grey proved reluctant to countenance the breakup of the Habsburg Empire in favor of Italy, Romania, or future Serbian territorial claims.[43]

In 1913, a prominent group of pro-Yugoslav Croatian politicians, fearing imprisonment in the event of war between the Dual Monarchy and Serbia, agreed to form a committee in exile to promote the idea of South Slav unity. These men, the most prominent of whom were the Dalmatians Ante Trumbić, Frano Supilo, and Ivan Meštrović, fled to Italy shortly after the war broke out and formed the Yugoslav Committee. The Yugoslav Committee operated with the full diplomatic support of the Serbian government, and its members maintained close contact with Serbian legations in the Entente capitals. They worked to promote the idea of post-war South Slav unity and the creation of a federated South Slav state that would combine Serbia with the Austro-Hungarian Empire's South Slav territories. When the initial negotiations between the Entente and Italy failed, the Yugoslav Committee moved to London, hoping to influence the course of negotiations between the Entente and Italy.[44] Several of its members visited France, hoping to sway public opinion in favor of the Yugoslav idea.

In mid-September 1914, prior to leaving Italy, Ivan Meštrović, Frano Supilo, and Ante Trumbić met jointly with the Entente Ministers in Rome in a meeting arranged by the Serbian Minister.[45] The purpose of the meeting was to assure the Entente Ministers that all of Dalmatia was settled by a "Serbian element" that desired unification with Serbia. Bošković reported:

> As our Dalmatians [Meštrović, Supilo, Trumbić] were Catholics and Croats, it had a strong impact on the English Ambassador. They spoke to him about the greater Serbian idea. The English Ambassador said that he will inform his government about everything, and that they had nothing to fear about the greater pretensions of Italy, because he doesn't believe it will go further than Trieste and one part of Istria.[46]

In the course of the meeting, Russia's Minister Krupenski also assured them that they had nothing to fear from the Italians, as Italy was interested only in Trieste.

The Triple Alliance knew full well of the danger posed by an Italian entry into the war. Germany and Austria-Hungary also realized that they were at a disadvantage in terms of territory they could offer, and could only hope for Italian neutrality, in exchange for which the Triple Alliance offered the Albanian port of Valona, and to rectify Austria-Hungary's Friulian border with Italy.[47]

By early October, Italy's position was still far from clear. In an effort to prevent Italy from taking the Dual Monarchy's South Slav regions, Frano Supilo suggested creating an independent Croatia from parts of Bosnia-Herzegovina, Dalmatia, and Slovenia. Fearing the Entente would promise the Dalmatian seacoast to Italy, Pašić suggested the Yugoslav Committee broach the idea of giving autonomy to Slovenia, Croatia, and Dalmatia within the Austro-Hungarian framework.[48] Russia, meanwhile, refused to make any promises to Italy regarding Trieste, while Germany wanted Trieste to remain a part of the Dual Monarchy. Serbia's Minister to Petrograd, Miroslav Spalajković, told Russian Foreign Minister Sazonov of Serbia's position that "Trieste doesn't belong to Italy or Austria-Hungary, but to our Serbo-Croato-Slovenian state." He stated that it would be best to have a strong Serbia on the Adriatic, which would prevent German influence from reaching Trieste.[49]

In mid-October, the English Minister in Rome James Rennell Rodd told the Serbs that in his opinion a lasting post-war peace would not be secured unless the Serb-Croat question was settled. Of particular concern were objections among Catholic circles in both France and Italy, who—in the event of the post-war creation of a South Slav state—wanted autonomy for Croatia. The English however, opposed the creation of a state on a purely religious basis. They did feel, however, that greater thought should be given to varying degrees of autonomy within an expanded post-war Serbia. Reassuring Bošković, Rodd stressed that Italian pretensions to the eastern coast of the Adriatic went no further than Trieste.[50]

By mid-November, Serbia was receiving mixed signals on the issue of Trieste and the Dalmatian coast. On the one hand, Russia's Minister to Rome, Krupenski, now hinted to Bošković that Serbia might not receive the Dalmatian coast. Instead, Serbia would probably receive an outlet on the Adriatic in northern Albania. On the other hand, the Italian Minister in Niš, Nicola Squitti di Palermiti e Guarna, told Pašić that Italy wanted nothing beyond Trieste. This prompted Pašić to comment: "it seems strange that the Russian Ambassador is willing to give Italy more than it wants."[51] In spite of Krupenski's new willingness to reward Italy with Dalmatia, Russia remained enthusiastic about a post-war South Slav state with Serbia at its head.[52]

On October 29, following almost a month of Turkish border provocations in the Caucasus, the Ottoman Empire launched a surprise naval attack on the Russian Black Sea ports of Odessa, Sevastopol, Theodosia, and Novorosijsk. This act brought Turkey into the war on the side of the Triple Alliance, diverted Russian troops away from Galicia and Prussia to the Caucasus, and closed the Dardanelles to Entente shipping, hitherto the most important and direct route to Russia. The partially completed Thessaloniki–Niš–Prahovo rail line now became the most direct route for the Entente to ship supplies to Russia during winter months. Turkey's entry into the war also increased Bulgaria's strategic importance. Russia wished to bring

Bulgaria into the war on the side of the Entente, both to relieve the potential danger to Serbia's southeast flank, and to place pressure on Turkey. Yet, the price of Bulgarian alliance would require that Serbia surrender substantial portions of Macedonia to Bulgaria.

The Turkish entry into the war also had repercussions for the Balkans, especially those areas with large Islamic populations, such as Bosnia-Herzegovina, Kosovo, Macedonia, and Sandžak. The Sultan, who was also Caliph of all Muslims, published a Fatwa. At Friday prayers on December 11 in Sarajevo's main mosque, the Begova džamija, the Reis-ul-Ulema, Džemaludin Efendi Ćaušević, in the company of all the Muftis from Bosnia-Herzegovina, read the Sultan's Fatwa in Turkish, then a version translated into Croatian. The Fatwa called on all Muslims to fight together with Austria-Hungary and Germany, and referred to the war taking place as *Jihad* (holy war). In an effort to solidify pro-Habsburg, anti-Serb fervor among Bosnia-Herzegovina's Muslim population, German and Croat papers printed articles about Turkey's efforts under the heading "Holy War."[53] Sarajevo's newspapers called on all Muslims, without regard to age or social status, to enter into "war against those who are marked as enemies of Islam."[54]

In response to Russian pressure to reach a settlement with Bulgaria, in mid-August Pašić had offered to give Bulgaria all of Macedonia east of the Bregalnica River, provided Bulgaria maintained good relations with Serbia until the end of the war, and provided Serbia received compensation of Austro-Hungarian territories "settled by Serbo-Croats" that included coastal territory.[55] Serbia stated it would do anything the Entente asked of it, provided the other signatories of the Treaty of Bucharest made similar sacrifices. Pašić also demanded any discussions of realigning the borders in Macedonia be kept secret, or they would cause the fall of his government.[56] In spite of continued Entente pressure on Serbia to make territorial concessions to Bulgaria, Sofia refused to join the Entente unless it received the contested areas of Macedonia prior to joining.

Throughout the fall, tension between Serbia and Bulgaria increased. The President of Bulgaria's government, Radoslavov, was convinced the Triple Alliance would win the war and was rumored to have signed a secret agreement with Austria-Hungary and Germany in which Bulgaria would attack Macedonia.[57] Bulgarian-sponsored *komite* continued to conduct disruptive guerilla raids inside Macedonia and destroyed key bridges, tunnels, and other sections of Serbia's vital rail link with Thessaloniki, while the Bulgarian press mounted an anti-Serbian campaign, justifying the *komite* raids. Bulgaria's behavior became so threatening that at the end of October Pašić brought it to the attention of the Entente, stating that if the behavior continued, it could lead to Serbian military action.[58]

On October 30, Pašić used Turkey's entry into the war to suggest Bulgaria find territorial compensation at Turkish expense: the Greek and Romanian governments did likewise. All of Bulgaria's neighbors hoped Sofia would gain satisfaction from Turkish territory, and thereby bring an end to their disagreements with Bulgaria. Russia also pressured Bulgaria to join the Entente and attack Turkey. Although Radoslavov declined, he promised Bulgaria would remain strictly neutral and not attack Serbia.[59]

In early November, Russia began serious discussions with Sofia about specific demands for Bulgarian entry into the war on the side of the Entente. These discussions proved fruitless and aggravating. Serbia continued to insist on its position of August 21: that it would give Bulgaria eastern Macedonia up to the Bregalnica River, provided Bulgaria remained neutral and maintained good relations with Serbia until the war's end. Even then, Serbian transfer of Macedonian territory was contingent upon Serbia receiving Habsburg lands in a final peace settlement.

Unknown to the Entente, Bulgaria was already firmly entrenched in the Triple Alliance's camp. It continued negotiations about a possible pact with the Entente primarily out of fear that its other Balkan neighbors—Greece, Romania, and Serbia—would use this as an excuse to dismember Bulgaria.[60]

As the autumn wore on, Serbia's international position remained uncertain. Although Romania now appeared more inclined to entertain Entente overtures and Greece continued to maintain cordial neutrality, Bulgaria remained as threatening as ever. Turkey's entry into the war meant Russian troops would be distracted from the Carpathians and Prussia, possibly freeing additional Austro-Hungarian troops for the Balkan Front. Also of great concern, Serbia's allies were shutting it out of discussions with Italy, in which predominantly Slav lands were being offered as an incentive to bring Italy into the war on the side of the Entente.

The Second Army's withdrawal from Mačva

Charged with defending a front that stretched from Loznica to Obrenovac, Stepa Stepanović's Second Army was stretched thin. The flat Mačva region offered little natural cover from Austro-Hungarian artillery fire, and Stepanović's casualties were high. To worsen matters, the Second Army faced not only the Austro-Hungarian Fifth Army, but also General Krauss' Combined Corps. Throughout the second half of September and all of October, the Second Army endured an unremitting artillery bombardment, against which it lacked sufficient shells to answer. As early as September 24, Stepa warned the High Command of the difficulties he faced in holding the flat, marshy Mačva Peninsula. Yet in spite of the artillery bombardment and Austro-Hungarian superiority, the Second Army managed to contain the Fifth Army to its small bridgehead at Pričinović.

The situation changed suddenly on October 22, when Potiorek received an erroneous intelligence report that Russia was sending 35,000 soldiers up the Danube to aid Serbia. Feeling an urgent need to act before the arrival of Russian reinforcements, Potiorek decided to immediately launch a new offensive.[61] On the afternoon of October 24, the Fifth Army attacked the Serbian Second Army near Parašnica, where it broke the Ravnje Detachment's front and forced Morava I to withdraw a short distance. Expecting reinforcements, the commander of the Ravnje Detachment launched a counterattack the next day, which was beaten back by heavy artillery fire.

Now running critically low on ammunition, Stepanović informed the High Command that each howitzer battery had only seventy-two shells per cannon, and that each field artillery battery had approximately 255 shells per cannon.[62] On October 26, the Fifth Army continued its attack near Radenković, but was repulsed with heavy losses. The attacks continued on October 27 with an artillery barrage that demolished the Serbian forward trenches.[63] The Habsburg bombardment was so fierce that the commander of Morava I reported men going crazy from the shelling.[64] Lacking sufficient artillery ammunition, and facing an enemy force twice the size of his own, Stepanović tried to shorten his lines. Lacking sufficient troops and artillery to defend the entire line, Stepa ordered the Army to withdraw a short distance on October 27.[65]

The inability to respond to the overwhelming Austro-Hungarian artillery bombardments finally took its toll on Stepanović. Unable to watch his troops slaughtered by the incessant Habsburg artillery while Serbian batteries sat silent, Stepanović sent his resignation to the High Command:

> All my petitions up until now about the dangerous situation, due to a lack of artillery ammunition, as well as requests that howitzers be sent to me, have not had any success, even though some of these were an expression of despair. I have not received howitzer batteries, and little or no artillery ammunition has been sent to me. Currently, the situation is like this: the opponent, with more powerful artillery, destroys trenches and buries soldiers, people die, and I don't have reserves to replace the losses, nor have I the necessary ammunition to conduct a battle and lessen the losses ... Because of this situation, the daily worries for artillery ammunition have spent me and broken my strength, so that I feel completely powerless and incapable to further command the Army. Therefore, I request that I be immediately released from this duty. It is in the general interest that you send me a replacement as quickly as possible.[66]

Alarmed by this development, Putnik—who was himself nearly paralyzed by emphysema—immediately placed a telephone call to Stepanović. Putnik initially thought Stepa was tendering his resignation because he had lost the Parašnica region. When Putnik found out the real reason—artillery ammunition shortages—he upbraided Stepanović: "this is terrible what you have done." Stepa's conversation with Putnik was heated, and—according to Stepa's own record—laced with profanity. During the course of the conversation, Putnik asked Stepa whom he wanted as his replacement, and told him that the High Command would send all the artillery ammunition it had: unfortunately, Serbia lacked sufficient artillery ammunition for its army. Toward the end of the conversation, Putnik said: "if we don't have artillery ammunition, we will resist with rifles." He then said "courage friend, courage!," to which Stepa replied: "I have never lacked courage; just give me the means for battle." Stepanović then withdrew his resignation.[67]

On October 28, Stepanović asked the High Command about the possibility of withdrawing the Second Army to more defensible positions and received tentative approval.[68] Meeting with his divisional commanders on October 29, they reached the conclusion that the Second Army could no longer defend its present line in the face of continuing artillery bombardments. On October 30, Stepanović decided to abandon the Mačva Peninsula and withdraw the Second Army to Mount Cer.[69] Stepa informed the High Command of his decision, stated that the lack of artillery ammunition was the primary reason for the withdrawal, and added that the morale of the second and third levy troops in the Ravnje Detachment was at low levels, following outbreaks of madness caused by unceasing artillery bombardment. Putnik approved the withdrawal, but informed Stepa that the new line must be held, and that "it cannot even be thought to withdraw from that line."[70]

The Second Army withdrew on the night of October 30 to a new defensive line, running roughly from Mišar on the southeast outskirts of Šabac, to Lešnica in the west. During the withdrawal, the NCOs in the Parašnica and Ravanica Detachments lost control over their men and the troops fled in complete disarray. The Second Army's withdrawal was complicated by the many refugees clogging the main roads. One soldier recorded: "children wail and mothers become upset. Mothers carry their children who are still nursing at the breast."[71] The sight of thousands of women, children, and old men suffering by the roadside further worsened the morale of the withdrawing Serbian forces. Another soldier noted: "women and children wail and run after us because they fear the bestiality of the Austrian soldiers." At the sound of incoming artillery shells, the refugees would scream hysterically, further unnerving the soldiers.[72] Unseasonably warm and dry weather, dry roads, and a bright moon, which made it possible to see at night "as at day," only slightly lessened the plight of the refugees. In contrast to the refugee-choked roads, the villages and towns of Mačva were completely deserted.[73]

The Second Army's new defensive line—some 40 kilometers shorter than the previous line—was anchored by Mount Cer on its left wing. The Second Army deployed its forces with Timok II on the left, Morava I in the center, and Timok I on the right. Timok II's position on the left wing was especially crucial: it was centered on the hilltop of Vidojevica, and was vital to maintaining links between the Second and Third Armies. Knowing that further withdrawal was not an option, the Second Army dug in and awaited the next Austro-Hungarian attack. As the Second Army withdrew, desertion became pronounced: on November 1, over 400 men disappeared from Šumadija I's 10th Regiment.[74]

On to Valjevo

Having pushed the Serbian Second Army out of Mačva, Potiorek now decided to mount a general offensive with all his forces, scheduled for November 6. Now, for the first time since the war began, all the Austro-Hungarian Balkan Armies would make a simultaneous, coordinated attack. At the beginning of November, *Balkanstreitkräfte* consisted of 276 battalions and thirty-two cavalry squadrons, totaling 285,000 men and 600 cannon. The Serbian operational army consisted of 142 under-strength battalions and thirty-nine cavalry squadrons, totaling barely 200,000 men and 298 cannon.[75] The men were underfed, under-equipped, partially clothed, and the artillery had largely run out of ammunition.

According to Potiorek's plan, the Fifth Army—comprised of von Scheuchenstuel's VIII Corps and Krauss' Combined Corps—would push south from Šabac toward Valjevo and encircle the Serbian Second Army's right wing. From the south, Wurm's XVI Corps would drive northeast toward Valjevo via Krupanj and Pecka and encircle the Serbian First Army's left wing. The remainder of the Fifth and Sixth Armies—von Rhemen's XIII and von Appel's XV Corps—would mount frontal attacks on the Serbian Third Army. If the offensive succeeded, the Austro-Hungarian pincers would meet near Valjevo and encircle the Serbian Second and Third Armies in the Jadar valley and Mačva.

The November 6 offensive began with a two-hour artillery bombardment, said to be the heaviest thus far. The ammunition shortage meant the Serbian artillery was unable to answer even "to every hundredth shell."[76] In the north, the Second Army beat back all Austro-Hungarian assaults. To the south, the Third and First Armies repelled most of the Habsburg assaults in heavy hand-to-hand fighting, yet at heavy cost: the Third Army's Combined Division lost 1,126 men during the day, while Drina I lost 1,173 men. By late afternoon, heavy losses forced the Combined Division to withdraw from its positions on Gučevo across the Štira River. In spite of heavy losses, Drina I held its positions. Farther south, the XV Corps overran the forward positions of Danube I and Morava II, forcing both to withdraw.

Drina I spent the next day, November 7, beating off Austro-Hungarian assaults. By evening the division had lost over 1,000 men and withdrew from its positions, forcing other units of the Third Army to follow to avoid being outflanked. Farther south, the XVI Corps—now returned from repelling the Užice Army in Bosnia—pushed the First Army's overwhelmed Ljubovija Detachment back toward Pecka, threatening to drive a wedge between the First Army and the Užice Army and turn the First Army's flank.

The withdrawal of Drina I and the Combined Division from Gučevo exposed the Second Army's left flank to the Austro-Hungarian forces entering the Jadar valley. Even though the Second Army held its positions for a second day, the Third Army's withdrawal forced the Second Army's Timok II to abandon Vidojevica, leaving Cer and the Jadar valley wide open. The reasons for Timok II's withdrawal from Vidojevica were not apparent to the Serbian troops. Rumors swept the Second Army that Timok II had fled without a fight—that the Austro-Hungarian Army considered Timok II an easy opponent and chose to attack it, knowing it would collapse.[77]

The Serbian Army's morale was wavering, and desertions—especially among troops from the Drina divisional region—increased sharply. As the front collapsed, the city of Valjevo experienced problems with deserters. The High Command alerted military officials throughout the region to be on the lookout for deserters, and the chief of the Valjevo military station was instructed to examine the orders of all soldiers who presented themselves for bread rations.[78] At this time King Petar approached *Vojvoda* Putnik, telling him of his desire to visit the front on November 9 and 10. Putnik told the King: "You can't go to the front, your highness . . . because there you will hear that the soldiers curse you, Pašić, and me."[79]

A separate peace

Exasperated by the lack of artillery ammunition, clothing, and other equipment, Putnik sent a letter to Military Minister Stefanović on November 7 in which he reported:

> An ugly perspective for the future is foreseen, due entirely to the shortage in artillery ammunition, which becomes more burdensome and unbearable each day. The enemy is equipped with a great superiority in artillery and artillery ammunition. It can be confidently said, that in regard to the great persistence and praiseworthy sacrifices of our officers, under-officers, and enlisted men, we would not have had to leave even one position, if only we had sufficient ammunition.[80]

Not only were the rank and file becoming demoralized, so too was Serbia's highest military leader.

As the Austro-Hungarian assault continued unabated, on November 8 Crown Prince Aleksandar Karađorđević presided at a joint meeting of the Serbian government's Council of Ministers and the High Command in Valjevo. Pašić had called the meeting at Putnik's insistence, to allow Putnik to explain the gravity of Serbia's position. A desperate Putnik spoke to Pašić, the Crown Prince, and the assembled Ministers in somber tones, telling them the Second Army had been forced to withdraw from Mačva due to the lack of artillery ammunition. He also made it clear that the First and Third

Armies had withdrawn from Gučevo and Boranja the previous day because "[t]hey were unable to further withstand the rain of shells, mortars, and large cannon, which the Austro-Hungarian army possesses in abundance, and ours answer only to every hundredth shell."[81]

Putnik said all the army's divisions were at or below half strength, and they had lost 40–60 percent of the NCOs. Snow would begin to fall any day and the Serbian soldiers wore only rags. The months-long fighting had destroyed the morale and fighting spirit of the soldiers, who had had no opportunity for leave or rest. The situation was so bad that Putnik envisioned withdrawing from Valjevo and abandoning Belgrade as soon as Potiorek's forces renewed their offensive.

Putnik told the assembled officials that all prior High Command efforts at intervening with the government and Serbia's allies had been in vain. Putnik then dropped a bombshell and suggested they either seek a separate peace with Austria-Hungary or surrender:

> The opportunities of the army for resistance are few, and the final result of the development of events under these circumstances could only be either a separate peace with Austria-Hungary, or a cessation of defense, since we don't have any ammunition.[82]

Faced with the option of a separate peace or surrender, the government ministers declared they would continue the struggle until they ran out of resources. Pašić promised the government would spare no effort to get ammunition and supplies from the Entente.[83]

The government—which had evidently been unaware of the severity of the ammunition and matériel problem—immediately began a flurry of diplomatic activity designed to garner matériel support from the Entente. Pašić told his Ministers in Petrograd, London, and Paris to warn the allies of Serbia's impending collapse, and to remind them that if Serbia fell, two Austro-Hungarian Armies consisting of seven battle-hardened Corps would be freed for duty on other fronts. Pašić also sent out a gloomy government circular in which he predicted the fall of Serbia and forecast a situation worse than that of 1813, when Russia withdrew its troops from Serbia and left it open to Ottoman reoccupation. Pašić said: "If in the shortest time we don't receive field artillery and howitzer ammunition, then there will come an unavoidable catastrophe for the entire army and for Serbia."[84]

In response, on November 12, a concerned French government ordered the Schneider factory to immediately send Serbia 20,000 shells for field artillery and 10,000 shells for mountain guns—requisitioned from a shipment intended for Mexico. That same day, a boat sailed from Marseilles carrying some 500 shells and 10,000 fuses, all from an earlier order. The High Command informed Pašić the number was far too small.[85] Russia also tried to send shells, but was hampered by the supply situation: neither Bulgaria nor Romania would allow Russian military equipment to transit their territory via train. Therefore, all supplies had to travel from Odessa to the Danube. On the Danube, they traveled by barge to the Serbian port of Prahovo, where they were loaded on narrow-gauge trains. After Turkey entered the war, its Black Sea fleet gunboats posed a threat to the Russian supply convoys.

The army hemorrhages

On the night of November 9/10, Putnik ordered the battered Serbian Army to pull back to defensive positions around Valjevo. On November 10, the Austro-Hungarian forces continued their offensive. Under heavy attack, the Serbian First and Third Armies began to waver. The large number of refugees, the incessant bombardment, and deteriorating weather demoralized Serbia's troops even further. Lieutenant Ćurović of the Morava I Division recorded:

> The withdrawal of our troops is having a bad effect on the morale of the soldiers. We all know we have no artillery ammunition, and we know that every position is temporary, and that an order for withdrawal will come quickly. Exhaustion is great among us all, because we march by night and fortify positions by day.[86]

As morale fell and desertions increased, the exhausted Serbian Army continued its withdrawal toward Valjevo. The Third Army's was the most difficult, because it "was completed through the territory from which its troops were drawn [recruited], and which was now falling into enemy hands." As the troops withdrew from their home regions, the temptation to leave the ranks and protect their families grew.[87] Many units now withdrew without orders, merely following other withdrawing units. Confusion and chaos were rampant. Those who refused to withdraw without orders were ridiculed by withdrawing troops who called out: "What are you waiting for? Why aren't you moving?"[88]

Valjevo was now jammed with over 100,000 refugees. The High Command gathered five divisions near the city in a vain effort to launch a counter-offensive. Živko Pavlović, Chief of the Operational Section of the High Command, said that they failed "to implement this idea due to the fallen and wavering state of morale among our troops, because of the extreme shortage of clothing, footwear, and shelter, the enormous shortages of artillery ammunition, and the constant deterioration of the First Army."[89]

Facing impending encirclement by the Austro-Hungarian Fifth and Sixth Armies, lacking artillery ammunition, a strong natural defensive position, and with his army suffering from low morale and desertion, on November 11 Putnik ordered all Armies to prepare to withdraw across the Kolubara and Ljig rivers, roughly 25–30 kilometers east of Valjevo. He ordered that in their wake they destroy all train tracks, roads, bridges, telegraph and telephone lines. All livestock and food was to be driven off or requisitioned, so as to deny it to the Austro-Hungarian troops.[90] Putnik ordered the Serbian Army to establish a new defensive line on the right banks of the Kolubara and Ljig rivers, and the slopes of two mountains: Suvobor and Maljen. According to Putnik's instructions, the Second Army was to act as a base for the withdrawal of the First and Third Armies: only after the other two Armies withdrew was Stepanović's Second Army to withdraw behind the Kolubara.[91]

On November 12, a strong, cold wind began blowing. By the next morning, snow and cold rain fell throughout much of western Serbia. The snow melted rapidly, turning roads and paths to a sea of mud.[92] That same day, in a letter that made clear reference to the army's pressing manpower needs, General Mišić ordered all divisional and regional commanders to take the "severest measures" to deal with deserters.[93] The extent of the problem became apparent when the chief of the Army's Transportation Section told the High Command it was impossible for the railway inspectors to arrest the soldiers deserting their units and returning home, due to their large numbers and the fact that many were armed. To complicate matters, during their travels these soldiers would loot entire villages in the rear. The chief of the Transportation Section asked the High Command to assign soldiers and officers to guard the roads leading to and from the front lines, as well as the railway stations, and labeled the desertion situation a "catastrophe."[94]

During the sixteen-day period between October 28 and November 13, the Serbian Army lost 63,017 men, as many as half of whom may have deserted.[95] A great many of the deserters were taking their rifles home with them at a time when the Serbian Army lacked sufficient weapons to arm its front-line troops.[96] The seriousness of the desertion undoubtedly contributed to Putnik's suggestions at the November 8 joint meeting of the High Command and the Council of Ministers that Serbia seek a separate peace with Austria-Hungary.[97]

On November 14, General Živojin Mišić, Putnik's aide-de-camp, replaced the incapacitated Petar Bojović as commander of the First Army. Bojović had been wounded in early September during the invasion of Srem, and his wound had failed to heal: he had spent the last twenty days in bed, and by early November could no longer command his troops. That same day, von Frank's rapidly advancing Fifth Army took Obrenovac and a bridge over the Tamnava River, causing confusion on the Second Army's right wing. Stepanović heard rumors that the Third Army's right wing was withdrawing and called Putnik to ask for instructions. Putnik told Stepa that the Third Army had not yet withdrawn, and that Stepa should coordinate his withdrawal with Jurišić-Šturm. An angry Stepanović—fearing his right wing would be exposed if he waited—insisted they had nothing to agree upon, and that the order for cooperation should come from the High Command. In response, Putnik simply said "good-bye" and hung up the receiver.[98]

With his right flank exposed near Obrenovac, and under the erroneous impression that the Third Army had withdrawn leaving his left flank open, Stepa withdrew the entire Second Army toward the Kolubara. Initially, Stepa feared the Habsburg forces would trap the Second Army in the Kolubara valley: high waters had flooded most of the valley and the bridges, leaving only the Ub–Lajkovac–Lazarevac–Aranđelovac road open. The Second Army was, however, able to withdraw safely across the Kolubara on the night of November 14/15.[99]

Stepanović's uncoordinated and early withdrawal left the Third Army's right flank exposed to the west of Valjevo, and forced the First and Third Armies to withdraw in haste and disorder. The Austro-Hungarian forces failed to detect the gap created by the Second Army's withdrawal, and both the First and Third Armies escaped. As the First Army withdrew in mid-November, it battled cold weather, mountainous terrain, and poor or non-existent roads. The troops were cold, hungry, and lacked rifle and artillery ammunition. Colonel Živko Pavlović, Putnik's new aide-de-camp on the High Command, noted:

> The consequences of this were terrible: individuals, and even entire units intentionally absented themselves and gave up without resistance to the enemy. Discarding weapons, protests and self-mutilation, especially among the troops of the Danube II Division, became more frequent. In the rear of the army were seen a mass of soldiers with the refugees.[100]

Fortunately for Serbia, Potiorek's Sixth Army did not comprehend the seriousness of Serbia's situation or take advantage of it. Rather, it took a three-day rest to regroup and replenish, allowing the Serbian First Army to withdraw unscathed.

By now, entire battalions and regiments were deserting *en masse*. On November 14, *Vojvoda* Putnik wrote Military Minister Stefanović:

> In the latter period there has begun a blatant separation of soldiers from their commands and a return to their homes. Police and local officials do not have sufficient strength to capture these deserters and return them to their commands. I ask . . . that the police authorities undertake and use all, even the ultimate measures, to find the deserters and return them to their commands.[101]

That same day, the commander of the Timok divisional region complained to the High Command of insufficient police to apprehend deserters: many police stations had only one gendarme on duty—usually physically unfit for military service.[102] Serbia had 4,331 gendarmes, of whom 3,429 were assigned to the new regions, where they were charged with bringing order to the semi-anarchic situation that had existed in Macedonia during the last decades of Ottoman rule, as well as dealing with local rebellions and cross-border raids by Albanian and Bulgarian *komite*. Of the remaining 902 gendarmes, 252 were in Belgrade, and an additional fifty were on duty at the royal court. This left only 600 gendarmes to police all of old Serbia.[103]

As withdrawing troops mingled with fleeing refugees along the muddy roads and crowded bridges, they created chaos and confusion, and many became lost. Of increasing concern was the effect the refugees had on the morale of the soldiers, particularly the troops of Drina I and Drina II, when they saw mothers "leave their children at the side of the road and flee, unable to carry them further."[104] In spite of the problems and general confusion associated with the pull-back, the Serbian forces withdrew without incurring casualties from the Austro-Hungarian forces. Some units, such as Šumadija I, even withdrew in good order, with drums and bugles playing.[105] Nonetheless, when taken as a whole, the Serbian Army was in a desperate state.

As the Habsburgs advanced, entire villages—fearing imminent enemy occupation and atrocities—began to evacuate, often on the basis of rumors spread by deserters. This created further disease, starvation, and death for many peasants and hindered the movement of the Serbian Army. Pašić wrote Putnik that entire villages moved without adequate food or shelter, and that small children died by the wayside due to the extreme conditions.[106] One soldier repeatedly wrote in his diary of "refugees, refugees. The horrible pictures of war."[107] The Serbian government and private relief organizations were over-extended and unable to assist with food or shelter.

As morale deteriorated, the army hemorrhaged. On November 16, while driving to his new post as commander of the First Army, General Mišić saw large numbers of armed soldiers walking home across the fields in the Army's rear area en route to Kragujevac.[108] Third Army commander General Jurišić-Šturm reported that two-thirds (approximately 400 men) of the 4th battalion, 17th Regiment (Užice) of the Drina I Division deserted. The soldiers simply donned peasant clothes, dropped their weapons and left.[109] The breakdown in order affected the troops who remained: during the withdrawal from Valjevo across the Kolubara River, the Timok I Division plundered the town of Lazarevac.[110] That same day, the chief of the Mladenovac train station arrested 120 deserters, including a lieutenant from the 16th Regiment (Bitolj), first levy.[111]

Slowed by the poor weather and muddy roads, the Austro-Hungarian forces failed to keep pace with the withdrawing Serbian forces, and the Serbian Army escaped intact across the Ljig and Kolubara rivers. On November 16, von Appel's XV Corps entered the abandoned city of Valjevo. The same day, advance units of von Frank's Fifth Army reached the Kolubara River.

CHAPTER NINE

The Battle on the Kolubara

Doš'o Švaba sve do Ralje,
A od Ralje nikud dalje;
Doš'o Švaba sve do Ljiga,
A kod Ljiga zaglibi ga.

The Schwabie came all the way to Ralja,
But didn't go any further;
The Schwabie came all the way to Ljig,
And at Ljig he got stuck.

—SERBIAN POPULAR SONG

The eve of battle

As the victorious *Balkanstreitkräfte* entered Valjevo, Potiorek gave the weary Sixth Army a much needed three-day rest, and with good reason. *Balkanstreitkräfte* had lost almost 130,000 men since early September and now needed reinforcements and supplies. Incessant rains and snow transformed the roads of Mačva and the Jadar valley into a muddy quagmire, exacerbating the Army's supply. By November 14, mud made the road from Ub to Valjevo impassable by horse. Other roads were so bad that the VIII, XIII, and Combined Corps relied on a single road from Šabac for all their supplies. To the south, the Sixth Army's operational area lacked a single passable road. Just as victory seemed at hand, a supply shortage loomed.

The Kolubara River, normally an oversized stream, became a raging torrent that flooded the land along both sides.[1] To further aggravate matters, the retreating Serbian Army had taken all livestock and food with it. If the

Habsburg Fifth Army pressed across the Kolubara, it would capture the rail line running south from Obrenovac along the Kolubara river valley to Valjevo, thus ensuring a direct rail link to the Sava River.[2]

Hearing of the disarray and confusion in the Serbian Army, and under the impression it was routed and in headlong retreat toward Kragujevac and Aranđelovac, Potiorek cancelled the rest for the Fifth Army and ordered it and von Rhemen's XIII Corps (newly transferred to Potiorek's Sixth Army) to pursue the Serbian forces and take the heights east of the Kolubara. Austro-Hungarian intelligence reported that only rearguard units stood between Potiorek and Belgrade. Potiorek anticipated capturing Belgrade within days—hopefully by December 3, the sixty-sixth anniversary of Emperor Franz Joseph's ascension to the throne.

As Serbia's army crumbled, Germany's *OberKommando* pressured Potiorek to quickly seize northern Serbia to assure river transport between the Triple Alliance and its Balkan allies, Turkey and Bulgaria. The *OberKommando* also wanted Potiorek to quickly seize the eastern mining regions of Bor and Majdanpek.[3] Confident of a quick and final victory, Potiorek pushed his weary troops forward.

So sure was Potiorek of success that on November 17 he spoke with Generals Korbatin and Marterer about establishing an administration following Serbia's capitulation. This discussion included which parts of Serbia and Montenegro to permanently annex to the Empire. Potiorek wanted all of Mačva, and the regions along the Sava, Danube, and Drina rivers. Macedonia would be given to Bulgaria, and Romania would receive the Timok river valley. An Austrian general would administer the Croatian lands, and the Austrian and Hungarian administrative sections of the Empire would evenly split Bosnia-Herzegovina. In keeping with its pre-war southward expansion plans, the Dual Monarchy would also occupy the Sandžak as far south as Mitrovica in Kosovo.

Yet all was not as Potiorek hoped. On November 16, while advancing slowly through mud, rain, snow, and floods, the Fifth Army's lead cavalry and infantry units encountered strong Serbian resistance on the east bank of the Kolubara River. Potiorek initially disbelieved the officers who reported the Serbian Army had dug in, thinking the Fifth Army faced only rearguard units, and bad weather and flooding prevented the capture of the rail line. Yet Potiorek's officers were correct. The battered and exhausted Serbian Army was not in full retreat. Rather, it had dug in along the right banks of the Kolubara and Ljig rivers, and was offering fierce resistance.

What became known as the Battle on the Kolubara (November 16 to December 15) was fought over a wide geographic area that encompassed the area bordered by the Danube and Sava rivers on the north, the Kolubara River on the west, the Western Morava on the south, and the Great Morava on the east. Most of the battlefield was filled by the heavily forested Rudnik mountain range, where the peaks of Maljen and Suvobor on the western end formed an east–west barrier between the Kolubara and Western Morava valleys. To the north of Rudnik, the peaks of Venčac, Bukulja, Kosmaj, and Avala formed a barrier between the Danube, Sava, Kolubara, and Greater Morava rivers. This mountain chain was approximately 50–60 kilometers in depth and lacked good roads. It separated the Mačva plain and Kolubara river basin from the Western Morava and Great Morava watersheds. This natural barrier was enhanced by the Kolubara and Ljig rivers forming natural moats on its western slopes.

"Once more into the breach . . ."

Putnik—with the help of his new aide-de-camp Colonel Živko Pavlović—established a defensive line along an arc that ran south from Obrenovac along the right bank of the Kolubara and Ljig rivers. The terrain worked in Serbia's favor.

Near Mount Rudnik at the town of Ljig, the line departed from the Ljig River, turned west and followed the northern mountain slopes of Suvobor and Maljen. The Kolubara had several channels along its length and followed a relatively broad and marshy, meandering flood plain. The rains and melting snows in the mountains had caused the Kolubara to reach flood stage; much of the Kolubara valley from its mouth at the Sava, to its confluence with the Ljig, was underwater and many bridges were awash. Serbian destruction of the remaining bridges channeled the Austro-Hungarian troops to a series of well-known fords and into defensive corridors. The right bank of the Kolubara and Ljig rivers was higher than the left bank, giving Serbian troops the additional advantage of high ground.

The Sixth Army would be forced to advance uphill on the northern mountain slopes of Maljen, Suvobor, and Rudnik, through heavily wooded terrain. The few roads were usually impassable during winter. Only Habsburg units with trained mountain formations—such as the XV and XVI Corps—would be able to advance effectively. The terrain would also diminish the Habsburg advantage in artillery and shorten the Serbian Army's front to 200 kilometers.

On the Serbian Army's right flank, General Mihailo Živković's Defense of Belgrade numbered some 19,000 men and forty-seven cannon and was deployed along the Sava and Danube, from the mouth of the Kolubara to Grocka, east of Belgrade.[4] On the right wing, the 4,500-man Obrenovac Detachment held a short stretch between the Sava and the Marica stream, just east of Obrenovac. Stepanović's Second Army (Morava I, Timok I, Šumadija I, and the Cavalry Division) numbered 67,000 officers and men, and 138 cannon. It stretched southward from the Marica stream in the north to a small village on the Ljig, just south of the confluence of the Ljig and Kolubara rivers.

In the center, Jurišić-Šturm's Third Army (Drina II, Timok II, and the Combined Division) numbered 53,000 officers and men, and eighty cannon.

It defended the Ljig from the base of Mount Rudnik to the village of Moravci.[5]

On the Serbian left wing, Živojin Mišić's First Army (Danube I, Danube II, Drina I, Morava II, and the Maljen Detachment) numbered 44,000 men and eighty cannon, and deployed along the northern slopes of Suvobor and Maljen. On the army's left flank, the Užice Army (Morava II and various small detachments) had 25,000 men and officers, and fifty-five cannon to defend the Drina from Užice to Kadinjača. Although this line offered strong natural defenses, there was a gap between the First Army and the Užice Army. Because the Austro-Hungarian forces responsible for this sector of the front were taking a three-day rest, they did not attempt to exploit this hole.

By now, the Serbian Army numbered approximately 215,000 demoralized men—a number rapidly diminishing due to desertion—and 400 cannon, most of which lacked ammunition.[6] This meant Serbia had only one soldier to defend every meter of front. There was no strategic reserve: reinforcements could come only by pulling troops from elsewhere on the line. This forced Putnik to rely on quick, reliable evaluations of the situation and make rapid decisions.[7] Serbia's High Command had another concern: the Austro-Hungarians always seemed to know of Serbian movements in advance.[8]

From the standpoint of natural defenses, the weakest point on the defensive line was Čovka, a hilly formation in a bend at the confluence of the Ljig and Kolubara rivers. There were two fords in the immediate vicinity of Čovka (Bedi Brod and Dabin Brod), and it was a logical point for an Austro-Hungarian attack. Putnik ordered Stepanović "that Čovka must be held at all costs."[9]

Mišić's First Army—now dug in on Maljen and Suvobor—was in dire straits. During its withdrawal from Valjevo in a series of night marches, many of its units became lost, or simply melted away. The rapidly disappearing Drina I had been reduced to approximately 5,500 men, of which only the 6th Regiment was considered reliable; most of the 5th Regiment had deserted, and the 3rd Supernumerary Regiment had only 680 soldiers. The Second Army, where one officer said the "morale is falling all the more," was only slightly better off, with Morava I facing the worst discipline problems.[10]

In Jurišić-Šturm's Third Army, Drina II had less than half its strength—5,500 men—and its soldiers despised their newly issued Russian Mosin rifles. The only reliable unit in the Division was the 3rd Regiment; even officers were deserting in the remainder of the Division. Only the Combined Division was considered somewhat reliable. However, it lacked sufficient rifles for its men, and many of its soldiers—fighting in the mountains during the second half of November—lacked shoes or boots, and wore only pants and shirts.[11]

To the Austro-Hungarians it appeared none of the Serbian soldiers wanted to fight. On the eve of the decisive encounter between an exhausted and disintegrating Serbian Army and a victorious, advancing Austro-Hungarian Army, the Serbian soldiers were throwing down their weapons and going home.

Facing the Serbian Army were von Frank's Fifth Army and Potiorek's Sixth Army. On the left wing, the Fifth Army's Combined (XVII) Corps—under the direction of the able General Alfred Krauss—consisted of the 7th and 29th *K.u.k.* Divisions, and the 104th *Landsturm* Brigade. The Combined Corps faced the Obrenovac Detachment and the Second Army's Šumadija I and Cavalry Division. To the Combined Corps' right was General von Scheuchenstuel's VIII Corps, facing the Second Army's Timok I and Morava I Divisions. It included the 9th *K.u.k.* Division and the 21st *Honved* Division. Von Frank's Fifth Army could field some 97,000 men in 127 battalions with approximately 200 cannon.

To the right of VIII Corps was Potiorek's Sixth Army, with General von Rhemen's XIII Corps, newly transferred from the Fifth Army, which consisted of the 36th *K.u.k.* Division and the 42nd *Honved* Division, and faced Jurišić-Šturm's weak Third Army along the Ljig. To the right, General von Appel's XV Corps faced the First Army's Danube I and Morava II Divisions. Its 1st and 48th *K.u.k.* Divisions consisted entirely of mountain brigades, while the 40th *Honved* Division was a regular infantry formation. Further right, General Wurm's XVI Corps faced Danube II on Maljen. This was an unusually heavy army corps, featuring the 18th, Combined, and 50th *K.u.k.* Divisions, each of which had in its formation four mountain brigades. Potiorek's Sixth Army had at its disposal a total of some 144,000 men in 160 battalions and 336 cannon.

Excluding garrison troops, the combined Fifth and Sixth Armies fielded operational forces of approximately 237,000 men with 600 cannon. Unlike the Serbian forces, the Habsburg troops did not appear to suffer from severe morale and desertion problems.[12] Importantly, they had artillery ammunition and more cannon.

After seizing Valjevo, Potiorek planned to take Maljen and Suvobor, penetrate between the Užice and First Armies, and enter the Western Morava valley. He would then take Užice and drive toward Kragujevac in the heart of Serbia. The terrain was formidable, but Potiorek considered the mountain troops of the XV and XVI Corps equal to the task. Simultaneously, the Fifth Army's Combined Corps would push toward Belgrade. Putnik's plan was defensive; he hoped to stabilize the front and the rapidly disintegrating army until new stocks of artillery ammunition arrived from France. If and when artillery ammunition arrived, the Serbian Army would go on the offensive.[13]

Across the Kolubara

After the initial encounter between the Fifth Army and Stepanović's Second Army, Habsburg forces spent the next several days probing the Second

Army's line and shelling its positions, while trying—unsuccessfully—to bridge the swollen Kolubara in the face of Serbian artillery fire.[14] As rain and snow continued to fall, skirmishes continued, with forward positions changing hands several times.

On the left wing, Mišić's First Army established positions along a 25-kilometer front on the northern slopes of Maljen and Suvobor. Mišić left only Danube II and the Maljen Detachment to hold the entire ridge, and his other Divisions (Morava II, Danube I, and Drina I) along the Valjevo–Mionica–Gornji Milanovac road, already well defended by Jurišić-Šturm's Third Army. This weakened and exposed the First Army's left flank. Putnik's aide-de-camp Živko Pavlović criticized this as "flawed, because it did not offer the conditions for persistent and long-lasting resistance."[15]

The mountainous terrain and lack of roads on Maljen and Suvobor meant that most movement occurred through forests, and along mountain trails and tracks, giving an advantage to mountain warfare units. The Serbian First Army had only seven mountain cannon when it left Valjevo; given the steep angles of fire in the mountains, regular field artillery was near useless. Poor roads meant food and ammunition supplies were dwindling quickly. On Maljen the snowfall was so heavy that some positions appeared threatened by the weather.

Desertion further sapped the First Army. Danube II commander General Miloš Vasić informed Mišić that on November 18 two battalions from his 8th Regiment had abandoned their positions, and that the town of Mionica

PHOTO 19 *Third levy troops on guard.*

was full of numerous first and second levy deserters waiting for Austro-Hungarian troops to arrive so they could surrender. Vasić told Mišić: "from everything, it appears that the troops, and unfortunately, even the officers, will not fight. The evil is so great that it is difficult to find a drug for it." The officers of one company, when ordered to occupy positions abandoned by the 8th Regiment, swore at the officer reading the order and fled with their troops.[16] Concerned about the desertion epidemic sweeping the army, Crown Prince Aleksandar issued a royal order on November 18 creating *Depovske Komande* to apprehend the large numbers of NCOs and enlisted deserters.[17]

The Užice Army, tasked with protecting the First Army's left flank, pulled back from Bajina Bašta on the Drina, and now defended a line in the mountains some 8 kilometers west of Užice, with only weak forces between its main body and the First Army. That same day Mišić—sensing weakness in Potiorek's Sixth Army—suggested to Putnik that the First Army launch an offensive. The High Command approved, but a lack of artillery ammunition combined with bad weather to prevent an assault.[18] By day's end, Danube II's 8th Regiment lost over 1,000 men, most of whom surrendered.[19]

Potiorek continued to receive reports that bolstered his impression the Serbian Army was in full flight. The Austro-Hungarian Minister in Sofia reported that only rearguard elements remained on the Kolubara to protect the withdrawal of the Serbian Army. Acting on this report, Potiorek ordered his troops to resume the offensive on November 22, and for the Fifth Army to advance toward Belgrade on November 23. However, after receiving reports of determined Serbian resistance along the Kolubara on November 18, Potiorek ordered the Fifth Army to begin its advance on November 19.[20]

On November 19, the assault began in earnest. The VIII Corps crossed the Kolubara under cover of a heavy artillery bombardment, and by day's end the 9th Division and 21st Divisions succeeded in establishing bridgeheads on the right bank of the Kolubara.[21]

To the south along the First Army's front, the XV and XVI Corps pushed Danube II up the northern slopes of Maljen. But Danube II faced a second threat; on the afternoon of November 19, Mišić reported to the High Command that bad weather had hit the Division hard: roads were covered in snow and mud; the troops—lacking tents or other shelter—were literally covered with snow and had little winter clothing. Impassable roads meant no food and ammunition at the front. Mišić told Putnik that Danube II's troops no longer obeyed their officers, and in some cases had actually threatened them with weapons.[22]

November 19 was a particularly bad day for desertion. Almost 400 armed soldiers of the 12th Regiment passed through the town of Slatina; in Paraćin, large numbers of armed soldiers wandered the town, shooting, throwing hand grenades, and causing havoc. One soldier threw a hand grenade that seriously wounded a woman and three other people. Paraćin's military commander—evidently unaware of the scope of desertion, and not knowing of the previous order to disarm all soldiers returning to the rear— requested that soldiers not be sent to the rear with weapons.[23] The High Command's Transportation Section informed the Operational Section of a large group of armed soldiers heading home near the town of Aranđelovac,[24] while Second Army commander Stepanović reported that between 8:00 and 9:00 am an entire company of the 11th Regiment was arrested at the Baroševac train station after becoming belligerent with the station commander.[25]

The next day the Maljen Detachment, which held the First Army's left flank, was dislodged from some of its positions.

Heavy fighting continued along the Second Army's front near Čovka, with Morava I and Timok I bearing the brunt. By day's end, the VIII Corps had widened its bridgehead and the Kolubara had flooded Morava I's forward trenches, forcing a withdrawal.[26] The Third Army's front was relatively quiet, as the Ljig's high waters prevented a crossing. On November 20, seven days after the first snowfall, a group of deserters arrested at a train station asked only that they be given bread, *opanci*, and shirts: they expressed regret at leaving their units and said they would gladly return to service, but they were returning home to get food and clothing.[27]

To strengthen Morava I's collapsing left wing, Putnik ordered the Third Army to take the offensive on November 21, assisted by the Second Army's Morava I. The offensive, however, sputtered; high water levels, the lack of bridging equipment, and a lack of artillery ammunition prevented the Third Army from moving. Putnik, however, insisted Stepanović attack as scheduled.[28] Timok II arrived at Morava I's rear area on November 21, its troops exhausted from a forced night march. During its march, it passed through Drina II, whose soldiers were deserting in droves. The large numbers of deserters caused one Serbian officer from Timok II to write: "We have no army!"[29] Timok II and Morava I overran the forward Austro-Hungarian trenches that afternoon. Further north along the Kolubara, the Second Army's Timok I, Šumadija I, and Cavalry Divisions repelled numerous Habsburg attacks.[30] Along the Ljig, XIII Corps attacked the Third Army in earnest, but high water, bad weather, and a stubborn defense prevented a crossing. To the west, the XV and XVI Corps attacked along the entire Maljen–Suvobor Front. As the day wore on, XVI Corps gradually pushed the First Army off Maljen.

For the Serbian High Command, the only bright note was that the bad weather and steep terrain affected the ability of the Habsburg forces to resupply their units around Maljen and Suvobor. Interrogations of Austro-Hungarian prisoners revealed that Serbia's soldiers weren't the only ones facing difficulties: many front-line soldiers in the XIII Corps had not eaten bread in two or three days, many were falling ill, and most of the units were under half strength. The weather and mud-choked roads were now beginning to affect Habsburg forces.[31]

The near constant fog along the First Army's mountainous front dampened Serb spirits, while allowing Habsburg forces to approach Serbian lines undetected and launch surprise attacks. Serbian soldiers were so demoralized that in many instances they simply broke and ran, even when attacked by much smaller units.[32]

And desertion continued. On November 20, 359 men from the 7th Regiment of the Danube II Division were apprehended: they claimed their commanding officer, Captain Kojić, had been poisoned and their battalion disbanded. Captain Kojić had in fact been killed in battle, and the men were all deserters.[33] That same day the commander of the Šumadija divisional region informed the High Command that he had found 300 men of the 12th Regiment between Slatina and Kraljevo; they claimed their entire regiment had deserted.[34] On November 22, two entire platoons deserted from the 1st Regiment, along with seventeen men and two NCOs from the regimental transportation section.[35]

The scale of the exodus became apparent in a letter Nikola Pašić wrote to Putnik on November 21. Pašić said, "their number is enormous," and noted that the problem had hit troops from the Kragujevac, Rudnik, Užice, Podrinje, Valjevo, and Belgrade regions. To halt the hemorrhage, the High Command issued various orders to all the divisional and regional commanders in the territory of Old Serbia. One of the first of these, dated November 22, established third levy Četnik units in the rear areas, whose sole purpose was to apprehend deserters. They were to escort all "lost" soldiers to the local military commander, who would return them to their units. The Četniks had authority to shoot and kill any deserters who attempted to escape. Civilian authorities that attempted to shield or conceal deserters would be arrested and judged as accomplices to desertion.[36] Referring directly to the "blatant voluntary separation of soldiers from operational units and away from the battlefield," General Mišić ordered the High Command's Transportation Section to guard all roads and railways, and to coordinate this with the local gendarmerie and Ministry of Internal Affairs. In the future any soldier leaving his unit had to carry a stamped pass, signed by his unit's senior NCO.[37] But these measures had little immediate effect.

On November 22, XV and XVI Corps continued pushing the First Army back up the northern slopes of Maljen and Suvobor. Lacking a strategic reserve, Putnik could only shift units around. Hoping to take advantage of Potiorek's distraction with the Sixth Army's offensive, Putnik ordered the Second, Third, and Užice Armies to prepare for a general offensive,[38] which he saw as the only possible solution to the rapidly disintegrating situation.[39] Yet neither the Second nor Third Army succeeded in completing preparations.

The Serbian Second Army's forces at Čovka were engaged in heavy fighting with the Fifth Army's VIII Corps along the Kolubara. In a telephone conversation with Živko Pavlović, Stepanović said the Austro-Hungarian attacks prevented preparation for an offensive: the Second Army could not launch an attack before noon the following day.[40] Following heavy fighting that same day, the Fifth Army pushed the Cavalry Division back to the heights overlooking the Kolubara, while the Third Army wavered under XIII Corps' attacks.

The next day, November 23, the Fifth and Sixth Armies continued the offensive. All Austro-Hungarian Army Corps launched simultaneous and coordinated attacks along the entire front.[41] Amidst falling rain and snow, heavy fighting broke out along the entire Kolubara–Ljig–Maljen Front, where attempts to dig trenches proved futile, as they quickly filled with mud and water.[42] In the mountains, snow blocked roads and turned streams into torrents. The mud and weather hampered both sides, and fires could not be lit for five days.[43] That morning under cover of fog, the XV and XVI Corps pressed their assault on the First Army's left wing, pushing the Maljen Detachment and Danube II off the Maljen summit. This threatened the Užice Army's rear and right flank and forced it to abandon the city of Užice.

To the north along the Kolubara, the Combined and VIII Corps pressed their attacks against Stepanović's Second Army. Near Obrenovac, the 104th *Landsturm* Brigade crossed the Kolubara with close artillery support from a river monitor on the Sava. Although able to establish a small bridgehead, the 104th failed to take the heights east of the Kolubara, and lost at least 400 men, who were taken prisoner by the Obrenovac Detachment.[44] The 29th Division pushed back the Cavalry Division from its defensive positions on the east bank of the Kolubara and established a bridgehead. Further south at Čovka, all VIII Corps attacks were repulsed.

As the situation on the Serbian First Army's front worsened, Putnik urged Stepanović to hasten preparations for the planned offensive, stating:

> In regard to the situation on the battlefield and the state of our troops in general, especially the state of the troops of the First Army, the only way out of this difficult situation is to cross onto a general offensive as soon as possible, otherwise it will be all too late.[45]

But the extreme shortage of artillery ammunition made any offensive unrealistic.

On November 24, both sides engaged in attacks and counterattacks along the entire line. When not defending against the unremitting Habsburg attacks, the Second and Third Armies tried to prepare for an offensive, while the First and Užice Armies fought off the advancing XVI Corps. On Maljen, the First Army's left wing faced new attacks, as the Maljen Detachment—now cut off from the main body of the First Army—withdrew down the mountain. On the First Army's left flank, the Užice Army withdrew to set up defensive positions around Čačak, almost 90 kilometers by road east of the Drina. In spite of the First Army's worsening situation, Austro-Hungarian prisoners disclosed that XVI Corps was short on food, and that many of its companies were reduced to 100 men. The constant fighting and supply problems were taking their toll on both sides.[46]

On the Second Army's front, the Habsburg Combined Corps dislodged the Cavalry Division from its main defensive line on the heights east of the Kolubara; the Cavalry Division commander refused to speak with Stepanović on the telephone, and kept moving his headquarters, so his brigades were unable to receive orders from Division Headquarters. The situation became so confused that Brigade commanders began calling Second Army headquarters for instructions, bypassing the divisional commander entirely.[47]

In the face of this onslaught, Putnik's desired offensive just couldn't seem to come together. Timok I complained that the mud was so deep that whenever a wagon or cannon left the road it immediately bogged down. It also complained it lacked bridging material to cross the Kolubara. It did report, however, that interrogations of Austro-Hungarian prisoners revealed they had not eaten bread for five days.[48] Šumadija I reported that much of the Kolubara valley was still underwater and that their infantry and artillery could not advance without taking heavy casualties; engineers needed another four to five days to repair the roads and bridges along the Division's front.[49] At Čovka, Morava I couldn't fortify its positions; water kept filling the trenches, and cases of frostbite among the enlisted men were now reaching 100 per day.[50]

On the evening of November 24, snow and rain began falling once again.

The Serbian collapse

On November 25, following one of the most concentrated and heavy artillery bombardments to date, the VIII Corps dislodged Morava I from its positions at Čovka and crossed the Kolubara. Morava I's 1st Regiment lost close to 1,000 men, many of whom deserted.[51] Although Morava I was stronger than the 9th Division—having received two regiments from Timok II in addition to its regular compliment of four regiments—high desertion, incessant artillery bombardment, lack of food, and lack of artillery ammunition demoralized the troops, causing defeat.[52] But the crossing also cost the 9th Division dearly: during the preceding nine days it had suffered over 300 dead and 2,925 wounded.[53]

As Morava I began to fall back, Stepanović ordered a counterattack. General Ilija Gojković, Morava I's commander refused, noting they were having difficulty withdrawing their artillery through the mud. Morava I and Timok I withdrew some 7 kilometers to a new line, where Stepanović ordered Gojković to defend the new positions to the last man, even if it meant "sacrificing the division."[54]

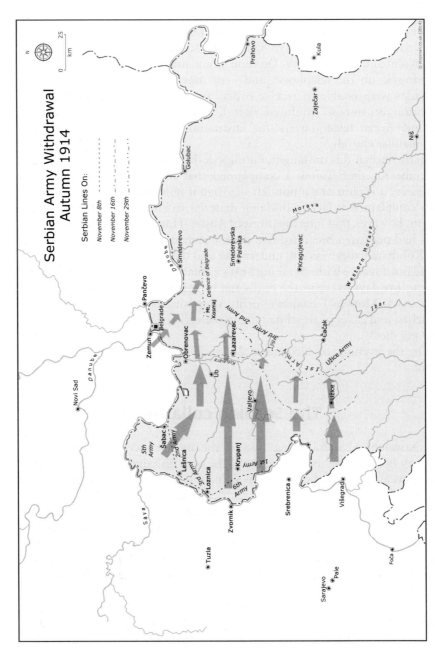

MAP 6 *Serbian Army withdrawal, autumn 1914.*

As Morava I withdrew, Putnik now anticipated losing Belgrade and ordered Mihailo Živković, the Commander of the Defense of Belgrade, to withdraw as soon as his position appeared untenable. The new line would be some 40 kilometers south of the capital near Mount Kosmaj.[55]

Morava I's withdrawal exposed the Third Army's right flank and forced Timok II to withdraw to the Kremnica River. Putnik demanded that Stepanović and Jurišić-Šturm hold their new positions, as failure would mean the loss of Belgrade. In contrast to the other Serbian commanders, Jurišić-Šturm reported that even though he lacked artillery ammunition, telephone and telegraph cables for communications, and all units were seriously under strength, he could attack the following day—Timok II excepted, which lacked many officers and NCOs.

However, on the First Army's front, XVI Corps had now completely pushed the Maljen Detachment and Danube II from Maljen's summit and ridge. As morale worsened, the troops of the 9th Regiment refused to fight; the First Army could only withdraw.[56]

For Serbia, November 25 was grim; the army lost thirty-two field guns, two mountain guns, and three *de Bange* guns, along with almost 4,000 shells, with most of the losses occurring in the First Army.[57] Only three quick-firing M910 120-mm howitzer batteries were still operational, the other five having been withdrawn to the rear for lack of ammunition.[58]

Early on the morning of November 26 under cover of darkness, thick fog, and snowstorms, XV Corps attacked the First Army's right wing (Drina I and Morava II) on the right bank of the Ljig and pushed it back to the divide between the Kolubara and Western Morava watersheds. As XVI Corps continued pushing the Maljen Detachment further down the slopes of Maljen, First Army's morale sank even lower. The rebellious 9th Regiment had only 639 men; some third levy battalions 180 men; Drina I Division fewer than 4,200 enlisted men; and that day alone over 500 troops went "missing" from the battlefield, prompting Mišić to report that "entire companies no longer exist."[59]

Mišić decided it was a mistake to keep withdrawing slowly and fighting for every inch of ground. His troops needed rest, new equipment, ammunition, time to re-equip with the new Russian Mosin rifles, and time to prepare defensive positions. To provide this breather, Mišić ordered the First Army to withdraw east to Gornji Milanovac in direct contradiction of High Command orders. He hoped to establish a new line running along Suvobor Mountain to the northeast of Gornji Milanovac.[60]

Along the lower Kolubara, the Obrenovac Detachment came under heavy attack from river monitors on the Sava, which fired over 3,000 artillery shells and destroyed the detachment's trenches. This enabled the 104th *Landsturm* Brigade to cross the Kolubara at its mouth and dislodge the Obrenovac Detachment, horribly weakening the Second Army's right wing.[61]

The First Army's withdrawal and the pull-back of the Obrenovac Detachment meant that the Third and Second Armies would also have to withdraw. It also meant that Belgrade would now fall. The Serbian military was in a state of collapse.

On the morning of November 26, Putnik informed Military Minister Stefanović that Belgrade would probably fall to the Austro-Hungarian troops and would be evacuated shortly. Putnik asked Stefanović to inform the government ministers.[62] Referring to Belgrade's relatively indefensible position, Putnik is reputed to have told Stefanović: "It is not my fault that the capital is placed there, where a frontier blockhouse used to be."[63]

Concerned about the effect the loss of Belgrade would have on morale, on November 26, Putnik again ordered Stepanović's Second Army to attack. Putnik was convinced a purely defensive position on the Kolubara would fail, and that the only way to relieve the pressure was to launch an offensive.[64] Yet the unrelenting Austro-Hungarian attacks since November 22 meant that it was all the Second and Third Armies could do to hold their positions. Both Armies had been pushed back by VIII Corps at Čovka. The XIII Corps attacks against the Third Army and the withdrawal of the First Army from Maljen had forced the Third Army's left wing to withdraw. It was only a matter of time before the current line would collapse. Finally acknowledging the futility of the Serbian position, Putnik issued a new order at 9:30 pm, establishing a new defensive line.[65]

Back in the rear, an explosion rocked the train station at Aranđelovac: deserters in a train wagon carrying rifle ammunition inadvertently set fire to a bag of gunpowder, blowing up the wagon and killing several people.[66]

As the First Army's rearguard fought a delaying action on the slopes of Maljen during the night of November 26/27, Putnik asked Mišić to halt the First Army's withdrawal and give the Third Army's left wing time to withdraw. Mišić mollified Putnik by saying: "I am doing and will do everything that can be done to the limits of possibility, to hold the positions, especially of Drina I."[67] Mišić's assurances notwithstanding, there was nothing the First Army could do to stop XVI and XV Corps.

Heavy fighting continued again on November 27. As the First Army attempted to hold its positions, its right wing suffered heavy losses; Drina I was particularly affected, losing 889 men in one day, mostly to desertion.[68] While the First Army fought its rearguard action, the troops' morale worsened and Drina I withdrew, exposing the Third Army's left flank, forcing its withdrawal.

On the night of November 27/28, XIII Corps launched a determined assault against Jurišić-Šturm's Third Army. Following heavy fighting, entire Serbian units ran out of rifle ammunition and the 14th Regiment fled. After losing 850 men, Timok II withdrew in disarray; not a single unit had maintained order, and most of the troops had fled to the hills and forests. By nightfall, only two companies of soldiers remained.[69] For the next 36 hours, Timok II ceased to exist as a combat unit.[70]

At dawn on November 28, the Habsburg 42nd Division attacked the Combined Division's right wing under cover of thick fog, quickly broke through, and threatened to encircle the entire Division. The fleeing troops of Timok II had sown chaos and confusion along the Combined Division's left wing, which in turn began to panic and flee. In the Third Army, only Drina II held. However, it too had to withdraw to prevent encirclement.

Hoping to strengthen the Second Army along the Kolubara, Putnik ordered the Obrenovac Detachment to attack the 29th Division on the heights at Konatica to relieve pressure on the Cavalry Division. Advancing through thick pre-dawn fog, the Cavalry Division and the Obrenovac Detachment drove the 29th from its positions. After counterattacks by both sides, the Serbs withdrew with four captured cannon and 765 prisoners, even though the Cavalry Division lost 141 men to desertion.[71] Timok I successfully repelled all attacks by the 21st Division and captured over 500 prisoners, but it was improbable it could hold much longer.

The loss of Čovka, the failure of the Cavalry Division to retake its positions along the Kolubara, and Timok I's worsening situation forced Stepanović to re-evaluate the Second Army's position. Late that morning he ordered the Army to prepare for an orderly withdrawal to a new line.[72]

To the south on the slopes of Maljen, XVI Corps attacked and nearly destroyed the Maljen Detachment, which lost over 1,000 men in one day and abandoned the mountain and its position on the First Army's left wing. The loss of Maljen meant the Užice Army's rear was now exposed, as was the First Army's left flank on Suvobor. Only heavy snow in the mountains prevented XVI Corps from exploiting this gap. The defense of Suvobor was now untenable.

On Suvobor, Danube I had lost over 1,800 men since November 24. The Division lacked NCOs, which worsened discipline. When the Habsburg attack came on November 28, it broke the Division's line. The situation with Morava II and Danube II was similar. On the First Army's left wing, Danube II lost contact with the rest of the Army; under heavy attack, its troops fled the front. While attempting to halt the flight, the commander of the 3rd Regiment was wounded by his own troops and captured. The commander of the 15th Regiment was captured at his regimental headquarters. The only remaining ranking officers—the divisional commander and the commander of the 14th Regiment—eventually reassembled a regimental size force, all that remained of Danube II.

On Suvobor, XV Corps turned the First Army's right wing, pushing back Drina I, whose battalions had been reduced to company size. With its flanks threatened from the left and right, and having lost contact with the Third Army and the Užice Army, the First Army's position was now completely untenable. Unable to further defend the mountains dividing the Kolubara and Western Morava watersheds, Mišić ordered his divisional commanders to withdraw toward Gornji Milanovac, beginning early next morning. Mišić told the High Command:

I find that it is wiser to begin the gradual withdrawal to new positions in [good] order early tomorrow, rather than wait and be forced to do this in disorder. The new position is half as long and we will be able to offer strong resistance to the enemy on it. I beg for an urgent answer, and I will carry out every other order of the High Command with especial energy if my above-mentioned opinion is not adopted, removing from myself responsibility for the results.[73]

Mišić then called Putnik. There followed a heated two-hour telephone call, in which Putnik threatened, cajoled, and pleaded with Mišić to hold his current positions. Mišić refused, stating that some of his regiments had less than 600 men, that they had little artillery and rifle ammunition, no winter clothing or shelter, and little food. Putnik finally agreed with Mišić, and approved the withdrawal.[74] Because of Mišić's withdrawal, Putnik was now forced to withdraw the Užice Army toward Čačak to protect its right flank and rear, leaving the Western Morava river valley open to the Austro-Hungarian Sixth Army.

The First Army began withdrawing from its positions on Suvobor during the night of November 28/29. Due to thick fog, XVI Corps failed to notice the withdrawal, and did not begin pursuing until 9:00 am on the morning of November 29. This permitted an unhindered withdrawal. That same day, Stepanović also decided he could no longer hold; he called Putnik and told him the Second Army and Obrenovac Detachment would have to withdraw to the defensive line Putnik had laid out in his order of November 16.[75] Knowing this meant losing the capital, and conscious of the political and diplomatic ramifications, Putnik asked Stepa to poll his divisional commanders and ask them if they could hold. Stepa did so: to a man they answered in the negative.

The ramifications of the Second Army's withdrawal were far-reaching. Putnik informed Military Minister Stefanović that "Belgrade must be abandoned, and this will make impossible the defense of the entire Danube line: all of northern Serbia will have to be abandoned." Putnik also requested the Serbian government seek urgent help from its allies.[76] Putnik then ordered the Defense of Belgrade to withdraw to its previously prepared positions to the south of the city at Kosmaj and Varovnica, along with the Obrenovac Detachment.[77]

Desertion now became critical. On November 29, Stepanović informed the High Command that the Second Army was arresting approximately fifty deserters per day: he did not say how many men they were unable to arrest. According to Stepanović, many of the deserters were arguing and shooting at the gendarmes; they feared only patrols of officers. Some deserters had thrown hand grenades, and one NCO spread panic by riding through a village on horseback yelling, "Run! The Germans are coming!" Stepanović reported that many of the deserters were thought to be congregating in Aranđelovac.[78] Desertion had crippled the Drina I and Danube I Divisions. Each should have had 16,000 men, but at the end of November Drina I had approximately 4,020, while Danube I had only 4,930.[79]

Early on the morning of November 30, prior to the Defense of Belgrade's withdrawal, the French naval battery at Belgrade fired all 240 of its remaining 140-mm shells at the Austro-Hungarian artillery batteries around Zemun in less than one hour, causing great destruction and panic.[80] As the Serbian Army left the city, it blew up bridges and other structures deemed of potential use to the Habsburg Army. Most of Belgrade's civilian population fled. The number of refugees was not large; four months of near-constant Austro-Hungarian artillery bombardment had caused the city's population to shrink from 90,000 to approximately 7,000–8,000 residents.[81]

During the night of November 29/30, the First, Second, Third, and Užice Armies began withdrawing to new defensive positions, and there was little contact with Habsburg forces. The Serbs spent the next several days fortifying their positions in preparation for the expected Austro-Hungarian attack. One infantry officer from Morava I recorded:

We withdraw and don't know when the end will be. We all know we don't have artillery ammunition, and that the opponent has much. Many claim they are sick and because of that go to the rear. Food is irregular and the weather is cold. The soldiers have no clothes, and there are sections [of the front] where it is completely impossible to hold, where the soldiers' legs are constantly wet.[82]

Potiorek's grand maneuver

As the Serbs abandoned Belgrade, Potiorek ordered the Habsburg Fifth Army's Combined Corps to turn the Serbian Army's right flank, and then drive south, attacking the Serbian Army from the rear. This move required the entire Fifth Army to swing north through Belgrade and then turn south, hitting the Serbian forces at Kosmaj. The Fifth Army would then be positioned to enter the Morava valley. Potiorek anticipated this would take between three and four days, during which time the Serbian and Austro-Hungarian forces would essentially be disengaged.

Potiorek conducted this maneuver at the behest of the German High Command, which wanted the Orient Express rail line to Turkey and Bulgaria reopened.[83] Since the arrival of the Russian naval mission in September, and British and French naval missions in October and November, the allies had deployed naval cannon, mines, and torpedoes around Belgrade, effectively shutting the Danube to all river traffic between the Habsburg Empire and Turkey. Reliant on the Central Powers for most of its military supplies, Turkey found it difficult to resupply its front-line units, which were now fighting the Russians in Armenia and the British in the Near East. For Germany it was essential that Turkey remain in the war and continue to divert Russian troops from the Eastern Front and British colonial troops from the Western Front.

Yet all was not well with *Balkanstreitkräfte*. In spite of its success in pushing back the Serbian Army and taking large swathes of Serbian territory, it had paid a high price. Like the Serbs, the Austro-Hungarian forces had been fighting since November 8, and had slogged through mud, rain, snow, and mountainous terrain against fierce resistance. The Fifth and Sixth Armies were still supplied mostly from Bosnia, creating a long umbilical cord that stretched from across the Drina through the mud of the Jadar valley and Mačva, the flooded Kolubara river valley, and into the snow-covered mountains. The further Potiorek advanced, the further his troops were from their supply base. By late November, food shortages were common. Clothing and equipment—worn from months of use—began to fall into disrepair. As cold weather arrived, disease began to spread: by late November, the Sixth Army's XV Corps was losing 500 to 600 soldiers daily to sickness.[84]

The Serbian High Command's policy of taking all livestock and food was paying dividends. As Habsburg forces ran low on supplies, many soldiers left their units—already at half strength—to scavenge for food. Morale fell. Manpower shortages began to be felt as the Empire sent untrained conscripts directly to the front, some in their forties. Many Austro-Hungarian soldiers—tired and worn out by the cold and the fighting—began to surrender willingly to the retreating Serbian forces.[85]

For Putnik and the Serbian Army, the Fifth Army's maneuver to the north through Belgrade was a welcome relief. Although Putnik was unaware of Potiorek's plans, it meant a chance for the Serbian forces to rest and resupply. Not only did Serbian forces receive a break from the constant shelling and fighting, the withdrawal from the Kolubara and Ljig shortened the Serbian front by over 40 kilometers.

Potiorek's decision to send the Fifth Army through Belgrade and surround the Serbian forces coincided with a major miracle for Serbia. In late November and early December, field-artillery ammunition finally began to arrive: 20,000 shells from Greece, and almost double that from France, giving the Serbian Army a much-needed shot in the arm.[86] The French shells, however, were 2.5 millimeters too long, so they had to be hurriedly disassembled in Niš, sent to the royal arsenal in Kragujevac where they were shortened, and then returned to Niš for final assembly. A locomotive was kept waiting under full steam at the train station in Niš: whenever 300 shells were completed, the train was dispatched to Kragujevac. Another two to three locomotives were kept under steam in Niš to transport the shells to the front. In this manner, the Serbian Army received 11,000 artillery shells in the last few days of November.[87] The arrival of 75-mm artillery ammunition at the front meant the Serbian artillery no longer needed to account for every shell. Small quantities of clothing and shoes also began to arrive, as did fresh replacement soldiers.

Serbian morale was particularly improved by the arrival of a 1,300-strong battalion of under-officer cadets from the cadet school in Skopje. Prior to embarking for the front, Crown Prince Aleksandar addressed them, ending his speech with a rousing cry of "not one step backward." Highly patriotic and imbued with a fervor unseen since the earliest days of the war, these new arrivals were spread throughout the Serbian Army. Their presence had a marked impact on the morale of the war-weary troops.[88] Desperate for manpower, the High Command sent large numbers of gendarmes to the front, as well as recruits from the "New Regions" of Kosovo, Macedonia, Sandžak, and southern Serbia.

New drastic disciplinary measures caused many deserters to return to their units, further strengthening the army's ranks. Putnik issued order no. 7723, which toughened Serbia's policy toward deserters. Prior to this time, the army had usually returned deserters to their units. Now, anyone who left the front line was considered a deserter, and the penalty was death. The only valid reason for leaving the front lines was a serious wound: all who left and were not seriously wounded were to be court-martialed. This included Serbian soldiers captured by the enemy, except for those who were seriously wounded when captured.[89]

Since the withdrawal on November 30, Austro-Hungarian and Serbian forces had been out of contact, except for occasional reconnaissance patrols and a few localized skirmishes. Potiorek's forces awaited the completion of the Fifth Army's encircling maneuver prior to renewing their offensive.

It appears this short rest, the arrival of supplies, the infusion of replacement troops, and the visible presence of quantities of artillery shells had a salutary effect on Serbian morale. After two days, the troops of Mišić's First Army were dancing the *Kolo*—a folk dance—around their campfires.[90]

This should not be interpreted as an overnight transformation of a rag-tag, war-weary force into a well-equipped, well-rested army. Quite the contrary; the beleaguered First Army had been reduced to a skeleton force of 22,000 men: Drina I had 5,129 men, Danube I 4,930 men, Danube II 5,129 men, and Morava II 7,921 men.[91] And the High Command noted that Serbian troops continued to desert and flee the battlefield, even when attacked by much smaller and weaker Austro-Hungarian units.[92]

While Putnik knew of the growing discipline and supply problems among the Austro-Hungarian troops, he also knew that Serbian soldiers were psychologically better suited to offense than defense, and that an offensive would substantially raise morale. Putnik decided it was time for Serbia to take the initiative and launch an offensive.

Mišić reached the same conclusion. Acting on reports from his divisional commanders that described XVI Corps as suffering from low morale and lack of supplies, as well as reports describing a significant improvement in the First Army's morale following its three-day rest, Mišić decided the time

PHOTO 20 *General Živojin Mišić.*

was ripe for a counteroffensive. At 4:30 pm on December 2, Mišić telephoned the High Command and told Živko Pavlović, and later Putnik, that he intended to launch an attack with the First Army the following day. Mišić asked Putnik for support from Stepanović's Second Army. After verifying Mišić's intent, Putnik approved the attack and ordered Stepanović and Jurišić-Šturm to also go on the offensive on December 3.[93]

CHAPTER TEN

One man's triumph, another man's victory

Early on the morning of December 2, an Austro-Hungarian detachment from Novi Sad's Petrovaradin fortress crossed the Sava and entered Belgrade without encountering resistance. That same day, Potiorek ordered Fifth Army commander General von Frank to prepare a triumphal entry into Belgrade for December 3. The previous day, December 1, Potiorek met with the newly appointed Imperial governor for Serbia, General Stephen Sarkotić—the Croatian commander of the 42nd *Honved* "Devil's Division"—to discuss arrangements for administering occupied Serbia. Advance parties of the Fifth Army spent the night of December 2 hurriedly placing large Austro-Hungarian banners and flags on the Kalemegdan fortress and throughout the city. Franz Josef's sixty-sixth anniversary as Emperor would be celebrated the next day in grand style. Victory seemed assured.

In the South Slav parts of the Empire, the celebrations had already begun. In Trebinje, a concert was held the evening of December 2 to honor the Emperor. Kapellmeister Riedl and his orchestra played pieces by Beethoven, Swendsen, and Grieg, and 1,200 Krone was collected for charity. In Dubrovnik, a large parade was held that included the local *Schutzkorps* battalion, the city's 6th Company, and over 1,000 representatives of the city's guilds and civic organizations.

December 3, 1914 was a momentous day. Potiorek sent a congratulatory anniversary greeting to the Emperor, in which he personally announced the occupation of Belgrade. For Potiorek, the Fifth Army's triumphant entry into Belgrade on the Emperor's anniversary was a vindication. As the Fifth Army's Combined Corps paraded through Belgrade with General von Frank at its head, bands played and banners waved. Franz Ferdinand was avenged and Mount Cer forgotten. Belgrade's small German and Hungarian community turned out to greet the conquering troops with wine, cookies, and bread.[1] In honor of the Emperor's anniversary, Potiorek ordered a one-day rest for all soldiers and sailors participating in the parade. As an occupying force, the Fifth Army went to work with Germanic efficiency. By the third day of occupation, the Fifth Army had restored electricity to much of Belgrade and repaired the trolley lines between the Kalemegdan and Trg Slavija. That same day they began to hang Serbian civilians on a gallows erected across from the Hotel Moskva on *Terazije*, one of Belgrade's most prominent squares.[2] Three other gallows were established for public executions: on the upper Kalemegdan fortress, Čubara, and Karaburma. In the Empire, railways began booking special trains from Budapest and Vienna to Zemun to allow tourists to sightsee in the newly captured city.[3]

Potiorek received a telegram from the Turkish government, informing him the Sultan had awarded him a medal. In Vienna and Budapest, the newspapers triumphantly proclaimed victory over Serbia and a complete defeat of the Serbian Army. As far as Potiorek knew, the entire Serbian Army was in full flight, an opinion shared by Serbia's allies. The end of Potiorek's long Balkan campaign to vindicate himself and repair his reputation was finally in sight.

But the campaign was not over, and the end arrived in an entirely unexpected manner. Around noon on December 3, Potiorek received reports at his headquarters in Koviljača of a Serbian attack against the XVI Corps, which he dismissed as an isolated action. At 7:45 pm, General von Frank received a surprising report at his staff headquarters in the Serbian royal palace. The Serbian Army had not collapsed and was not retreating to the interior. Rather, there was heavy fighting along the Fifth and Sixth Army fronts. General von Frank immediately cancelled all leave.[4]

At 7:00 am on the morning of December 3, after a heavy bombardment from its newly resupplied artillery, the Serbian Army began its long-awaited offensive. In the north, Stepanović's Second Army attacked the XIII and VIII Corps east of Lazarevac, while Jurišić-Šturm's Third Army on Rudnik attacked the much stronger XV Corps. Both Armies ran into fierce resistance; after hand-to-hand fighting, only small gains were made at a few points.

North of Gornji Milanovac, Mišić's First Army attacked the XVI Corps along its entire front. Under cover of heavy fog, the First Army's troops advanced most of the way to the Habsburg lines undetected. As the fog lifted, Serbian artillery began a devastating barrage against the Austro-Hungarian positions. Many Habsburg units broke and fled in disarray. On the First Army's right wing and center, Drina I, Morava II, and Danube I attacked the Austro-Hungarian Combined Division. On the First Army's left wing, Danube II attacked the 50th Division. In the center, Morava II and Danube I quickly broke the Combined Division's front lines and pushed it back 3 kilometers onto the southeast slopes of Suvobor. In the course of one day, the First Army captured over 400 prisoners, four mountain howitzers, one machine gun, and 1,000 artillery shells. The malaise and poor morale that had for so long plagued the First Army seemed to have been replaced—literally overnight—by a new *esprit de corps*.[5]

The next day, December 4, the First Army continued its attack. Following a counterattack by the *K.u.k.* 1st Division, Mišić sent the Army reserve to the front, which broke the Austro-Hungarian lines. By day's end, the First Army had pushed the 1st, 50th, and Combined Divisions back an additional 3 kilometers up the slopes of Suvobor, and captured large numbers of prisoners and equipment. All three Austro-Hungarian divisions had broken at various points during the day, and their troops had fled in panic. The Serbian Second and Third Armies once again made only limited progress in their attacks. On the Serbian Army's new northern front, the Defense of Belgrade reported a heavy Austro-Hungarian buildup, as the Habsburg Fifth Army's encircling maneuver began to near completion.

Given the poor performance of the XVI Corps over the previous two days, it was now questionable whether or not the Sixth Army could hold until von Frank finished his encircling maneuver in the north. Not realizing the extent of the problems in XVI Corps, Potiorek ordered von Frank to continue the Fifth Army's maneuver around the Serbian Army's northern flank.

On December 5, the First Army renewed its attack on XVI Corps with an early morning assault. After an intense artillery bombardment, the First Army broke the Austro-Hungarian lines on Suvobor. Habsburg troops fled in disarray as the XVI Corps literally disintegrated under the assault; soldiers discarded their weapons and equipment in their haste to escape. Fearing the First Army was advancing too rapidly, Putnik ordered Mišić to halt and allow the Second and Third Armies time to press their attacks and catch up. Mišić ordered his division commanders to halt their advance as soon as they reached the summit of Suvobor.[6]

Ignoring this order, Danube I commander General Milivoje Anđelković pressed his troops forward. By 11:00 pm, Danube I had overrun the summit of Suvobor, and penetrated more than 10 kilometers into the XVI Corps rear, where it wreaked havoc on the retreating Austro-Hungarian columns. During the day, the First Army captured four machine guns, three cannon, two mountain howitzers, over 1,800 prisoners, and large amounts of equipment.[7] The entire XVI Corps was now in disarray and fleeing. Its collapse left a hole in the Austro-Hungarian line, which threatened the rear areas of the XV and XIII Corps.

Stepanović's Second Army continued to assault the VIII and XIII Corps, with few results. By the end of the day, Morava I had made only small gains and captured 200 prisoners. Šumadija I did better, taking an important hill and capturing 700 prisoners. The Cavalry Division captured 200 prisoners. In spite of these local successes, the Second Army, Serbia's strongest, failed to make significant progress. Because of this, Putnik ordered Stepanović to halt his offensive and send Timok I to assist the Defense of Belgrade on the Serbian right flank near Kosmaj.

The Third Army met with some success on December 5, largely because the XVI Corps' collapse forced the 48th Division to withdraw to protect its right flank and rear from the First Army. Timok II pressed the 48th as it withdrew 4 kilometers to new positions. An officer in Timok II testified to the effectiveness of Serbia's newly resupplied artillery: "We passed along the trenches where the Austrians were. Dead—soldier upon soldier, all from shrapnel."[8] To the west, the Užice Army attacked the 18th Division for a third straight day, suffering heavy losses. Nonetheless, the XVI Corps' collapse forced the 18th Division to withdraw toward Valjevo to protect its left flank and rear.

On December 5, Potiorek first learned the XVI Corps had broken and was in full flight. Many of it brigades were reduced to between 800 and 1,000 men. Although he had equipment and supplies in ample quantity, Potiorek lacked men. On December 5, he asked AOK for a division's worth of unequipped men, whom he would equip and send to the front to fill the hole left by the XVI Corps. The AOK, which was using the last of its reserves to halt a Russian offensive in Galicia, turned down Potiorek's request. A desperate Potiorek then urged General von Frank to speed the Fifth Army's maneuver against the Serbian flank and rear, so as to relieve pressure on the Sixth Army.

At dawn on December 6, the First Army continued pursuing the retreating XVI Corps. On the Army's right wing, Drina I and Morava II turned north and attacked the XV Corps in its right flank, and reached the right bank of the Ljig. In the center, Danube I ran into heavy resistance, but by evening had broken across the mountain crests and was pursuing the Austro-Hungarian forces toward Mionica in the Kolubara river valley. By dark, forward elements of Danube I had entered Mionica, throwing panic into the XV Corps rear area. On the First Army's left wing, Danube II pushed the Habsburg forces back to the crest of Maljen. As it advanced, the First Army came across large quantities of discarded cannons, caissons, rifles, machine guns, ammunition, supply wagons, field hospitals, field kitchens, and other military equipment. On December 6, the First Army captured over 1,300 prisoners, four doctors, six mountain cannon and four field artillery pieces, and more than 100 supply wagons.[9]

The Užice Army, which now faced only light Austro-Hungarian opposition following the 18th Division's withdrawal, took little action during the day and allowed the remaining Habsburg forces to begin withdrawing toward the Drina. Nonetheless, it captured 560 prisoners. Because of the unclear situation on the Užice Army's front, as well as the Third Army's lack of progress, Mišić halted the First Army's advance for the day.

Around 10:30 am on December 6, Potiorek received a telephone call from XVI Corps commander General Wurm, informing him the XVI Corps had been completely destroyed, and the 1st Division ceased to exist as a fighting unit. Prior to this time, Potiorek was completely unaware of the scale of the Sixth Army's catastrophe, thinking there were only a few minor setbacks. Taken aback, Potiorek ordered the Sixth Army to withdraw and regroup on the left bank of the Kolubara River, where it could hold the Serbian Army while the Fifth Army swung around and attacked the Serbian forces from the rear. But the Fifth Army was three days late, and the Sixth Army had already begun a preliminary evacuation of Valjevo. What started as a local offensive by the First Army designed to boost Serbian morale had now become a rout of strategic significance.

On December 6, Putnik continued the crackdown on desertion, which had by now cost the Serbian Army nearly 60,000 men, one-quarter of the army's entire enlisted strength. He ordered the commanders of all divisional regions to form special units of third levy volunteers to apprehend deserters. These units were to patrol the roads leading to and from the battle areas; any deserter who attempted to flee was to be shot.[10] The issue of deserters, refugees, and loiterers was further confused by the presence of numerous soldiers in the rear areas carrying large sums of money and conducting private errands and shopping for their officers. These soldiers carried legitimate passes and often overstayed their passes or didn't return. The number of these errand-boys was growing to such an extent that it crowded the transport and harmed the operational army. The High Command ordered all errand-boys be apprehended and returned to their units, and the responsible officers punished.[11] The High Command was also concerned by the rear area behavior of all soldiers—not merely deserters. Evidently, a serious problem existed with soldiers shooting their weapons from passenger and freight trains, destroying telephone and telegraph lines; these activities were disrupting the army's communications.[12]

On the night of December 6/7, a battalion of Drina I crossed the Ljig, and without firing a shot captured an entire company. The 6th Regiment then continued on to the village of Cvetanovci, where it surprised the 28th *Landwehr* Regiment and captured 1,600 prisoners, ammunition, rifles and machine guns, and freed 500 Serbian soldiers who had been taken prisoner. In one instance, a single under-strength Serbian company of fifty-seven men captured six officers, an entire battalion of the 28th regiment (417 men), one field battery of six cannon with all its caissons, three machine guns, and 300 supply wagons. Several Habsburg officers committed suicide rather than be captured by the Serbian forces. The remainder of Drina I pursued the 40th Honved Division. By day's end, the 40th had ceased to exist as a fighting unit, and Drina I had captured three officers, 852 men, seven gun carriages, sixteen field cannon, thirty caissons, one field kitchen, and an artillery depot.[13]

Early on the morning of December 7, the remainder of the First Army continued pursuing the disintegrating XVI Corps. At 5:00 am, Danube II took the peak of Maljen and continued onward to cut the road from Valjevo to Užice. The First Army advance meant that the Austro-Hungarian troops in the Western Morava valley—near Užice—were now completely cut off from any contact with the Habsburg forces in the Kolubara valley. At 10:20 am, Putnik ordered the First Army to continue pursuing the Habsburg Sixth Army troops toward Valjevo and the Kolubara River.[14] Danube I pursued the 1st, 50th, and Combined Divisions from Mionica toward the Kolubara, while sending part of its forces toward Valjevo. Continuing to harass and drive the XVI Corps before it, the First Army captured more than 6,000 prisoners and forty-five cannon during the course of the day.[15] In the XVI Corps' rear at Valjevo, what had begun as an organized withdrawal from the city by the Sixth Army now turned into a general panic.[16]

On the left bank of the Ljig, Drina I and Morava II joined forces with the Third Army in pushing XV Corps back toward the Kolubara. As the First Army struck the XV Corps in its flank and rear, Jurišić-Šturm's Third Army now made substantial progress against the XV Corps, which withdrew to protect its rear and flanks from the First Army. As the Third Army advanced with increasing rapidity against the XV Corps, Captain Milorad Marković of the often-struggling Timok II wrote: "We are pursuing: us, the 13th Regiment. Irony."[17]

Around 10:00 am on December 8, having already crossed the Kolubara, lead elements of Danube I entered Valjevo and captured 150 prisoners. The remnants of XVI Corps managed to regroup and expel Danube I from Valjevo. The XVI Corps then set up defensive positions around Valjevo for the night, while the main body of Danube I and Danube II crossed the Kolubara and continued in pursuit of XVI Corps. The XVI Corps was now in dire straits: General Wurm informed Potiorek his Corps needed to withdraw from Serbia entirely and take a two-week rest.[18] Along the Third Army's front, the remainder of XV Corps managed to withdraw across the Kolubara on the night of December 8/9 under strong Serbian pressure.

On December 9, Mišić renewed the attack against the Habsburg rearguard around Valjevo. The First Army quickly broke through the Austro-Hungarian lines and pursued the Habsburg forces toward the border, as the XVI and XV Corps fled toward Šabac, Loznica, and Pecka. On December 10, as the extent of the XVI and XV Corps' rout finally became evident, Putnik ordered all Serbian Armies to engage in an energetic pursuit of the Austro-Hungarian troops. The First Army would continue pursuing the Sixth Army through Mačva, while the Second and Third Armies—which had now redeployed to face the Fifth Army—would advance toward Belgrade. They would join the Defense of Belgrade in an offensive against the Fifth Army on December 11.[19]

Lacking sufficient troop strength to mount an offensive along the entire front, Putnik ordered Mišić to halt at Valjevo. Mišić, however, had his own ideas, and ordered the First Army to continue its pursuit of the retreating Habsburg forces. Bad weather and muddy roads complicated the Austro-Hungarian withdrawal: as the remnants of the defeated Sixth Army arrived in Šabac on December 12, they left behind roads strewn with horses, carts, field hospitals, artillery, ammunition, aircraft, motor cars, field kitchens and bakeries, ambulances, caissons, and every imaginable piece of equipment necessary for the operation of a modern field army.

As the Habsburg forces fled, Mišić divided the First Army into three groups to pursue the retreating foe. Drina I advanced due north from Valjevo toward the Sava, while Danube I and II advanced toward the Drina along both sides of Mount Cer via Mačva and the Jadar valley.[20] A jubilant Živojin

Mišić telegrammed the Serbian High Command that "the disintegration of the enemy is complete."[21] In what had now became a foot race to the Drina and Sava rivers, the First Army pursued the Habsburg forces through Mačva and western Serbia. Over the next several days, the First Army encountered little or no resistance, while capturing 11,550 prisoners, sixteen howitzers, sixty-six cannon, and numerous supply wagons, caissons, gun carriages, motorcars, bakeries, field kitchens, ammunition, rifles, and machine guns. On December 13, units of the victorious First Army entered Šabac, Loznica, and Lešnica. With the exception of prisoners of war, not one Austro-Hungarian soldier remained in western Serbia. The Sixth Army had been routed and destroyed.

Potiorek's gamble

When the Second Army failed to make headway against von Frank's Fifth Army, a pessimistic Stepanović deemed the Second Army's positions unsuitable for defense, and asked Putnik for permission to withdraw. Given the spectacular successes of the First and Third Armies, Putnik angrily refused. On December 6, the Austro-Hungarian forces intercepted one of Stepa's gloomy dispatches to Putnik. Acting on the basis of Stepa's negative assessment, Potiorek decided the entire Serbian Army was withdrawing toward Aranđelovac: but when Krauss' Combined Corps ran into stiff Serbian resistance near Mount Kosmaj, it became apparent this was not the case.

On December 7, Potiorek was still unaware of the full extent of the disaster facing the Sixth Army. Potiorek expected the Fifth Army to break through to the Serbian rear at any moment, and destroy the Serbian Army. The setback to the Sixth Army would be only temporary.

On the same day, December 7, Putnik ordered the Third Army to pursue the retreating XV Corps along the left bank of the Ljig River with the Combined Division and Timok II. Drina II was to advance along the right bank of the Ljig toward Čovka and hit the XIII Corps in its right flank.

With the Third Army distracting attention from the Second Army's front, Stepanović now went on the offensive. Around midnight on December 7/8, Morava I drove the Austro-Hungarian 36th Division from the battlefield in disarray.

On December 8, Stepanović ordered the Second Army to attack the Habsburg forces and pursue them toward Lazarevac. However, other developments forced Stepanović to halt the offensive. The Fifth Army had finally begun its long-awaited attack, and had broken through the Defense of Belgrade's lines at Kosmaj. Lacking reserves, Putnik transferred Morava I from the Second Army to the Serbian right flank, where it would assist the Defense of Belgrade. With Stepanović unable to continue, XIII Corps used the night of December 8/9 to withdraw across the Kolubara, saving the

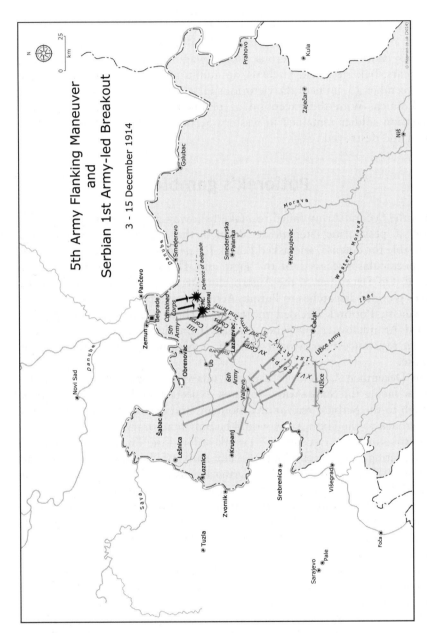

MAP 7 *Fifth Army flanking maneuver and Serbian First Army-led breakout, December 1914.*

isolated 36th and 42nd Divisions from certain destruction. That same day Putnik ordered the Third Army to turn north and attack the Fifth Army's right wing. Now both the Second and Third Armies would attack von Frank's Fifth Army, leaving Mišić's First Army to deal with the Habsburg forces in western Serbia.

When the Fifth Army swung into action near Kosmaj, it did do so piecemeal, and its units entered battle sequentially. The VIII Corps launched the first attacks on December 4, at the initiative of its commander, General Scheuchenstuel, but without success. Potiorek had intended for VIII Corps to wait for the Combined Corps—which comprised the Fifth Army's main force—and attack simultaneously, but it got lost on the roads south of Belgrade, and its tired troops did not arrive at the front until the evening of December 5. As a result, its attacks the next day were ineffective. The Fifth Army's chief of staff, Major General Gerabek, wrote that the troops were "so exhausted that even without a battle they can barely advance."[22]

On December 7, the Combined Corps and VIII Corps launched a series of unsuccessful attacks on Serbian positions around Kosmaj. The defenders were the Defense of Belgrade, the Obrenovac Detachment, and Timok I, which had arrived the previous evening from the Second Army. With the exception of Timok I, most of the defenders were second and third levy troops.

On December 8, the Combined Corps attacked Kosmaj, with Serb forces beating back numerous charges by the 104th *Landsturm* Brigade. However, a surprise attack by the VIII Corps' 7th Division dislodged two companies of third levy soldiers, who fled their trenches leaving behind ten cannon.[23] This created a hole in the line and forced Serbian troops to withdraw from Kosmaj. The Kosmaj Detachment attempted to retake Kosmaj, but after its commander Lieutenant Colonel Antonije Milošević died in a counterattack, the unit became leaderless and fled the battlefield. By 1:00 pm, the Austro-Hungarian troops had taken all of Kosmaj, driving a wedge between the Second Army's right flank and the Obrenovac Detachment's left flank. Only the arrival of Timok I prevented the entire line from breaking. Late on the afternoon of December 8, the Kosmaj Detachment's new commander, Colonel Dušan Tufegđić, counterattacked and retook some of the positions on Kosmaj's lower slopes. Tufegđić's small success caused the Austro-Hungarian troops to flee Kosmaj. In their wake, the Habsburg forces left behind over 1,000 dead, and the Kosmaj Detachment captured over 1,000 prisoners. Still unaware of the extent of the First Army's success against Potiorek's Sixth Army, Putnik became concerned because he lacked a strategic reserve to reinforce his right flank; he ordered Morava I to leave the Second Army and reinforce the Defense of Belgrade.

On December 9, the 7th Division resumed the assault on Kosmaj, but failed to dislodge the defenders. Having suffered heavy losses, and now aware of the catastrophe that had befallen the Sixth Army, von Frank ordered his Army to withdraw towards Belgrade, where it would cross the Danube and Sava and leave the XIII Corps to maintain a bridgehead around Belgrade. Potiorek also ordered—somewhat tardily—the remnants of XV and XVI Corps to withdraw toward Šabac. The XIII Corps was to withdraw toward Obrenovac, where it would rejoin the Fifth Army and defend the Austro-Hungarian bridgehead around Belgrade. Potiorek hoped a withdrawal and a three-day rest would allow his army to continue the offensive at a later date.

At noon on December 9, he informed the AOK of his orders withdrawing the Sixth and Fifth Armies, and the need for a three-day rest for XVI and XV Corps.[24] In a separate letter to the chief of the Imperial Chancellory, General Bolfras, Potiorek admitted "openly and without reserve that this withdrawal is a perceptible and great defeat." Ever hopeful, Potiorek suggested that an infusion of 55,000 troops would rectify the situation.[25]

On December 11, the repositioned Second and Third Armies, along with the Defense of Belgrade, attacked north toward Belgrade. The Third Army and the Defense of Belgrade ran into stiff Austro-Hungarian resistance and went nowhere. The Second Army broke the 21st Division's right wing, exposing the 9th Division's left flank. This breakthrough effectively destroyed VIII Corps' defensive line, forced the entire Corps to withdraw, and destroyed any realistic plan of maintaining an Austro-Hungarian bridgehead at Belgrade.[26] Sensing an impending Habsburg collapse, and dissatisfied with the pace of the Second and Third Armies' advance, at 7:30 pm Putnik ordered Stepanović and Jurišić-Šturm to "quicken the pace of the attacks, as much as possible, so that the enemy not be given time to fortify Belgrade."[27]

On December 12, Serbian troops broke through along the entire front. On the left wing, the Third Army took over 1,000 prisoners. In the center, the Second Army captured over 500 prisoners, and forced the 9th and 21st Divisions to withdraw. In spite of several Austro-Hungarian counterattacks, Timok I took Paraćanski Vis, the controlling piece of high ground between Kosmaj and Avala. Fierce Habsburg resistance was quickly suppressed by Serbian artillery. Šumadija I and the Obrenovac Detachment also advanced. On the Serbian right wing, the Defense of Belgrade broke the 29th Division's line.

Upon learning of the Serbian breakthrough on December 12, von Frank ordered the Fifth Army to withdraw toward Avala. The fog of war meant that not all Habsburg units received the order in time, resulting in an uneven withdrawal. VIII Corps began after midnight; XIII Corps began on the morning of December 13; the Combined Corps received the order to withdraw just as the Defense of Belgrade made a charge that broke the 29th Division's 58th Brigade. Later that morning, the Defense of Belgrade attacked the 104th *Landsturm* Brigade at Ralja: within moments, most of the 1,500-man Brigade surrendered.[28]

The Third Army broke through the Fifth Army's right wing, and XIII Corps failed to stabilize its front. The Combined Division and Drina II broke through the 9th Division 14 kilometers southwest of Belgrade. Desperate to hold the line, von Rhemen sent the XIII Corps reserve into battle, but it quickly broke and ran, with Šumadija I pursuing the fleeing units into the Topćider river valley. Although Stepanović ordered the pursuit to continue, the divisional commander chose to halt and rest for the evening, allowing the Austro-Hungarian forces to escape.[29] During the afternoon, von Frank began to withdraw all his forces to the immediate vicinity of the Belgrade bridgehead. Although not encountering particularly heavy resistance from the withdrawing Austro-Hungarian forces, the Serbian units advanced slowly, giving Habsburg forces time to reach the bridgehead. The most notable event on the Defense of Belgrade's front was the death of Major Rista Sandalj, killed while leading his battalion in a charge. A hero of the Balkan Wars, Sandalj was renowned for his discipline, honesty, and Spartan life.[30]

At 3:00 pm, Stepanović ordered Timok I to advance toward Belgrade via Avala and Kumodraž. It captured the 7th Division's rearguard—the 21st *Jäger* Battalion—at Avala, a large hill on the outskirts of Belgrade. By this point, the Fifth Army had fewer than 40,000 men.

The catastrophic collapse of what only a few days earlier had been a major Austro-Hungarian triumph loomed large at the Imperial Court. In Vienna, the AOK became concerned that a defeat would threaten the Empire's security along its entire southern border. On December 13, the AOK telegrammed Potiorek at Petrovaradin, stating that a complete collapse and defeat on the southern front must be avoided at all costs. On the one hand, the AOK wanted to hold Belgrade, both for reasons of prestige, as well as for the diplomatic and political leverage this would give the Empire in the Balkans. On the other hand, the AOK expressed concern that the Fifth Army be preserved to protect the Empire's southern borders. This telegram came from Archduke Friedrich himself, who said that the defeat of the Fifth Army must be avoided "at all costs," so that the Monarchy wouldn't leave its southern border undefended.[31]

Potiorek forwarded the telegram to von Frank, and then informed him he no longer stood by his earlier decision to defend Belgrade at all costs. If von Frank thought he could not hold Belgrade without incurring a high cost in men and matériel, he was free to withdraw the Fifth Army. Von Frank replied: "I cannot guarantee one or the other," and decided to evacuate the city.[32]

Early on the morning of December 14, the Third Army renewed its attack on the Habsburg Fifth Army's right wing along a line stretching from Rakovica to Košutnjak and Žarkovo. This sector of the Belgrade bridgehead was heavily defended by infantry, artillery, and river monitors, as it lay closest to the Austro-Hungarian pontoon bridge across the Sava at *Ada Ciganlija*. In spite of heavy resistance, by evening Drina I had taken the western edge of the Rakovica Forest.

In the center, the Second Army started from Avala, with Timok I pushing aside heavy fortifications at Torlak by using concentrated artillery fire. The bombardment was so fierce that the defending troops threw down their arms and fled—some in the direction of the advancing Serbs. During the encounter, Timok I captured an entire battalion. In the afternoon, Timok I passed through *Vojvoda* Stepanović's birthplace—the village of Kumodraž on the heights overlooking Belgrade. The Šumadija I Division advanced quickly; by evening it had reached Dedinje.

Morava I continued attacking the Austro-Hungarian left wing and forced the 29th Division to withdraw hastily to the ferry across the Danube at Višnjica. The remnants of the 29th crossed the Danube at Višnjica or retreated to Belgrade, where they crossed the Sava on pontoon bridges. As Morava I approached Višnjica, it came under heavy fire from river monitors on the Danube.

On the morning of December 14, von Frank telephoned Potiorek—who was now across the river in Zemun—and told him the situation was desperate: he could no longer hold Belgrade. At noon, von Frank ordered all his commanders to withdraw across the Sava at nightfall. Not knowing of von Frank's order to withdraw, but hoping to save Belgrade from destruction, Putnik ordered all Serbian forces to hold their positions on the heights above the city at Košutnjak, Kumodraž, Dedinje, and Banjica. Only the Cavalry Division and one regiment from Šumadija I could enter the city the following day.

This delay was a blessing for the Habsburg forces, as the ground between the heights and the city center offered no positions to establish a defense. The city was open for the taking, and the roads leading to the bridges were crowded with fleeing soldiers in commandeered wagons and carts. Putnik's order to halt on the heights allowed the confused and disorganized Fifth Army to cross the river unhindered.[33] During the night of December 14/15, the Fifth Army succeeded in withdrawing most of its troops across the Sava.

When the Cavalry Division entered Belgrade on the morning of December 15, it encountered only a few Austro-Hungarian rearguard soldiers, who had failed to withdraw in time. At 10:45 am, the Fifth Army dynamited the bridges across the Sava. The only Habsburg troops remaining on Serbian soil were now prisoners of war.

CHAPTER ELEVEN

The aftermath

Čika Pera jaše konja bela,
za njim ide Srbadija cela

Uncle Pete [King Petar] rides a white horse,
All the Serbs follow behind him.
—SERBIAN POPULAR SONG

The price of victory

At 9:40 am on the morning of December 15, 1914, Serbia's aged King, Petar Karađorđević, entered his devastated capital by motorcar. As the King rode down the main street, the sound of rifle fire echoed throughout the "white city." While the Cavalry Division skirmished with the Austro-Hungarian rearguard, artillery shells from the Habsburg batteries at Beanija and Zemun rained down on Belgrade. At the intersection of Kneza Mihaila and Kralja Petra streets, the King passed a group of armed Austro-Hungarian soldiers who were surrendering to Serbian troops. The King's goal was the Saborna Church on the hill by the edge of the Kalemegdan fortress. With shells still falling on the city, King Petar attended a brief service, giving thanks for the liberation of Belgrade and the tremendous Serbian victory over the Austro-Hungarian Army.[1] At 10:45 am, shortly after the King left the service, the Fifth Army blew the last of the bridges across the Sava, a kilometer down the hill from the Saborna Church.

The withdrawing Fifth Army took with it an enormous amount of war booty. Many of Belgrade's homes were looted of their belongings at the direct order of Austro-Hungarian officers: the Fifth Army piled the plunder onto wagons and carted it across the Sava into Austria-Hungary. Von Frank's Fifth Army blew up the city's power plant, and in direct contravention of the

Hague Convention took with it a large number of civilian hostages, including Stefan Bisers, the director of Belgrade's Society for Trolleys and Lighting. Without Bisers' technical expertise, it would be many weeks before Belgrade once again had light.[2]

The victory came at an enormous cost, both to the vanquished and the victor. In a few short months, the war transformed Austria-Hungary's once-proud *Balkanstreitkräfte* from a modern, well-equipped field army of over 450,000 men, into a demoralized, defeated remnant numbering barely half that. The army that only two weeks previously staged an elaborate victory triumph on the streets of Belgrade, now crawled away in abject and utter defeat. The extent of the Dual Monarchy's loss proved staggering. During the Battle on the Kolubara, the Serbian Army captured 323 officers, 43,000 enlisted men, 142 cannon, twenty-nine gun carriages, 386 caissons, seventy-one machine guns, 60,000 rifles, two airplanes, three cash boxes, five motor cars, thirty-seven hospital wagons, 3,500 supply wagons loaded with ammunition and other matériel, fifty-two field kitchens, forty-five field bakeries, engineering equipment, and 4,000 horses.[3]

But prisoners and equipment were not the only thing the *Kaiserlich und Königlich* army left behind in Serbia. As the First Army entered Valjevo, it found typhus, diphtheria, and cholera among the 3,400 Austro-Hungarian soldiers in that town's hospital.

All told, during the first five months of the war the Austro-Hungarian Empire lost 273,805 men (7,592 officers and 266,212 enlisted) on the Balkan Front, approximately one-half of one percent of its pre-war population. Of this number, 28,276 were killed, 122,122 wounded, and 74,000 captured.[4] What was to have been a quick and easy victory over a rag-tag, third-rate Balkan state, had turned into disaster.

In Vienna, the defeat was seen as a profound military, political, and diplomatic catastrophe that threatened the very integrity of the Empire's southern borders. In spite of the Fifth Army's successful withdrawal from Belgrade, it lacked equipment, men, and most importantly, a will to fight. For the immediate future it was in no shape to mount successful resistance to an invasion, should Serbia decide to cross the Sava and invade. In Bosnia-Herzegovina, the Sixth Army ceased to exist for all intents and purposes: those units that escaped Mišić's First Army withdrew to the north of the Sava through Šabac, and left the Drina completely undefended. Bosnia-Herzegovina, the Dual Monarchy's most potentially unstable province, now lacked a defense other than a few small, poorly equipped garrisons and *Schutzkorps*. The Habsburg Empire's southern border lay open to an Entente invasion. If the Serbian Army chose to attack, nothing would stand between it, Sarajevo, and Zagreb, save a few small garrison forces. If the Serbian Army attacked to the north, it would be able to march virtually unopposed as far as Novi Sad and the Petrovaradin fortress. Fearing the worst, the AOK hurriedly prepared to repel a Serbian invasion.

Despite the complete collapse of its southern front, the Dual Monarchy had no reason to fear a Serbian invasion. The victory on the Kolubara aside, the Serbian Army was unable to mount an offensive operation. Even during the best of times, Serbia's army was woefully unprepared for an invasion of Austria-Hungary. Now after five months of constant fighting, the weather and the enemy had all taken their toll on the physical and psychological state of the Serbian Army. Although enthused by the victory, the emotional and physical costs had been too great. The Battle on the Kolubara used most of the artillery ammunition recently arrived from France, and the army's matériel state was as bad as ever, alleviated only slightly by the large quantities of captured Habsburg matériel. In addition, Serbia had incurred disproportionately high manpower losses. With a population less than one-tenth the size of Austria-Hungary's, Serbia lost a total of 165,557 men in 1914, or 3.5 percent of its pre-war population. Of this number, 22,276 were killed, 96,122 wounded, and 45,159 missing. For such a small country, the price of victory was almost Pyrrhic.[5]

The Austro-Hungarian prisoners infected with typhus, diphtheria, and cholera quickly infected the Serbs. In spite of numerous medical missions sent by Serbia's allies, during the remainder of the winter and spring these diseases cost Serbia nearly as many lives—160,000—as the battlefield casualties during the first five months of war.[6] So widespread was the epidemic that the American journalist John Reed, visiting Serbia in the spring of 1915, called it "the country of death" and "the country of typhus."[7] The ensuing epidemics, which ravaged Serbia's military and civilian population alike, further weakened the country's ability to support military operations. Yet Serbia did not suffer these epidemics alone: retreating Habsburg soldiers carried disease back to Bosnia-Herzegovina and Srem, causing large numbers of deaths along the Dual Monarchy's southern border during the winter of 1914–1915.[8]

The western portions of the country—the fertile Mačva region in particular—were laid barren by the ravages of war. Most of the previously existing primitive infrastructure had been destroyed, either as the Serbian Army retreated or as the Austro-Hungarian Army advanced. Bridges, telephone and telegraph wires, and train tracks were destroyed; crops were ripped up and trampled; over 2,000 homes were razed, and numerous others were burned and looted; numerous cities—including Loznica, Šabac, Valjevo, and Belgrade—were plundered, shelled, and burned. And then there were the unspeakable atrocities against the civilian population. Serbia was deeply wounded and desperately needed time to recover.

On December 21, Oskar Potiorek, who had by now presided over three major disasters—security for the Archduke Ferdinand and his wife Sophie, and the humiliating defeats on Mount Cer and the Kolubara River—resigned in disgrace and was pensioned, along with the Fifth Army's commander General von Frank. The Archduke Eugene replaced Potiorek as commander of *Balkanstreitkräfte*, while Croatian General Sarkotić assumed operational command of the Empire's forces in Dalmatia and Bosnia-Herzegovina.

In sharp contrast to the disgraced Potiorek, people throughout Serbia and the Entente heaped praise on the "Hero of Suvobor," Živojin Mišić, who was quickly promoted to the rank of *Vojvoda* for his performance during the Battle of Kolubara.

In mid-December, the Balkan Front fell silent as the combatants licked their wounds. The two sides remained behind their pre-war boundaries, with the exception of the upper Drina's east bank near Višegrad, Goražde, and Foča, which the Serbian and Montenegrin forces continued to occupy. Once again the Drina, Sava, and Danube rivers assumed their age-old function as borders.

As the Dual Monarchy's Balkan forces rebuilt and re-equipped during the winter and spring of 1915, the Empire's attention was distracted by other events, which kept it from pursuing a new campaign against Serbia. By mid-December 1914, Russian General Brusilov's Army group had penetrated deep into the Carpathians, almost to the Pannonian Plain. By the end of March 1915, the enormous fortress at Przemysl fell to the Russians, causing the alarmed Germans to send aid to the Dual Monarchy. The British landing at Gallipoli in April 1915 threatened to push Greece closer to the Entente. And Italy's entry into the war in late May of 1915 forced the Empire to divert some of its Balkan forces to the Italian front, opening up an entirely new threat to the Habsburg fleet at Pula and Kotor. Given the threat that the Russians, Italians, and British posed to the Dual Monarchy, Vienna could ill afford to spare valuable troops on another campaign against Serbia. The Balkan Front would remain quiet until October of 1915.

To the non-combatant go the spoils

On December 7, 1914, as word began to filter back to Niš about the remarkable extent of Mišić's victory, the Serbian government publically declared its official war aims in the "Niš Declaration." Drafted by the Yugoslav Committee, the declaration called for uniting Serbs, Croats, and Slovenes in one state, at the expense of the Habsburg Empire. For the first time, the government officially announced what had been semi-officially spoken and written since the war's outbreak. The territories outlined in the document were identical to those sought by Belgrade, and it referred to Serbia as "Piedmont."[9]

In the days following the Niš Declaration, the Serbian press openly trumpeted Serbia's claims: Slovenia, Istria, Trieste, Dalmatia, Bosnia-Herzegovina, Croatia, Srem, Banat, Bačka, Baranja, and Slavonia. On December 22, the Belgrade daily newspaper *Politika* ran an article with the banner headline "The Future of the Slavs," in which it called for a union of Croats, Serbs, Slovenes, and Bulgarians. The following day another article, headlined "Our Pretensions" by the historian Stanoje Stanojević, argued that in light of Serbia's magnificent battlefield victories, it was no longer appropriate to be humble about Serbia's political aims.[10]

Although a great many issues remained regarding the future South Slav state, in the heady days following the victory at Kolubara, these were put aside to be resolved at a later date.[11]

As Serbia entered 1915, it did so with a new sense of military and political confidence, as well as a sense of purpose: the unification of the Balkan Peninsula's Slavs into one state. Yet, Serbia's newly proclaimed war aims to the contrary, during the coming months the Entente continued to negotiate with Italy. By late March, the Entente promised Italy all of Dalmatia, Istria, and Trieste, which was confirmed in the Treaty of London on April 26, 1915. The very lands Serbia had counted on as part of a post-war South Slav state were now being given to an ostensible ally, and one that had yet to enter the fight.

On the international stage, Serbia became more assertive about its ambitions for a post-war Greater Serbia or Yugoslavia. The destruction of the Habsburg Empire, for so long an unspoken and unlikely wish, now became a realistic and achievable goal. At the same time, Serbia confronted the horrible reality left in the wake of the 1914 campaigns: its manpower and matériel losses could not be easily replaced. Serbia's allies were slow to respond with the matériel necessary to rebuild the ragged army and restock empty warehouses.

On the Balkan Peninsula itself, Serbia's neighbors all took careful note of Serbia's two convincing victories over a Great Power, the mighty Habsburg Empire. Overnight, the Serbian Army earned a reputation as a force to be reckoned with, one capable of defeating a Great Power. The Serbian victory increased pro-Entente sentiment in Romania. Greece became more amenable to the shipment of Entente military supplies to Russia and Serbia via Thessaloniki. Bulgarian agitation in the press and along the border calmed somewhat. And the Albanian population along the Macedonian and southern Serbian borders became more subdued.

For Austria-Hungary, the events on the Balkan Front in 1914 were a tremendous embarrassment, disappointment, and humiliation. What was to have been a quick and easy campaign to avenge Franz Ferdinand, eradicate the Balkan upstart, remove the threat of South Slav nationalism to the Empire's internal political arrangements, bring security to the Empire's southern borders, and enable the Empire to continue its southward expansion with a railway to Thessaloniki, had turned into a debacle of epic proportions. A second-rate, agrarian Balkan power of 4.5 million people had humbled an industrialized Empire of 50 million. To worsen matters, the war had expanded far beyond Vienna's original intention of a localized Balkan conflict, in which the future existence of Serbia was at stake. By late 1914, with all the Great Powers embroiled in the war, there existed the distinct possibility that the very existence of Austria-Hungary was now at stake.

Why Austria-Hungary lost

Heretofore, the only explanations of the Austro-Hungarian Empire's poor performance have come from the Empire's apologists, who attempted to attribute the defeat to pre-war military unpreparedness, a shortage of modern military equipment and training, a lack of combat experience, and superior Serbian military prowess. Yet the reasons for the Serbian victories at Cer and Kolubara are as different from one another as is the reason for the Habsburg triumph in Mačva in early November. All three major battles—on Mount Cer, on the Drina, and along the Kolubara—were decided by different factors that had little to do with the state of readiness of Austria-Hungary's pre-war army.

In early August 1914, the operational forces of *Balkanstreitkräfte* outnumbered the Serbian operational army by as much as three to one. Even after the AOK transferred the Second Army to Galicia, the Habsburg Army still had more troops, and maintained a more than three-to-one advantage in artillery. Not only did the Austro-Hungarian Army far outnumber that of Serbia, but its weaponry, equipment, and supply situation were in most respects far superior to Serbia's. In marked contrast to accounts of the Serbian Army, one does not find accounts of barefoot or moccasin-clad, half-uniformed Habsburg troops advancing into battle carrying black powder, single-shot rifles.

Some Habsburg apologists have concentrated on superior Serbian artillery as an explanation for the debacle. Yet the Habsburg forces maintained a more than three-to-one advantage in artillery throughout 1914. Unlike the Serbian Army, the Habsburg forces did not suffer massive ammunition shortages. Nor are they reported to have withdrawn entire batteries from the front, due to a lack of ammunition. One former Austro-Hungarian artillery officer, Michael Elmannsberger, claimed that at the beginning of the war the Habsburg artillery had "high standards in firing technique," and "up to the end of the war the Austro-Hungarian artillery exceeded in firing technique all others with whom they came in contact." It appeared that "the thorough peace-time training of the young officers in firing instructions was amply repaid."[12] We must therefore look beyond the physical preparations of the Austro-Hungarian Army to find the causes for Serbia's victory, and the Dual Monarchy's defeat.

In assessing the Balkan Front in 1914, the Habsburg rank and file appear to have fought bravely and to the extent of their capabilities. Their equipment appears to have been modern and in ample supply. The answers to why Austria-Hungary failed must be found in other places. Indeed, there are ample reasons for Habsburg failure, both on a strategic and tactical level. On the strategic level, the common factors in the two Habsburg defeats were poor strategic planning and poor leadership. On the tactical level, the most important reasons are the lack of tactical integration of the superior Austro-Hungarian artillery and Habsburg infantry doctrine.

The overall Habsburg plan for mobilization and invasion was flawed from the outset. The Empire's mobilization plan called for *Minimalgruppe B*—the Fifth and Sixth Armies—to concentrate the bulk of its forces in Bosnia-Herzegovina, along the west bank of the Drina River. Given the rugged, easily defensible terrain of eastern Bosnia-Herzegovina, the Empire stationed far more troops there than a defensive posture would warrant. The overwhelming Habsburg superiority in mountain formations and mountain artillery, as well as the mountainous terrain, which leant itself to defense, meant that only one Army at most was needed to protect Bosnia-Herzegovina from invasion.

A second flaw in the plan dealt with the invasion route. Rather than attack Serbia at its most vulnerable point, the Morava river valley, Potiorek's invasion plan called for choosing the least hospitable terrain, crossing the Drina and advancing through the marshy and mountainous terrain of western Serbia. Given the lack of passable roads, the muddy conditions, and the easily defensible mountainous terrain, such a route gave every advantage to the defenders and no advantage to the invaders.[13] Such a route also presented logistical problems: the Empire had only three rail lines running toward Serbia's western border. After crossing the border, the Habsburg forces were forced to use horse-drawn carts to supply the army. As the Austro-Hungarian Army advanced deeper into Serbia, supply routes lengthened, winter set in, and the roads became impassable: it was only a matter of time before Mother Nature became as significant an obstacle to the Habsburg forces as the Serbian Army.

A far easier and more logistically justifiable route would have been to cross the Sava and Danube rivers and attack from the north, directly toward the mouth of the Morava. This route offered almost 45 kilometers of a relatively flat and wide valley, before encountering the first rough terrain. In such terrain, the Empire's superiority in artillery would tip the scales in its favor. And given the logistical demands of a modern field army, the eight rail lines running up to the Empire's southern borders along the Sava and Danube rivers, as well as the rail line running directly from Zemun the entire length of the Morava valley, made a northern invasion route the logical choice.

An earlier Habsburg general, Louis of Baden, used this route successfully in 1690 when fighting the Turkish Empire. At various times during 1914, both Generals von Frank and Krauss argued with Potiorek that this northern route should be followed, all to no avail.[14] In October 1915, when German Field Marshall August von Mackensen led a joint German/Austro-Hungarian invasion of Serbia, this northern route was used with surprising ease and success. Indeed, it was Potiorek's choice of direction that some Austro-Hungarian apologists subsequently blamed for the Empire's defeat.[15]

In addition to bad strategic planning, poor Austro-Hungarian generalship helped the Serbian forces to win the victory. At the outset of the first invasion on August 12, Potiorek ordered the Fifth Army to invade Serbia before the Sixth Army completed its concentration, and while the status of the Second

Army remained uncertain. This decision, largely a result of political concerns, meant that the Fifth Army's attack was not coordinated with the other two Armies, and that it bore the brunt of the Serbian counterattack alone. By the time the Sixth and Second Armies entered battle on the left and right wings, it was too late: the Austro-Hungarian center had collapsed and was in full retreat.

During the battle along the Kolubara, poor leadership also played a primary role in the debacle. In mid-November after seizing Valjevo, Potiorek ignored his generals, who claimed their armies needed rest and replenishment. Potiorek placed little stock in his generals' reports that the Serbian Army had dug in along the banks of the Kolubara and Ljig rivers. He also ignored the increasingly poor state of supply and morale among the Austro-Hungarian forces and concentrated solely on an imagined Serbian collapse. Rather than allow his armies the rest and resupply they so badly needed, Potiorek looked to the political consequences of capturing Belgrade in time for the anniversary of the Emperor's coronation. To achieve this goal, he pushed his increasingly ragged and depleted forces to the point where their matériel and numerical superiority no longer afforded them an advantage.

On the tactical level, the Austro-Hungarian Army misused and wasted what should have been its primary and overwhelming advantage: its artillery. Austro-Hungarian artillery was divided among advancing columns, and, with few exceptions, was never used on the divisional level, or in concentration against Serbian strong points. The commanders of artillery brigades rarely used their artillery in concert. On one of the few occasions when the Habsburg forces coordinated and concentrated their artillery fire, the breakout from Mačva against Stepanović's Second Army, the Serbian troops literally melted away before the intense Habsburg artillery barrage, and the Fifth Army advanced with few casualties. Many Habsburg infantry officers did not appreciate artillery's power and use, and were often unwilling to wait for the artillery to soften up a target prior to an attack. Prior to an engagement, "the artillery received either none or only meaningless orders, and then as the fight progressed, usually nothing more."[16] This meant Habsburg infantry often attacked Serbian positions without artillery support.

Habsburg infantry doctrine also contributed to the Balkan debacle. In addition to attacking frequently without artillery support, the infantry often advanced in massed formations and columns, which caused particularly high losses during the Battle of Mount Cer. Some Austro-Hungarian officers thought they could break holes in the Serbian Front by using massed human bodies.[17]

Another problem was the lack of an effective pursuit. On those occasions when the Habsburg troops forced the Serbian soldiers to withdraw or retreat, the Habsburg forces were slow to follow. During 1914, there are few examples of Austro-Hungarian units pursuing a retreating Serbian unit. On numerous occasions, the Habsburg forces broke the Serbian lines and caused the Serbian troops to flee in panic and disarray. Yet they always allowed the Serbian forces ample time to withdraw unmolested to new defensive positions.

During battles, the Austro-Hungarian infantry always opened rifle fire at long range. As the infantry approached the Serbian trenches, it would often fall silent for hours at a time, because the advancing troops had fired all their rifle ammunition. The infantry would then dig in at the point where they ran out of ammunition and wait until fresh ammunition arrived. The Habsburg troops lacked training with hand grenades and used them infrequently. So too, the Habsburg forces lacked sufficient numbers of cavalry, and did not use effectively the cavalry they did have.

All told, strategic and tactical mistakes and poor generalship combined to weaken Austria-Hungary's war-making ability. The Dual Monarchy's misuse of artillery and infantry, as well as grave strategic errors, significantly reduced the Empire's overwhelming advantage in manpower and artillery. Yet, in the end, much of the blame for Austria-Hungary's Balkan debacle rests squarely on the shoulders of Oskar Potiorek.

Why Serbia won

As we examine the Balkan Front from Serbia's perspective, an unusual picture emerges. In August 1914, the conflict between Serbia and Austria-Hungary was a mismatch of the worst sort. On paper it appeared that the Dual Monarchy would quickly demolish Serbia's ramshackle army. Only a fool would have predicted Serbian victories of such enormous proportions. Yet somehow, Serbia managed not only to defeat the Habsburg forces, but to do so convincingly. The reasons for Serbia's success may be found only partially in Austro-Hungarian mistakes. The primary reason for Serbia's success was brilliant strategy by the Chief of Serbia's High Command, *Vojvoda* Radomir Putnik, and numerous officers willing to take the initiative on the field of battle. Other reasons for success include good generalship, the army's tactical doctrines, battlefield experience from the Balkan Wars, and the psychological makeup of the Serbian soldier.

Vojvoda Putnik's strategy recognized that Serbia had insufficient troop strength to defend its borders in forward positions. The placement of the Serbian forces took full advantage of the mountainous terrain along the Drina River and other natural defenses. So too, the use of third levy soldiers and irregular units for forward defense and guerrilla actions gave Serbia an edge.

Unlike Potiorek, Putnik based the Serbian Army's movements and positions on military not political concerns. The late decision to defend Belgrade at the outbreak of war, together with Putnik's decision in late November to abandon the capital, demonstrate the Serbian High Command was not a hostage to politics. During the course of 1914, this translated into a calculated willingness to allow key cities—such as Valjevo, Belgrade, Šabac,

Obrenovac, Uice, and Loznica—to fall to the enemy, often without a fight, when those cities' positions were deemed unsuitable for further defense. The only politically motivated action undertaken by the Serbian High Command, the ill-advised invasion of Srem, ended in failure and weakened Serbia's defenses along the Drina at a critical moment.

Putnik (and Mišič during his tenure as aide-de-camp to Putnik) constantly sought opportunities to counter Austro-Hungarian advances with Serbian offensives. Serbia's generals, experienced in the Balkan Wars, were familiar with the effect of an offensive, both on the enemy and on the morale of their own troops. For this reason, Serbia's High Command ordered numerous counterattacks precisely at moments when the Austro-Hungarian forces expected the Serbian Army to be in full retreat. These counterattacks forced the Austro-Hungarian forces to maintain constant vigilance, even when following retreating Serbian forces.

Serbia benefited from having able, battle-tested generals. There is no question that the leadership of Stepa Stepanović and Živojin Mišić turned the tide in the Serbian victories at Cer and Kolubara. So too, there can be little question that General Jurišić-Šturm performed heroic service with his Third Army, the weakest of the three main Serbian field armies. Both during the Battle on Mount Cer and the Battle on the Drina, his Third Army bore the brunt of the Austro-Hungarian assault. Yet both times Jurišić-Šturm managed to hold off overwhelming forces until the arrival of reinforcements, all the while inflicting heavy losses on the enemy. Perhaps of greatest importance, these leaders consistently took the initiative, and when they disagreed with a High Command directive, would argue their position strongly to Putnik.

On a tactical level, Serbia's army benefited heavily from the Balkan Wars, and had incorporated the wartime experiences into its military doctrines. The Serbian artillery, although heavily outnumbered by the Austro-Hungarian artillery, operated in close contact with the infantry, which had "an almost superstitious reverence for artillery fire."[18] The Serbian Army frequently dragged its cannon into the front trenches for direct fire against the enemy. The outnumbered Serbian batteries always delivered effective fire against the Austro-Hungarian troops and artillery, often causing panic and disarray in the Habsburg ranks.

The Serbian infantry made heavy use of hand grenades, usually to the consternation of the Habsburg troops.[19] The Serbian Army learned of this through interrogations of prisoners. Acting on this information, the High Command ordered the officers—when charging—to give the command to throw hand grenades very loudly, simply to demoralize the enemy.

A primary source of Serbian tactical supremacy seems to have come from the infantry's defensive doctrines, which mirrored those of the High Command's strategy. Serbia's defense was both passive and active. When the Habsburg troops attacked, Serbian forward pickets and outposts would attempt to channel the charges along certain corridors. As the enemy approached, Serbian artillery opened up, often from the forward trenches.

Sometimes the Serbian defenders purposely abandoned forward positions to give the impression of retreat. When the Habsburg troops came upon the main defensive positions, Serbian forces—usually in battalion strength— would counterattack along the flanks of the charging Habsburg troops, often encircling them. As the Austro-Hungarian troops broke and ran, the Serbian troops would then pursue, with the aim of following the enemy into his lines and seizing his forward positions. The fleeing troops, closely pursued by Serbian infantry, would often sow panic in the Habsburg lines. On many occasions, the Serbian Army used the tactic of such a passive/active defense to rout superior forces from their positions. As a result, any time the Habsburg forces mounted an infantry assault on a Serbian position, it carried the risk of a strong counterattack and loss of Habsburg positions.

On a larger scale, the Serbian forces incorporated these tactics on the Divisional and Army levels. It was precisely these tactics of pursuit that enabled the Serbian forces to break the Fifth Army on Mount Cer, and the Sixth Army on Suvobor and Maljen.

A final yet significant contributing factor to Serbia's victories lay in the psychological makeup of the Serbian soldiers. Hardy, battle-hardened, and possessing enormous initiative, they continued to fight under conditions that would have destroyed lesser forces. The Austro-Hungarian Combined Corps commander General Alfred Krauss said: "I viewed them and view them now as soldiers, as the strongest of all our enemies . . . They gave our troops much more trouble than the Russians, Rumanians, and Italians."[20] Unlike the Habsburg troops, the Serbian soldiers were fighting on their home territory to protect their country from a foreign invasion. This gave the Serbian troops both an edge and a disadvantage.

For some reason, unknown to observers, but commented on by many, Serbian soldiers became demoralized when forced to spend long periods of time on the defensive. Although the unremitting artillery bombardment during the period of trench warfare affected morale, being on the defensive seemed to take as great a toll as did Habsburg artillery. General Mišić noticed a significant morale boost on December 3 when his troops went on the offensive, even before the First Army's significant breakthrough had occurred. Simply going on the offensive proved psychologically healthy for the troops.

A post-mortem

In assessing the factors that led to Serbia's victory and Austria-Hungary's defeat in 1914, foremost is the military leadership on both sides. The victory was the result of brilliant Serbian generalship and a sound defensive strategy. The Serbian generals—battle tested during the Balkan Wars—knew the capabilities of their troops, and were experienced in maneuver, unlike their Habsburg counterparts, who had only experienced peacetime exercises. The

Serbian High Command, under the direction of *Vojvoda* Putnik, formulated a defensive strategy based on a thorough knowledge of and familiarity with Serbia's topography, as well as an understanding of the larger strategic goals: protecting the Morava–Vardar corridor and preventing the Habsburg Second Army from being transported to the Eastern Front.

This does not imply that all the decisions of Serbia's High Command were perfect. Modern historians and military specialists have criticized the Serbian High Command for bowing to Entente pressure to invade Srem and leaving the Drina relatively unguarded. So too, questions have been raised about the wisdom of the High Command decision to continue fighting at Mačkov Kamen after it became apparent that Potiorek's Sixth Army was not in flight. Furthermore, Stepa Stepanović has come under criticism for his decision to abandon Mačva and his Army's sluggish performance during the Battle along the Kolubara.

In contrast to Serbia's defensive strategy, Potiorek's strategy was politically motivated. Wishing to achieve a victory by the Emperor's birthday (August 18), and hoping to avenge the personal embarrassment of the Sarajevo assassination, he spurred his forces into battle at the earliest possible moment, prior to their being in a state of complete readiness. Because these forces were able to enter combat only sequentially, Potiorek squandered Austria-Hungary's quantitative and qualitative superiority by sending his men into battle piecemeal, without mutual support. Political motives also entered into Potiorek's decision—against the advice of his generals—to advance toward Belgrade immediately after the capture of Valjevo. The impending anniversary of the Emperor's coronation (December 3) put a special cachet on capturing the Serbian capital by that date. This decision to advance before his troops were ready, directly contributed to the defeat along the Kolubara. And once again, during the battle along the Kolubara, Austro-Hungarian forces frequently attacked in an uncoordinated and piecemeal fashion, such as at Varovnica and Kosmaj.

In any battle or campaign, each side is bound to make a number of mistakes or errors, in its strategy, tactics, decision-making, and execution of movement. Many battles are won or lost when a combatant skillfully and quickly exploits his opponent's weakness or errors. Unfortunately for the Dual Monarchy, during the summer, fall, and winter of 1914, its military leaders made more than their share of serious errors.

Fortunately for Serbia, its High Command and army were led by military leaders of an extremely high caliber. The planning of Radomir Putnik, and the daring, energetic, and innovative performances of Živojin Mišić, Stepa Stepanović, Petar Bojović, and Pavle Jurišić-Šturm, enabled the Serbian Army to reduce the enormous Austro-Hungarian advantage in arms and men to a point where Serbia's beleaguered army actually stood a fighting chance.

In the end, the first five months of hostilities on the Balkan Front provided the Entente with two notable and much needed victories over the Triple Alliance, while diverting hundreds of thousands of Habsburg troops desperately needed on other fronts. These victories ended the immediate danger to Serbia's survival as a state, and provided fuel for the fires of national expansion and the unification of the Balkan Peninsula's Slavs in one state.

In addition, Serbia's eleven-year-old political struggle against Austro-Hungarian hegemony, as well as its now open struggle for larger ethnic and nationalist goals, began for the first time to open serious ethnic and religious rifts among the Balkan Peninsula's Slavs. Questions hitherto submerged under the Imperial umbrellas of Austria-Hungary and Turkey were now brought into the open, as the question of national, religious, and ethnic allegiance arose within Bosnia-Herzegovina, Croatia, Dalmatia, Slavonia, Slovenia, and Vojvodina. To whom did Serbs, Croats, and Muslims in the Habsburg Empire owe their loyalty: a Greater Serbia, the Habsburg Emperor, an independent Croatian state, or a South Slav state? Did the peninsula's Muslim Slavs owe allegiance to the Sultan in Istanbul? Some of the ill will generated by these loyalty questions would have far-reaching ramifications for the South Slav lands throughout the twentieth century.

As the diplomats in Rome, London, Paris, and Petrograd argued over the shape of the post-war world, the competing claims for ethnic, national, and religious loyalty became increasingly contradictory and confusing. When these claims contradicted the aspirations of a Great Power, such as Italy's claims for the Dalmatian coast, Serbia's role in the Entente became quite clear: it was not a full partner. In the case of the Habsburg Empire's boundaries, British insistence on maintaining the pre-war status quo left Serbia's aspirations—as well as those of many other South Slavs—in the shadow of Great Power diplomacy. This status as a second-class ally was clearly reflected in the Entente's efforts to pressure Serbia to make territorial compensation to both Bulgaria and Italy, in the hope of bringing both these countries into the war on the side of the Entente.

Serbia entered 1915 with a war-ravaged economy, an exhausted and worn-out army, and the status of second-class ally. But, unlike the situation five months previously in July 1914, its very existence was no longer at stake. The new year brought with it the possibility of an eventual Entente victory, and the liberation and unification of the Habsburg Empire's South Slavs with Serbia. In January 1915, the Entente still thought the war would end quickly, and Serbia—basking in the Pyrrhic glory of its victory—looked forward to the realization of the aims first enumerated by Ilija Garašanin in 1844.

Eleven months later, the picture would be radically different. Serbia's army would begin its long retreat through Albania, abandoning the country to Bulgaria, Germany, and the Dual Monarchy. The very future of an independent Serbia would be brought into question.

But in September 1918 the war would come full circle, and Serbia would play a crucial role in the events that forced the Central Powers to surrender. The outcome would be a new South Slav state, whose history is still being debated.

NOTES

Introduction

1   After the war, the Royal Yugoslav Army General Staff compiled a large multi-volume work entitled *Veliki rat Srbije za oslobođenje i ujedinjenje Srba, Hrvata i Slovenaca* (*The Great War of Serbia for the Liberation and Unification of Serbs, Croats, and Slovenes*). This was in many respects identical in layout and focus to the later official Austrian government (Österreichischen Bundesministerium für Heereswesen und vom Kriegsarchiv) publication *Österreich-Ungarns letzter Krieg 1914–1918*, 7 vols, Edmund Glaise von Horstenau, ed., Verlag Militärwissenschaftlichen Mitteilungen (Vienna, 1931–1938).

2   The most recent well-known work to posit this idea is Christopher Clark's *The Sleepwalkers: How Europe Went to War in 1914*, Penguin (London, 2013), p. xxi.

3   The Franco-Serbian offensive on the Salonika Front on September 14, 1918 broke the Central Powers' defensive lines and left the back door open to Budapest, Vienna, and Berlin, forcing Austria-Hungary and Germany to sue for peace.

4   The most prominent post-war Habsburg apologists include: Franz Conrad von Hötzendorff, *Aus Meiner Dienstzeit, 1906–1918*, vols III, IV, V, VI, Rikola Verlag (Vienna, 1923); Edmund Glaise Horstenau, ed., *Österreich-Ungarns letzter Krieg 1914–1918*, vols I, II, Verlag Militärwissenschaftlichen Mitteilungen (Vienna, 1931); August von Cramon, *Unser Österreichisch-ungarischer Bundesgenosse im Weltkrieg*, 2nd revised edition, E.S. Mittler (Berlin, 1922); August von Cramon and P. Fleck, *Deutschlands Schicksalbund mit Österreich-Ungarn*, Verlag für Kulturpolitik (Berlin, 1932); Alfred Krauss, *Die Ursachen Unserer Niederlage*, Lehmann (Munich, 1921); Wilhelm Czermak, *In Deinem Lager war Österreich: Die Österreichisch-ungarische Armee, wie man sie nicht kennt*, W.G. Korn (Breslau, 1938).

5   Gunther Rothenberg, "The Habsburg Army in the First World War: 1914–1918," in Bela K. Király and Nandor F. Dreisiger, eds, *East Central European Society in World War I*, Social Science Monographs (Boulder, CO, 1985), p. 289.

6   See portrayals of Habsburg readiness in István Deák, "The Habsburg Army in the First and Last Days of World War I: A Comparative Analysis," in Bela K. Király and Nandor F. Dreisiger, eds, *East Central European Society in World War I*, Social Science Monographs (Boulder, CO, 1985); István Deák, *Beyond*

Nationalism: A Social and Political History of the Habsburg Officer Corps, 1848–1918, Oxford University Press (New York, 1990). Janos Decsy, "The Habsburg Army on the Threshold of Total War," in Bela K. Király and Nandor F. Dreisiger, eds, *East Central European Society in World War I*, Social Science Monographs (Boulder, CO, 1985); Rudolf Jerabek, *Potiorek: General im Schatten von Sarajevo*, Verlag Styria (Graz, 1991); Robert A. Kann, Bela Király, and Paula S. Fichtner, eds, *The Habsburg Empire in World War I*, Columbia University Press (New York, 1977); Gunther Rothenberg, *The Army of Francis Joseph*, Purdue University Press (West Lafayette, IN, 1976); Gunther Rothenberg, "The Habsburg Army in the First World War: 1914–1918," in Bela K. Király and Nandor F. Dreisiger, eds, *East Central European Society in World War I*, Social Science Monographs (Boulder, CO, 1985); A.J.P. Taylor, *The Habsburg Monarchy 1809–1918*, Harper (New York, 1965). In fairness it should be pointed out that modern historians, most notably István Deák and Gunther Rothenberg, have dispelled the myth of ethnic disloyalty among the Empire's soldiers.

7   Gunther E. Rothenberg, "The Austro-Hungarian Campaign Against Serbia in 1914," *Journal of Military History*, 53(2): 127–146 (April 1989), p. 145.

8   Rothenberg, *The Army of Francis Joseph*, p. 182.

9   Rothenberg, "The Austro-Hungarian Campaign," p. 134.

10 "Resüme über die Serbische Armee im Feldzeug 1912–13," Chef d. Gestb., Evidenzbureau, No. 1274, Kriegsarchiv (Vienna).

11 Cramon, *Unser Österreichisch-ungarischer*, p. 200.

12 Arhiv Srpske pravoslavne crkve, Crkvena opština Sarajevo (Stara Srpska Pravoslavna Crkva Sv. Arhanđela Mihaila i Gavrila), hereafter ASPC/COS. *Ljetopis Srpskih Osnovnih i Više Djevojačke Škole u Sarajevu, 31 augusta 1898 do 28 juna 1914*, entry for June 16 (old calendar), 1914. In Bosnia, the Habsburg Monarchy continued the Turkish practice of recording people by religion, as opposed to nationality. Thus, the categories of Catholic and Protestant could refer to any number of national groups from throughout the Empire as well as Bosnians.

13 Paul Miller, "Yugoslav Eulogies: The Footprints of Gavrilo Princip," The Carl Beck Papers in Russian and East European Studies, No. 2304, University Library Systems, University of Pittsburgh (Pittsburgh, PA, 2014), p. 14.

14 Dragoslav Ljubibratić, *Mlada Bosna i Sarajevski atentat*, Muzej grada Sarajeva (Sarajevo, 1964), p. 7. See also David James Smith, *One Morning in Sarajevo: 28 June 1914*, Phoenix (London, 2009), pp. 282–285.

15 "Otkrivanje spomen-ploče Gavrilu Principu," *Oslobođenje* (Sarajevo, May 4, 1945). See also Miller, "Yugoslav Eulogies: The Footprints of Gavrilo Princip," p. 25.

16 Miller, "Yugoslav Eulogies: The Footprints of Gavrilo Princip," p. 35.

17 Emily Gunzburger Makaš, "Museums and the History and Identity of Sarajevo," paper presented at the European Association for Urban History's 11th International Conference on Urban History, *Cities and Societies in Comparative Perspective*, August 29 to September 1, 2012, Prague, Czech Republic.

18 The author resided in both Bosnia and Herzegovina and Serbia in the decade leading up to the commemoration and followed these events closely.

19 The author was shown some of this diplomatic correspondence on the condition that he not disclose the source. He has also seen third-party diplomatic cables from another EU member state regarding the Franco-Austrian disagreement, this too with the provision that he not disclose the source. Some of these documents remain in his possession.

20 These included the University of Utah, the Research Center for the Humanities of the Hungarian Academy of Sciences, the Institute for Balkan Studies and Thracology at the Bulgarian Academy of Sciences, the Institute for National History in Macedonia, the Institute for Recent History in Slovenia, and the Croatian Institute for History. Funding was provided by the Deutsche Forschungsgemeinschaft, the Hungarian Academy of Sciences, and the Canton of Sarajevo.

21 Author's conversations with conference organizer Husnija Kamberović from the Institut za istoriju in Sarajevo, and diplomats from EU member states.

22 "Prvo autonomija, pa samostalnost," *B92*, June 28, 2014. http://www.b92.net/info/vesti/index.php?yyyy=2014&mm=06&dd=28&nav_category=11&nav_id=869254 [Accessed June 28, 2014].

Chapter 1: A Sunday in Sarajevo

1 Franz Josef's official title was Seiner Kaiserlichen und Königlich Apostolischen Majestät. Franz Joseph I, von Gottes Gnaden Kaiser von Österreich; Apostolischer König von Ungarn, König von Bohmen, von Dalmatien, Kroatien, Slavonien, Gallizien, Lodomerien und Illyrien; König von Jerusalem, etc.; Erzherzog von Österreich; Großherzog von Toskana und Krakau; Herzog von Lothringen, von Salzburg, Steyer, Kärnten, Krain und der Bukowina; Großfürst von Siebenbürgen, Markgraf von Mähren; Herzog von Ober- und Niederschlesien, von Modena, Parma, Piacenza und Guastalla, von Auschwitz und Zator, von Teschen, Friaul, Ragusa und Zara; gefürsteter Graf von Habsburg und Tirol, von Kyburg, Görz und Gradiska; Fürst von Trient und Brixen; Markgraf von Ober- und Niederlausitz und in Istrien; Graf von Hohenembs, Feldkirch, Bregenz, Sonnenberg, etc.; Herr von Triest, von Cattaro und auf der windischen Mark; Großwojwod der Wojwodschaft Serbien, etc., etc. As shown in *Bosnischer Bote/Bosanski Glasnik 1914: Universal-Hand- und Adreszbuch für Bosnien und die Hercegovina*, Kommissionsverlag der Kais. Kön. Hof- und Staatsdruckerei in Wien (Vienna, 1914), p. 55.

2 The Heller was the subunit of the Austro-Hungarian Krone. One hundred Heller equaled one Krone.

3 *Bosnischer Bote/Bosanski Glasnik 1914.*

4 *Programm für die Reise Ihrer Hoheit der durchl. Frau Herzogin Sophie von Hohenberg nach der Bosnien und der Hercegovina vom 24. bis 30. Juni. 1914.* Document Inv. Broj R225 from the collection of the Nacionalna i univerzitetska Biblioteka Bosne i Hercegovine (NUBBiH).

5   The headline reads "Hoher Besuch." *Bosnische Post*, June 25, 1914, no. 142.
    Newspapers published in Sarajevo at the time included *Srpska Riječ, Istina,
    Hrvatski Dnevnik, Hrvatski List, Sarajevski List*, and *Vakat*.

6   Vladimir Dedijer, *Sarajevo 1914*, 1st edition, Prosveta (Belgrade, 1966),
    pp. 523–524.

7   See note 6.

8   Today's *ulica Zelenih beretki*.

9   Today's *Štrosmajerova*.

10 *Bosnische Post*, June 26, 1914, no. 143. The source for this is Borivoje Jevtić, a
    student at the time, but who himself gave post-facto contradictory reports on
    details of the assassination. A number of authors, including Dedijer, have
    labeled Jevtić's account unreliable. Jevtić's oft-reprinted statement from June
    29, 1929 in the *New York World* about the assassination contradicts a number
    of established facts and appears full of embellishments.

11 Letter of May 4/17, 1914, from Jovanović to Pašić, Arhiv Srbije, Ministarstvo
    Inostranih Dela—Političko Odeljenje (hereafter AS, MID-PO), 1914, V-I/1,
    II/349.

12 This information was compiled from numerous Sarajevo newspaper reports on
    the Duchess's activities.

13 Joachim Remak, *Sarajevo: The Story of a Political Murder*, Criterion Books
    (New York, 1959), p. 108.

14 *Programm für die Reise Ihrer Hoheit der durchl.*

15 Today's US Embassy and University of Sarajevo campus.

16 Peter F. Sugar, *Industrialization of Bosnia-Hercegovina, 1878–1918*, University
    of Washington Press (Seattle, WA, 1963), pp. 5, 15.

17 Robert J. Donia, *Sarajevo: A Biography*, Hurst (London, 2006), p. 64. See also
    Bosnischer Bote/Bosanski Glasnik 1914, p. 481.

18 *Bosnischer Bote/Bosanski Glasnik 1914*, pp. 489–490.

19 Miloš Ković, "The Beginning of the 1875 Serbian Uprising in Herzegovina:
    The British Perspective," *Balcanica*, XLI: 55–71 (Belgrade, 2010).

20 Hamdija Kapidžić, *Agrarno pitanje u Bosni i Hercegovini za vrijeme
    austrougarske uprave (1878–1918)*, Radovi—vol. XLIX, Odjeljenje društvenih
    nauka—vol. 16, ANUBiH (Sarajevo, 1973), p. 113.

21 According to the 1910 census, there were 1,898,044 residents (824,021 Serbs,
    611,884 Muslims, 433,480 Catholics, 11,247 Jews, and 6,247 Evangelical
    Protestants). See *Bosnischer Bote/Bosanski Glasnik 1914*. See also the web site
    for the *Zavod za statistiku Federacije BiH* (http://www.fzs.ba/popis.htm)
    [Accessed March 26, 2014].

22 Ferdo Hauptman, "Privreda i društvo Bosne i Hercegovine u doba Austro-
    Ugarske vladavine (1878–1918)," in Enver Redžić, ed., *Prilozi za istoriju
    Bosne i Hercegovine II*, vol. LXXiX, ANUBiH (Sarajevo, 1987), pp. 198–200.

23 Quoted in Luigi Albertini, *The Origins of the War of 1914*, 3 vols, translated
    and edited by Isabella M. Massey, Oxford University Press (London, 1953),
    vol. 2, p. 6.

24 See note 23, p. 24.

25 For those wishing an in-depth account of the day of the assassination, perhaps the best accounts of the plotters and the visit are found in volume 2 of Luigi Albertini's *The Origins of the War of 1914*, Oxford University Press (London, 1953); Vladimir Dedijer's *Sarajevo 1914*, 2nd edition, Prosveta (Belgrade, 1978); and Joachim Remak's *Sarajevo: The Story of a Political Murder*, Criterion Books (New York, 1959). Two other well-researched works that focus on the personal lives of the royal couple and the conspirators, respectively, are: Greg King and Sue Woolmans' *The Assassination of the Archduke: Sarajevo 1914 and the Romance that Changed the World*, Macmillan (London, 2013); and David James Smith's *One Morning in Sarajevo: 28 June 1914*, Phoenix (London, 2009).

26 *Bosnische Post*, June 29, 1914, no. 145.

27 Entry of June 15/28, 1914, *Zapisnik odborskih sednica za vreme od 1/I 1913 do 21/XII 1926*, ASPC/COS.

28 *Bosnische Post*, June 29, 1914, no. 145.

29 Vladimir Ćorović, *Crna knjiga: patnje Srba Bosne i Hercegovine za vreme svetskog rata 1914–1918*, 3rd edition, Udruženje ratnih dobrovoljaca 1912–1918. godine, njihovih potomaka i poštovalaca (Belgrade, 1996), p. 32.

30 See note 29, pp. 38–39.

31 *Bosnische Post*, June 29, 1914, no. 145a.

32 Ćorović, *Crna knjiga*, p. 40.

33 Entry for June 16/29, 1914, *Ljetopis Srpskih Osnovnih i Vise Djevojačke Škole u Sarajevu, 31 August 1898 do 28 Maja 1914*, ASPC/COS.

34 *Bosnische Post*, June 29, 1914, no. 145a.

35 See note 34.

36 See note 34.

37 *Bosnische Post*, June 30, 1914, no. 145a.

38 Ćorović, *Crna knjiga*, p. 42.

39 Burial records from *Groblje Koševo 1912–1925*, entry for June 21/July 11 1914; see also *Djelovodni Protokol 1912–1916*, entry for June 30/July 13, 1914, ASPC/COS.

40 *Sarajevski List*, July 1, 1914.

41 *Bosnische Post*, June 29, 1914, no. 145a.

42 This involved an incident in which Montenegrin authorities arrested a number of men crossing the border from Serbia carrying bombs. It is thought that they may have been involved in a plot to kill King Nikola. Leon Trotsky, *The War Correspondence of Leon Trotsky: The Balkan Wars, 1912–1913*, Pathfinder Press (New York, 1980), pp. 113–114.

43 *Bosnische Post*, June 30, 1914, no. 146.

44 *Sarajevski List, Vanredno Izdanje*, July 1, 1914, no. 134.

45 Remak, *Sarajevo: The Story of a Political Murder*, p. 55.

46   Dolph W.A. Owings, *The Sarajevo Trial*, Documentary Publications (Chapel Hill, NC, 1984), vol. I, p. xvii.

47   *Sarajevski List*, July 4, 1914, no. 137.

48   Ivan Kranjčević, *Uspomene jednog učesnika u Sarajevskom atentatu*, Svjetlost (Sarajevo, 1954), pp. 22–24.

49   The most insightful studies of the development of the student movement in Bosnia-Herzegovina prior to 1914 were written by two of Gavrilo Princip's schoolmates, Ivan Kranjčević and Dragoslav Ljubibratić. Kranjčević received a ten-year sentence for his part in the plot, which he served with Princip in Theresienstadt. Dragoslav Ljubibratić was a contemporary of the conspirators and associated with most of them from his school days. He wrote biographies of both Princip and Gaćinović.

50   Enver Redžić, "Omladinski pokret i sarajevski atentat," in Enver Redžić, ed., *Prilozi za istoriju Bosne i Hercegovine*, vol. 2, ANUBiH (Sarajevo, 1987), pp. 306–307. For further discussion, see Dušan Bataković's "The Balkan Piedmont—Serbia and the Yugoslav Question," *Dialogue*, 10: 25–73 (Paris, 1994).

51   Dragoslav Ljubibratić, *Mlada Bosna i Sarajevski atentat*, Muzej grada Sarajeva (Sarajevo, 1964), p. 96.

52   Owings, *The Sarajevo Trial*, p. 194.

53   Testimony of Ivan Kranjčević during the trial shows some of these nuances. Owings, *The Sarajevo Trial*, pp. 203–215.

54   *Bosnische Post*, February 19, 1912, no. 40; *Bosnische Post*, February 20, 1912, no. 41; *Bosnische Post*, February 21, 1912, no. 42.

55   *Bosnische Post*, February 21, 1912, no. 42.

56   Gérard Chaliand and Arnaud Blin, "The Golden Age of Terrorism," in Gérard Chaliand and Arnaud Blin, eds, *The History of Terrorism: From Antiquity to Al Qaeda*, University of California Press (Berkeley, CA, 2007), pp. 175–196.

57   Dedijer, *Sarajevo 1914*, 2nd edition, vol. 1, p. 31.

58   The "Propaganda of the Deed" was a popular anarchist idea stemming from the writings of such philosophers as Peter Kropotkin and Mikhail Bakunin.

59   Owings, *The Sarajevo Trial*, pp. 54–56.

60   Ljubibratić, *Mlada Bosna i Sarajevski atentat*, p. 113.

61   Predrag Palavestra, "Young Bosnia: Literary Action 1908–1914," *Balcanica*, XLI: 155–184 (Belgrade, 2011), p. 155.

62   Albertini, *The Origins of the War of 1914*, vol. 2, p. 23.

63   Ljubibratić, *Mlada Bosna i Sarajevski atentat*, p. 113.

64   Telegram of July 5/18, 1914, from Serbia's Foreign Ministry to all embassies. Published in Vladimir Dedijer and Života Anić, eds., *Dokumenti o spoljnoj politici Kraljevine Srbije, 1903–1914*, vol. VII, no. 1 (January 1/14–April 30/May 13, 1914); no. 2 (May 1/14–July 22/August 4, 1914) (Belgrade, 1980), p. 595.

65 Telegram of June 23/July 6, 1914, from Jovanović to Pašić, AS, MID-PO, 1914, V-I, 411, Fasc. 659. See also the two telegrams from Jovanović to Pašić of 16/19 June, 1914, published in Dedijer and Anić, eds, *Dokumenti o spoljnoj politici Kraljevine Srbije, 1903–1914*, pp. 422–423.

66 Communication of Herr Hoflehner to Count Berchtold, July 6, 1914, published in Stationery Office, *War 1914: Punishing the Serbs*, Crown Publishers (London, 1915), pp. 9–10.

67 Letter of July 1/14, 1914 to all Serbian embassies. Telegram of July 1/14, 1914 to all Serbian embassies. Published in Dedijer and Anić, eds., *Dokumenti o spoljnoj politici Kraljevine Srbije, 1903–1914*, pp. 553–555.

68 Telegram of July 5/18, 1914, from Serbia's Foreign Ministry to all embassies. Published in Dedijer and Anić, eds, *Dokumenti o spoljnoj politici Kraljevine Srbije, 1903–1914*, p. 595.

Chapter 2: A third Balkan war?

1 See documents nos. 10855 and 10862 in Ludwig Bittner and Hans Ubersberger, eds., *Österreich-Ungarns Aussenpolitik Von Der Bosnischen Krise 1908 Bis Zum Kriegsausbruch 1914: Diplomatische Aktenstücke Des Österreichisch-Ungarischen Ministeriums Des Äussern* (Vienna, 1930), vol. XIII, pp. 811–812, pp. 823–824 (hereafter ÖUAP).

2 Andrej Mitrović, *Srbija u prvom svetskom ratu*, Srpska književna zadruga (Belgrade, 1984), p. 82. Other sources quoted him as saying "Austria has declared war on us. That is her finish. God will give us victory." See Slavko Gavrilović et al., *Istorija Srpskog naroda*, vol. VI–2, Srpska književna zadruga (Belgrade, 1983), p. 38.

3 Telegram from Pašić to London Embassy, July 15/28, 1914, from the collection of Jovan Jovanović Pižon, Arhiv Jugoslavije (AJ) 80–7–352.

4 Leon Trotsky, *The War Correspondence of Leon Trotsky: The Balkan Wars, 1912–1913*, Pathfinder Press (New York, 1980), p. 79.

5 Joachim Remak, *The Origins of World War I, 1871–1914*, Holt, Rinehart & Winston (New York, 1967), p. 112.

6 For the original French-language text of the ultimatum, see ÖUAP vol. VIII, pp. 515–517, document no. 10395. For the full English-language translation, see Michael Boro Petrovich, *A History of Modern Serbia*, Harcourt Brace Jovanovich (New York, NY, 1976), vol. II, p. 614.

7 Jan G. Beaver, *Collision Course: Franz Conrad von Hötzendorf, Serbia, and the Politics of Preventive War*, Lulu Press (Raleigh, NC, 2009), p. 243.

8 ÖUAP, vol. VIII, p. 596, document no. 10526.

9 Luigi Albertini, *The Origins of the War of 1914*, translated and edited by Isabella M. Massey, Oxford University Press (London, 1953), vol. 2, p. 347.

10 Dušan P. Stefanović, "Pred buru. . . (Beograd u prvim danima svetskoga rata," in *Agonija Beograda u svetskom ratu*, Štamparija "Jedinstvo" (Belgrade, 1931), p. 4.

11 Đorđe Ćutković, "Spontani branioci Beograda 1914 godine," in *Agonija Beograda u svetskom ratu*, Štamparija "Jedinstvo" (Belgrade, 1931), p. 27.

12 Andrej Mitrović, "Albanci u politici Austro-Ugarske prema Srbiji 1914–1918," in *Srbi i Albanci u XX veku*, Naučni skupovi Srpske akademije nauka i umetnosti, vol. LXI, odeljenje istorijskih nauka, vol. 20 (Belgrade, 1991), p. 113.

13 *ÖUAP*, vol. VIII, p. 660, document no. 10646.

14 The original Serbian response is found in *ÖUAP*, vol. VIII, pp. 660–663, document no. 10648.

15 Kaiser Wilhelm II wrote that the Serbian response to the Austro-Hungarian ultimatum was "a brilliant performance for a time limit of only 48 hours. This is more than one could have expected! A great moral success for Vienna: but with it every reason for war drops away." See Sidney Bradshaw Fay, *The Origins of the World War*, Macmillan (New York, 1928), vol. II, p. 348.

16 Christopher Clark, *The Sleepwalkers: How Europe Went to War in 1914*, Penguin (London, 2013), pp. 464–466.

17 Stefanović, "Pred buru . . . (Beograd u prvim danima svetskoga rata," p. 7.

18 Arhiv Srpske akademije nauka i umetnosti (hereafter ASANU), Istorijska zbirka, Broj: 8701. Diary of Dušan Stefanović (hereafter *DDS*), p. 1.

19 Stefanović, "Pred buru . . . (Beograd u prvim danima svetskoga rata," p. 7.

20 Vladimir Dedijer and Života Anić, eds., *Dokumenti o spoljnoj politici Kraljevine Srbije, 1903–1914*, vol. VII, no. 1 (January 1/14– April 30/May 13, 1914); no. 2 (May 1/14–July 22/August 4, 1914) (Belgrade, 1980), document no. 538. See also *ÖUAP*, vol. VIII, p. 657, document no. 10642.

21 *Hrvatski dnevnik*, July 28, 1914, no. 170; Franz Conrad von Hötzendorff, *Aus Meiner Dienstzeit, 1906–1918*, Rikola Verlag (Vienna, 1923), vol. IV, p. 130; Dimitrije Djordjević, "Vojvoda Putnik, the Serbian High Command, and Strategy in 1914," in Bela K. Király and Nandor F. Dreisiger, eds, *East Central European Society in World War I*, East European Monographs (Boulder, CO, 1985), p. 572.

22 Sava Skoko, *Vojvoda Radomir Putnik*, Beogradski izdavačko-grafički zavod (Belgrade, 1984), vol. 2, p. 33.

23 Telegram 23 July 23/August 5, 1914, Arhiv Srbije, Ministarstvo Inostranih Dela—Političko Odeljenje (hereafter AS, MID-PO), 1914, I-I/16, V/428.

24 Dimitrije Djordjević, "Vojvoda Radomir Putnik," in Bela K. Király and Nandor F. Dreisiger, eds, *East Central European Society in World War I*, East European Monographs (Boulder, CO, 1985), p. 234.

25 *DDS*, entry for July 25, 1914.

26 See note 25, entry for July 26, 1914.

27 See note 25, entry for July 26, 1914.

28 A good overview of part of this period may be found in Wayne Vucinich, *Serbia between East and West, 1903–1908*, Stanford University Press (Palo Alto, CA, 1954).

29 Dušan Bataković, "Ilija Garašanin's 'Načertanije': A Reassessment," *Balcanica*, XXV–1: 157–183 (Belgrade, 1994). See also Radoš Ljušić, "Ilija Garašanin on Serbia's Statehood," *Balcanica*, XXXIX: 131–174 (Belgrade, 2008).

30 Nebojša Vuličević, "Odbor za škole i učitelje u Staroj Srbiji: osnivanje, organizacija i ciljevi (1868–1876)," *Srpske studije*, 4: 209–230 (Belgrade, 2013).

31 Translation from Bataković's "Ilija Garašanin's 'Načertanije': A Reassessment."

32 See Gunther Rothenberg's three excellent works on the topic: *The Austrian Military Border in Croatia, 1522–1747*, University of Illinois Press (Urbana, IL, 1960); *The Military Border in Croatia, 1740–1881: A Study of an Imperial Institution*, University of Chicago Press (Chicago, IL, 1966); and "The Habsburg Army in the Napoleonic Wars," *Military Affairs: The Journal of Military History, Including Theory and Technology*, 37(1): 1–5 (February 1973).

33 Juraj Križanić, *Politika*, Blackwell (Oxford, 1985).

34 The most noted leaders of this movement were Ljudevit Gaj, Antun Mažuranić, and Vjekoslav Babukić.

35 Perhaps the best study of Austria-Hungary's efforts to push south toward Thessaloniki may be found in Andrej Mitrović, *Prodor na Balkan: Srbija u planovima Austro-Ugarske i Nemačke, 1908–1918*, Zavod za uđbenike (Belgrade, 2011). For an English-language discussion of Vienna's plans for a rail line to Thessaloniki, see Kenneth Morrison and Elizabeth Roberts, *The Sandžak: A History*, Hurst (London, 2014), pp. 69–70, 76, 79–83.

36 Trotsky, *The War Correspondence of Leon Trotsky*, p. 18.

37 Jovan Hadži-Vasiljević, *Pokret Srba i Bugara u Turskoj posle srpsko-turskih ratova 1876. i 1877.–1878 godine i njegove posledice (1878.–1882.)*, Nova štamparija Davidović (Belgrade, 1908).

38 Uroš Šešum, "Društvo protiv Srba 1897–1902. Metodi i mere bugarske diplomatije, Egzarhije i Bugarsko-makedonsko odrinske revolucionarne organizacije protiv širenja srpskog uticaja u Južnoj Staroj Srbiji i Makedoniji 1897–1902," *Srpske studije*, 4: 77–103 (Belgrade, 2013). For a description of the cultural and political organizations in place to support these efforts, see Vukašin Dedović, *Rad Srbije na zaštiti državnih i nacionalnih interesa u Makedoniji od 1885. do 1913. godine*, Doctoral dissertation, Faculty of Philosophy, University of Belgrade (Belgrade, 2010).

39 Dragoslav Ljubibratić, *Mlada Bosna i Sarajevski atentat*, Muzej grada Sarajeva (Sarajevo, 1964), p. 33.

40 There are three reputed versions of the text of this document. Vasa Kazimirović, *Crna Ruka: ličnosti i događaju u Srbiji od prevrata 1903. do Solunskog procesa 1917. godine*, Prometej (Novi Sad, 2013), pp. 91–93. Živan Živanović, *Politička istorija Srbije*, G. Kon (Belgrade, 1925), vol. IV, pp. 343–347. Dragiša Vasić, *Devetsto treća*, Tucović (Belgrade, 1925). See also David McKenzie, *Apis: The Congenial Conspirator: The Life of Colonel Dragutin T. Dimitrijević*, East European Monographs (Boulder, 1989), p. 35.

41 Kazimirović, *Crna Ruka*, p. 19. McKenzie, *Apis: The Congenial Conspirator*, pp. 31–49.

42 Kazimirović, *Crna Ruka*, p. 146.

43 Suzana Rajić, "The Russian Secret Service and King Alexander Obrenović of Serbia (1900–1903)," *Balcanica*, XLIII: 143–168 (Belgrade, 2012), pp. 159–165.

44 Živojin Mišić, *Moje uspomene*, Beogradski izdavačko-grafički zavod (Belgrade, 2010), pp. 189–200.

45 Great Britain's position on this matter is examined in Francis Radovich, "The British Court and Relations with Serbia," *East European Quarterly*, 14: 461–468 (Winter 1980). See also Slobodan G. Markovich, *British Perceptions of Serbia and the Balkans, 1903–1906*, Dialogue (Paris, 2000), pp. 63–88.

46 Dušan Bataković, "Storm over Serbia: The Rivalry between Civilian and Military Authorities (1911–1914)," *Balcanica*, XLIV: 307–350 (Belgrade, 2013), pp. 307–356. McKenzie, *Apis: The Congenial Conspirator*, pp. 51–63.

47 Albertini, *The Origins of the War of 1914*, vol. 2, pp. 25–26.

48 Elizabeth Roberts, *Realm of the Black Mountain: A History of Montenegro*, Hurst (London, 2007), p. 278.

49 Andrej Mitrović, *Prodor na Balkan: Srbija u planovima Austro-Ugarske i Nemačke, 1908–1918*, Zavod za udbenike (Belgrade, 2001), p. 240.

50 Vladimir Dedijer, *Sarajevo 1914*, 2nd edition, Prosveta (Belgrade, 1978), vol. 1, p. 160.

51 Mitrović, *Prodor na Balkan* (2001), pp. 234–238.

52 Strachan, Hew. *The First World War: vol. 1: To Arms*, Oxford University Press (Oxford, 2001), p. 69.

53 Telegram of June 2/15, 1914, from Serbian Ambassador to Istanbul Đorđević to Nikola Pašić, AS, MID-PO, 1914, P-III/15, X/144.

54 Mitrović, *Prodor na Balkan* (2001), pp. 234–238.

55 See note 54, p. 242.

56 Dušan Bataković, *Prelude to Sarajevo: The Serbian Question in Bosnia and Herzegovina 1878–1914*, Serbian Academy of Sciences and Arts (Belgrade, 1996).

57 Telegram of July 12, 1914, from Serbia's General Consul in Budapest to the Ministry of Foreign Affairs, in Dedijer and Anić, eds., *Dokumenti o spoljnoj politici Kraljevine Srbije, 1903–1914*, p. 313.

58 Bataković, "Storm over Serbia," pp. 311–314.

59 Bataković, "The Balkan Piedmont," pp. 25–73.

60 Bataković, "Storm over Serbia," pp. 311–314.

61 Biljana Vučetić, "Pogledi na organizaciju Srpske odbrane u Makedoniji u 1906. godini," *Vesnik*, LVI: 37 (Belgrade, 2010), pp. 165–170; Dedović, *Rad Srbije*.

62 The classic account of tensions between Serbia and the Dual Monarchy during this period is Dimitrije Đorđević's *Carinski rat Austro-Ugarske i Srbije, 1906–1911*, Istorijski institut (Belgrade, 1962).

63 Rothenberg, *The Army of Francis Joseph*, p. 140.

64 Morrison and Roberts, *The Sandžak*, p. 79. See also Mitrović, *Prodor na Balkan* (Belgrade, 2011).

65 Ljubibratić, *Mlada Bosna i Sarajevski atentat*, p. 34.

66 See note 65, pp. 35–36.

67 Maude M. Holbach, *Bosnia and Herzegovina: Some Wayside Wanderings*, J. Lane (London, 1910), pp. 152–153; *The National Question in Yugoslavia: Origins, History, Politics*, Cornell University Press (Ithaca, NY, 1988), p. 367.

68 Albertini, *The Origins of the War of 1914*, vol. 1, pp. 291–292. The Austro-Hungarian note of July 23, 1914 declared that Serbia's failure to follow this earlier declaration was the reason for the ultimatum. See the text of this declaration in ÖUAP, vol. VIII, p. 515, document no. 10395.

69 Mitrović, *Prodor na Balkan* (Belgrade, 2011).

70 Conrad, *Aus Meiner Dienstzeit, 1906–1918*, vol. I, pp. 531–532.

71 Even as late as early July 1914 Habsburg officials were discussing a rail line from Bosnia to Albania. Telegram of May 20/June 2, 1914, from Serbian Ambassador Živojin Balugđić in Athens to MID, in Dedijer and Anić, eds, *Dokumenti o spoljnoj politici Kraljevine Srbije, 1903–1914*, p. 271.

72 Mitrović, *Prodor na Balkan*, pp. 96–130 (Belgrade, 2011).

73 John D. Treadway, *The Falcon and Eagle: Montenegro and Austria-Hungary, 1908–1914*, Purdue University Press (Purdue, IL, 1983), pp. 135–158.

74 Letter of June 12/25, 1914, from Serbia's Minister to Vienna Jovan M. Jovanović to Nikola Pašić, AS, MID-PO, 1914, P-III/15, X/171.

75 Mitrović, "Albanci u politici Austro-Ugarske prema Srbiji 1914–1918," p. 113. For an examination of Austria-Hungary's policy towards the Albanians during the war, see Dušan T. Bataković, "Podaci Srpskih vojnih vlasti o Arbanaškim prvacima 1914," in *Mešovita građa*, XVII–XVIII: 188–206 (Belgrade, 1988); Robert Schwanke, "Das Albanische Schulwesen und Oesterreich-Ungarn waehrend des I. Weltkriegs," in *Dissertationes Albanicae*, vol. XIII, Band Rudolf Trofenik (Munich, 1971).

76 Simeon Damianov, "Bulgaria's Decision to Enter the War: Diplomatic Negotiations, 1914–15," in Bela K. Király and Nandor F. Dreisiger, eds, *East Central European Society in World War I*, East European Monographs (Boulder, CO, 1985), p. 163.

77 Letter of April 16/29, 1914, from Jovanović to Pašić, AS, MID-PO, 1914, V-I/2, II/421.

78 Quoted in Damianov, "Bulgaria's Decision to Enter the War," p. 164.

79 Letter of June 10/23, 1914, from Jovanović to Pašić, AS, MID-PO, 1914, O-IV/14, VIII/64.

80 Telegram of July 4/17, 1914, from Gavrilović to Ministry of Foreign Affairs, AS, MID-PO, 1914, O-IV/27, VIII/717.

81 Letter of June 12/23, 1914, from Jovanović to Pašić, AS, MID-PO, 1914, P-III/15, X/171. See also letter of June 10/23, 1914, from Jovanović to Pašić, AS, MID-PO, 1914, O-IV/14, VIII/64.

82 Letter of June 12/25, 1914, from Jovanović to Pašić, AS, MID-PO, 1914, P-III/15, X/169.

83 Letter of June 13/26, 1914, from Jovanović to Pašić, AS, MID-PO, 1914, P-III/15, X/182–183. Prince Wilhelm von Wied abandoned the throne on September 3, 1914 in the face of local uprisings.

84 Letter of June 21/July 3, 1914, from Đorđević to Pašić, AS, MID-PO, 1914, P-III/15, X/190. See also telegram of June 10/23, 1914, from Đorđević to Pašić, AS, MID-PO, 1914, P-III/15, X/164.

85 Serbian support for Romania was certain to influence Bucharest's attitudes toward a conflict between Belgrade and Vienna and armaments shipments coming up the Danube to Serbia. Telegram of July 8/21, 1914, from Stanojević to Pašić, AS, MID-PO, 1914, O-IV/10, VIII/25. Telegram of July 10/23, 1914, from Paču to Boško Čolak-Antić, AS, MID-PO, 1914, O-IV/23, VIII/644. Telegram of July 10/23, 1914, from Stanojević to Pašić, AS, MID-PO, 1914, O-IV/23, VIII/645.

86 Telegram of July 10/23, 1914, from Paču to Čolak-Antić, AS, MID-PO, 1914, O-IV/23, VIII/644.

87 Telegram of June 14/27, 1914, from Živojin Balugđić to Pašić, AS, MID-PO, 1914, O-IV/20, VIII/544.

88 Letter of June 1/14, 1914, from the General Staff to the Ministry of Foreign Affairs, AS, MID-PO, 1914, I-I/16, V/396–397. Letter of June 14/27, 1914, from the Military Ministry to the Ministry of Foreign Affairs, AS, MID-PO, 1914, I-I/16, V/410. Letter of June 28/July 11, 1914, from the Military Ministry to Ministry of Foreign Affairs, AS, MID-PO, 1914, I-I/16, V/419.

89 Letter of May 9/22, 1914, from Jovanović to Pašić, AS, MID-PO, 1914, O-IV/19, VIII/87.

90 See note 89.

91 Telegram of May 12/25, 1914, from Balugđić to Pašić, AS, MID-PO, 1914, O-IV/19, VIII/155.

92 Telegram of June 6/19, 1914, from Đorđević to Pašić, AS, MID-PO, 1914, O-IV/4, VII/589–592.

93 Telegram no. 443 of June 30/July 13, 1914, from Đorđević to Pašić, AS, MID-PO, 1914, O-IV/4, VII/693–697.

94 Telegram of July 1/14, 1914, from Pašić to Đorđević, AS, MID-PO, 1914, F–160, no. 209, Pov. #449.

95 Arhiv Vojnoistorijskog instituta (hereafter AVII), Fond 3, Kutija 208, Regbr. 6/18, Fasc 1.

96 Letter of May 15/28, 1914, from Ministry of Internal Affairs to Ministry of Foreign Affairs, AS, MID-PO, 1914, V-I/1, II/352.

97 Telegram of June 7/20, 1914, from Milanković to Ministry of Foreign Affairs, AS, MID-PO, 1914, V-I/1, II/347.

98 Letter of May 27/June 9, 1914, from Military Ministry to Ministry of Foreign Affairs, AS, MID-PO, 1914, V-I/1, II/356.

99 Letter of June 2/15, 1914, from Military Ministry to Ministry of Foreign Affairs, AS, MID-PO, 1914, V-I/1, II/366–367.

100 Greg King and Sue Woolmans, *The Assassination of the Archduke: Sarajevo 1914 and the Romance that Changed the World*, Macmillan (London, 2013), p. 162.

101 Letter of May 29/June 11, 1914, from the Military Ministry to Ministry of Foreign Affairs, AS, MID-PO, 1914, V-I/1, II/358–360. Letter of 2/15 June 2/15, 1914, from Military Ministry to Ministry of Foreign Affairs, AS, MID-PO, 1914, V-I/1, II/366–367.

102 Letter of May 29/June 11, 1914, from the Military Ministry to the Ministry of Foreign Affairs, AS, MID-PO, 1914, V-I/1, II/358–360.

Chapter 3: Parallel structures and hostile neighbors

1 Dušan T. Bataković, "Storm over Serbia: The Rivalry between Civilian and Military Authorities (1911–1914)," *Balcanica*, XLIV: 307–350 (Belgrade, 2013), p. 317.

2 Vasa Kazimirović, *Crna Ruka: ličnosti i događaju u Srbiji od prevrata 1903. do Solunskog procesa 1917. godine*, Prometej (Novi Sad, 2013), pp. 257–271.

3 See note 2, p. 275.

4 The full text of the Black Hand's constitution and rulebook may be found in Radovan M. Drašković, *Pretorijanske težnje u Srbiji*, Žagor (Belgrade, 2006), pp. 120–127.

5 The ten were: Bogdan Radenković (civilian); Čedomir Popović; Vojislav Tankosić; Ljubomir Jovanović (civilian); Velimir Vemić; Dragutin Dimitrijević Apis; Ilija Radivojević; Ilija Jovanović Pčinjski; Milan Vasić; and Milan Gr. Milovanović Pilac.

6 Milan Ž. Živanović, *Pukovnik Apis: Solunski proces hiljadu Devetsto sedamnaeste; prilog za proučavanje političke istorije Srbije od 1903 do 1918 god.*, Savremena Administracija (Belgrade, 1955), p. 201.

7 Kazimirović, *Crna Ruka*, p. 341.

8 Luigi Albertini, *The Origins of the War of 1914*, translated and edited by Isabella M. Massey, Oxford University Press (London, 1953), vol. 2, p. 31.

9 Milovanović was Prime Minister of Serbia from 1911 until his untimely death in 1912. Živanović, *Pukovnik Apis*, p. 191.

10 Bataković, "Storm over Serbia," p. 328.

11 Dragoslav Ljubibratić, *Mlada Bosna i Sarajevski atentat*, Muzej grada Sarajeva (Sarajevo, 1964), p. 39.

12 See note 11, p. 40.

13 David McKenzie, *Apis: The Congenial Conspirator: The Life of Colonel Dragutin T. Dimitrijević*, East European Monographs (Boulder, 1989), pp. 72–73.

14 Albertini, *The Origins of the War of 1914*, vol. 2, pp. 64–65.

15 Ljubibratić, *Mlada Bosna i Sarajevski atentat*, pp. 36–39; Albertini, *The Origins of the War of 1914*, vol. 2, p. 25.

16 For an overview of Franz Ferdinand's ideas about restructuring the Empire, see Albertini, *The Origins of the War of 1914*, vol. 2, pp. 11–18.

17 Quoted in Albertini, *The Origins of the War of 1914*, vol. 2, pp. 19–21.

18 Vidoje Golubović, *Stare Kafane Beograda*, 3D+ (Belgrade, 2013).

19 Čedomir A. Popović, "Rad organizacije 'Ujedinjenje ili smrt,' Pripreme za Balkanski rat," *Nova Evropa*, XVI: 10 (November 26, 1927). See also Albertini, *The Origins of the War of 1914*, vol. 2, pp. 27–28.

20 Albertini, *The Origins of the War of 1914*, vol. 2, pp. 24, 28.

21 Albertini, *The Origins of the War of 1914*, vol. 2, p. 42.

22 Popović, Čedomir A., "Organizacija."

23 Vladimir Dedijer, "Sarajevo Fifty Years After," *Foreign Affairs*, July 1964.

24 Martin Pappenheim, *Ein geschichtlicher Beitrag zur Vorgeschichte des Attentates von Sarajevo: Gavrilo Princips Bekenntnisse; zwei Manuskripte Princips, Aufzeichnungen seines Gefängnispsychiaters Dr. Pappenheim aus Gesprächen von Feber bis Juni 1916 über das Attentat, Princips Leben und seine politischen und sozialen Anschauungen*, R. Lechner (Vienna, 1926). "Dr. Pappenheim's Conversations with Princip: Confessions of the Assassin Whose Deed Led to the World War," edited by Hamilton Fish Armstrong, in *Current History*, August 1927. See also David James Smith, *One Morning in Sarajevo: 28 June 1914*, Phoenix (London, 2009), pp. 264–267.

25 McKenzie, *Apis: The Congenial Conspirator*, p. 129.

26 Albertini, *The Origins of the War of 1914*, vol. 2, p. 42.

27 McKenzie claims 20,000 Dinars, Albertini 26,000 Dinars. McKenzie, *Apis: The Congenial Conspirator*, p. 74; Albertini, *The Origins of the War of 1914*, vol. 2, p. 32.

28 McKenzie, *Apis: The Congenial Conspirator*, p. 99.

29 Dedijer, "Sarajevo Fifty Years After."

30 Bataković, "Storm over Serbia," pp. 328–329.

31 Vladimir Dedijer, *Sarajevo 1914*, 2nd edition, Prosveta (Belgrade, 1978), p. 7.

32 Dedijer, "Sarajevo Fifty Years After."

33 Milan Ž. Živanović, "Istina o 'Austrijskom špijunu' Radu Malobabić," *Politika*, no. 12218 (February 11, 1946).

34 Letter of June 8/21, 1914, from Head of the General Staff Intelligence Section Dragutin Dimitrijević "Apis" to the Main General Staff Operational Department, in Vladimir Dedijer and Života Anić, eds, *Dokumenti o spoljnoj politici Kraljevine Srbije, 1903–1914*, vol. VII, no. 1 (January 1/14–April 30/ May 13, 1914); no. 2 (May 1/14–July 22/August 4, 1914) (Belgrade, 1980), pp. 363–365.

35 See note 34, p. 365.

36 Dedijer, "Sarajevo Fifty Years After."

37 M. Ljuba Jovanović, *The Murder of Sarajevo: Translation of an Article*, British Institute of International Affairs (London, 1925), p. 3.

38 Albertini, *The Origins of the War of 1914*, vol. 2, pp. 93–94.

39 Letter of June 14/27, 1914, from Commander Prvanović to the Commander of the V Odsek of Border Troops in Banja Koviljača, in Dedijer and Anić, eds, *Dokumenti o spoljnoj politici Kraljevine Srbije, 1903–1914*, pp. 363–365, 415.

40 Letter of June 15/28, 1914, from Vulović to Prvanović, in Dedijer and Anić, eds, *Dokumenti o spoljnoj politici Kraljevine Srbije, 1903–1914*, p. 421.

41 Kazimirović, *Crna Ruka*, p. 354; Joachim Remak, *Sarajevo: The Story of a Political Murder*, Criterion Books (New York, 1959), pp. 77–78.

42 Dolph W.A. Owings, *The Sarajevo Trial*, Documentary Publications (Chapel Hill, NC, 1984), vol. I, p. 121.

43 Ljubibratić, *Mlada Bosna i Sarajevski atentat*, p. 203.

44 Dedijer, "Sarajevo Fifty Years After."

45 Remak, *Sarajevo*, pp. 194–198.

46 Quoted in Vladimir Dedijer, *The Road to Sarajevo*, MacGibbon & Kee (London, 1967), p. 398.

47 Vladimir Dedijer, *Sarajevo 1914*, 1st edition, Prosveta (Belgrade, 1966), p. 685.

48 Albertini, *The Origins of the War of 1914*, vol. 2, pp. 82–86.

49 Dedijer, *Sarajevo 1914*, 2nd edition, Prosveta (Belgrade, 1978), vol. 2, pp. 217–224.

50 Živanović, *Pukovnik Apis*, p. 203.

51 Nikola Popović, *Odnosi Srbije i Rusije u prvom svetskom ratu*, Narodna knjiga (Belgrade, 1977), p. 59.

52 Christopher Clark, *The Sleepwalkers: How Europe Went to War in 1914*, Penguin (London, 2013), pp. 430–432.

53 Andrej Mitrović, *Serbia's Great War, 1914–1918*, Hurst (London, 2007), p. 47.

54 See note 53, p. 47.

55 See note 53, p. 47.

56 Margaret MacMillan, *The War that Ended Peace: The Road to 1914*, Random House (New York, 2013), p. 584.

57 Telegram of July 13/26, 1914, from Miroslav Spalajković to Pašić, AS, MID-PO, 1914, P-III/15, pov. 2789.

58 Telegram of July 13/26, 1914, from Spalajković to Pašić, AS, MID-PO, 1914, P-III/15, pov. 2789.

59 This is reflected in the title of the Royal Yugoslav government's official account of the war, *The Great War of Serbia for the Liberation and Unification of the Serbs, Croats, and Slovenes*. Ministarstvo vojske i mornarice, Glavni Đeneralštab. *Veliki rat Srbije za oslobođenje i ujedinjenje Srba, Hrvata i Slovenaca* (Belgrade, 1924). For more on the evolution of Serbia's wartime goals, see Milorad Ekmečić, *Ratni ciljevi Srbije, 1914*, Srpska književna zadruga (Belgrade, 1973).

60 Letter of July 1/14, 1914, from Ljubomir Mihailović in Rome to Pašić, AS, MID-PO, 1914, I-I/10, IV/462.

61 Letter of August 4/17, 1914, from Italy's Ambassador in Belgrade to Pašić, AS, MID-PO, 1914, I-I/10, IV/459.

62 Mitar Đurišić, *Bitka na Drini 1914*, Vojnoistorijski institut (Belgrade, 1969), p. 23.

63 Nikola Popović, *Odnosi Srbije i Rusije u prvom svetskom ratu*, p. 221.

64 Telegram of July 18/31, 1914, from Mateja-Mata Bošković to Pašić, AS, MID-PO, F-XII/5, pov. 3041.

65 Nikola Popović, *Odnosi Srbije i Rusije u prvom svetskom ratu*, p. 223.

66 Telegram of August 4/17, 1914, from Spalajković to Pašić, AS, MID-PO, F-XII/5, pov. 3678.

67 Đurišić, *Bitka na Drini 1914*, p. 22.

68 Telegram of July 15/28, 1914, from Pašić to Balugđić, AS, MID-PO, 1914, F-XI/3, pov. 2836.

69 Telegram of July 20/August 2, 1914, from Balugđić to Pašić, AS, MID-PO, 1914, O-II/1, VII/48. Telegram of July 23/August 5, 1914, from Balugđić to Pašić, AS, MID-PO, 1914, O-II/1, VII/51.

70 Simeon Damianov, "Bulgaria's Decision to Enter the War: Diplomatic Negotiations, 1914–15," in Bela K. Király and Nandor F. Dreisiger, eds, *East Central European Society in World War I*, East European Monographs (Boulder, CO, 1985), p. 160. Ljuben Berov, "The Bulgarian Economy during World War I," in Bela K. Király and Nandor F. Dreisiger, eds, *East Central European Society in World War I*, East European Monographs (Boulder, CO, 1985), p. 170.

71 Letter of July 18/31, 1914, from Čolak-Antić to Pašić, AS, MID-PO, 1914, V-I/2, II/473.

72 Telegram of July 15/28, 1914, from Serbian Consul in Thessaloniki to Pašić, AS, MID-PO, 1914, V-I/2, II/461. Letter of July 15/28, 1914, from Ministry of Internal Affairs to Pašić, AS, MID-PO, 1914, V-I/2, II/457.

73 Telegram of July 16/29, 1914, from Čolak-Antić to Pašić, AS, MID-PO, 1914, V-I/2, II/463. Telegram of July 16/29, 1914, from Balugđić to Pašić, AS, MID-PO, 1914, V-I/2, II/460.

74 Letter of July 18/31, 1914, from Čolak-Antić to Pašić, AS, MID-PO, 1914, V-I/2, II/473.

75 Telegram of July 17/30, 1914, from Serbia's Consul in Thessaloniki Vitrović to Pašić, AS, MID-PO, 1914, V-I/2, II/465.

76 Telegram of July 17/30, 1914, from Balugđić to Pašić, AS, MID-PO, 1914, V-I/2, II/464.

77 Telegram of July 18/31, 1914, from Serbian envoy Ristić in Bucharest to Pašić, AS, MID-PO, 1914, V-I/2, II/467.

78 Telegram of July 18/31, 1914, from Ristić to Pašić, AS, MID-PO, 1914, V-I/2, II/468.

79 Telegram of July 19/August 1, 1914, from Čolak-Antić to Pašić, AS, MID-PO, 1914, V-I/2, II/470.

80 Telegram of July 23/August 5, 1914, from Čolak-Antić to Pašić, AS, MID-PO, 1914, F-XV/12, pov. 3269.

81 This squadron was commanded by Rear Admiral Ernest Troubridge, later the commander of the British Naval Mission to Serbia. See Charles E.J. Fryer, *The Royal Navy on the Danube*, East European Monographs (Boulder, CO, 1988), pp. 44–53.

82 Pašić's response to Balugđić's telegram of July 17/30, 1914, AS, MID-PO, 1914, F–13/238. See also Đurišić, *Bitka na Drini 1914*, p. 20.

83 Đurišić, *Bitka na Drini 1914*, p. 20.

84 Nikola Popović, *Odnosi Srbije i Rusije u prvom svetskom ratu*, p. 141.

85 Letter of July 10/23, 1914, from Military Minister Dušan Stefanović to Pašić, AS, MID-PO, 1914, O-II/1, VII/64.

86 Letter of June 22/July 5, 1914, from the Military Ministry to Ministry of Foreign Affairs, AS, MID-PO, 1914, V-I/1, II/373. Letter of June 20/July 3, 1914, from Military Ministry to Ministry of Foreign Affairs, AS, MID-PO, 1914, V-I/1, II/375.

87 Letter of July 7/20, 1914, from Military Ministry to Ministry of Foreign Affairs, AS, MID-PO, 1914, V-I/1, II/383.

88 Letter of July 15, 1914, from Military Minister Stefanović to Pašić, AS, MID-PO, 1914, N-II/1, VI/447. Telegram of July 18, 1914, from Čolak-Antić in Sofia to Ministry of Foreign Affairs, AS, MID-PO, 1914, N-II/1, VI/449.

89 Telegram of July 22, 1914, from Balugđić to Ministry of Foreign Affairs, AS, MID-PO, 1914, N-II/1, VI/462.

90 Letter of July 1/14, 1914, from Stefanović to Pašić, AS, MID-PO, 1914, V-I/2, II/451. Letter of July 5/18, 1914, from Ministry of Internal Affairs to Ministry of Foreign Affairs, AS, MID-PO, 1914, V-I/2, II/453.

91 Petar Opačić, "Genocidna Politika Austrougarske protiv Srpskog narod i Srbije u prvom svetskom ratu kao platforma za genocid u drugom svetskom ratu," in Petar Opačić, Savo Skoko, Radomir Rakić, and Milovan Ćurčić, eds, *Genocid nad srbima u dvadestom veku* (Belgrade, 1992), p. 17.

92 See note 91, pp. 16–18. See also Vladimir Ćorović, *Crna knjiga: patnje Srba Bosne i Hercegovine za vreme svetskog rata 1914–1918*, 3rd edition, Udruženje ratnih dobrovoljaca 1912–1918. godine, njihovih potomaka i poštovalaca (Belgrade, 1996).

93 Opačić, "Genocidna Politika," p. 18.

94 In Zagreb these were: *Slobodna Riječ, Narodno Jedinstvo, Srpsko Kolo, Olsobogjenje, Privrednik*, and *Vihor*; in Osijek *Volksrecht*; in Šid *Pravo Naroda*; in Petrovaradin *Sloboda*; in Vinkovci *Svjetlost*; and in Mitrovica *Hrvatski branik. Hrvatski dnevnik*, July 29, 1914, no. 171.

95 See Borivoje Milošević, "Progon Pravoslavnog sveštenstva Bosanske krajine u Prvom svetskom ratu," *Srpske Studije*, 4 (Belgrade, 2013).

96 For example, Todor Rijić was shot after the train on which he was held came under fire. *Hrvatski dnevnik*, August 10, 1914, no. 186.

97 *Hrvatski dnevnik*, August 6, 1914, no. 180; *Hrvatski dnevnik*, August 8, 1914, no. 183.

98 *Hrvatski dnevnik*, August 25, 1914, no. 206.

Chapter 4: "A peasant mob"

1   Boris Kršev, *Finansijska politika Jugoslavije 1918–1941*, Prometej (Novi Sad, 2007), p. 172.

2   Savo Skoko and Petar Opačić, *Vojvoda Stepa Stepanović, u ratovima Srbije 1876–1918*, Beogradski izdavačko-grafički zavod (Belgrade, 1983), p. 309.

3   Savo Skoko, *Vojvoda Radomir Putnik*, Beogradski izdavačko-grafički zavod (Belgrade, 1984), vol. I, p. 19; Gale Stokes, "Milan Obrenović and the Serbian Army," in Bela K. Király and Nandor F. Dreisiger, eds, *East Central European Society in World War I*, Social Science Monographs (Boulder, CO, 1985), p. 565; Borislav Ratković, "Srpska vojska u Balkanskim ratovima 1912–1913 i u prvom svetskom ratu," *Vojnoistorijski glasnik*, 1/2: 56–86 (Belgrade, 1993), pp. 65, 69.

4   International Commission to Inquire into the Causes and Conduct of the Balkan Wars. *The Other Balkan Wars: A 1913 Carnegie Endowment Commission Inquiry in Retrospect with a New Introduction and Reflections on the Present Conflict by George F. Kennan*, Carnegie Endowment for International Peace (Washington, DC, 1993).

5   Živojin Mišić, *Moje Uspomene*, edited by Savo Skoko, Beogradski izdavačko-grafički zavod (Belgrade, 1978), pp. 189–196.

6   Vasa Kazimirović, *Crna Ruka: ličnosti i događaju u Srbiji od prevrata 1903. do Solunskog procesa 1917. godine*, Prometej (Novi Sad, 2013), pp. 563–594; Dušan T. Bataković, "Storm over Serbia: The Rivalry between Civilian and Military Authorities (1911–1914)," *Balcanica*, XLIV: 307–350 (Belgrade, 2013), pp. 336–345; Radovan M. Drašković, *Pretorijanske težnje u Srbiji*, Žagor (Belgrade, 2006), pp. 171–189.

7   Kazimirović, *Crna Ruka*, pp. 576–577; see also Skoko, *Vojvoda Radomir Putnik*, vol. I, p. 22.

8   Quoted in Vladimir Dedijer, *Sarajevo 1914*, 2nd edition, Prosveta (Belgrade, 1978), vol. 2, p. 124. Albertini, *The Origins of the War of 1914*, translated and edited by Isabella M. Massey, Oxford University Press (London, 1953), vol. 2, p. 63.

9   Diary of Jovan Jovanović-Pižon, August 5/18, 1914, Arhiv Jugoslavije (hereafter AJ), 80–54–492.

10 Telegram of June 6/19, 1914, from Đorđević to Pašić, AS, MID-PO, 1914, O-IV/4, VII/589–592. Telegram no. 443 of June 30/July 13, 1914, from Đorđević to Pašić, AS, MID-PO, 1914, O-IV/4, VII/693–697.

11   Alex N. Dragnich, *Serbia, Nikola Pašić, and Yugoslavia*, Rutgers University Press (New Brunswick, NJ, 1974), p. 107.

12   Arhiv Vojnoistorijskog instituta (hereafter AVII), Fond 3, Kutija 352, RegBr. 3/2, Fasc. 1.

13   AVII, Fond 3, Kutija 2, RegBr. 29a, Fasc. 1. *Formacija celokupne vojske*, Ministarstvo vojno (Belgrade, 1903), pp. 246–247. Gale Stokes, "Milan Obrenović and the Serbian Army," in Bela K. Király and Nandor F. Dreisiger, eds, *East Central European Society in World War I*, Social Science Monographs (Boulder, CO, 1985), p. 556.

14   Leon Trotsky, *The War Correspondence of Leon Trotsky: The Balkan Wars, 1912–1913*, Pathfinder Press (New York, 1980), p. 61.

15   Aleksandar Stojićević, *Istorija naših ratova za oslobođenje i ujedinjenje od 1912–1918 god. (Tok operacija i primena snabdevanja)*, N. Kovačević (Belgrade, 1932), p. 22.

16   AVII, Fond 3, Kutija 2, RegBr. 29a, Fasc. 1. *Formacija celokupne vojske*.

17   After the Balkan Wars, five new divisional regions were created in Macedonia, Kosovo, and the Sandžak of Novi Pazar. These were the Bitolj, Bregalnica, Vardar, Kosovo, and Ibar regions. At the outbreak of war, these divisional regions existed only on paper and were unable to field battle-ready divisions. During 1914 their primary function was to recruit and train soldiers from the "New Regions" to be sent to existing military formations.

18   AVII, Fond 3, Kutija 2, RegBr. 29a, Fasc. 1. *Formacija celokupne vojske*.

19   See note 18.

20   See note 18, pp. 246–247. The company-level third levy units were to be fleshed out with as many men as were available (*koliko bude*), but the smallest sized company was to have at least fifty-eight men.

21   Albert A. Nofi, "Comparative Divisional Strengths during World War I: East Central European Belligerents and Theaters," in Bela K. Király and Nandor F. Dreisiger, eds, *East Central European Society in World War I*, Social Science Monographs (Boulder, CO, 1985).

22   AVII, Fond 3, Kutija 237, RegBr. 1, 4, 5, Fasc. 1; AVII, Fond 3, Kutija 237, RegBr. 20, Fasc. 2. *Pregled gubitaka u ratu 1914 i 1915 godine*. Compare these with losses in AVII, Fond 3, Kutija 237, RegBr. 7, Fasc. 1, which gives a figure of 160,343.

23   AVII, Fond 3, Kutija 237, RegBr. 2–7, Fasc. 1.

24   Vuk Obradović, "Puške sistema Mosin u naoružanju Srpske vojske tokom prvog svetskog rata," *Vesnik*, LVI: 37 (Belgrade, 2010), p. 80.

25   Živko Pavlović, *Bitka na Jadru avgusta 1914 god.*, Grafički zavod Makarije (Belgrade, 1924), p. 605 (hereafter *BNJ*).

26   Charles J. Vopicka, *Secrets of the Balkans: Seven Years of a Diplomatist's Life in the Storm Centre of Europe*, Rand McNally (Chicago, IL, 1921), p. 34.

27   Obradović, "Puške," p. 80.

28   Mitar Đurišić, "Neki ekonomski problemi Srbije U ratnoj 1914. Godini," *Vojnoistorijski glasnik*, 4: 3–57 (Belgrade, 1964), p. 4.

29　Information on infantry weapons can be found in: AVII, Fond 3. Kutija 55, RegBr. 2/40, Fasc. 1; AVII, Fond 3, Kutija 2, RegBr. 29a, Fasc. 1. *Formacija celokupne vojske*; Pavlović, *BNJ*, p. 53; W.H.B. Smith, *Small Arms of the World*, 10th edition, A & W Visual Library (Harrisburg, PA, 1973); Ian V. Hogg, *The Illustrated Encyclopedia of Artillery: An A–Z Guide to Artillery Techniques and Equipment throughout the World*, Chartwell (Secaucus, NJ, 1987); Stokes, "Milan Obrenović and the Serbian Army."

30　AVII, Fond 3, Kutija 352, RegBr. 12/16, 17, 21, Fasc. 1.

31　AVII, Fond 3, Kutija 237, RegBr. 2, Fasc. 4. Austrian sources claim a figure of 216 machine guns: Edmund Glaise von Horstenau, ed., *Österreich-Ungarns letzter Krieg 1914–1918*, Verlag Militärwissenschaftlichen Mitteilungen (Vienna, 1931), vol. I, Beilage 7 (hereafter *ÖULK*).

32　Nofi, "Comparative Divisional Strengths during World War I," p. 263.

33　Pavlović, *BNJ*, pp. 80–95.

34　Details of Serbia's cannon purchase from France are found in Dimitrije Đorđević, *Carinski rat Austro-Ugarske i Srbije, 1906–1911*, Istorijski institut (Belgrade, 1962). Technical details of these cannon are found in the 1907 edition of *Löbells Jahresberichte*, a German annual that kept track of military developments around the world. The type of cannon the Schneider company offered for export may be found in the Schneider catalogue for 1914, *Matériels d'artillerie et bateaux de guerre*. Thanks to Dr. Bruce Gudmundsson for providing these materials.

35　VAS, FVKS, Popisnik 3, Kutija 237, RegBr. 2, Fasc. 4. Austro-Hungarian sources claim the Serbian Army had 542 cannon: *ÖULK*, vol. 1, Beilage 7. They may have been counting the obsolete pieces still in fortress service, or disregarded the cannon Serbia sent to Montenegro.

36　VAS, FVKS, Popisnik 3, Kutija 352, RegBr. 7/1, Fasc. 1. High Command document of August 13, 1914, a *Danglis* battery was to have approximately twenty-one men with four cannon, 145 horses, and 100 shells per gun. See VAS, FVKS, Popisnik 3, Kutija 352, RegBroj. 13/2, Fasc. 2. The Danglis fired a lighter shell than the 75-mm field gun, and so required its own ammunition. *Poznavanje artileriskog materijala*, Artileriska oficirska škola (Belgrade, 1934), p. 24.

37　VAS, FVKS, Popisnik 3, Kutija 237, RegBr. 2, Fasc. 4.

38　VAS, FVKS, Popisnik 3, Kutija 352, RegBr. 7/1, Fasc. 1; Pavlović, *BNJ*, p. 54.

39　Albin Kutschbach, *Die Serben im Balkankrieg 1912–1913 und im Kriege gegen die Bulgaren*, Franckh (Stuttgart, 1913), pp. 95–96. Kutschbach reports that Serbia captured cannon from the Bulgarians during the Second Balkan War. These included eleven quick-firing 75-mm field guns (probably the *Schneider* M1904), thirty *Krupp* field guns (not quick-firing—possibly the 9-cm FK M97), along with seven mountain guns. One of the weapons in use was a Turkish 150-mm "Carigradski Ostragan," a breech-loading *Krupp* piece captured in 1878. See VAS, FVKS, Popisnik 3, Kutija 352, RegBroj. 12/38, Fasc. 1. See AVII, Fond 3, Kutija 352, RegBr. 7/1, Fasc. 1, order from the High Command Operational Department to the Artillery Department dated September 28, 1914. See also Dragoljub Dinić, *Poznavanje naoružanja Kraljevine Jugoslavije i njenih suseda*, Štamparija "Dom" (Belgrade, 1936), p. 87.

40   VAS, FVKS, Popisnik 3, Kutija 50, RegBr. 1/77, Fasc. 1. Telegram of November 4/17, 1914, from 3rd Army commander General Pavle Jurišić-Šturm to High Command.

41   Captured Turkish weapons were formed into a three-battery unit called the "Krupp Field Division," which was initially sent to the Morava I Division. A second Krupp artillery division was soon formed and sent to Morava II. The Krupp pieces were later supplemented and replaced with captured Habsburg artillery depending on availability of ammunition. By early November 1914, there were: two Krupp field divisions, totaling six batteries, three of which had been withdrawn to the rear due to a lack of ammunition; three Austro-Hungarian field batteries (which replaced the withdrawn Turkish Krupp batteries); one battery of Austro-Hungarian 104-mm guns; and one three-gun battery of Turkish mountain guns. VAS, FKVS, Kutija 50, RegBr. 1/19, Fasc. 1. General Staff Order of July 19, 1914. VAS, FKVS, Popisnik 3, Kutija 50, RegBr. 1/7, Fasc. 1. Telegram of July 29/August 11, 1914, from the High Command to 2nd Army commander Stepanović. VAS, FKVS, Popisnik 3, Kutija 50, RegBr. 1/39, Fasc. 1. Telegram of August 4/17, 1914, from the High Command to the commander of the 2nd Krupp Field Artillery Division. VAS, FKVS, Popisnik 3, Kutija 352, RegBr. 7/1, Fasc. 1, and Kutija 50, RegBr. 1/63. Letter of October 12/25, 1914, from the Chief of the Artillery Technical Section to the High Command. See the letter from the Head of the Artillery Department of the High Command to the Chief of Staff of the High Command, with attached "Pregled Stanje municije artiljerijske i puščane" of October 22/November 4, 1914, in VAS, FVKS, Popisnik 3, Kutija 72, RegBr. 5/11, Fasc. 2.

42   Ivan B. Mijatović and Nebojša D. Đokić, "Gradska opsadna artiljerija Vojske Kneževine i Kraljevine Srbije," *Vesnik*, LVIII: 39 (Belgrade, 2012). These included domestically manufactured 4-pounders based on the *La Hitte* system and four batteries of Turkish iron *Krupp* guns, two of which were 90 mm and two 80 mm, all captured in 1878, probably the Krupp C/64 80-mm 4-pounder. Dinić, *Poznavanje*, p. 87.

43   Đurišić, "Neki ekonomski problem," p. 4.

44   AVII, Fond 3, Kutija 352, RegBr. 4/1, Fasc.1.

45   Telegram of July 1/14 1914, from Mihailović to Pašić, AS, MID-PO, 1914, I-I/10, IV/455.

46   AVII, Fond 3, Kutija 237, RegBr. 4, Fasc.1. Svetozar A. Đorđević, *Kroz ratne vihore: prvi svetski rat i Srpska avijatika*, Izdanje autora (Belgrade, 1967), p. 21. Austrian sources claim Serbia had eight aircraft at the outset of the war. They may have confused the Serbian aircraft with a squadron of eight French aircraft dispatched to Serbia in late December 1914. See *ÖULK*, vol. I, Beilage 7.

47   Đorđević, *Kroz ratne*, p. 21.

48   Čedomir Janić, "Nastanak, razvoj i dejstva Srpske avijatike u periodu 1912–1916," in Vujović, Vojislav, ed., *Srpska Avijatika 1912–1918*, Muzej jugoslovenskog vazduhoplovstva (Belgrade, 1993), p. 37.

49   Telegram of July 22/August 4, 1914, from Transportation Section to High Command, AVII, Fond 3, Kutija 50, RegBr. 7/3, Fasc. 7.

50 Letter of August 17/30, 1914, from High Command to the Chief of the Operational Section, AVII, Fond 3, Kutija 50, RegBr. 7/8, Fasc. 7.

51 Đorđević, *Kroz ratne*, pp. 32–33. Janić, "Nastanak," p. 38.

52 AVII, Fond 3, Kutija 208, RegBr. 6/18, Fasc 1.

53 See note 52.

54 See note 52.

55 See note 52.

56 See note 52.

57 See note 52.

58 AVII, Fond 3. Kutija 208, RegBr. 9/1, Fasc. 2. A report from General Gojković, honorary adjutant to King Petar on May 20, 1914, on the readiness of the Morava I and II Divisions. The Morava I Division was missing most of its non-commissioned officers and officers, who had remained in Macedonia. Pavlović, *BNJ*, pp. 56–57.

59 Letter of April 25/May 8, 1914, from Stefanović to Pašić, AS, MID-PO, 1914, O-II/1, VII/67.

60 Letter of March 6/19, 1914, from Vesnić to Pašić, AS, MID-PO, 1914, A-III/6, II/297.

61 Pavlović, *BNJ*, p. 605.

62 Stojićević, *Istorija*, p. 301.

63 Pavlović, *BNJ*, pp. 56–60.

64 Letter of September 2/15, 1914, from Stefanović to Pašić, AS, Predsedništvo Ministarskog Saveta (hereafter PMS), 1914, Fasc. 1.

65 Letter dated December 19, 1914/January 1, 1915, from the President of the Skupština to Pašić, AS, PMS, 1914, Fasc. 1.

66 As many as 3,000 craftsmen may have been released from military duty for this task. Letter of September 2/15, 1914, from Military Minister Stefanović to Pašić, AS, PMS, 1914, Fasc.1.

67 Dimitrije Djordjević, "Vojvoda Putnik, the Serbian High Command, and Strategy in 1914," in Bela K. Király and Nandor F. Dreisiger, eds, *East Central European Society in World War I*, East European Monographs (Boulder, CO, 1985), p. 570.

68 Quoted in Đurišić, "Neki ekonomski problem," p. 9.

69 Letter of June 1/14, 1914, from the General Staff to the Ministry of Foreign Affairs, AS, MID-PO, 1914, I-I/16, V/396–397. Letter of June 14/27, 1914, from the Military Ministry to the Ministry of Foreign Affairs, AS, MID-PO, 1914, I-I/16, V/410. Letter of June 28/July 11, 1914, from the Military Ministry to Ministry of Foreign Affairs, AS, MID-PO, 1914, I-I/16, V/419.

70 Vopicka, *Secrets of the Balkans*, p. 34.

71 Letter of July 15/28, 1914, from Stefanović to Pašić, AS, MID-PO, 1914, I-I/1, III/202.

72 Letter of July 15/28, 1914, from Stefanović to Pašić, AS, MID-PO, 1914, N-II/1, VI/447.

73 Krauss, Alfred, *Die Ursachen Unserer Niederlage*, Lehmann (Munich, 1921), pp. 152–153.

74 Stojićević, *Istorija*, p. 301.

75 Vopicka, *Secrets of the Balkans*, p. 34.

76 See note 75, p. 33.

77 AVII, Fond 3, Kutija 237, RegBr. 2, Fasc. 4. Pavlović claims the Serbian Army had rifles for only 180,000 men. This figure must refer to the "rapid fire," bolt action, magazine-fed weapons. Pavlović, *BNJ*, p. 95. Austro-Hungarian estimates vary. The AOK gives a figure of 200,000 rifles (*ÖULK*, vol. I. Beilage 7), while Conrad gives a much higher figure of 272,000 rifles, but was using the term to refer to soldiers. *Aus Meiner Dienstzeit, 1906–1918*, Rikola Verlag (Vienna, 1923), vol. IV, p. 301.

78 AVII, Fond 3, Kutija 237, RegBr. 2, Fasc. 4.

79 *ÖULK*, vol. I, pp. 63–69.

80 Trotsky, *The War Correspondence of Leon Trotsky*, p. 62.

81 Letter of April 3/16 1914, from Stefanović to Pašić, AS, MID-PO, 1914, V-I/1, II/336–337. Letter of April 22/May 5, 1914, from Stefanović to Pašić, AS, MID-PO, 1914, V-I/1, II/338–339.

82 Diary of Dušan Stefanović (hereafter *DDS*), July 27, 1914.

83 *DDS*, July 26, 1914.

84 *Politika*, July 14, 1914.

85 *DDS*, July 27, 1914. See also *Politika*, July 15/28, 1914, as quoted in Miomir Milenović, "Objava rata i prvi napad Austrijanaca na Beograd: kako je u Beogradu izgledao prvi dan Evropskog rata," in *Agonija Beograda u svetskom ratu*, Štamparija "Jedinstvo" (Belgrade, 1931), p. 17.

86 Đorđe Ćutković, "Spontani branioci Beograda 1914 godine," in *Agonija Beograda u svetskom ratu*, Štamparija "Jedinstvo" (Belgrade, 1931), p. 31.

87 Milenović, "Objava rata," p. 17.

88 See note 87, p. 19.

89 Ćutković, "Spontani branioci Beograda 1914 godine," p. 33.

90 *Politika*, July 15/28, 1914.

91 Milenović, "Objava rata," p. 20.

Chapter 5: The guns of July

1 Dušan P. Stefanović, "Pred buru . . . (Beograd u prvim danima svetskoga rata," in *Agonija Beograda u svetskom ratu*, Štamparija "Jedinstvo" (Belgrade, 1931), p. 4.

2 See note 1, p. 10.

3 Telegram dated July 16/29, 1914, from Anđelković to High Command, AVII, Fond 3, Kutija 54, RegBr. 1/1, Fasc. 1. Telegram dated July 16/29, 1914, from Anđelković to High Command, AVII, Fond 3, Kutija 54, RegBr. 1/2, Fasc. 1.

4   Silvija Đurić and Vidosav Stevanović, eds, *Golgota i vaskrs Srbije 1914–1915*, IRO "Beograd" (Belgrade, 1990), p. 37.

5   Stefanović, "Pred buru . . . (Beograd u prvim danima svetskoga rata," p. 11.

6   See note 5, p. 12.

7   See note 5, p. 11.

8   Đurić and Stevanović, eds, *Golgota i vaskrs Srbije 1914–1915*, p. 37.

9   Đorđe Ćutković, "Spontani branioci Beograda 1914 godine," pp. 33–36. The troops may have come from the 1st *Landsturm* infantry regiment stationed at Petrovaradin. Ćutković refers to it as the 1st *Domobran* regiment. Edmund Glaise von Horstenau, ed., *Österreich-Ungarns letzter Krieg 1914–1918*, Verlag Militärwissenschaftlichen Mitteilungen (Vienna, 1931), vol. I, p. 68 (hereafter *ÖULK*). Austro-Hungarian sources are silent on the issue and have never acknowledged this engagement took place, although Conrad makes brief and cryptic mention of a Serbian attack on some Habsburg steamers. Franz Conrad von Hötzendorff, *Aus Meiner Dienstzeit, 1906–1918*, Rikola Verlag (Vienna, 1923), vol. IV, p. 142 (hereafter *AMD*).

10   Stefanović, "Pred buru . . . (Beograd u prvim danima svetskoga rata," p. 12.

11   Telegram of July 16/29, 1914, from Anđelković to High Command, AVII, Fond 3, Kutija 54, RegBr. 1/1, Fasc. 1.

12   Telegram of July 17/30, 1914, from Anđelković to High Command, AVII, Fond 3, Kutija 54, RegBr. 1/4, Fasc. 1.

13   Telegram of July 17/30, 1914, from Anđelković to High Command, AVII, Fond 3, Kutija 54, RegBr. 1/4, Fasc. 1.

14   Letter of July 16/29, 1914, from Stefanović to Pašić, AS, MID-PO, 1914, V-I/1, II/389. Letter of July 21/August 3, 1914, from Stefanović to Pašić, AS, MID-PO, 1914, V-I/1, II/393. Letter of July 22/August 4, 1914, from Ministry of Internal Affairs to Pašić, AS, MID-PO, 1914, V-I/1, II/398. Telegram of July 16/29, 1914, from commandant in Zaječar to Military Ministry, AS, MID-PO, 1914, V-I/2, II/462.

15   Rodolphe Archibald Reiss, *Report Upon the Atrocities Committed by the Austro-Hungarian army During the First Invasion of Serbia, Submitted to the Serbian Government by R. A. Reiss*, English translation by F.S. Copeland, Simpkin, Marshall, Hamilton, Kent & Co. (London, 1916), p. 21.

16   Telegram of July 17/30, 1914, from Pašić to all Serbian legations, AS, MID-PO, 1914, V-I/1, II/386.

17   Predrag Marković, "Razaranja Beograda u Prvom svetskom ratu," in *Srbija 1918. Godine i stvaranje jugoslovenske države*, Zbornik radova Istorijskog institut (Belgrade, 1989), vol. 5, p. 44.

18   *Depeša*, July 21/August 3, 1914.

19   Telegram of July 23/August 5, 1914, from Anđelković to High Command, AVII, Fond 3, Kutija 56, RegBr. 31/1, Fasc. 1.

20   Đurić and Stevanović, eds, *Golgota i vaskrs Srbije 1914–1915*, p. 39.

21 Slavko Mihajlović, "Oblaci nad gradom," reprinted in Đurić, Silvija, and Stevanović, Vidosav, eds, *Golgota i vaskrs Srbije 1914–1915*, IRO "Beograd" (Belgrade, 1990), p. 118.

22 Marković, "Razaranja Beograda u Prvom svetskom ratu," p. 44. Reiss, *Report*, p. 18.

23 Reiss, *Report*, p. 19.

24 *Hrvatski dnevnik*, August 27, 1914, no. 210.

25 *Depeša*, July 22/August 4, 1914.

26 *Depeša*, July 23/August 5, 1914.

27 *Depeša*, July 22/August 4, 1914.

28 Marković, "Razaranja Beograda u Prvom svetskom ratu," p. 44.

29 Mihajlović, "Oblaci nad gradom," p. 123.

30 *Depeša*, July 22/August 4, 1914.

31 *Depeša*, July 23/August 5, 1914.

32 The Carpathian and Italian Fronts were the only areas outside of the Balkans where fighting occurred in mountainous regions. Although the Ardennes is heavily forested and hilly, there were no major mountains.

33 Douglas Johnson Wilson, *Battlefields of the World War, Western and Southern Fronts: A Study in Military Geography*, Oxford University Press (New York, 1921), p. 573.

34 See note 33, p. 575.

35 Nikola Popović, *Odnosi Srbije i Rusije u prvom svetskom ratu*, Narodna knjiga (Belgrade, 1977), pp. 123–124. Charles E.J. Fryer, *The Royal Navy on the Danube*, East European Monographs (Boulder, CO, 1988), pp. 67–77.

36 Andrej Mitrović, "Centralne sile i strategijske saobraćajnice na Balkanu 1915. Godine," *Zbornik radova*, 4, Istorijski institut (Belgrade, 1986).

37 Ministarstvo vojske i mornarice, Glavni Đeneralštab. *Veliki rat Srbije za oslobođenje i ujedinjenje Srba, Hrvata i Slovenaca* (Belgrade, 1924), vol. I, p. 25 (hereafter *VRS*).

38 Letter and twenty-six page report on the state of Serbia's railroads for wartime mobilization and supply purposes from Colonel Pešić of the General Staff to Military Minister Stefanović of July 20, 1914, AVII Fond 3, Kutija 208, RegBr. 6/18, Fasc 1. For a British analysis of Serbia's railroads, see Fryer, *The Royal Navy on the Danube*, pp. 67–77.

39 Mitrović, "Centralne sile," pp. 199–201.

40 In 1910, the Austro-Hungarian Army prepared highly detailed hydrographic maps of the Drina and its fords. AVII, Fond 3, Kutija 57.

41 Ivo Andrić's famous bridge at Višegrad was on a stretch of the Drina that was bordered by Austro-Hungarian territory on both sides.

42 *VRS*, vol. I, pp. 26, 31.

43 Telegram of July 28/August 10, 1914, from Pašić to Spalajković, AS, MID-PO, 1914, FII, 44/1914, 131/211.

44 Dimitrije Djordjević, "Vojvoda Putnik, the Serbian High Command, and Strategy in 1914," in Bela K. Király and Nandor F. Dreisiger, eds, *East Central European Society in World War I*, East European Monographs (Boulder, CO, 1985), p. 576.

45 Tadija Pejović, "Moje uspomene i doživljaji 1892–1919," reprinted in Đurić and Stevanović, p. 31.

46 Dimitrije Djordjević, "Vojvoda Radomir Putnik," in Bela K. Király and Nandor F. Dreisiger, eds, *East Central European Society in World War I*, East European Monographs (Boulder, CO, 1985), p. 230.

47 See High Command Directive No. 1. Str. Pov. OBr. 796, in Aleksandar Stojićević, *Istorija naših ratova za oslobođenje i ujedinjenje od 1912–1918 god. (Tok operacija i primena snabdevanja)*, N. Kovačević (Belgrade, 1932), p. 319.

48 Stojićević, *Istorija naših ratova*, p. 318.

49 Djordjević, "Vojvoda Radomir Putnik," p. 234.

50 Milić Milićević and Ljubodrag Popović, *Generali Vojske kneževine i Kraljevine Srbije*, Vojna Knjiga (Belgrade, 2003), pp. 255–259.

51 Gojko Nikoliš, ed., *Ratni dnevnik Dr. Svetislava Barjaktarovića*, Srpska akademija nauka i umetnosti (Belgrade, 1987), p. 15.

52 AVII, Fond 3, Kutija 237, RegBr. 2, Fasc. 4.

53 Živko Pavlović, *Bitka na Jadru avgusta 1914 god.*, Grafički zavod Makarije (Belgrade, 1924), p. 95 (hereafter *BNJ*).

54 AVII, Fond 3, Kutija 237, RegBr. 2, Fasc. 4. See *ÖULK*, vol. I, Beilage 7.

55 *ÖULK*, vol. I, pp. 16–25, pp. 91–110, Beilage 4, 6, 7. *AMD*, vol. IV, pp. 266–277, pp. 279–304, Anlage 7, 8, 9, 16. Rudolf Jerabek, *Potiorek: General im Schatten von Sarajevo*, Verlag Styria (Graz, 1991), pp. 97–106.

56 *ÖULK*, vol. I, Beilage 4.

57 Slavko Pavičić, *Hrvatska vojna i ratna poviest i prvi svjetski rat*, Hrvatska knjiga (Zagreb, 1943), pp. 283–284.

58 Richard B. Spence, "The Yugoslav Role in the Austro-Hungarian Army, 1914–1918," in Bela K. Király and Nandor F. Dreisiger, eds, *East Central European Society in World War I*, Social Science Monographs (Boulder, CO, 1985), p. 357.

59 See note 58, p. 359.

60 Sergej Vrišer, *Uniforme v zgodovini: Slovenija in sosednje dežele*, Partizanska knjiga (Ljubljana, 1987), color plates 14, 15, 22.

61 Richard B. Spence, "Die Bosniaken Kommen!: The Bosnian-Hercegovinian Formations of the Austro-Hungarian Army, 1914–1918," in Richard B. Spence and Linda R. Nelson, eds, *Scholar, Patriot, Mentor: Historical Essays in Honor of Dimitrije Djordjević*, East European Monographs (Boulder, CO, 1992), pp. 302–304.

62 National mix varied widely depending on the area of recruitment. The 1st regiment, raised from the regions surrounding Sarajevo, was 40 percent Serb, 40 percent Muslim, and 10 percent Croat. The 2nd Regiment, raised from the

Banja Luka region, was over 60 percent Serb. The 3rd regiment from Tuzla had over 50 percent Muslims, many Serbs, and only a few Croats. The 4th regiment from Mostar was around 50 percent Croat, 20 percent Muslim, with the remainder Serbs. Spence, "Die Bosniaken Kommen!," pp. 303–304.

63 Spence, "Die Bosniaken Kommen!," p. 304.

64 The Sixth Army had a larger number of batteries than the Fifth Army, yet a smaller number of cannon. This may be explained by the preponderance of mountain units in the Sixth Army. *ÖULK*, vol. I, pp. 64–65. *AMD*, vol. IV, Anlage 9.

65 Details from Fryer, *The Royal Navy on the Danube*.

66 *ÖULK*, vol. I, pp. 63–69.

67 Pavlović, *BNJ*, pp. 71–73.

68 Savo Skoko and Petar Opačić, *Vojvoda Stepa Stepanović, u ratovima Srbije 1876–1918*, Beogradski izdavačko-grafički zavod (Belgrade, 1983), p. 321.

69 *AMD*, vol. IV, pp. 340–341.

70 *ÖULK*, vol. I, pp. 103–104.

71 The boats were *Morava*, *Šumadija* with 51 passengers, *Deligrad* with 150 passengers, and *Krajina* with 21 passengers and wheat. *Hrvatski dnevnik*, August 10, 1914, no. 186. *Sausalito News*, vol. XXX, no. 31, August 1, 1914.

72 Pavlović, *BNJ*, p. 106.

73 Skoko, *Vojvoda Radomir Putnik*, vol. II, p. 47.

74 Pavlović, *BNJ*, p. 113. High Command, OBr. 1093, OBr. 1107, July 30/August 12, 1914.

75 Third Army, OBr. 329, July 30/August 12, 1914.

76 Pavlović, *BNJ*, p. 117.

77 See note 76, p. 115.

78 See note 76, p. 118.

79 High Command, OBr. 1109, July 30/August 12, 1914.

80 High Command, OBr. 1111, July 30/August 12, 1914.

81 Pavlović, *BNJ*, p. 121.

82 Svetozar A. Đorđević, *Kroz ratne vihore: prvi svetski rat i Srpska avijatika*, Izdanje autora (Belgrade, 1967), p. 22. Pavlović, *BNJ*, p. 122.

83 Pavlović, *BNJ*, p. 123.

84 See note 83, p. 122.

Chapter 6: Lightning on Mount Cer

1 Gunther Rothenberg, *The Army of Francis Joseph*, Purdue University Press (West Lafayette, IN, 1976), p. 183.

2 Franz Conrad von Hötzendorff, *Aus Meiner Dienstzeit, 1906–1918*, Rikola Verlag (Vienna, 1923), vol. IV, p. 337 (hereafter *AMD*). Rudolf Jerabek,

Potiorek: General im Schatten von Sarajevo, Verlag Styria (Graz, 1991), pp. 110–116.

3   *AMD*, vol. IV, pp. 355–356.

4   See note 3, p. 363.

5   Savo Skoko, *Vojvoda Radomir Putnik*, Beogradski izdavačko-grafički zavod (Belgrade, 1984), vol. II, pp. 43–44.

6   *AMD*, vol. IV, p. 387. Živko Pavlović, *Bitka na Jadru avgusta 1914 god.*, Grafički zavod Makarije (Belgrade, 1924), pp. 125–126 (hereafter *BNJ*).

7   Pavlović, *BNJ*, p. 125.

8   See note 7, pp. 124–125.

9   Skoko, *Vojvoda Radomir Putnik*, vol. II, p. 44.

10 *AMD*, vol. IV, p. 370.

11 Skoko, *Vojvoda Radomir Putnik*, vol. II, p. 46.

12 See note 11, p. 46.

13 Rodolphe Archibald Reiss, *Report Upon the Atrocities Committed by the Austro-Hungarian army During the First Invasion of Serbia, Submitted to the Serbian Government by R. A. Reiss*, English translation by F.S. Copeland, Simpkin, Marshall, Hamilton, Kent & Co. (London, 1916), p. 148. See also Pavlović, *BNJ*, p. 137.

14 Pavlović, *BNJ*, p. 133. Third Army to High Command, OBr. 398, August 13/26, 1914.

15 Pavlović, *BNJ*, p. 134. Third Army to High Command, OBr. 403, July 31/ August 13, 1914.

16 Skoko, *Vojvoda Radomir Putnik*, vol. II, p. 65.

17 See note 16, p. 66.

18 See note 16, p. 66.

19 *AMD*, vol. IV, p. 385.

20 Skoko, *Vojvoda Radomir Putnik*, vol. II, p. 67.

21 See note 20, p. 68.

22 *AMD*, vol. IV, pp. 396–397.

23 Skoko, *Vojvoda Radomir Putnik*, vol. II, p. 70.

24 Mihailo Vojvodić and Dragoljub Živojinović, eds., *Veliki rat Srbije, 1914–1918*, Srpska književna zadruga (Belgrade, 1970), p. 18.

25 Skoko, *Vojvoda Radomir Putnik*, vol. II, p. 71.

26 See note 25, p. 71.

27 Egon Erwin Kiš, *Zapiši to Kiš*, reprinted in Silvija Đurić and Vidosav Stevanović, eds, *Golgota i vaskrs Srbije 1914–1915*, IRO "Beograd" (Belgrade, 1990), p. 99.

28 Edmund Glaise von Horstenau, ed., *Österreich-Ungarns letzter Krieg 1914–1918*, Verlag Militärwissenschaftlichen Mitteilungen (Vienna, 1931), vol. I, pp. 121–122 (hereafter *ÖULK*).

29 See note 28, p. 100.

30 Pavlović, *BNJ*, p. 216. Serbian High Command figures for August show the Combined Division as having a full strength of roughly 14,000 men and 350 officers. AVII, Fond 3, Kutija 237. RegBr. 2, Fasc. 4. Skoko claims the division lost almost a third of enlisted strength and almost half its officers. This would indicate approximately 9,000 men. His source for this figure is unknown. Skoko, *Vojvoda Radomir Putnik*, vol. II, p. 71.

31 Skoko, *Vojvoda Radomir Putnik*, vol. II, p. 75.

32 *ÖULK*, vol. I, pp. 125–126. See also *AMD*, vol. IV, pp. 412–414.

33 The IV, VIII, and XIII Corps had eight divisions and four combined brigades (115 battalions, 18 squadrons, 400 cannon) against a Serbian force comprised of six infantry divisions and one cavalry division (94 battalions, 30 squadrons, 108 cannon).

34 *Hrvatski dnevnik*, August 27, 1914, no. 210.

35 Slavko Pavičić, *Hrvatska vojna i ratna poviest i prvi svjetski rat*, Hrvatska knjiga (Zagreb, 1943), pp. 266–268.

36 *Hrvatski dnevnik*, September 3, 1914, no. 221.

37 Skoko, *Vojvoda Radomir Putnik*, vol. II, p. 84.

38 See note 37, p. 84.

39 See note 37, pp. 85–86.

40 *Hrvatski dnevnik*, August 29, 1914, no. 214.

41 Kiš, *Zapiši to Kiš*, p. 110.

42 Skoko, *Vojvoda Radomir Putnik*, vol. II, p. 90.

43 See note 42, p. 91.

44 Reiss, *Report*, p. 21.

45 Pavičić, *Hrvatska vojna i ratna poviest i prvi svjetski rat*, p. 266. The diary of an Austro-Hungarian captain, found on his corpse on August 19, describes how the 53rd Regiment looted one village and committed other atrocities. AVII, Fond 3, Kutija 51, RegBr. 5/15, Fasc. 3.

46 *Hrvatski dnevnik*, August 27, 1914, no. 210.

47 AVII, Fond 3, Kutija 51, RegBr. 5/25, Fasc. 3.

48 AVII, Fond 3, Kutija 51, RegBr. 5/25, Fasc. 3. This is a brochure distributed to Habsburg troops on behavior towards Serbia's civilian population.

49 *Politika*, August 17/30, 1914.

50 *Hrvatski dnevnik*, August 29, 1914, no. 214

51 *Hrvatski dnevnik*, August 27, 1914, no. 210.

52 "To sum up, there was . . . no single article in the Convention of 1907 which was not violated, to a greater or lesser degree, by all the belligerents." International Commission to Inquire into the Causes and Conduct of the Balkan Wars. *The Other Balkan Wars: A 1913 Carnegie Endowment Commission Inquiry in Retrospect with a New Introduction and Reflections on the Present Conflict by George F. Kennan*, Carnegie Endowment for International Peace (Washington, DC, 1993), p. 233.

53   *Hrvatski dnevnik*, September 1, 1914, no. 217.

54   ASANU, Br. 14580. Diary of Mirko R. Ćurović, August 8/21, 1914 (hereafter DMĆ).

55   Reiss, *Report*, p. 143.

56   See note 55, p. 142.

57   International Commission, *The Other Balkan Wars*, p. 223.

58   Gojko Nikoliš, ed., *Ratni dnevnik Dr. Svetislava Barjaktarovića*, Srpska akademija nauka i umetnosti (Belgrade, 1987), p. 18.

59   *Depeša*, August 9/21 and 11/23, 1914.

60   DDS, Diary of Dušan Stefanović, August 20, 1914.

61   *Politika*, August 17/30, 1914.

62   Richard B. Spence, "The Yugoslav Role in the Austro-Hungarian Army, 1914–1918," in Bela K. Király and Nandor F. Dreisiger, eds, *East Central European Society in World War I*, Social Science Monographs (Boulder, CO, 1985), p. 359.

63   DMĆ, August 8/21, 1914.

64   *Politika*, August 18/30, 1914.

Chapter 7: The Battle on the Drina, invasion of Srem, and Mačkov Kamen

1   Mitar Đurišić, "Neki ekonomski problemi Srbije U ratnoj 1914. Godini," *Vojnoistorijski glasnik*, 4: 3–57 (Belgrade, 1964), pp. 5–30.

2   AVII, Fond 3, Kutija 237, RegBr. 2, Fasc. 4.

3   *Hrvatski dnevnik*, August 6, 1914, no. 180.

4   AVII, Fond 3, Kutija 56, RegBr. 17/2, 4, Fasc. 2.

5   AS, MID-PO, 1914, O-II/1, VII/67.

6   AVII, Fond 3, Kutija 56, RegBr. 17/7, Fasc. 2. AVII, Fond 3, Kutija 237, RegBr. 2–7, Fasc. 1.

7   AVII, Fond 3, Kutija 56, RegBr. 17/9, Fasc. 2.

8   AVII, Fond 3, Kutija 209, RegBr. 1, Fasc. 1, p. 219, OBr. 4017.

9   Diary of Dušan Stefanović, August 14, 1914 (hereafter DDS).

10   Telegram of July 28/August 10, 1914, from Pašić to Spalajković, AS, MID-PO, 1914, FII, 35/1914, 132/1.

11   Mihailo Vojvodić and Dragoljub Živojinović, eds, *Veliki rat Srbije, 1914–1918*, Srpska književna zadruga (Belgrade, 1970), p. 19.

12   DDS, August 14, 1914.

13   Telegram of August 12/25, 1914, from Spalajković to Pašić, AS, MID-PO, 1914, FII, 35/1914, 132/10.

14 Telegram of August 22/September 4, 1914, from Pašić to Spalajković, AS, MID-PO, 1914, FII, 35/1914, 132/13.

15 Letter of September 2/15, 1914, from the Russian Ministry of Foreign Affairs to the Serbian Legation in Petrograd, AS, MID-PO, 1914, FII, 35/1914, 132/15.

16 AVII, Fond 3, Kutija 79, Broj. 3/5.

17 DDS, p. 48.

18 Gojko Nikoliš, ed., *Ratni dnevnik Dr. Svetislava Barjaktarovića*, Srpska akademija nauka i umetnosti (Belgrade, 1987), p. 15.

19 Vuk Obradović, "Puške sistema Mosin u naoružanju Srpske vojske tokom prvog svetskog rata," *Vesnik*, LVI: 37 (Belgrade, 2010), p. 84.

20 Edmund Glaise von Horstenau, ed., *Österreich-Ungarns letzter Krieg 1914–1918*, Verlag Militärwissenschaftlichen Mitteilungen (Vienna, 1931), vol. I, pp. 607–608 (hereafter *ÖULK*).

21 Ministarstvo vojske i mornarice, Glavni Đeneralštab. *Veliki rat Srbije za oslobođenje i ujedinjenje Srba, Hrvata i Slovenaca* (Belgrade, 1924), vol. II, pp. 72–73 (hereafter *VRS*). See also AVII, Fond 3, Kutija 79, RegBr. 3/24.

22 Savo Skoko and Petar Opačić, *Vojvoda Stepa Stepanović, u ratovima Srbije 1876–1918*, Beogradski izdavačko-grafički zavod (Belgrade, 1983), p. 369.

23 See note 22, p. 371.

24 *Politika*, September 1/14, 1914.

25 DDS, August 9, 1914.

26 Mitar Đurišić, *Bitka na Drini 1914*, Vojnoistorijski institut (Belgrade, 1969), pp. 82–88. Skoko and Opačić, *Vojvoda Stepa Stepanović*, p. 373. Savo Skoko, *Vojvoda Radomir Putnik*, Beogradski izdavačko-grafički zavod (Belgrade, 1984), vol. II, p. 112.

27 Đurišić, *Bitka na Drini 1914*, pp. 59–60.

28 *ÖULK*, vol. I, p. 616.

29 Telegram August 24/September 6, 1914, from Živković to High Command, AVII, Kutija 54, RegBr. 2/5, Fasc. 1.

30 Telegram August 28/September 10,1914, AVII, Fond 3, Kutija 54, RegBr. 2/13, Fasc. 1.

31 *Politika*, August 28/September 10, 1914.

32 Slavko Mihajlović, "Oblaci nad gradom," reprinted in Đurić, Silvija, and Stevanović, Vidosav, eds, *Golgota i vaskrs Srbije 1914–1915*, IRO "Beograd" (Belgrade, 1990), p. 118.

33 Telegram August 28/September 10, 1914, AVII, Kutija 54, RegBr. 2/13, Fasc. 1.

34 *Politika*, August 29/September 11 and August 30/September 12, 1914. See also *Depeša*, August 30/September 12 and August 31/September 13,1914.

35 Rudolf Jerabek, *Potiorek: General im Schatten von Sarajevo*, Verlag Styria (Graz, 1991), pp. 133–142.

36 Letter of August 24, 1914, from Bolfras to Conrad. Franz Conrad von Hötzendorff, *Aus Meiner Dienstzeit, 1906–1918*, Rikola Verlag (Vienna, 1923), vol. IV, pp. 549–550.

37 Report from Major General Gustav Goglia on the readiness of the Serbian Army. AVII, Fond 3, Kutija 51, RegBr. 5/26, Fasc. 3.

38 1st, 18th, 40th, 48th, and 50th Divisions, the 13th Mountain Brigade, and the 109th Combined Brigade.

39 9th, 21st, 36th, and 42nd Divisions, and the 104th *Landsturm* Brigade.

40 7th and 29th Divisions, the 14th Mountain Brigade, and the 12th, 27th, and 32nd *Landsturm* Regiments.

41 Skoko, *Vojvoda Radomir Putnik*, vol. II, pp. 114–115.

42 After Cer, Potiorek replaced von Giesl with von Scheuchenstuel, former commander of the 9th *K.u.k.* Division.

43 DMĆ, August 26/September 8, 1914.

44 DMĆ, August 27/September 9, 1914. See also Skoko and Opačić, *Vojvoda Stepa Stepanović*, p. 377.

45 Nikoliš, ed., *Ratni dnevnik Dr. Svetislava Barjaktarovića*, p. 18.

46 As quoted in Skoko and Opačić, *Vojvoda Stepa Stepanović*, p. 378.

47 Nikoliš, ed., *Ratni dnevnik Dr. Svetislava Barjaktarovića*, p. 18.

48 AVII, Fond 3, Kut. 79, Broj. 5/33.

49 DMĆ, September 8/21, 1914.

50 Đurišić, *Bitka na Drini 1914*, pp. 156–157.

51 See note 50, pp. 155, 159.

52 See note 50, pp. 153–154, 219.

53 The middle and upper river is fordable at numerous places. The Habsburg forces had detailed hydrographic surveys of the depth, water speed, and character of river bottoms. See AVII, Fond 3, Kutija 57.

54 Đurišić, *Bitka na Drini 1914*, p. 220.

55 See note 54, pp. 170–171.

56 See ÖULK, vol. I, p. 613. See also *VRS*, vol. II, pp. 154–155.

57 AVII, Fond 3, Kutija 73, RegBr. 5/32. See also Đurišić, *Bitka na Drini 1914*, p. 174.

58 Dimitrije Djordjević, "Vojvoda Putnik, the Serbian High Command, and Strategy in 1914," in Bela K. Király and Nandor F. Dreisiger, eds, *East Central European Society in World War I*, East European Monographs (Boulder, CO, 1985), p. 581.

59 Đurišić, *Bitka na Drini 1914*, pp. 197–198.

60 See *VRS*, vol. II, pp. 272–289 and ÖULK, vol. I, pp. 628–631.

61 *VRS*, vol. II, p. 276.

62 Đurišić, *Bitka na Drini 1914*, p. 170.

63 Skoko and Opačić, *Vojvoda Stepa Stepanović*, p. 388.

64 The Serbs considered their artillery useless during this engagement. The Habsburg forces, however, considered it the most effective encountered to date. Đurišić, *Bitka na Drini 1914*, pp. 203–204.

65 *VRS*, vol. II, pp. 297–298.

66 Đurišić, *Bitka na Drini 1914*, pp. 203–204.

67 *VRS*, vol. II, p. 299.

68 Austrian sources give a figure of 20,000 men. *ÖULK*, vol. I, p. 630. Serbian sources place Sixth Army losses as high as 30,000 men. Skoko, *Vojvoda Radomir Putnik*, vol. II, p. 132.

69 Vladimir Dedijer, Ivan Božić, Sima Ćirković, and Milorad Ekmečić, *History of Yugoslavia*, McGraw-Hill (New York, 1974), p. 480.

70 Skoko and Opačić, *Vojvoda Stepa Stepanović*, p. 391.

71 Đurišić, *Bitka na Drini 1914*, p. 209.

72 Rodolphe Archibald Reiss, *Report Upon the Atrocities Committed by the Austro-Hungarian army During the First Invasion of Serbia, Submitted to the Serbian Government by R. A. Reiss*, English translation by F.S. Copeland, Simpkin, Marshall, Hamilton, Kent & Co. (London, 1916), pp. 2–12.

73 Đurišić, *Bitka na Drini 1914*, p. 210.

74 See note 73, p. 210.

75 *ÖULK*, vol. I, p. 628.

76 Djordjević, "Vojvoda Putnik," p. 580.

77 Skoko and Opačić, *Vojvoda Stepa Stepanović*, p. 390.

78 Đurišić, *Bitka na Drini 1914*, pp. 212–213 and f. 202. See also Djordjević, "Vojvoda Putnik," p. 580.

79 Skoko and Opačić, *Vojvoda Stepa Stepanović*, p. 393.

Chapter 8: Defeat and hemorrhage

1 Telegram of September 9/22, 1914, from Odbrana Beograda to High Command, AVII, Fond 3, Kutija 54, RegBr. 2/47, Fasc. 1; AVII, Fond 3, Kutija 54, RegBr. 2/40, Fasc. 1.

2 Joksim P. Gajić, "Odbrana Beograda 1914," in *Agonija Beograda u svetskom ratu*, Štamparija "Jedinstvo" (Belgrade, 1931), p. 24.

3 Telegram of September 11/24, 1914, from Odbrana Beograda to High Command, AVII, Fond 3, Kutija 54, RegBr. 2/45, Fasc. 1. AVII, Fond 3, Kutija 51, RegBr. 5/30, Fasc. 3.

4 Telegram of September 13/26, 1914, from Odbrana Beograda to High Command, AVII, Fond 3, Kutija 54, RegBr. 2/50, Fasc. 1.

5 Telegram of September 16/29, 1914, from Odbrana Beograda to High Command, see note 4, Fond 3. Kutija 54, Regbr. 2/57, Fasc. 1.

6 Telegram of September 11/24, 1914, to High Command from Odbrana Beograda, AVII, Fond 3, Kutija 54, RegBr. 2/45, Fasc. 1.

7 Savo Skoko, *Vojvoda Radomir Putnik*, Beogradski izdavačko-grafički zavod (Belgrade, 1984), vol. II, p. 134.

8 Telegram of September 23, 1914, from Berchtold to Conrad. Franz Conrad von Hötzendorff, *Aus Meiner Dienstzeit, 1906–1918*, Rikola Verlag (Vienna, 1923), vol. IV, p. 851.

9 Ministarstvo vojske i mornarice, Glavni Đeneralštab. *Veliki rat Srbije za oslobođenje i ujedinjenje Srba, Hrvata i Slovenaca* (Belgrade, 1924), vol. III, pp. 67–71 (hereafter *VRS*). Edmund Glaise von Horstenau, ed., *Österreich-Ungarns letzter Krieg 1914–1918*, Verlag Militärwissenschaftlichen Mitteilungen (Vienna, 1931), vol. I, pp. 640–647 (hereafter *ÖULK*).

10 DDS, October 11, 1914. Skoko, *Vojvoda Radomir Putnik*, p. 134.

11 *VRS*, vol. III, pp. 110–112. *ÖULK*, vol. I, p. 654.

12 Letter of November 1/14, 1914, from Military Minister Stefanović to Nikola Pašić, AS, PMS, 1914, Fasc. 1. For a more detailed discussion of Montenegro during the First World War, see Novica Rakočević, *Crna Gora u prvom svjetskom ratu, 1914–1918*, Istorijski institut u Titogradu (Cetinje, 1969).

13 *VRS*, vol. III, pp. 6, 14–15, 22–23. AVII, Fond 3, Kutija 77, RegBr. 3/8.

14 Telegram of September 19/October 2, 1914, from Spalajković to Pašić, AS, MID-PO, Fond 1914, Fascikla II, Redni Broj 1–41-FII, 44/1914, 130/354.

15 Mitar Đurišić, "Neki ekonomski problemi Srbije U ratnoj 1914. Godini," *Vojnoistorijski glasnik*, 4 (Belgrade, 1964), p. 9. Aleksandar Stojićević, *Istorija naših ratova za oslobođenje i ujedinjenje od 1912–1918 god. (Tok operacija i primena snabdevanja)*, N. Kovačević (Belgrade, 1932), pp. 306–307.

16 Telegram of October 11/24, 1914, from Šajinović in Odessa to Spalajković in Petrograd, AS, MID-PO, 1914, Fascikla I, Redni Broj 1–26-FI, 26/1914. AS, MID-PO, 1914, Fascikla II, Redni Broj 1–41-FII, 35/1914. Đurišić, "Neki ekonomski," p. 12.

17 Mihailo Vojvodić and Dragoljub Živojinović, eds., *Veliki rat Srbije, 1914–1918*, Srpska književna zadruga (Belgrade, 1970), p. 55. Savo Skoko and Petar Opačić, *Vojvoda Stepa Stepanović, u ratovima Srbije 1876–1918*, Beogradski izdavačko-grafički zavod (Belgrade, 1983), p. 397.

18 DMĆ, October 11/24, 1914.

19 Skoko and Opačić, *Vojvoda Stepa Stepanović*, p. 395.

20 Slavko Pavičić, *Hrvatska vojna i ratna poviest i prvi svjetski rat*, Hrvatska knjiga (Zagreb, 1943), pp. 287–288.

21 Skoko and Opačić, *Vojvoda Stepa Stepanović*, p. 396.

22 DMĆ, October 13/26, 1914 and October 14/27, 1914.

23 Skoko and Opačić, *Vojvoda Stepa Stepanović*, p. 397.

24 DDS, September 29, 1914.

25 Gojko Nikoliš, ed., *Ratni dnevnik Dr. Svetislava Barjaktarovića*, Srpska akademija nauka i umetnosti (Belgrade, 1987), p. 19 (hereafter *RDSB*).

26 DMĆ, September 14/27, 1914.

27 DMĆ, October 13/26, 1914.

28 Ludwig Elmannsberger, "The Austro-Hungarian Artillery in the World War," *Coast Artillery Journal*, 62(3): 192–206 (Fort Monroe, VA, 1925), p. 199.

29 DMĆ, October 31/November 13, 1914, November 7/20, 1914, and November 8/21, 1914.

30 See VA, FVKS, Popisnik 3, Kutija 237, RegBr. 1, 4, 5, Fasc. 1. VA, FVKS, Popisnik 3, Kutija 237, RegBr. 20, Fasc. 2. *Pregled gubitaka u ratu 1914 i 1915 godine*. VA, FVKS, Popisnik 3, Kutija 237, RegBr. 7, Fasc. 1.

31 Quoted in Skoko and Opačić, *Vojvoda Stepa Stepanović*, p. 401.

32 Telegram of October 12/25, 1914, from High Command to Jurišić-Šturm, VA, FVKS, Popisnik 3, Kutija 50, RegBr. 1/62, Fasc.1. Telegram of October 8/21, 1914, from High Command to Bojović, VA, FVKS, Popisnik 3, Kutija 50, RegBr. 1/59, Fasc. 1. Telegram of October 15/28, 1914, from High Command to Artillery Technical Section, VA, FVKS, Popisnik 3, Kutija 50, RegBr. 1/64, Fasc. 1.

33 Skoko, *Vojvoda Radomir Putnik*, vol. II, p. 137. The shortage became so acute that Morava I's Lieutenant Marko Ćurović recorded in his diary the number of bullets his regiment fired daily. DMĆ for October.

34 DMĆ, September 14/27, 1914.

35 DMĆ, October 13/26, 1914.

36 Interrogatory letter of December 19, 1914/January 1, 1915, from the President of the National Assembly to Nikola Pašić, AS, PMS, 1914, Fasc. 1. At this time Serbia had only sufficient industrial and craft capacity to produce 80,000–100,000 *opanci* per month. Given the size of the army, an additional 300,000 *opanci* per month would have needed to be manufactured to equip all the troops.

37 France sent three 140-mm cannon from the battleship *Henri IV*, while Russia sent two obsolete 150-mm guns manufactured in 1867. Britain sent two batteries of 4.7-inch (120-mm) naval guns to Belgrade in early 1915. Charles E.J. Fryer, *The Royal Navy on the Danube*, East European Monographs (Boulder, CO, 1988), pp. 21, 23, 40.

38 Milorad Ekmečić, *Ratni ciljevi Srbije, 1914*, Srpska književna zadruga (Belgrade, 1973), p. 220.

39 Telegram of August 11/24, 1914, from Pašić to Bošković, AJ, 80–7–405.

40 Telegram of September 6/19, 1914, from Ristić to Pašić, AJ, 80–1–386.

41 Telegram of August 18/31, 1914, from Serbian Minister in Rome Ljubomir Mihajlović to Jovan Jovanović-Pižon, AJ, 80–1–251, 252, 253, 254.

42 Telegram of September 12/25, 1914, from Bošković to Pašić, AJ, 80–2–183. Telegram of September 18/31, 1914, from Mihajlović to Pašić, AJ, 80–1–255.

43 Telegram of September 6/19, 1914, from Bošković to Pašić, AJ, 80–2–178, 179, 180, 181.

44 For a brief survey of the Yugoslav Committee, see Milorad Ekmečić's "Serbian War Aims" and Gale Stokes' "The Role of the Yugoslav Committee in the Formation of Yugoslavia," both in Dimitrije Djordjević, ed., *The Creation of Yugoslavia, 1914–1918*, Clio Books (Santa Barbara, CA, 1980),

and Ivo J. Lederer's *Yugoslavia at the Paris Peace Conference: A Study in Frontiermaking*, Yale University Press (New Haven, CT, 1963).

45 Letter of September 30, 1914, from Frano Supilo to Ljubomir Mihajlović, in Dragovan Šepić, *Pisma i memorandumi Frana Supila (1914–1917)*, Naučno delo (Belgrade, 1967).

46 Telegram of September 18/31, 1914, Mihajlović to Pašić, AJ, 80-1-256, 257, 258, 259. The goals of the Yugoslav Committee differed somewhat from those of the Serbian government. Unlike Pašić, the Dalmatians wanted Trieste and Istria incorporated into a future South Slavic state.

47 Telegram of September 21/October 4, 1914, from Mihajlović to Pašić, AJ, 80-1-260.

48 Telegram of September 22/October 5, 1914, from Mihajlović to Pašić, AJ, 80-1-261.

49 Telegram of September 22/October 5, 1914, from Spalajković to Pašić, AJ, 80-2-461, 462.

50 Telegram of September 26/October 9, 1914, from Mihajlović to Pašić, AJ, 80-1-264, 265.

51 Telegram of October 31/November 13, 1914, from Bošković to Pašić, AJ, 80-2-186.

52 Letter of November 4/17, 1914, from Vesnić to Pašić, AJ, 80–2–51.

53 *Bosnische Post*, December 11, 1914, no. 282.

54 Petar Opačić, "Genocidna Politika Austrougarske protiv Srpskog narod i Srbije u prvom svetskom ratu kao platforma za genocid u drugom svetskom ratu," in Petar Opačić, Savo Skoko, Raadomir Rakić, and Milovan Ćurčić, eds, *Genocid nad srbima u dvadestom veku* (Belgrade, 1992), p. 17.

55 Letter of August 8/21, 1914, from Pašić to Čolak-Antić, AS, MID-PO, 1914, F-XIV, Br. 483.

56 Mitar Đurišić, *Bitka na Drini 1914*, Vojnoistorijski institut (Belgrade, 1969), p. 15.

57 See note 56, p. 392.

58 See note 56, p. 393.

59 Letter of October 19/November 1, 1914, from Čolak-Antić to Pašić, AS, MID-PO, 1914, F-XII, Br. 215.

60 Đurišić, *Bitka na Drini 1914*, p. 416.

61 See note 60, p. 299.

62 See note 60, p. 301.

63 DMĆ, October 14/27, 1914. *VRS*, vol. III, pp. 138–142.

64 Skoko and Opačić, *Vojvoda Stepa Stepanović*, p. 401.

65 *ÖULK*, vol. I, pp. 662–664.

66 *VRS*, vol. III, p. 145.

67 *VRS*, vol. III, pp. 145–147.

68 *VRS*, vol. III, pp. 162–164.

69 *VRS*, vol. III, pp. 165–167.

70 AVII, Fond 3, Kutija 58, RegBr. 1/37.

71 *RDSB*, p. 47.

72 DMĆ, October 17/30 and October 18/31 1914. *VRS*, vol. III, p. 168.

73 *RDSB*, pp. 43, 47.

74 AVII, Fond 3, Kutija 56, RegBr. 17/17, Fasc. 1.

75 Skoko and Opačić, *Vojvoda Stepa Stepanović*, p. 405.

76 See note 75, p. 406.

77 *RDSB*, pp. 50–51.

78 AVII, Fond 3, Kutija 56, RegBr. 17/13, Fasc. 1.

79 Quoted in Skoko, *Vojvoda Radomir Putnik*, vol. II, p. 144.

80 Text of letter quoted in Vojvodić and Živojinović, eds., *Veliki rat Srbije, 1914–1918*, p. 67.

81 Quoted in Skoko, *Vojvoda Radomir Putnik*, vol. II, p. 143. See also the undated circular of Nikola Pašić to all Serbian Ministers abroad, AS, MID-PO, 1914, F-XIX, Br. 6955.

82 Skoko and Opačić, *Vojvoda Stepa Stepanović*, pp. 408–409.

83 The best treatment of this meeting is in Đurišić, *Bitka na Drini 1914*, pp. 416–418.

84 Đurišić, "Neki ekonomski," p. 15.

85 See note 84, p. 20.

86 DMĆ, October 28/November 10, 1914.

87 Živko Pavlović, *Bitka na Kolubari*, 2 vols. (Belgrade, 1928, 1930), Part 1, sveska 1, p. 33 (hereafter *BNK*).

88 *RDSB*, p. 52.

89 *BNK*, Part 1, sveska 1, p. 14.

90 *BNK*, pp. 6–7. First Army OBr. 2759, October 31/November 13, 1914.

91 *BNK*, p. 5. High Command OBr. 6253, October 29/November 11, 1914, and High Command OBr. 6292, November 1/14, 1914.

92 *RDSB*, p. 54.

93 AVII, Fond 3, Kutija 55, RegBr. 6/9, Fasc. 3.

94 AVII, Fond 3, Kutija 55, RegBr. 6/11, Fasc. 3.

95 AVII, Fond 3, Kutija 237, RegBr. 4, Fasc.1. AVII, Fond 3, Kutija 237, RegBr. 5, Fasc. 1.

96 AVII, Fond 3, Kutija 55, RegBr. 2/19, Fasc. 1.

97 Skoko and Opačić, *Vojvoda Stepa Stepanović*, p. 408. Dimitrije Djordjević, "Vojvoda Putnik, the Serbian High Command, and Strategy in 1914," in Bela K. Király and Nandor F. Dreisiger, eds, *East Central European Society in World War I*, East European Monographs (Boulder, CO, 1985), p. 581.

98 *VRS*, vol. IV, p. 7.

99 *BNK*, Part 1, sveska 1, p. 56.

100 *BNK*, Part 1, sveska 1, p. 19.

101 AVII, Fond 3, Kutija 55, RegBr. 6/12, Fasc. 3.

102 AVII, Fond 3, Kutija 55, RegBr. 6/12, Fasc. 3.

103 Letter of September 29/October 12, 1914, Stefanović to Pašić, AS, PMS, 1914, Fasc. 1.

104 *RDSB*, p. 52.

105 *RDSB*, p. 55.

106 Letter of November 8/21, 1914, from Pašić to Putnik, AVII, Fond 3, Kutija 55, RegBr. 6/29, Fasc. 3.

107 *RDSB*, p. 52.

108 AVII, Fond 3, Kutija 56, RegBr. 17/18, Fasc. 1.

109 AVII, Fond 3, Kutija 55, RegBr. 6/13, Fasc. 3.

110 *RDSB*, p. 55.

111 AVII, Fond 3, Kutija 55, RegBr. 6/14, Fasc. 3.

Chapter 9: The Battle on the Kolubara

1 Alfred Krauss, "Uzroci našeg poraza," translated from the German "Die Ursachen Unser Niederlage" (Belgrade, 1938), reprinted in Silvija Đurić and Vidosav Stevanović, eds, *Golgota i vaskrs Srbije 1914–1915*, IRO "Beograd" (Belgrade, 1990), p. 390.

2 Savo Skoko and Petar Opačić, *Vojvoda Stepa Stepanović, u ratovima Srbije 1876–1918*, Beogradski izdavačko-grafički zavod (Belgrade, 1983), p. 410.

3 Edmund Glaise von Horstenau, ed., *Österreich-Ungarns letzter Krieg 1914–1918*, Verlag Militärwissenschaftlichen Mitteilungen (Vienna, 1931), vol. I, p. 713 (hereafter *ÖULK*).

4 AVII, Fond 3, Kutija 237, RegBr. 5, Fasc. 1.

5 See note 4.

6 High Command's records during this period are haphazard. Desertion may have caused the Serbian Army's troop strength to have fallen well below 190,000 by early December.

7 Živko Pavlović, *Bitka na Kolubari*, 2 vols. (Belgrade, 1928, 1930), Part 1, sveska 1, pp. 75–77 (hereafter *BNK*).

8 *BNK*, Part 1, sveska 1, p. 81. High Command OBr. 6,600, November 5/18, 1914.

9 Ministarstvo vojske i mornarice, Glavni Đeneralštab. *Veliki rat Srbije za oslobođenje i ujedinjenje Srba, Hrvata i Slovenaca* (Belgrade, 1924), vol. IV, p. 153 (hereafter *VRS*).

10 DMĆ, November 2/15, 1914.

11 *BNK*, Part 1, sveska 1, pp. 102–104.

12 *ÖULK*, vol. I, pp. 659–660.

13 *BNK*, Part 1, sveska 1, p. 79.

14 *ÖULK*, vol. I, p. 682. DMĆ, November 4/17, 1914. *BNK*, Part 1, sveska 1, p. 144. Second Army OBr. 3746, from Stepanović to High Command, November 5/18, 1914.

15 *BNK*, Part 1, sveska 1, p. 21.

16 *BNK*, Part 1, sveska 1, p. 97.

17 AVII, Fond 3, Kutija 209, RegBr. 1, Fasc. 1, p. 306, F_O Order No. 6394.

18 *BNK*, Part 1, sveska 1, p. 82. First Army OBr. 2853, from Mišić to High Command, November 5/18, 1914.

19 *ÖULK*, vol. I, p. 685.

20 *ÖULK*, vol. I, p. 686.

21 DMĆ, November 6/19, 1914. *BNK*, Part 1, sveska 1, p. 189. Second Army OBr. 3798, from Stepanović to High Command, November 6/19, 1914. *ÖULK*, vol. I, p. 687.

22 Danube II's commander, Miloš Vasić, reported a serious desertion problem, and had sent out patrols to the neighboring villages to scavenge food, *opanci*, and clothing for the soldiers. Without food or clothing, Danube II could not hold its positions. *BNK*, Part 1, sveska 1, p. 149. First Army OBr. 2878, from Mišić to High Command, November 6/19, 1914.

23 AVII, Fond 3, Kutija 56, RegBr. 17/19, Fasc. 1.

24 AVII, Fond 3, Kutija 55, RegBr. 6/19, Fasc. 3.

25 AVII, Fond 3, Kutija 55, RegBr. 6/20, Fasc. 3.

26 *VRS*, vol. IV, p. 185.

27 AVII, Fond 3, Kutija 55, RegBr. 6/21, Fasc. 3.

28 *BNK*, Part 1, sveska 1, p. 245. Third Army OBr. 2813, from Jurišić-Šturm to High Command, November 8/21, 1914.

29 Milorad Marković, "Ratni dnevnici," reprinted in Silvija Đurić and Vidosav Stevanović, eds., *Golgota i vaskrs Srbije 1914–1915*, IRO "Beograd" (Belgrade, 1990), p. 329. Diary entry for November 9/21, 1914.

30 *BNK*, Part 1, sveska 1, pp. 329–330. Morava I OBr. 1929 to Second Army at 02:20 hours, November 9/22, 1914. Morava I OBr. 1930 to Second Army at 06:40 hours, November 9/22, 1914.

31 *BNK*, Part 1, sveska 1, p. 283.

32 *VRS*, vol. IV, pp. 263–265.

33 AVII, Fond 3, Kutija 55, RegBr. 6/24–25, Fasc. 3.

34 AVII, Fond 3, Kutija 55, RegBr. 6/15, Fasc. 3.

35 AVII, Fond 3, Kutija 55, RegBr. 6/27, Fasc. 3.

36 AVII, Fond 3, Kutija 209, RegBr. 1, Fasc. 1, p. 306. DMĆ, November 27/December 10, 1914.

37 AVII, Fond 3, Kutija 56, RegBr. 17/10, Fasc. 2.

38 *VRS*, vol. IV, p. 311. High Command OBr. 6887, November 9/22, 1914.

39 *BNK*, Part 1, sveska 1, p. 302. High Command OBr. 6887 to all Armies at 13:00 hours, November 9/22, 1914.

40 *BNK*, Part 1, sveska 1, p. 359.

41 *ÖULK*, vol. I, p. 696.

42 *BNK*, Part 1, sveska 1, p. 333. Šumadija I OBr. 2396 to Second Army at 06:12 hours, November 10/23, 1914.

43 Skoko and Opačić, *Vojvoda Stepa Stepanović*, p. 425.

44 See note 43, p. 424.

45 *VRS*, vol. V, p. 42. High Command OBr. 6935 to Second Army qt 12:00 noon, 10/23 November 10/23, 1914.

46 *BNK*, Part 1, sveska 1, p. 423.

47 *BNK*, Part 1, sveska 1, p. 415. Second Army OBr. 3967 to High Command at 11:15 hours, November 11/24, 1914.

48 *BNK*, Part 1, sveska 1, p. 443. Timok I OBr. 1491 to Second Army at 11:35 hours, November 11/24, 1914.

49 *BNK*, Part 1, sveska 1, p. 445. Šumadija I OBr. 2439 to Second Army at 21:15 hours, November 11/24, 1914.

50 *BNK*, Part 1, sveska 1, p. 416. Second Army OBr. 3984 to High Command, November 11/24, 1914.

51 *BNK*, Part 1, sveska 1, p. 463. Second Army OBr. 4028 to High Command at 19:30 hours, November 12/25, 1914.

52 *BNK*, Part 1, sveska 2, p. 514. Morava I OBr. 2050 to Second Army, November 14/27, 1914.

53 *ÖULK*, vol. I, p. 697.

54 *BNK*, Part 1, sveska 2, p. 499. Second Army OBr. 4022 to Morava I at 14:38 hours, November 12/25, 1914. *VRS*, vol. V, pp. 87–88.

55 *BNK*, Part 1, sveska 1, p. 460. High Command OBr. 7122 to Defense of Belgrade, November 12/25, 1914.

56 *BNK*, Part 1, sveska 2, p. 526. First Army OBr. 3085 to High Command, November 12/25, 1914.

57 Letter from Putnik to Stefanović, December 5, 1914, VAS, FVKS, Popisnik 3, RegBr. 7/1, Fasc. 1. VAS, FVKS, Kutija 352, RegBr. 5/3, Fasc. 1, a report from the Artillery Department dated November 29/December 12, 1914 to the Operational Department.

58 Letter from Putnik to Stefanović, December 5, 1914, VAS, FVKS, Kutija 352, RegBr. 7/1, Fasc. 1.

59 *BNK*, Part 1, sveska 2, p. 527. First Army OBr. 3090 to High Command at 16:20 hours, November 13/26, 1914.

60 *VRS*, vol. V, p. 149. First Army OBr. 3107, November 13/26, 1914.

61 *BNK*, Part 1, sveska 2, p. 596. Obrenovac Detachment OBr. 1743 to High Command at 20:40 hours, November 13/26, 1914.

62 *BNK*, Part 1, sveska 2, p. 525. High Command OBr. 7149 to Military Ministry at 10:20 hours, November 13/26, 1914.

63 Dimitrije Djordjević, "Vojvoda Radomir Putnik," in Bela K. Király and Albert A. Nofi, eds, *East Central European War Leaders: Civilian and Military*, East European Monographs (Boulder, CO, 1988), p. 238.

64 *VRS*, vol. V, p. 167. High Command OBr. 7189 to Second Army at 17:30 hours, November 13/26, 1914.

65 *VRS*, vol. V, p. 168. High Command OBr. 7194 to all Armies at 21:30 hours, November 13/26, 1914.

66 *BNK*, Part 1, sveska 2, p. 593. Second Army OBr. 409 to High Command at 10:55 hours, November 14/27, 1914.

67 *BNK*, Part 1, sveska 2, p. 590. First Army OBr. 3144 to High Command at 00:35 hours, November 14/27, 1914.

68 *BNK*, Part 1, sveska 2, p. 613. Drina I OBr. 1644 to First Army at 21:45 hours, November 14/27, 1914.

69 *BNK*, Part 1, sveska 2, p. 693. *VRS*, vol. V, p. 243.

70 On November 29, the Commander of Timok II reported that the Division's total strength amounted to 1,400 rifles. *BNK*, Part 1, sveska 2, p. 761. Timok II OBr. 1290 to Third Army at 12:30 hours, November 16/29, 1914.

71 *BNK*, Part 1, sveska 2, p. 729. Second Army OBr. 4163 to High Command at 10:20 hours, November 16/29, 1914.

72 *BNK*, Part 1, sveska 2, p. 705. Second Army OBr. 4128 to High Command at 11:30 hours, November 15/28, 1914.

73 *BNK*, Part 1, sveska 2, pp. 647–648. First Army OBr. 3187 to High Command at 23:25 hours, November 15/28, 1914. First Army OBr. 3189 to High Command at 21:30 hours, November 15/28, 1914. See also *VRS*, vol. V, p. 259.

74 *VRS*, vol. V, p. 317. High Command OBr. 7325 to First Army at 01:00 hours, November 16/29, 1914.

75 *BNK*, Part 1, sveska 2, p. 533. High Command OBr. 7194, November 13/26, 1914.

76 *BNK*, Part 1, sveska 2, p. 726. High Command OBr. 7375 to Military Ministry at 17:38 hours, November 16/29, 1914. See also *VRS*, vol. V, p. 318.

77 *BNK*, Part 1, sveska 2, p. 726. High Command OBr. 7378 to Obrenovac Detachment at 21:00 hours, November 16/29, 1914.

78 AVII, Fond 3, Kutija 55, RegBr. 6/30, Fasc. 3.

79 By mid-December, the Drina I Division had replenished its ranks to 8,665 enlisted men. Yet the division showed 25,201 enlisted on the books, indicating that it had lost 16,536 men to a combination of factors: death, wounds, missing, and desertion, by far the highest losses of any single Serbian division. The next closest division is the Morava I with 11,382 and Šumadija with 6,975. All the remaining divisions have losses in the range of 4,000–6,000 enlisted men each. AVII, Fond 3, Kutija 237, RegBr. 6, Fasc. 1.

80   Charles E.J. Fryer, *The Royal Navy on the Danube*, East European Monographs (Boulder, CO, 1988), p. 23.

81   *Politika*, November 13/26, 1914.

82   DMĆ, November 8/21, 11/24, and 17/30, 1914.

83   ÖULK, vol. I, p. 713.

84   Skoko and Opačić, *Vojvoda Stepa Stepanović*, p. 432.

85   VRS, vol. V, p. 351. High Command OBr. 7448 to all Armies, November 17/30, 1914. ÖULK, vol. I, p. 706. DMĆ, November 14/27,1914.

86   Vasa Božidarović, "Još malo svetlosti na Kolubarsku bitku," *Ratnik* (Belgrade, 1922), p. 62. Mitar Đurišić, "Neki ekonomski problemi Srbije U ratnoj 1914. Godini," *Vojnoistorijski glasnik*, 4 (Belgrade, 1964), p. 24.

87   Serbian artillery was not completely resupplied. All 120-mm *De Bange* cannon were withdrawn from battle, for want of ammunition, as were all Schneider howitzers. *BNK*, Part 1, sveska 2, pp. 873–874, 911.

88   Miloje Simljanić et al., eds, *Skopski Đački bataljon, 1914: bataljon 1,300 kaplara*, Udruženje 1300 kaplara (Belgrade, 1941), p. xv.

89   AVII, Fond 3, Kutija 55, RegBr. 6/32, Fasc. 3.

90   Skoko and Opačić, *Vojvoda Stepa Stepanović*, p. 435.

91   *BNK*, Part 2, sveska 1, p. 2.

92   *BNK*, Part 1, sveska 2, p. 830. High Command OBr. 7462 to all Armies, November 18/December 1, 1914.

93   VRS, vol. V, p. 416. Milan Radenković, *Kolubarska bitka*, Vojno delo (Belgrade, 1959), pp. 187–190.

Chapter 10: One man's triumph, another man's victory

1   Slavko Mihajlović, "Oblaci nad gradom," reprinted in Silvija Đurić and Vidosav Stevanović, eds, *Golgota i vaskrs Srbije 1914–1915*, IRO "Beograd" (Belgrade, 1990), p. 118.

2   See note 1, p. 206.

3   Krsman Milošević, *Odbrane Beograda kroz vekove*, Savez potomaka ratnika Srbije 1912–1920 godine (Belgrade, 2012), p. 200.

4   Savo Skoko and Petar Opačić, *Vojvoda Stepa Stepanović, u ratovima Srbije 1876–1918*, Beogradski izdavačko-grafički zavod (Belgrade, 1983), p. 437.

5   Živko Pavlović, *Bitka na Kolubari*, 2 vols. (Belgrade, 1928, 1930), Part 2, sveska 1, p. 47 (hereafter *BNK*). Skoko and Opačić, *Vojvoda Stepa Stepanović*, p. 439.

6   *BNK*, Part 2, sveska 1, p. 221. First Army OBr. 3414 to all Division commanders at 12:15 hours, November 22/December 5, 1914.

7   *BNK*, Part 2, sveska 1, p. 244.

8   Milorad Marković, "Ratni dnevnici," reprinted in Silvija Đurić and Vidosav Stevanović, eds, *Golgota i vaskrs Srbije 1914–1915*, IRO "Beograd" (Belgrade, 1990), p. 334. Entry for November 23/December 6, 1914.

9   *BNK*, Part 2, sveska 1, p. 308.

10   AVII, Fond 3, Kutija 55, RegBr. 6/31, Fasc. 3.

11   Letter of September 10/23, 1914, from the chief of the High Command staff to the chief of the Operational Section of the High Command. AVII, Fond 3, Kutija 56, RegBr. 17/11, Fasc. 2.

12   AVII, Fond 3, Kutija 56, RegBr. 17/20, Fasc. 1.

13   *BNK*, Part 2, sveska 1, p. 341. Skoko and Opačić, *Vojvoda Stepa Stepanović*, p. 447.

14   *BNK*, Part 2, sveska 1. p. 336. High Command OBr. 7757 to all Armies at 10:20 hours, November 24/December 7, 1914.

15   *BNK*, Part 2, sveska 1. p. 371. First Army OBr. 3498 to High Command, November 25/December 8, 1914.

16   *BNK*, Part 2, sveska 1. p. 401. First Army OBr. 3516 to High Command, November 26/December 9, 1914.

17   Marković, "Ratni dnevnici," p. 335. Entry for November 24/December 7, 1914.

18   Edmund Glaise von Horstenau, ed., *Österreich-Ungarns letzter Krieg 1914–1918*, Verlag Militärwissenschaftlichen Mitteilungen (Vienna, 1931), vol. I, p. 735 (hereafter *ÖULK*).

19   Ministarstvo vojske i mornarice, Glavni Đeneralštab. *Veliki rat Srbije za oslobođenje i ujedinjenje Srba, Hrvata i Slovenaca* (Belgrade, 1924), vol. VII, p. 172 (hereafter *VRS*). High Command OBr. 7949 to all Armies, November 27/December 10, 1914.

20   *VRS*, vol. VII, p. 85. First Army OBr. 3519 to Division commanders, November 26/December 9, 1914.

21   *BNK*, Part 2, sveska 1, p. 401. First Army OBr. 3516 to High Command, November 26/December 9, 1914.

22   Skoko and Opačić, *Vojvoda Stepa Stepanović*, p. 454.

23   *ÖULK*, vol. I, p. 735.

24   *ÖULK*, vol. I, p. 740.

25   *ÖULK*, vol. I, p. 741.

26   *ÖULK*, vol. I, p. 744.

27   *VRS*, vol. VII, p. 230. High Command OBr. 7999 to Second and Third Armies, November 28/December 11, 1914.

28   *ÖULK*, vol. I, p. 746.

29   *VRS*, vol. VII, p. 281.

30   Milan Radenković, *Kolubarska bitka*, Vojno delo (Belgrade, 1959), p. 439. Dušan T. Bataković and Nikola B. Popović, eds, *Kolubarska Bitka*, Litera (Belgrade, 1989), p. 133.

31 *ÖULK*, vol. I, p. 747.

32 *ÖULK*, vol. I, pp. 748–749.

Chapter 11: The aftermath

1 *Politika*, December 8/21, 1914.

2 See note 1.

3 Živko Pavlović, *Bitka na Kolubari*, 2 vols. (Belgrade, 1928, 1930), Part 2, sveska 2, p. 864 (hereafter *BNK*).

4 Edmund Glaise von Horstenau, ed., *Österreich-Ungarns letzter Krieg 1914–1918*, Verlag Militärwissenschaftlichen Mitteilungen (Vienna, 1931), vol. I, pp. 759–760 (hereafter *ÖULK*).

5 AVII, Fond 3, Kutija 237, RegBr. 20, Fasc. 2. *Pregled Gubitaka u ratu 1914 i 1915 godine.*

6 Dragan Živojinović, "Serbia and Montenegro: The Home Front, 1914–1918," in Bela K. Király and Nandor F. Dreisiger, eds, *East Central European Society in World War I*, Social Science Monographs (Boulder, CO, 1985), p. 243.

7 John Reed, *The War in Eastern Europe*, Scribner's (New York, 1916), p. 29.

8 *ÖULK*, vol. I, p. 760.

9 Andrej Mitrović, *Serbia's Great War, 1914–1918*, Hurst (London, 2007), pp. 100–101.

10 *Politika*, December 9/22 and 10/23, 1914.

11 Mitrović, *Serbia's Great War*, pp. 100–101.

12 Ludwig Elmannsberger, "The Austro-Hungarian Artillery in the World War," *Coast Artillery Journal*, 62(3): 192–206 (Fort Monroe, VA, 1925), p. 197.

13 Krauss, "Uzroci našeg poraza," translated from the German "Die Ursachen Unser Niederlage" (Belgrade, 1938), reprinted in Silvija Đurić and Vidosav Stevanović, eds, *Golgota i vaskrs Srbije 1914–1915*, IRO "Beograd" (Belgrade, 1990), p. 378.

14 See note 13, pp. 386–387.

15 See note 13, p. 393.

16 Elmannsberger, "The Austro-Hungarian Artillery in the World War," p. 199.

17 Krauss, "Uzroci našeg poraza," p. 384.

18 Charles J. Vopicka, *Secrets of the Balkans: Seven Years of a Diplomatist's Life in the Storm Centre of Europe*, Rand McNally (Chicago, IL, 1921), p. 34.

19 Egon Erwin Kiš, *Zapiši to Kiš*, reprinted in Silvija Đurić and Vidosav Stevanović, eds, *Golgota i vaskrs Srbije 1914–1915*, IRO "Beograd" (Belgrade, 1990), p. 106.

20 Krauss, "Uzroci našeg poraza," p. 384.

BIBLIOGRAPHY

Unpublished sources

(AJ) Arhiv Jugoslavije
(AS) Arhiv Srbije
(ASANU) Arhiv Srpske akademije nauka i umetnosti
(AVII) Arhiv Vojnoistorijskog instituta
(VAS) Vojni Arhiv Srbije
(DDS) Diary of Dušan Stefanović in Arhiv SANU
(DMČ) Diary of Marko Čurović in Arhiv SANU
(ASPC/COS) Arhiv Srpske pravoslavne crkve, Crkvena opština Sarajevo (Stara
Srpska Pravoslavna Crkva Sv. Arhanđela Mihaila i Gavrila)
Papers of Jovan Jovanović Pižon
Arhiv Narodne i univerzitetske biblioteke Bosne i Hercegovine

Periodicals and newspapers

Sarajevski list (Sarajevo)
Hrvatski list (Sarajevo)
Bosnische Post (Sarajevo)
Bosanska Vila (Sarajevo)
Depeša (Belgrade)
Politika (Belgrade)

Published documentary collections

Bittner, Ludwig, and Hans Ubersberger, eds. *Österreich-Ungarns Aussenpolitik Von
Der Bosnischen Krise 1908 Bis Zum Kriegsausbruch 1914: Diplomatische
Aktenstücke Des Österreichisch-Ungarischen Ministeriums Des Äussern*
(Vienna, 1930).
*Bosnischer Bote/Bosanski Glasnik 1914: Universal-Hand- und Adreszbuch für
Bosnien und die Hercegovina*, Kommissionsverlag der Kais. Kön. Hof- und
Staatsdruckerei in Wien (Vienna, 1914).
Dedijer, Vladimir, and Anić, Života, eds. *Dokumenti o spoljnoj politici Kraljevine
Srbije, 1903–1914*, vol. VII, no. 1 (January 1/14– April 30/May 13, 1914); no. 2
(May 1/14–July 22/August 4, 1914) (Belgrade, 1980).

Horstenau, Edmund Glaise von, ed. *Österreich-Ungarns letzter Krieg 1914–1918*, vols. I and II, Verlag Militärwissenschaftlichen Mitteilungen (Vienna, 1931).

Ministarstvo vojske i mornarice, Glavni Đeneralštab. *Veliki rat Srbije za oslobođenje i ujedinjenje Srba, Hrvata i Slovenaca*. Several vols. (Belgrade, 1924).

Nikoliš, Gojko, ed. *Ratni dnevnik Dr. Svetislava Barjaktarovića*, Srpska akademija nauka i umetnosti (Belgrade, 1987).

Pavlović, Živko. *Bitka na Jadru avgusta 1914 god.*, Grafički zavod Makarije (Belgrade, 1924).

Pavlović, Živko. *Bitka na Kolubari*, 2 vols. (Belgrade, 1928, 1930).

Stationery Office. *War 1914: Punishing the Serbs*, Crown Publishers (London, 1915).

Šepić, Dragovan. *Pisma i memorandumi Frana Supila (1914–1917)* (Belgrade, 1967).

Šišić, Ferdo, ed. *Dokumenti o postanku Kraljevine Srba, Hrvata i Slovenaca 1914–1919* (Zagreb, 1920).

Vojvodić, Mihailo, and Živojinović, Dragoljub, eds. *Veliki rat Srbije, 1914–1918*, Srpska književna zadruga (Belgrade, 1970).

Published memoirs and campaign studies

Conrad von Hötzendorff, Franz. *Aus Meiner Dienstzeit, 1906–1918*, vols. I, III, IV, V, VI, Rikola Verlag (Vienna, 1923).

Stojićević, Aleksandar. *Istorija naših ratova za oslobođenje i ujedinjenje od 1912–1918 god (Tok operacija i primena snabdevanja)*, N. Kovačević (Belgrade, 1932).

Trotsky, Leon. *The War Correspondence of Leon Trotsky: The Balkan Wars, 1912–1913*, Pathfinder Press (New York, 1980).

Books and articles

Adams, John Clinton. *Flight in Winter*, Princeton University Press (Princeton, NJ, 1942).

Albertini, Luigi. *The Origins of the War of 1914*, 3 vols, translated and edited by Isabella M. Massey, Oxford University Press (London, 1953).

Aranđelović, Nikola J. *Vojvoda Stepa I. Stepanović*, publisher not identified (Belgrade, 1938).

Banac, Ivo. *The National Question in Yugoslavia: Origins, History, Politics*, Cornell University Press (Ithaca, NY, 1988).

Bataković, Dušan T. "Podaci Srpskih vojnih vlasti o Arbanaškim prvacima 1914," in *Mešovita građa*, XVII–XVIII: 188–206 (Belgrade, 1988).

Bataković, Dušan T. "Ilija Garašanin's 'Načertanije': A Reassessment," *Balcanica*, XXV–1: 157–183 (Belgrade, 1994).

Bataković, Dušan T. "The Balkan Piedmont—Serbia and the Yugoslav Question," *Dialogue*, 10: 25–73 (Paris, 1994).

Bataković, Dušan T. *Prelude to Sarajevo: The Serbian Question in Bosnia and Herzegovina 1878–1914*, Serbian Academy of Sciences and Arts (Belgrade, 1996).

Bataković, Dušan T. "Storm over Serbia: The Rivalry between Civilian and Military Authorities (1911–1914)," *Balcanica*, XLIV: 307–350 (Belgrade, 2013).

Bataković, Dušan T., and Popović, Nikola B., eds, *Kolubarska Bitka*, Litera (Belgrade, 1989).

Beaver, Jan G. *Collision Course: Franz Conrad von Hötzendorf, Serbia, and the Politics of Preventive War*, Lulu Press (Raleigh, NC, 2009).

Belić, Emilo. *Stepa Stepanović*, publisher not identified (Belgrade, 1938).

Belić, Vladimir. *Putnik*, Jugo-Istok (Belgrade, 1938).

Berov, Ljuben. "The Bulgarian Economy during World War I," in Király, Bela K., and Dreisiger, Nandor F., eds, *East Central European Society in World War I*, East European Monographs (Boulder, CO, 1985).

Božidarović, Vasa. "Još malo svetlosti na Kolubarsku bitku," *Ratnik* (Belgrade, 1922).

Chaliand, Gérard and Blin, Arnaud. "The Golden Age of Terrorism," in Chaliand, Gérard, and Blin, Arnaud, eds, *The History of Terrorism: From Antiquity to Al Qaeda*, University of California Press (Berkeley, CA, 2007).

Churchill, Winston. *The Unknown War: The Eastern Front*, Scribner's (New York, 1931).

Clark, Christopher. *The Sleepwalkers: How Europe Went to War in 1914*, Penguin (London, 2013).

Čorović, Vladimir. *Crna knjiga: patnje Srba Bosne i Hercegovine za vreme svetskog rata 1914–1918*, 3rd edition, Udruženje ratnih dobrovoljaca 1912–1918. godine, njihovih potomaka i poštovalaca (Belgrade, 1996).

Cramon, August von. *Unser Österreichisch-ungarischer Bundesgenosse im Weltkrieg*, 2nd revised edition, E.S. Mittler (Berlin, 1922).

Cramon, August von, and Fleck, P. *Deutschlands Schicksalbund mit Österreich-Ungarn*, Verlag für Kulturpolitik (Berlin, 1932).

Curtwright, Lynn H. "The Failure of British Policy in the Balkans in the Winter of 1914–1915, and its Impacts on the British War Effort," in Spence, Richard B., and Nelson, Linda R., eds, *Scholar, Patriot, Mentor: Historical Essays in Honor of Dimitrije Djordjević*, East European Monographs (Boulder, CO, 1992).

Čutković, Đorđe. "Spontani branioci Beograda 1914 godine," in *Agonija Beograda u svetskom ratu*, Štamparija "Jedinstvo" (Belgrade, 1931).

Czermak, Wilhelm. *In Deinem Lager war Österreich: Die Österreichisch-ungarische Armee, wie man sie nicht kennt*, W.G. Korn (Breslau, 1938).

Damianov, Simeon. "Bulgaria's Decision to Enter the War: Diplomatic Negotiations, 1914–15," in Király, Bela K., and Dreisiger, Nandor F., eds, *East Central European Society in World War I*, East European Monographs (Boulder, CO, 1985).

Deák, István. "The Habsburg Army in the First and Last Days of World War I: A Comparative Analysis," in Király, Bela K., and Dreisiger, Nandor F., eds, *East Central European Society in World War I*, East European Monographs (Boulder, CO, 1985).

Deák, István. *Beyond Nationalism: A Social and Political History of the Habsburg Officer Corps, 1848–1918*, Oxford University Press (New York, 1990).

Decsy, Janos. "The Habsburg Army on the Threshold of Total War," in Király, Bela K., and Dreisiger, Nandor F., eds, *East Central European Society in World War I*, East European Monographs (Boulder, CO, 1985).

Dedijer, Vladimir. "Sarajevo Fifty Years After," *Foreign Affairs*, July 1964.

Dedijer, Vladimir. *Sarajevo 1914*, 1st edition, Prosveta (Belgrade, 1966).

Dedijer, Vladimir. *The Road to Sarajevo*, MacGibbon & Kee (London, 1967).

Dedijer, Vladimir. *Sarajevo 1914*, 2nd edition, Prosveta (Belgrade, 1978).

Dedijer, Vladimir, Božić, Ivan, Ćirković, Sima, and Ekmečić, Milorad. *History of Yugoslavia*, McGraw-Hill (New York, 1974).

Dedović, Vukašin. *Rad Srbije na zaštiti državnih i nacionalnih interesa u Makedoniji od 1885. do 1913. godine*, Doctoral dissertation, Faculty of Philosophy, University of Belgrade (Belgrade, 2010).

Dinić, Dragoljub. *Poznavanje naoružanja Kraljevine Jugoslavije i njenih suseda*, Štamparija "Dom" (Belgrade, 1936).

Djordjević, Dimitrije, ed. *The Creation of Yugoslavia, 1914–1918*, Clio Books (Santa Barbara, CA, 1980).

Djordjević, Dimitrije. "Vojvoda Putnik, the Serbian High Command, and Strategy in 1914," in Király, Bela K., and Dreisiger, Nandor F., eds, *East Central European Society in World War I*, East European Monographs (Boulder, CO, 1985).

Djordjević, Dimitrije. "Vojvoda Radomir Putnik," in Király, Bela K., and Nofi, Albert A., eds, *East Central European War Leaders: Civilian and Military*, East European Monographs (Boulder, CO, 1988).

Donia, Robert J. *Sarajevo: A Biography*, Hurst (London, 2006).

Đorđević, Dimitrije. *Carinski rat Austro-Ugarske i Srbije, 1906–1911*, Istorijski institut (Belgrade, 1962).

Đorđević, Svetozar A. *Kroz ratne vihore: prvi svetski rat i Srpska avijatika*, Izdanje autora (Belgrade, 1967).

Dragnich, Alex N. *Serbia, Nikola Pašić, and Yugoslavia*, Rutgers University Press (New Brunswick, NJ, 1974).

Drašković, Radovan M. *Pretorijanske težnje u Srbiji*, Žagor (Belgrade, 2006).

Đukić, Svetozar S. "Odbrana Beograda i prelaz u Zemun 1914 god," in *Agonija Beograda u svetskom ratu*, Štamparija "Jedinstvo" (Belgrade, 1931).

Đurić, Antonije. *Za čast otadžbine: kako se Beograd borio u prvom svetskom ratu*, NIRO Književne novine (Belgrade, 1985).

Đurić, Silvija, and Stevanović, Vidosav, eds. *Golgota i vaskrs Srbije 1914–1915*, IRO "Beograd" (Belgrade, 1990).

Đurišić, Mitar. "Neki ekonomski problemi Srbije U ratnoj 1914. Godini," *Vojnoistorijski glasnik*, 4 (Belgrade, 1964).

Đurišić, Mitar. *Bitka na Drini 1914*, Vojnoistorijski institut (Belgrade, 1969).

Ekmečić, Milorad. *Ratni ciljevi Srbije, 1914*, Srpska književna zadruga (Belgrade, 1973).

Ekmečić, Milorad. "Serbian War Aims," in Djordjević, Dimitrije, ed., *The Creation of Yugoslavia, 1914–1918*, Clio Books (Santa Barbara, CA, 1980).

Elmannsberger, Ludwig. "The Austro-Hungarian Artillery in the World War," *Coast Artillery Journal*, 62(3): 192–206 (Fort Monroe, VA, 1925).

Fay, Sidney Bradshaw. *The Origins of the World War*, vol. II, Macmillan (New York, 1928).

Fryer, Charles E.J. *The Royal Navy on the Danube*, East European Monographs (Boulder, CO, 1988).

Gajić, Joksim P. "Odbrana Beograda 1914," in *Agonija Beograda u svetskom ratu*, Štamparija "Jedinstvo" (Belgrade, 1931).

Gavrilović, Slavko et al., *Istorija Srpskog naroda*, vol. VI–2, Srpska književna zadruga (Belgrade, 1983).

Golubović, Vidoje. *Stare Kafane Beograda*, 3D+ (Belgrade, 2013).

Gordon-Smith, Gordon. *From Serbia to Jugoslavia: Serbia's Victories, Reverses and Final Triumph, 1914–1918*, Putnam (New York, 1920).

Hađi-Vasiljević, Jovan. *Pokret Srba i Bugara u Turskoj posle srpsko-turskih ratova 1876. i 1877.–1878 godine i njegove posledice (1878.–1882.)*, Nova štamparija Davidović (Belgrade, 1908).

Hauptman, Ferdo. "Privreda i društvo Bosne i Hercegovine u doba Austro-Ugarske vladavine (1878–1918)," in Redžić, Enver, ed., *Prilozi za istoriju Bosne i Hercegovine II*, vol. LXXiX, ANUBiH (Sarajevo, 1987).

Hogg, Ian V. *The Illustrated Encyclopedia of Artillery: An A–Z Guide to Artillery Techniques and Equipment throughout the World*, Chartwell (Secaucus, NJ, 1987).

Holbach, Maude M. *Bosnia and Herzegovina: Some Wayside Wanderings*, J. Lane (London, 1910).

International Commission to Inquire into the Causes and Conduct of the Balkan Wars. *The Other Balkan Wars: A 1913 Carnegie Endowment Commission Inquiry in Retrospect with a New Introduction and Reflections on the Present Conflict by George F. Kennan*, Carnegie Endowment for International Peace (Washington, DC, 1993).

Iskruljev, Toša. *Raspeće Srpskog naroda u Sremu 1914 godine i Mađari*, Štamparija i knjigoveznica Jovanović i Bogdanov (Novi Sad, 1936).

Janić, Čedomir. "Nastanak, razvoj i dejstva Srpske avijatike u periodu 1912–1916," in Vujović, Vojislav, ed., *Srpska Avijatika 1912–1918*, Muzej jugoslovenskog vazduhoplovstva (Belgrade, 1993).

Jerabek, Rudolf. *Potiorek: General im Schatten von Sarajevo*, Verlag Styria (Graz, 1991).

Johnson, Douglas Wilson. *Battlefields of the World War, Western and Southern Fronts: A Study in Military Geography*, Oxford University Press (New York, 1921).

Jones, Fortier. *With Serbia into Exile: An American's Adventures with the Army that Cannot Die*, Century (New York, 1916).

Jovanović, M. Ljuba. *The Murder of Sarajevo: Translation of an Article*, British Institute of International Affairs (London, 1925).

Kamberović, Husnia. "Commemoration of the First World War in Bosnia and Herzegovina," *Prilozi Contributions*, 43, Institut za istoriju u Sarajevu (Sarajevo, 2014).

Kann, Robert A., Király, Bela, and Fichtner, Paula S., eds, *The Habsburg Empire in World War I*, Columbia University Press (New York, 1977).

Kapetan Bohte. *Poznavanje artileriskog materijala*, Artileriska oficirska škola (Belgrade, 1934).

Kapidžić, Hamdija. *Agrarno pitanje u Bosni i Hercegovini za vrijeme austrougarske uprave (1878–1918)*, Radovi—vol. XLIX, Odjeljenje društvenih nauka—vol. 16, ANUBiH (Sarajevo, 1973).

Kazimirović, Vasa. *Crna Ruka: ličnosti i događaju u Srbiji od prevrata 1903. do Solunskog procesa 1917. godine*, Prometej (Novi Sad, 2013).

King, Greg, and Woolmans, Sue. *The Assassination of the Archduke: Sarajevo 1914 and the Romance that Changed the World*, Macmillan (London, 2013).

Kiš, Egon Erwin. *Zapiši to Kiš*, reprinted in Đurić, Silvija, and Stevanović, Vidosav, eds., *Golgota i vaskrs Srbije 1914–1915*, IRO "Beograd" (Belgrade, 1990).

Ković, Miloš. "The Beginning of the 1875 Serbian Uprising in Herzegovina: The British Perspective," *Balcanica*, XLI: 55–71 (Belgrade, 2010).

Kranjčević, Ivan. *Uspomene jednog učesnika u Sarajevskom atentatu*, Svjetlost (Sarajevo, 1954).

Krauss, Alfred. *Die Ursachen Unserer Niederlage*, Lehmann (Munich, 1921).

Krauss, Alfred. "Uzroci našeg poraza," translated from the German "Die Ursachen Unser Niederlage" (Belgrade, 1938), reprinted in Đurić, Silvija, and Stevanović, Vidosav, eds., *Golgota i vaskrs Srbije 1914–1915*, IRO "Beograd" (Belgrade, 1990).

Križanić, Juraj. *Politika*, Blackwell (Oxford, 1985).

Kršev, Boris. *Finansijska politika Jugoslavije 1918–1941*, Prometej (Novi Sad, 2007).

Kutschbach, Albin. *Die Serben im Balkankrieg1912–1913 und im Kriege gegen die Bulgaren*, Franckh (Stuttgart, 1913).

Lazarević, Jelena. *Engleskinje u Srpskom narodu*, Izdanje Beogradskog zenskog drustva (Belgrade, 1929).

Lederer, Ivo J. *Yugoslavia at the Paris Peace Conference: A Study in Frontiermaking*, Yale University Press (New Haven, CT, 1963).

Leidinger, Hannes, Moritz, Verena, Moser, Karin and Dornik, Wolfram. *Habsburgs Scmutziger Krieg: Ermittlungen zu österreichisch-ungarischen Kriegsführung 1914–1918*, Residenz Verlag (Vienna, 2014).

Ljubibratić, Dragoslav. *Mlada Bosna i Sarajevski atentat*, Muzej grada Sarajeva (Sarajevo, 1964).

Ljušić, Radoš. "Ilija Garašanin on Serbia's Statehood," *Balcanica*, XXXIX: 131–174 (Belgrade, 2008).

Ludendorff, Erich von. *Ludendorff's Own Story, August 1914–November 1918*, 2 vols., Harper (New York, 1919).

Lukić, Đorđe. *Bitka na Drini*, Vojno delo (Belgrade, 1966).

MacMillan, Margaret. *The War that Ended Peace: The Road to 1914*, Random House (New York, 2013).

Makaš, Emily Gunzburger. "Museums and the History and Identity of Sarajevo," paper presented at the European Association for Urban History's 11th International Conference on Urban History, *Cities and Societies in Comparative Perspective*, August 29 to September 1, 2012, Prague, Czech Republic.

Marković, Milorad. "Ratni dnevnici," reprinted in Đurić, Silvija, and Stevanović, Vidosav, eds., *Golgota i vaskrs Srbije 1914–1915*, IRO "Beograd" (Belgrade, 1990).

Marković, Predrag. "Razaranja Beograda u Prvom svetskom ratu," in *Srbija 1918. Godine i stvaranje jugoslovenske države*, vol. 5, Zbornik radova Istorijskog institut (Belgrade, 1989).

Markovich, Slobodan G. *British Perceptions of Serbia and the Balkans, 1903–1906*, Dialogue (Paris, 2000).

McKenzie, David. *Apis: The Congenial Conspirator: The Life of Colonel Dragutin T. Dimitrijević*, East European Monographs (Boulder, 1989).

Mihajlović, Slavko. "Oblaci nad gradom," reprinted in Đurić, Silvija, and Stevanović, Vidosav, eds., *Golgota i vaskrs Srbije 1914–1915*, IRO "Beograd" (Belgrade, 1990).

Mijatović, Ivan B., and Đokić, Nebojša D. "Gradska opsadna artiljerija Vojske Kneževine i Kraljevine Srbije," *Vesnik*, LVIII: 39 (Belgrade, 2012).

Mijatović, Ivan B., and Đokić, Nebojša D. "Prvi pokušaji nabavke brzometnih topova u Srbiji," *Vesnik*, LIX: 40 (Belgrade, 2013).

Milenović, Miomir. "Objava rata i prvi napad Austrijanaca na Beograd: kako je u Beogradu izgledao prvi dan Evropskog rata," in *Agonija Beograda u svetskom ratu*, Štamparija "Jedinstvo" (Belgrade, 1931).

Milićević, Milić, and Popović, Ljubodrag. *Generali Vojske kneževine i Kraljevine Srbije*, Vojna Knjiga (Belgrade, 2003).

Miller, Paul. "Yugoslav Eulogies: The Footprints of Gavrilo Princip," The Carl Beck Papers in Russian and East European Studies, No. 2304, University Library Systems, University of Pittsburgh (Pittsburgh, PA, 2014), p. 14.

Milošević, Borivoje. "Progon Pravoslavnog sveštenstva Bosanske krajine u Prvom svetskom ratu," *Srpske Studije*, 4 (Belgrade, 2013).

Milošević, Krsman. *Odbrane Beograda kroz vekove*, Savez potomaka ratnika Srbije 1912–1920 godine (Belgrade, 2012).

Mišić, Živojin. *Moje Uspomene*, edited by Savo Skoko, Beogradski izdavačko-grafički zavod (Belgrade, 1978).

Mišić, Živojin. *Moje uspomene*, Beogradski izdavačko-grafički zavod (Belgrade, 2010).

Mitrović, Andrej. *Prodor na Balkan: Srbija u planovima Austro-Ugarske i Nemačke, 1908–1918*, Nolit (Belgrade, 1981).

Mitrović, Andrej. *Srbija u prvom svetskom ratu*, Srpska književna zadruga (Belgrade, 1984).

Mitrović, Andrej. "Centralne sile i strategijske saobraćajnice na Balkanu 1915. Godine," *Zbornik radova*, 4, Istorijski institut (Belgrade, 1986).

Mitrović, Andrej. "Albanci u politici Austro-Ugarske prema Srbiji 1914–1918," in *Srbi i Albanci u XX veku*, Naučni skupovi Srpske akademije nauka i umetnosti, vol. LXI, odeljenje istorijskih nauka, vol. 20 (Belgrade, 1991).

Mitrović, Andrej. *Prodor na Balkan: Srbija u planovima Austro-Ugarske i Nemačke, 1908–1918*, Zavod za udbenike (Belgrade, 2011).

Mitrović, Andrej. *Serbia's Great War, 1914–1918*, Hurst (London, 2007).

Morrison, Kenneth, and Roberts, Elizabeth. *The Sandžak: A History*, Hurst (London, 2014).

Nikoliš, Gojko, ed. *Ratni dnevnik Dr. Svetislava Barjaktarovića*, Srpska akademija nauka i umetnosti (Belgrade, 1987),

Nofi, Albert A. "Comparative Divisional Strengths during World War I: East Central European Belligerents and Theaters," in Király, Bela K., and Dreisiger, Nandor F., eds, *East Central European Society in World War I*, Social Science Monographs (Boulder, CO, 1985).

Noykov, Stilyan. "The Bulgarian Army in World War I, 1915–18," in Király, Bela K., and Dreisiger, Nandor F., eds, *East Central European Society in World War I*, Social Science Monographs (Boulder, CO, 1985).

Obradović, Vuk. "Puške sistema Mosin u naoružanju Srpske vojske tokom prvog svetskog rata," *Vesnik*, LVI: 37 (Belgrade, 2010).

Opačić, Petar. "Genocidna Politika Austrougarske protiv Srpskog narod i Srbije u prvom svetskom ratu kao platforma za genocid u drugom svetskom ratu," in Opačić, Petar, Skoko, Savo, Rakić, Radomir, and Ćurčić, Milovan, eds, *Genocid nad srbima u dvadestom veku* (Belgrade, 1992).

Owings, Dolph W.A. *The Sarajevo Trial*, vol. I, Documentary Publications (Chapel Hill, NC, 1984).

Palavestra, Predrag. "Young Bosnia: Literary Action 1908–1914," *Balcanica*, XLI: 155–184 (Belgrade, 2011).

Pappenheim, Martin. *Ein geschichtlicher Beitrag zur Vorgeschichte des Attentates von Sarajevo: Gavrilo Princips Bekenntnisse; zwei Manuskripte Princips, Aufzeichnungen seines Gefängnispsychiaters Dr. Pappenheim aus Gesprächen von Feber bis Juni 1916 über das Attentat, Princips Leben und seine politischen und sozialen Anschauungen*, R. Lechner (Vienna, 1926).

Pavičić, Slavko. *Hrvatska vojna i ratna poviest i prvi svjetski rat*, Hrvatska knjiga (Zagreb, 1943).

Pavlović, M. *Vojvode Mišić od Suvobora do Maribora*, Štamparska radionica Ministarstva Vojnog i Mornarice (Belgrade, 1922).

Pejović, Tadija. *"Moje uspomene i doživljaji 1892–1919"* (Belgrade, 1978), reprinted in Đurić, Silvija, and Stevanović, Vidosav, eds, *Golgota i vaskrs Srbije 1914–1915*, IRO "Beograd" (Belgrade, 1990).

Petrovich, Michael Boro. *A History of Modern Serbia*, 2 vols. Harcourt Brace Jovanovich (New York, NY, 1976).

Pisarev, Iu. A. *Serbiia i Chernogoriia v pervoi mirovoi voine*, Izdatel'stvo nauka (Moscow, 1968).

Popović, Čedomir A. "Rad organizacije 'Ujedinjenje ili smrt,' Pripreme za Balkanski rat," *Nova Evropa*, XVI: 10 (November 26, 1927).

Popović, Nikola. *Odnosi Srbije i Rusije u prvom svetskom ratu*, Narodna knjiga (Belgrade, 1977).

Popović, Nikola. *Jugoslovenski dobrovoljci 1914/1918, zbornik dokumenata*, Udruženje dobrovoljaca (Belgrade, 1980).

Radenković, Milan. *Kolubarska bitka*, Vojno delo (Belgrade, 1959).

Radovich, Francis. "The British Court and Relations with Serbia," *East European Quarterly*, 14: 461–468 (Winter 1980).

Rajić, Suzana. "The Russian Secret Service and King Alexander Obrenović of Serbia (1900–1903)," *Balcanica*, XLIII: 143–168 (Belgrade, 2012).

Rakočević, Novica. *Crna Gora u prvom svjetskom ratu, 1914–1918*, Istorijski institut u Titogradu (Cetinje, 1969).

Ranković, Živan J. *Vojvoda Radomir Putnik: Njegov život i rad*, Državna štamparija (Sarajevo, 1926).

Ratković, Borislav. "Srpska vojska u Balkanskim ratovima 1912–1913 i u prvom svetskom ratu," *Vojnoistorijski glasnik*, 1/2: 56–86 (Belgrade, 1993).

Redžić, Enver. "Omladinski pokret i sarajevski atentat," in Enver Redžić, ed., *Prilozi za istoriju Bosne i Hercegovine*, vol. 2, ANUBiH (Sarajevo, 1987).

Reed, John. *The War in Eastern Europe*, Scribner's (New York, 1916).

Reiss, R.A. (Rodolphe Archibald). *Report Upon the Atrocities Committed by the Austro-Hungarian army During the First Invasion of Serbia, Submitted to the Serbian Government by R. A. Reiss*, English translation by F.S. Copeland, Simpkin, Marshall, Hamilton, Kent & Co. (London, 1916).

Remak, Joachim. *Sarajevo: The Story of a Political Murder*, Criterion Books (New York, 1959).

Remak, Joachim. *The Origins of World War I, 1871–1914*, Holt, Rinehart & Winston (New York, 1967).

Roberts, Elizabeth. *Realm of the Black Mountain: A History of Montenegro*, Hurst (London, 2007).

Rothenberg, Gunther. *The Austrian Military Border in Croatia, 1522–1747*, University of Illinois Press (Urbana, IL, 1960).

Rothenberg, Gunther. *The Military Border in Croatia, 1740–1881: A Study of an Imperial Institution*, University of Chicago Press (Chicago, IL, 1966).

Rothenberg, Gunther. "The Habsburg Army in the Napoleonic Wars," *Military Affairs: The Journal of Military History, Including Theory and Technology*, 37(1): 1–5 (February 1973).

Rothenberg, Gunther. *The Army of Francis Joseph*, Purdue University Press (West Lafayette, IN, 1976).

Rothenberg, Gunther. "The Habsburg Army in the First World War: 1914–1918," in Király, Bela K., and Dreisiger, Nandor F., eds, *East Central European Society in World War I*, Social Science Monographs (Boulder, CO, 1985).

Rothenberg, Gunther. "The Austro-Hungarian Campaign Against Serbia in 1914," *Journal of Military History*, 53(2): 127–146 (April 1989).

Samogyi, Eva. "The Hungarian Honved Army and the Unity of the Habsburg Empire; The Honved Reform of 1904," in Király, Bela K., and Dreisiger, Nandor F., eds, *East Central European Society in World War I*, Social Science Monographs (Boulder, CO 1985).

Schwanke, Robert. "Das Albanische Schulwesen und Oesterreich-Ungarn waehrend des I. Weltkriegs," in *Dissertationes Albanicae*, vol. XIII, Band Rudolf Trofenik (Munich, 1971).

Šepić, Dragovan. *Pisma i memorandumi Frana Supila (1914–1917)*, Naučno delo (Belgrade, 1967).

Šešum, Uroš. "Društvo protiv Srba 1897–1902. Metodi i mere bugarske diplomatije, Egzarhije i Bugarsko-makedonsko odrinske revolucionarne organizacije protiv širenja srpskog uticaja u Južnoj Staroj Srbiji i Makedoniji 1897–1902.," *Srpske studije*, 4: 77–103 (Belgrade, 2013).

Simljanić, Miloje et al., eds. *Skopski Đački bataljon, 1914: bataljon 1,300 kaplara*, Udruženje 1300 kaplara (Belgrade, 1941).

Skoko, Savo. *Vojvoda Radomir Putnik*, 2 vols, Beogradski izdavačko-grafički zavod (Belgrade, 1984).

Skoko, Savo, and Opačić, Petar. *Vojvoda Stepa Stepanović, u ratovima Srbije 1876–1918*, Beogradski izdavačko-grafički zavod (Belgrade, 1983).

Slijepčević, Pero. "Bosna i Hercegovina u Svetskom Ratu," in Slijepčević, Pero, ed., *Napor Bosne i Hercegovine za oslobođenje i ujedinjenje*, Oblasni odbor narodne odbrane (Sarajevo, 1929).

Smith, David James. *One Morning in Sarajevo: 28 June 1914*, Phoenix (London, 2009).

Smith, W.H.B. *Small Arms of the World*, 10th edition, A & W Visual Library (Harrisburg, PA, 1973).

Spence, Richard B. "The Yugoslav Role in the Austro-Hungarian Army, 1914–1918," in Király, Bela K., and Dreisiger, Nandor F., eds, *East Central European Society in World War I*, Social Science Monographs (Boulder, CO, 1985).

Spence, Richard B. "Die Bosniaken Kommen!: The Bosnian-Hercegovinian Formations of the Austro-Hungarian Army, 1914–1918," in Spence, Richard B., and Nelson, Linda R., eds, *Scholar, Patriot, Mentor: Historical Essays in Honor of Dimitrije Djordjević*, East European Monographs (Boulder, CO, 1992).

Stanojević, Vladimir. *Istorija Srpskog vojnog saniteta* and *Naše ratno sanitetsko iskustvo*. Vojnoizdavački i novinski centar, Beograd; 1992.

Stefanović, Dušan P. "Pred buru . . . (Beograd u prvim danima svetskoga rata," in *Agonija Beograda u svetskom ratu*, Štamparija "Jedinstvo" (Belgrade, 1931).

Stojićević, Aleksandar. *Istorija naših ratova za oslobođenje i ujedinjenje od 1912–1918 god. (Tok operacija i primena snabdevanja)*, N. Kovačević (Belgrade, 1932).

Stokes, Gale. "The Role of the Yugoslav Committee in the Formation of Yugoslavia," in Djordjević, Dimitrije, ed., *The Creation of Yugoslavia, 1914–1918*, Clio Books (Santa Barbara, CA, 1980).

Stokes, Gale. "Milan Obrenović and the Serbian Army," in Király, Bela K., and
    Dreisiger, Nandor F., eds, *East Central European Society in World War I*, Social
    Science Monographs (Boulder, CO, 1985).
Strachan, Hew. *The First World War: vol. 1: To Arms*, Oxford University Press
    (Oxford, 2001).
Sturzenegger, C. *Serbien im Europäischen Kriege 1914/1915*, Art Institut Orell
    Füssli (Zurich,; 1916).
Sugar, Peter F. *Industrialization of Bosnia-Hercegovina, 1878–1918*, University of
    Washington Press (Seattle, WA, 1963).
Taylor, A.J.P. *The Habsburg Monarchy 1809–1918*, Harper (New York, 1965).
Treadway, John D. *The Falcon and Eagle: Montenegro and Austria-Hungary,
    1908–1914*, Purdue University Press (Purdue, IL, 1983).
Trotsky, Leon. *The War Correspondence of Leon Trotsky: The Balkan Wars,
    1912–1913*, Pathfinder Press (New York, 1980).
Vasić, Dragiša. *Devetsto treća*, Tucović (Belgrade, 1925).
Vopicka, Charles J. *Secrets of the Balkans: Seven Years of a Diplomatist's Life in
    the Storm Centre of Europe*, Rand McNally (Chicago, IL, 1921).
Višer, Sergej. *Uniforme v zgodovini: Slovenija in sosednje dežele*, Partizanska
    knjiga (Ljubljana, 1987).
Vučetić, Biljana. "Pogledi na organizaciju Srpske odbrane u Makedoniji u 1906.
    godini," *Vesnik*, LVI: 37 (Belgrade, 2010).
Vucinich, Wayne. *Serbia between East and West, 1903–1908*, Stanford University
    Press (Palo Alto, CA, 1954).
Vučo, Nikola. *Privredna istorija Srbije do prvog svetskog rata*, Naučna knjiga
    (Belgrade, 1955).
Vuličević, Nebojša. "Odbor za škole i učitelje u Staroj Srbiji: osnivanje,
    organizacija i ciljevi (1868–1876)," *Srpske studije*, 4: 209–230 (Belgrade, 2013).
Wilson, Douglas Johnson. *Battlefields of the World War, Western and Southern
    Fronts: A Study in Military Geography*, Oxford University Press (New York,
    1921).
Zelenika, Milan. *Rat Srbije i Crne Gore 1915*, Vojnoizdavački zavod "Vojno delo"
    (Belgrade, 1954).
Živanović, Milan Ž. *Pukovnik Apis: Solunski proces hiljadu Devetsto sedamnaeste;
    prilog za proučavanje političke istorije Srbije od 1903 do 1918 god.*, Savremena
    Administracija (Belgrade, 1955).
Živanović, Milan Ž. "Istina o 'Austrijskom špijunu' Radu Malobabić," *Politika*,
    no. 12218 (February 11, 1946).
Živanović, Živan, *Politička istorija Srbije*, G. Kon (Belgrade, 1925).
Živojinović, Dragan. "Serbia and Montenegro: The Home Front, 1914–1918," in
    Király, Bela K., and Dreisiger, Nandor F., eds, *East Central European Society in
    World War I*, Social Science Monographs (Boulder, CO, 1985).
Živojinović, Dragoljub. *Petar I Karađorđević, život i delo*, 2 vols, Beogradski
    izdavačko-grafički zavod (Belgrade, 1988).

INDEX